by PEACH-PIT

Translation: Christine Schilling
Lettering: Alexis Eckerman

ZOMBIE-LOAN Vol. 2 © 2004 PEACH-PIT / SQUARE ENIX. All
rights reserved. First published in Japan in 2004 by SQUARE ENIX
CO., LTD. English translation rights arranged with SQUARE ENIX
CO., LTD. and Hachette Book Group USA through Tuttle-Mori Agency,
Inc. Translation © 2007 by SQUARE ENIX CO., LTD.

Yen Press
Hachette Book Group USA
237 Park Avenue, New York, NY 10017

Visit our Web sites at www.HachetteBookGroupUSA.com and
www.YenPress.com.

Yen Press is a division of Hachette Book Group USA, Inc.
The Yen Press name and logo is a trademark of
Hachette Book Group USA, Inc.

First Edition: February 2008

10   9   8   7   6   5   4   3   2   1

BVG

Printed in the United States of America

all produced by
PEACH-PIT
Banri Sendou : Shibuko Ebara
main staff: Nao, Zaki
special thanks: Kinomin, Momiji, Bunbun, Takako, A.Kitamura
...and your reading.

TRANSLATION NOTES

p13
Onigiri are common, cheap snacks. They are seaweed-wrapped triangles of packed rice with various fillings.

p15
A *capsule hotel* is a hotel of extremely dense occupancy that provides its guests with a box-style room, the dimensions of which only allow its occupant to sleep.

p30
Utopia Serial Murder Case is a spoof on *Portopia Serial Murder Case* (*Portopia Renzoku Satsujin Jiken*), an old 8-bit murder mystery game created by Yuji Horii and released by Enix in 1983.

p39
"Lily" in Japanese is *yuri* which is also a genre of anime/manga involving girl-girl relationships.

p70
Bentou is a traditional Japanese boxed lunch usually containing rice, fish or meat, and one or more pickled or cooked vegetables.

p87
Gyuudon is a rice bowl with beef and vegetables on top.

p88
Osoreyama is a region in Japan famous for its *itako*, or shrine maidens. They specialize in acting as mediums for the deceased, missing, and other restless souls.

p100
Gamera is a famous monster in the Godzilla series.

p101
A *yankee* is a young delinquent or street punk.

p133
The *Pythagorean tetractys* was a sacred symbol of the Pythagorean brotherhood and consisted of an equilaterally triangular figure with ten points in four rows; the Hebrew tetractys replaces the points with the Hebrew letters of the tetragrammaton. The *Kabbalah* is a set of spiritual practices and beliefs which are supplementary to the Jewish religion and which play a significant role in Jewish mysticism. The *Sefer Yetzirah*, or "Book of Creation" in Hebrew, is its earliest known text.

p146
Squilla is a type of mantis shrimp. It's also known as mantis prawn.

p147
Himokyuu is a kind of *maki-zushi*, or wrapped sushi, that contains ark shell shellfish and cucumber. Ths inscription on Shito's teacup, *kotobuki*, can mean "longevity" or "congratulations."

p151
Ossan is a rude term for a middle-aged man. The misunderstanding occurs because Sawatari's first name is Otsu-san, which can easily be mispronounced.

p159
BL is an acronym for "boys love" and is a genre of Japanese entertainment that includes manga, anime, and video games depicting idealized male-male relationships, usually created by women for women.

p167
Tomobiki, the name of the building written on the stairs, can refer to two things: the first being that one's taking of that path will yield bad luck for one's friend; the second being a day where, no matter what one does, one can never win (or all efforts end in a draw). The former is the reason Chika and Shito fight all the way up the stairs, the latter the ironic result of their efforts.

p173
Shito uses incorrect kanji to say "offline chat" in Japanese; the characters he employs make similar sounds to the actual word, further stressing his computer illiteracy.

to be continued vol.3

ZOMBIE-LOAN

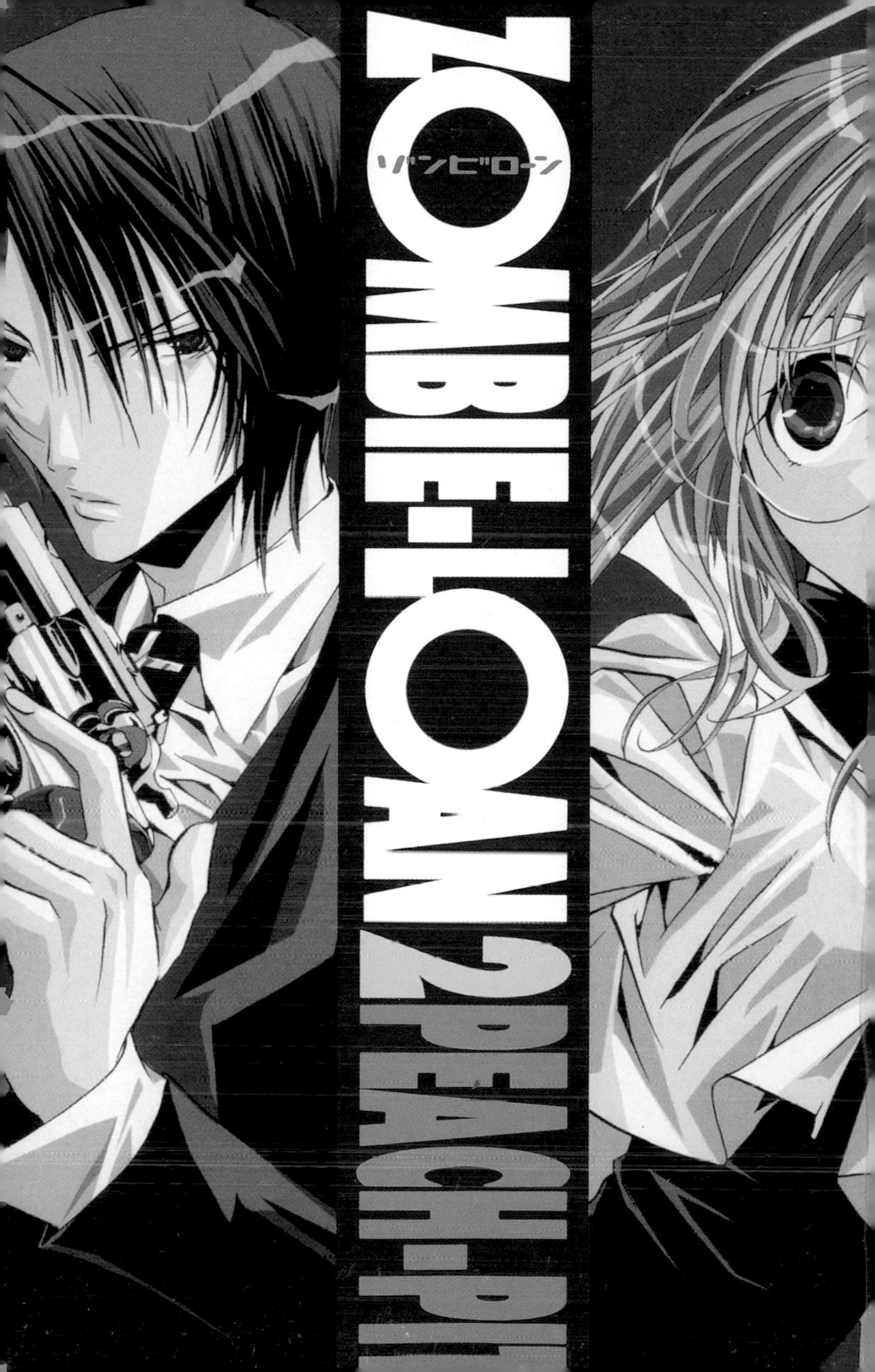
ZOMBIE-LOAN
ゾンビローン
2
PEACH-PIT

CONTENTS

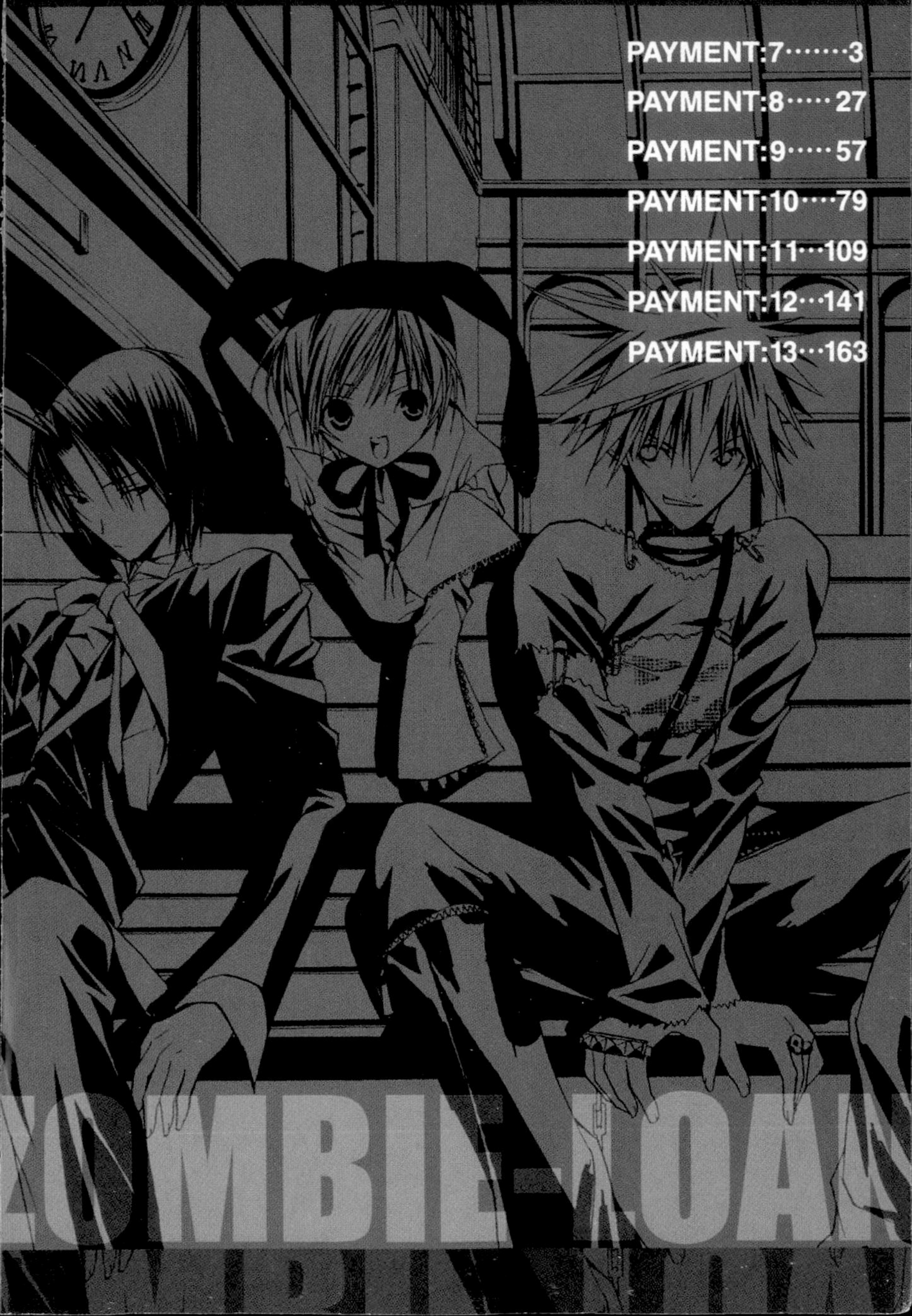

ZOMBIE-LOAN

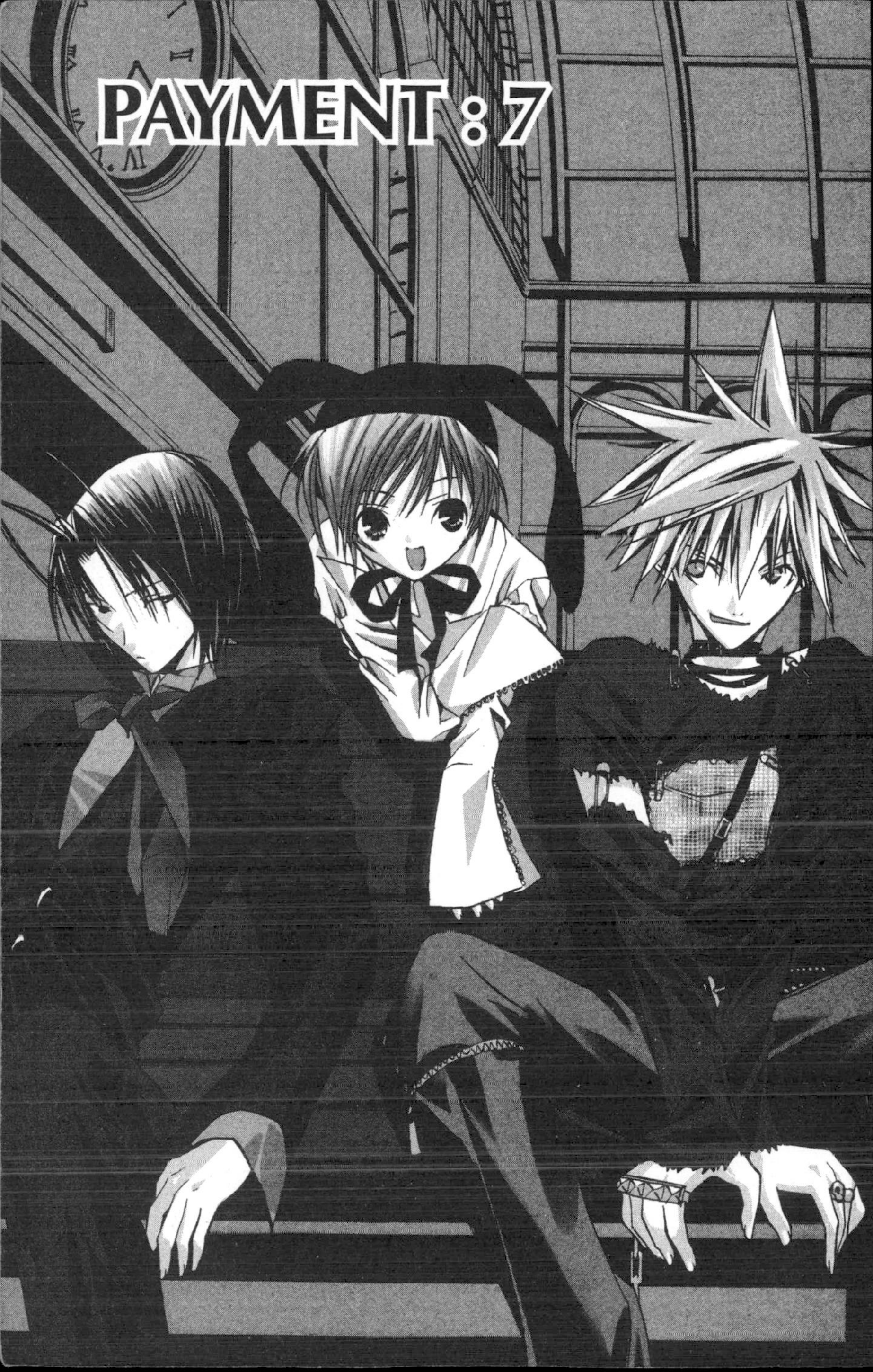
PAYMENT : 7

ZOMBIE-LOAN

http://p-pit.ktplan.ne.jp

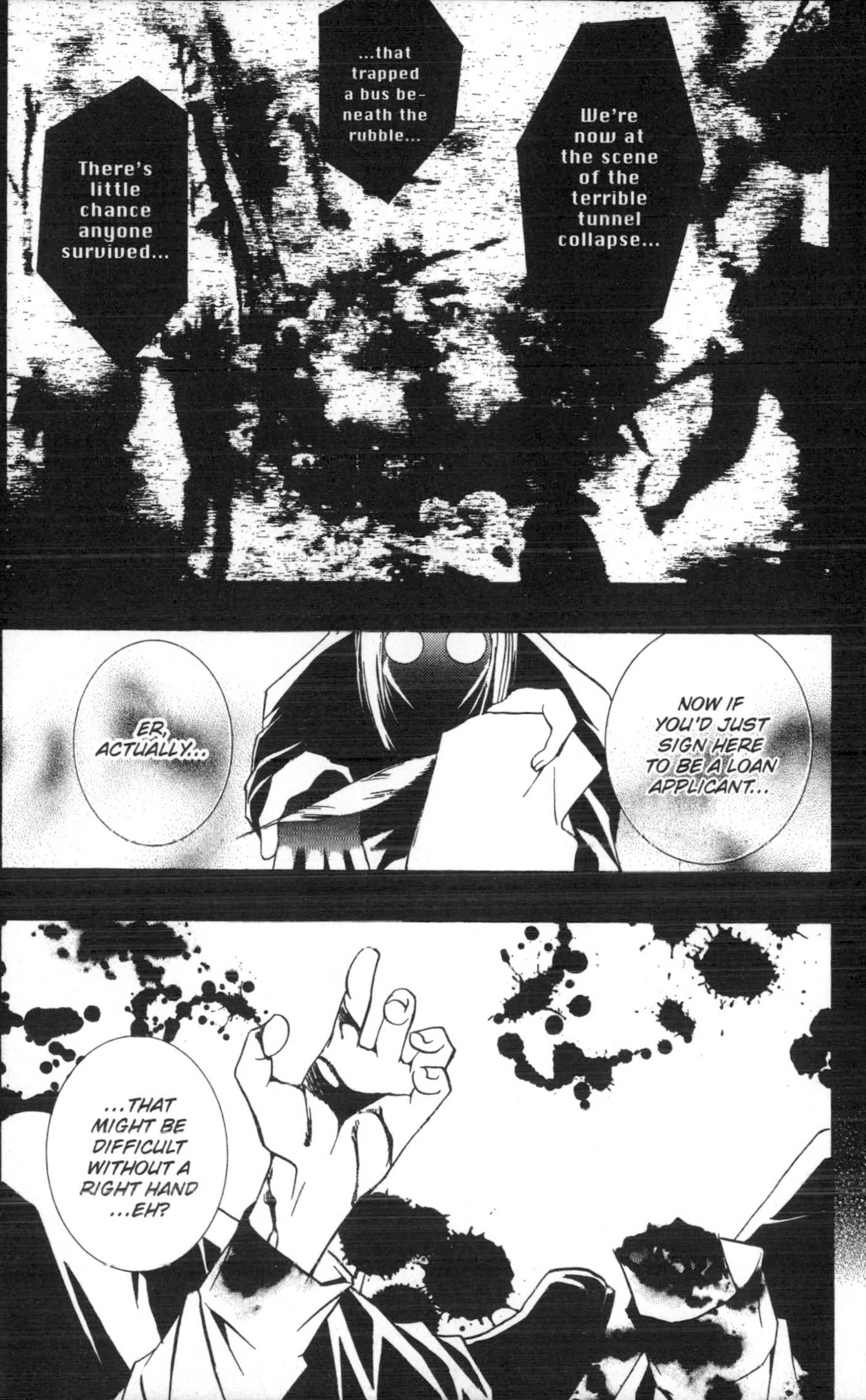
We're now at the scene of the terrible tunnel collapse...
...that trapped a bus beneath the rubble...
There's little chance anyone survived...
NOW IF YOU'D JUST SIGN HERE TO BE A LOAN APPLICANT...
ER, ACTUALLY...
...THAT MIGHT BE DIFFICULT WITHOUT A RIGHT HAND ...EH?

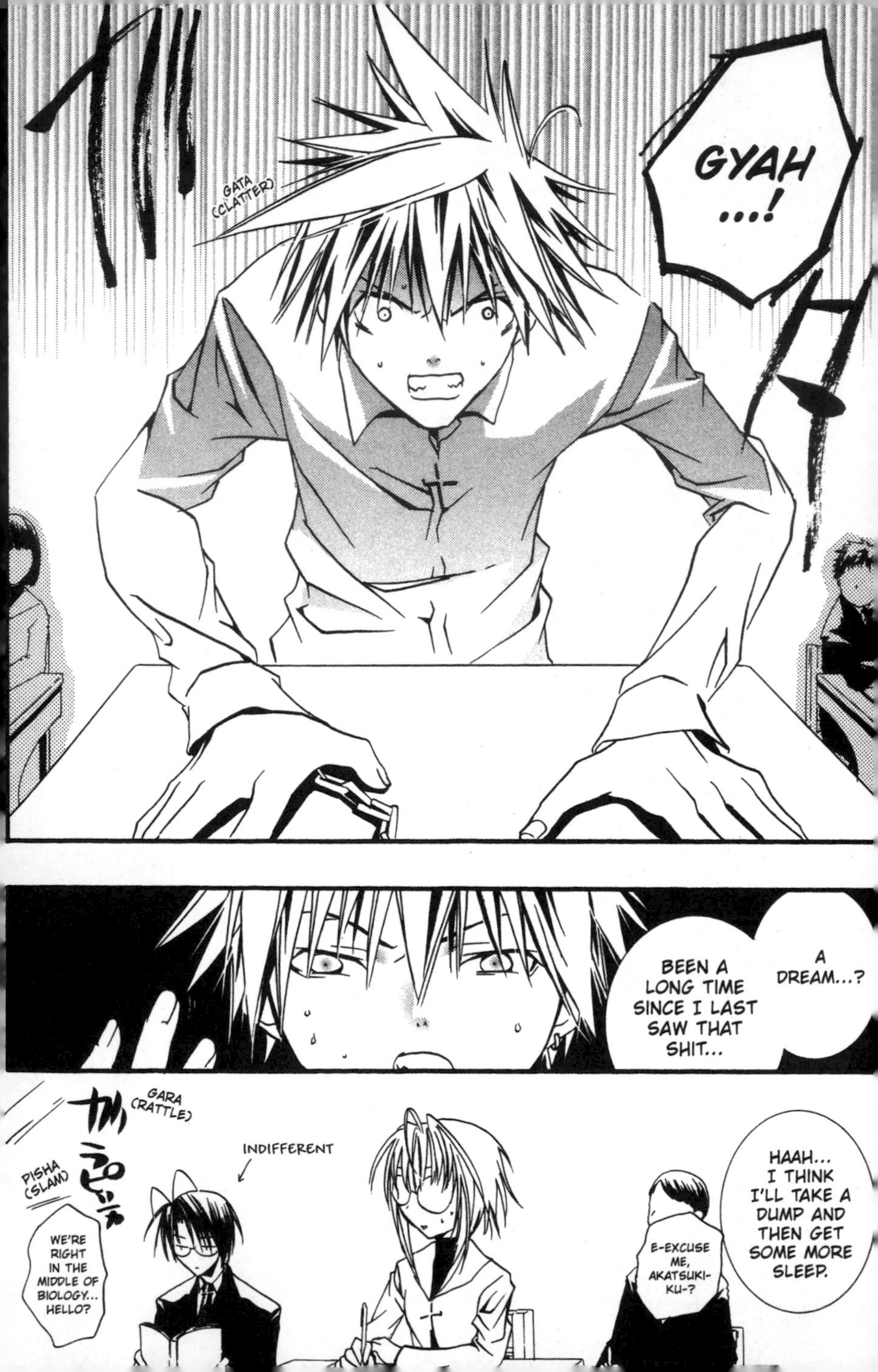
GYAH ...!
GATA (CLATTER)
A DREAM...?
BEEN A LONG TIME SINCE I LAST SAW THAT SHIT...
HAAH... I THINK I'LL TAKE A DUMP AND THEN GET SOME MORE SLEEP.
E-EXCUSE ME, AKATSUKI-KU-?
INDIFFERENT
GARA (RATTLE)
PISHA (SLAM)
WE'RE RIGHT IN THE MIDDLE OF BIOLOGY... HELLO?

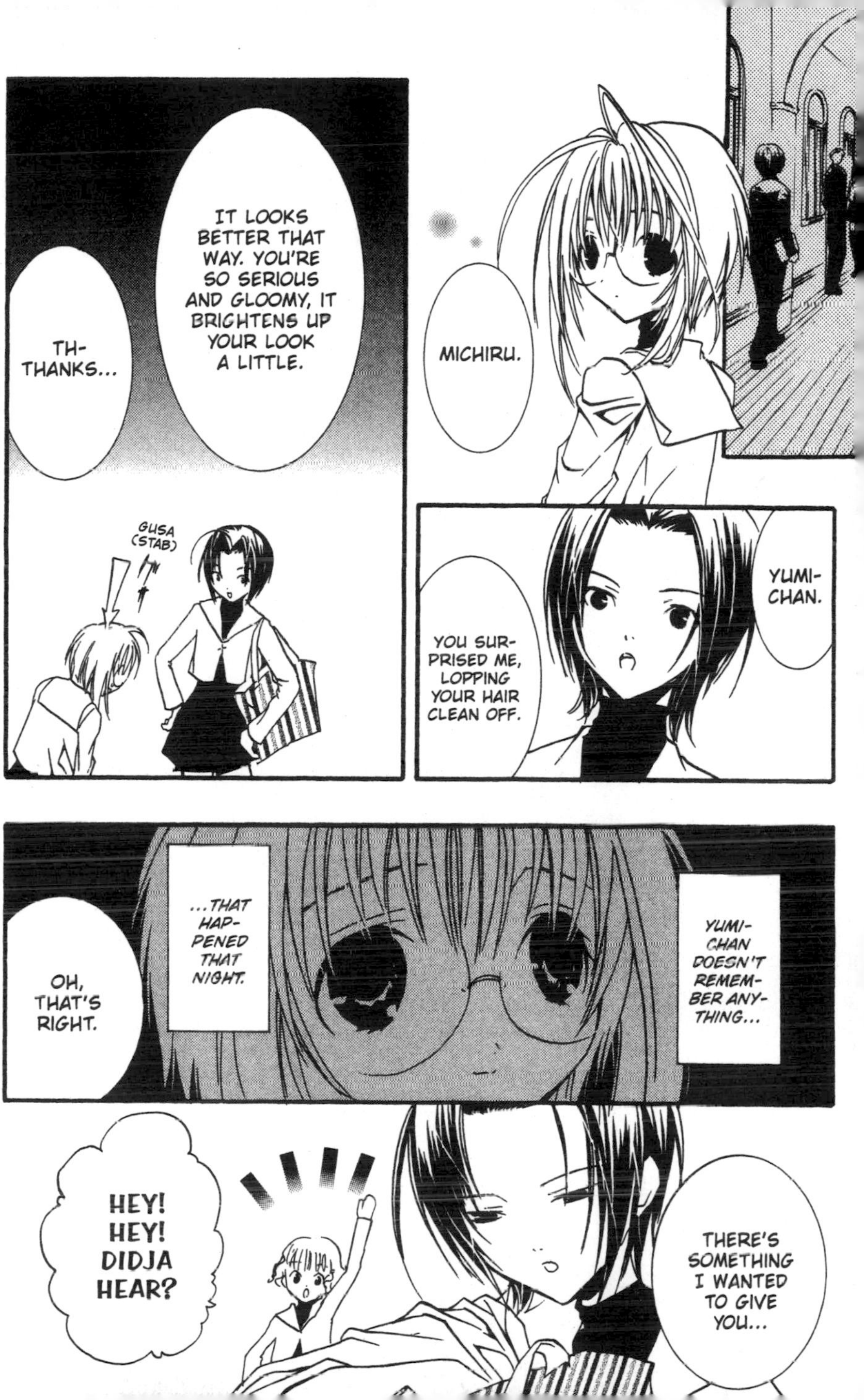
MICHIRU.
YUMI-CHAN.
YOU SURPRISED ME, LOPPING YOUR HAIR CLEAN OFF.
IT LOOKS BETTER THAT WAY. YOU'RE SO SERIOUS AND GLOOMY, IT BRIGHTENS UP YOUR LOOK A LITTLE.
TH-THANKS...
GUSA (STAB)
YUMI-CHAN DOESN'T REMEMBER ANYTHING...
...THAT HAPPENED THAT NIGHT.
OH, THAT'S RIGHT.
THERE'S SOMETHING I WANTED TO GIVE YOU...
HEY! HEY! DIDJA HEAR?

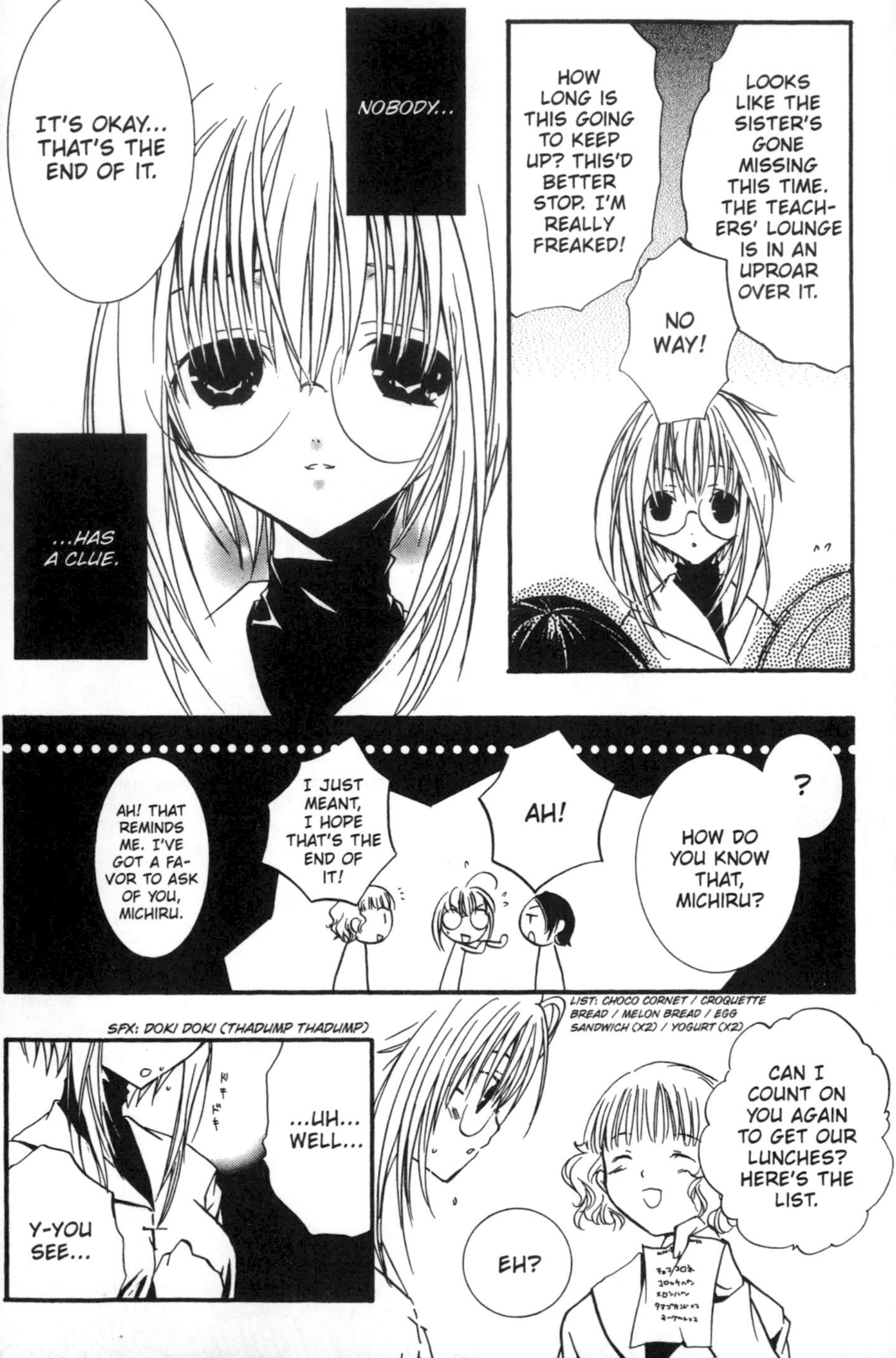
LOOKS LIKE THE SISTER'S GONE MISSING THIS TIME. THE TEACHERS' LOUNGE IS IN AN UPROAR OVER IT.
HOW LONG IS THIS GOING TO KEEP UP? THIS'D BETTER STOP. I'M REALLY FREAKED!
NO WAY!
NOBODY...
IT'S OKAY... THAT'S THE END OF IT.
...HAS A CLUE.
?
HOW DO YOU KNOW THAT, MICHIRU?
AH!
I JUST MEANT, I HOPE THAT'S THE END OF IT!
AH! THAT REMINDS ME. I'VE GOT A FAVOR TO ASK OF YOU, MICHIRU.
LIST: CHOCO CORNET / CROQUETTE BREAD / MELON BREAD / EGG SANDWICH (X2) / YOGURT (X2)
CAN I COUNT ON YOU AGAIN TO GET OUR LUNCHES? HERE'S THE LIST.
EH?
SFX: DOKI DOKI (THADUMP THADUMP)
...UH... WELL...
Y-YOU SEE...

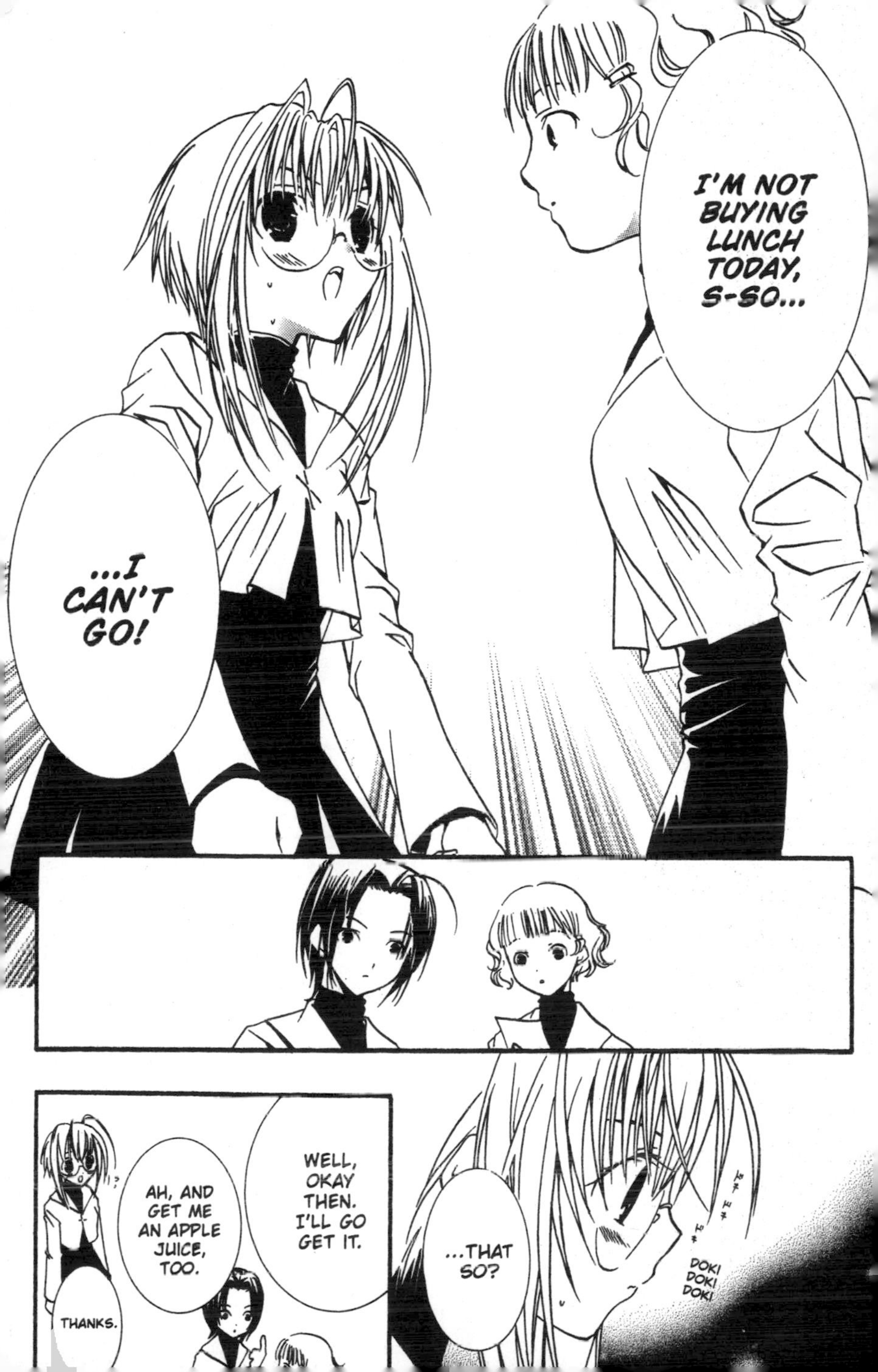
I'M NOT BUYING LUNCH TODAY, S-SO...
...I CAN'T GO!
DOKI DOKI DOKI
...THAT SO?
WELL, OKAY THEN. I'LL GO GET IT.
AH, AND GET ME AN APPLE JUICE, TOO.
THANKS.

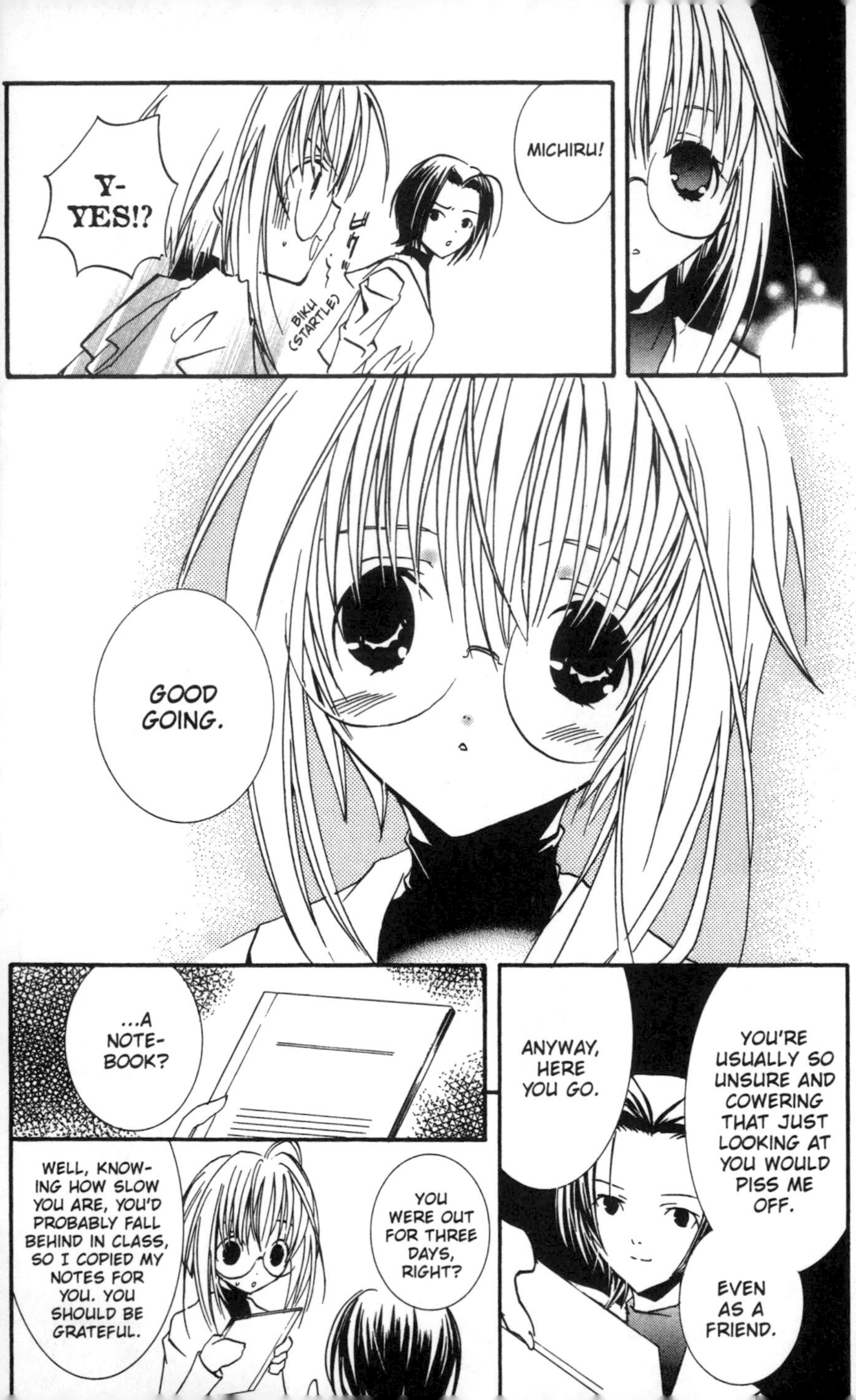
MICHIRU!
Y-
YES!?
BIKU (STARTLE)
GOOD GOING.
ANYWAY, HERE YOU GO.
YOU'RE USUALLY SO UNSURE AND COWERING THAT JUST LOOKING AT YOU WOULD PISS ME OFF.
EVEN AS A FRIEND.
...A NOTE-BOOK?
YOU WERE OUT FOR THREE DAYS, RIGHT?
WELL, KNOW-ING HOW SLOW YOU ARE, YOU'D PROBABLY FALL BEHIND IN CLASS, SO I COPIED MY NOTES FOR YOU. YOU SHOULD BE GRATEFUL.

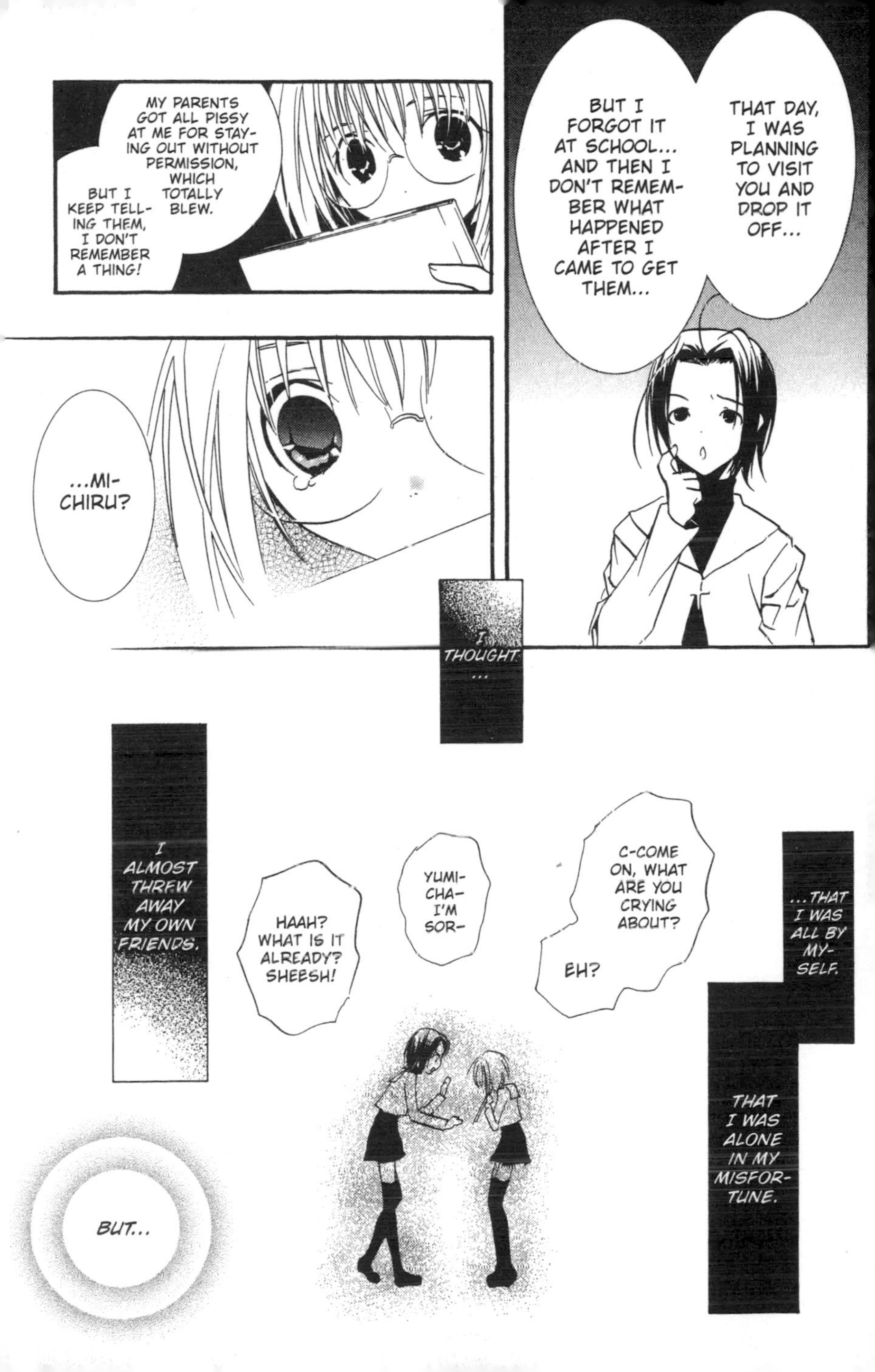
THAT DAY, I WAS PLANNING TO VISIT YOU AND DROP IT OFF...
BUT I FORGOT IT AT SCHOOL... AND THEN I DON'T REMEMBER WHAT HAPPENED AFTER I CAME TO GET THEM...
MY PARENTS GOT ALL PISSY AT ME FOR STAYING OUT WITHOUT PERMISSION, WHICH TOTALLY BLEW.
BUT I KEEP TELLING THEM, I DON'T REMEMBER A THING!
...MI-CHIRU?
I THOUGHT...
...THAT I WAS ALL BY MYSELF.
THAT I WAS ALONE IN MY MISFORTUNE.
C-COME ON, WHAT ARE YOU CRYING ABOUT?
EH?
YUMI-CHA- I'M SOR-
HAAH? WHAT IS IT ALREADY? SHEESH!
I ALMOST THREW AWAY MY OWN FRIENDS.
BUT...

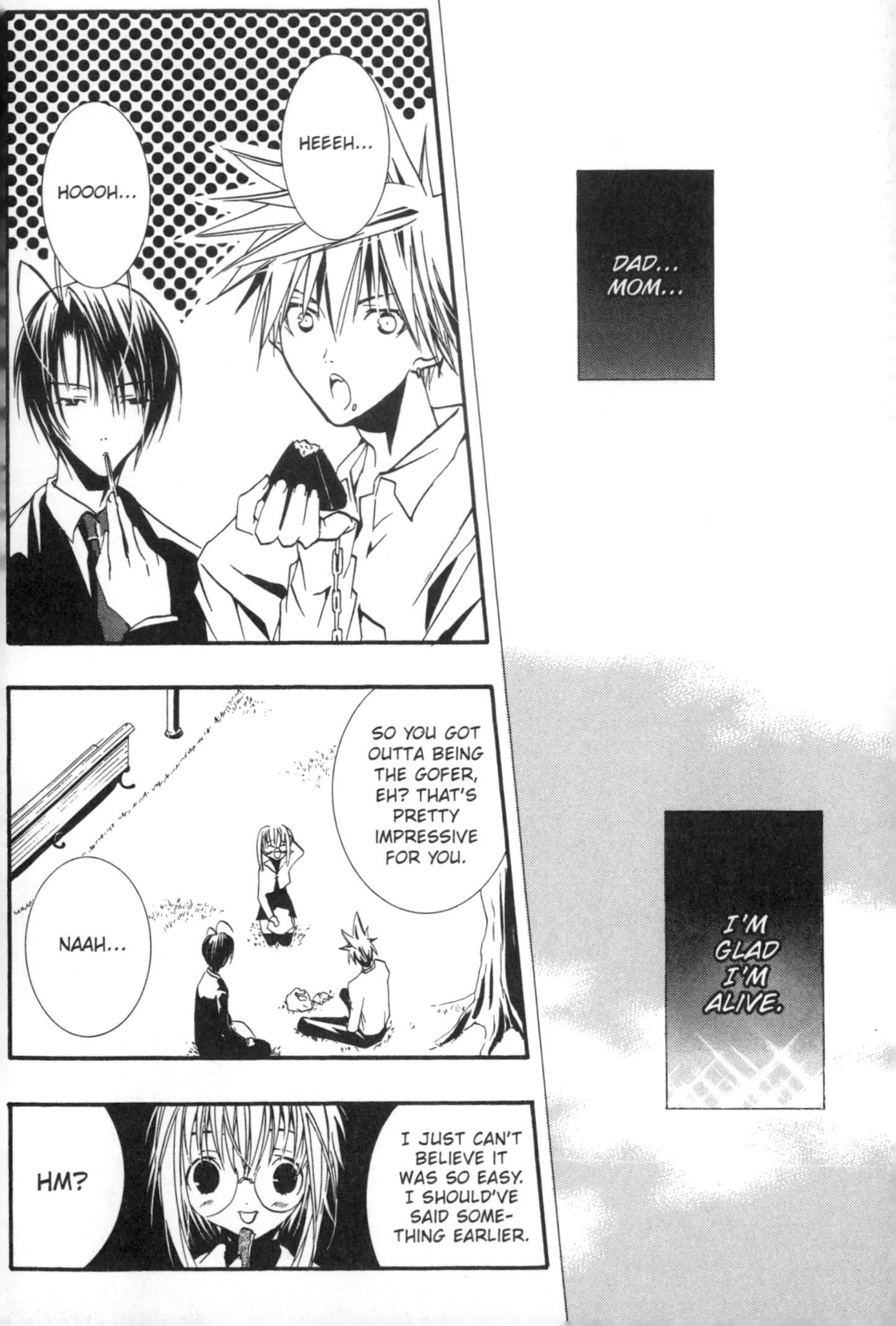
DAD... MOM...
I'M GLAD I'M ALIVE.
HEEEH...
HOOOH...
SO YOU GOT OUTTA BEING THE GOFER, EH? THAT'S PRETTY IMPRESSIVE FOR YOU.
NAAH...
I JUST CAN'T BELIEVE IT WAS SO EASY. I SHOULD'VE SAID SOME-THING EARLIER.
HM?

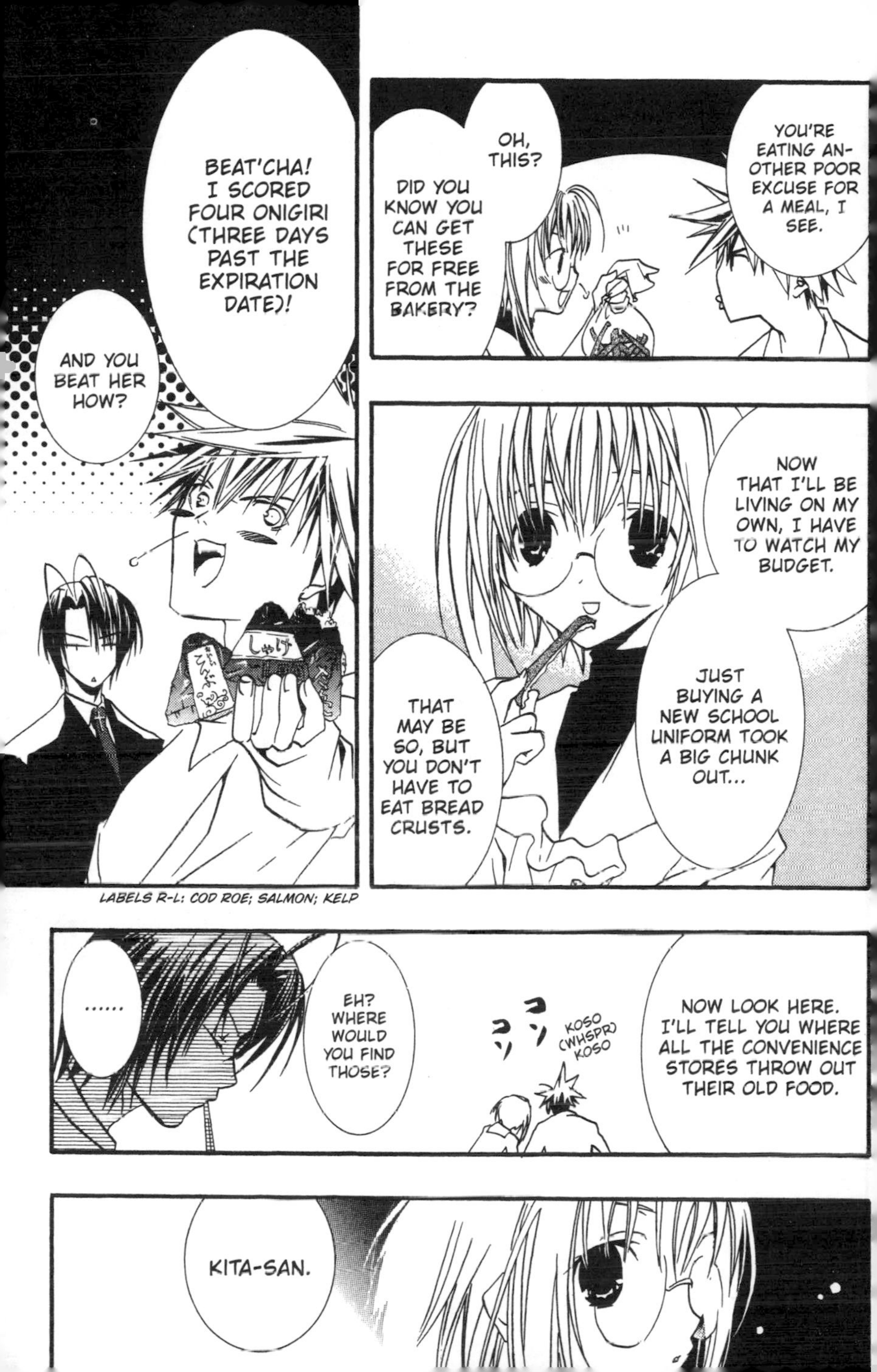
YOU'RE EATING AN-OTHER POOR EXCUSE FOR A MEAL, I SEE.
OH, THIS?
DID YOU KNOW YOU CAN GET THESE FOR FREE FROM THE BAKERY?
NOW THAT I'LL BE LIVING ON MY OWN, I HAVE TO WATCH MY BUDGET.
JUST BUYING A NEW SCHOOL UNIFORM TOOK A BIG CHUNK OUT...
THAT MAY BE SO, BUT YOU DON'T HAVE TO EAT BREAD CRUSTS.
BEAT'CHA! I SCORED FOUR ONIGIRI (THREE DAYS PAST THE EXPIRATION DATE)!
AND YOU BEAT HER HOW?
しゃけ
LABELS R-L: COD ROE; SALMON; KELP
NOW LOOK HERE. I'LL TELL YOU WHERE ALL THE CONVENIENCE STORES THROW OUT THEIR OLD FOOD.
KOSO (WHSPR) KOSO
EH? WHERE WOULD YOU FIND THOSE?
......
KITA-SAN.

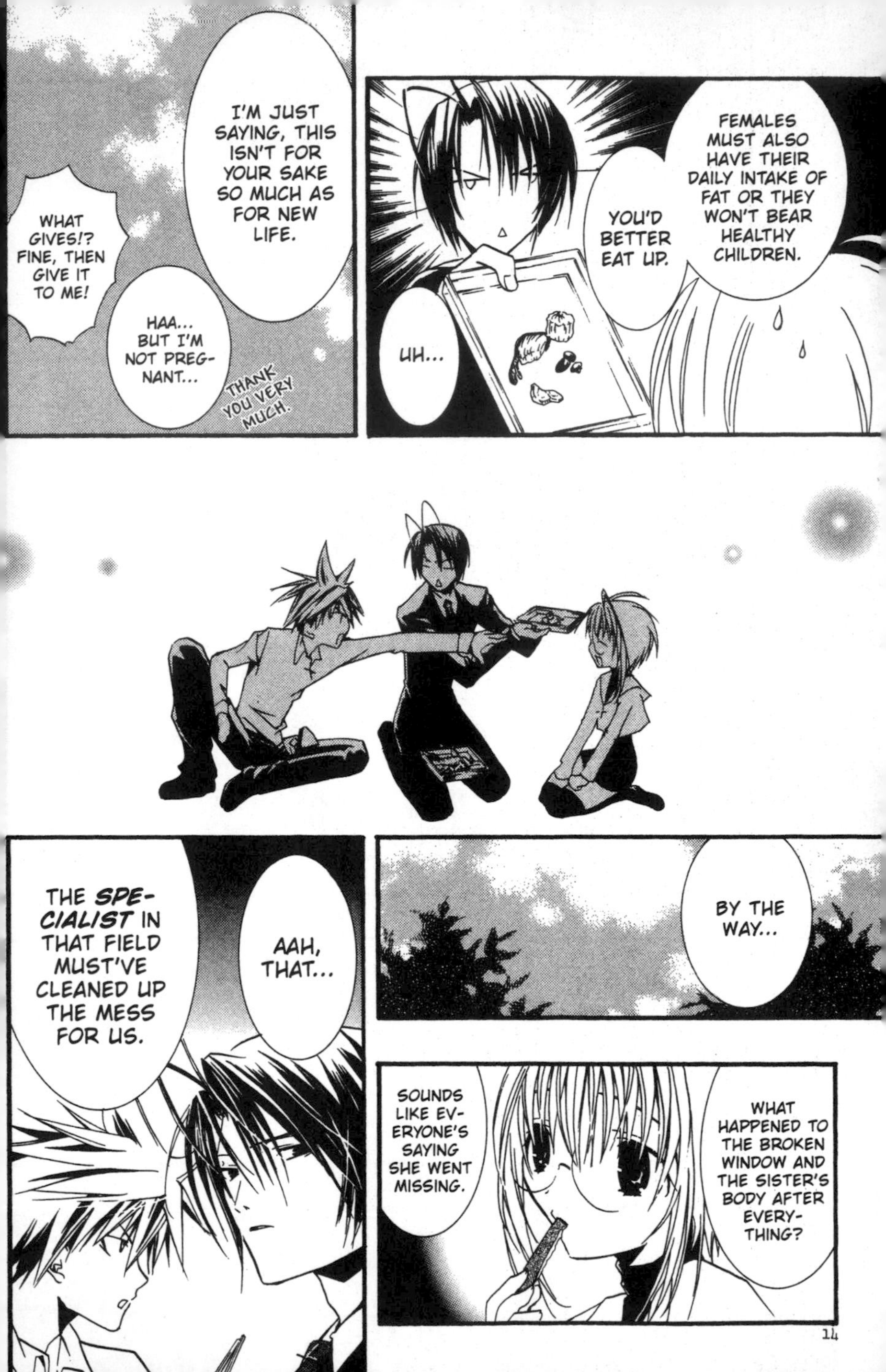
FEMALES MUST ALSO HAVE THEIR DAILY INTAKE OF FAT OR THEY WON'T BEAR HEALTHY CHILDREN.
YOU'D BETTER EAT UP.
UH...
I'M JUST SAYING, THIS ISN'T FOR YOUR SAKE SO MUCH AS FOR NEW LIFE.
WHAT GIVES!? FINE, THEN GIVE IT TO ME!
HAA... BUT I'M NOT PREGNANT...
THANK YOU VERY MUCH.
BY THE WAY...
WHAT HAPPENED TO THE BROKEN WINDOW AND THE SISTER'S BODY AFTER EVERYTHING?
SOUNDS LIKE EVERYONE'S SAYING SHE WENT MISSING.
AAH, THAT...
THE *SPECIALIST* IN THAT FIELD MUST'VE CLEANED UP THE MESS FOR US.

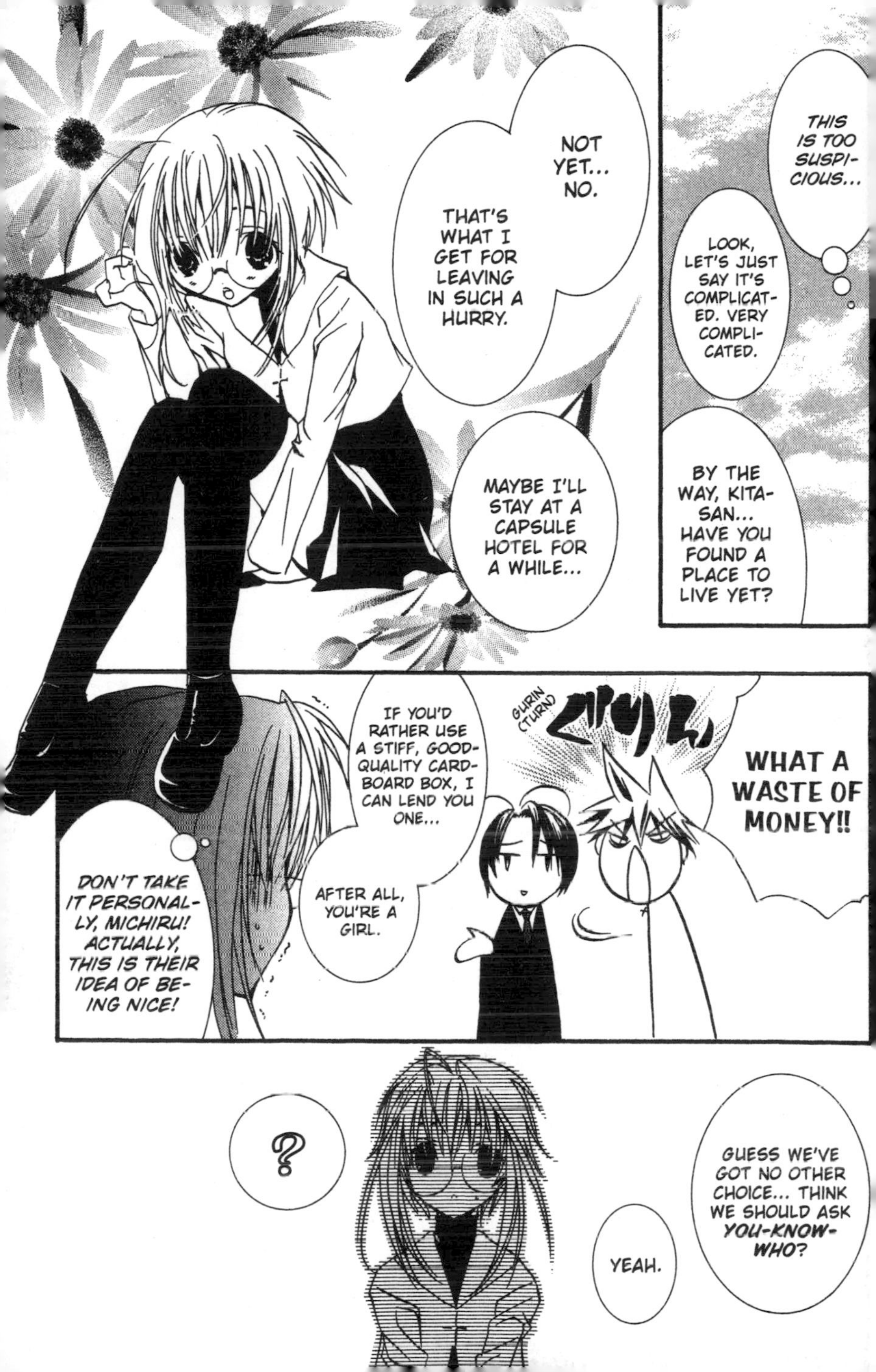
THIS IS TOO SUSPICIOUS...
LOOK, LET'S JUST SAY IT'S COMPLICATED. VERY COMPLICATED.
BY THE WAY, KITA-SAN... HAVE YOU FOUND A PLACE TO LIVE YET?
NOT YET... NO.
THAT'S WHAT I GET FOR LEAVING IN SUCH A HURRY.
MAYBE I'LL STAY AT A CAPSULE HOTEL FOR A WHILE...
WHAT A WASTE OF MONEY!!
GURIN (TURN)
IF YOU'D RATHER USE A STIFF, GOOD-QUALITY CARDBOARD BOX, I CAN LEND YOU ONE...
AFTER ALL, YOU'RE A GIRL.
DON'T TAKE IT PERSONALLY, MICHIRU! ACTUALLY, THIS IS THEIR IDEA OF BEING NICE!
GUESS WE'VE GOT NO OTHER CHOICE... THINK WE SHOULD ASK YOU-KNOW-WHO?
YEAH.
?

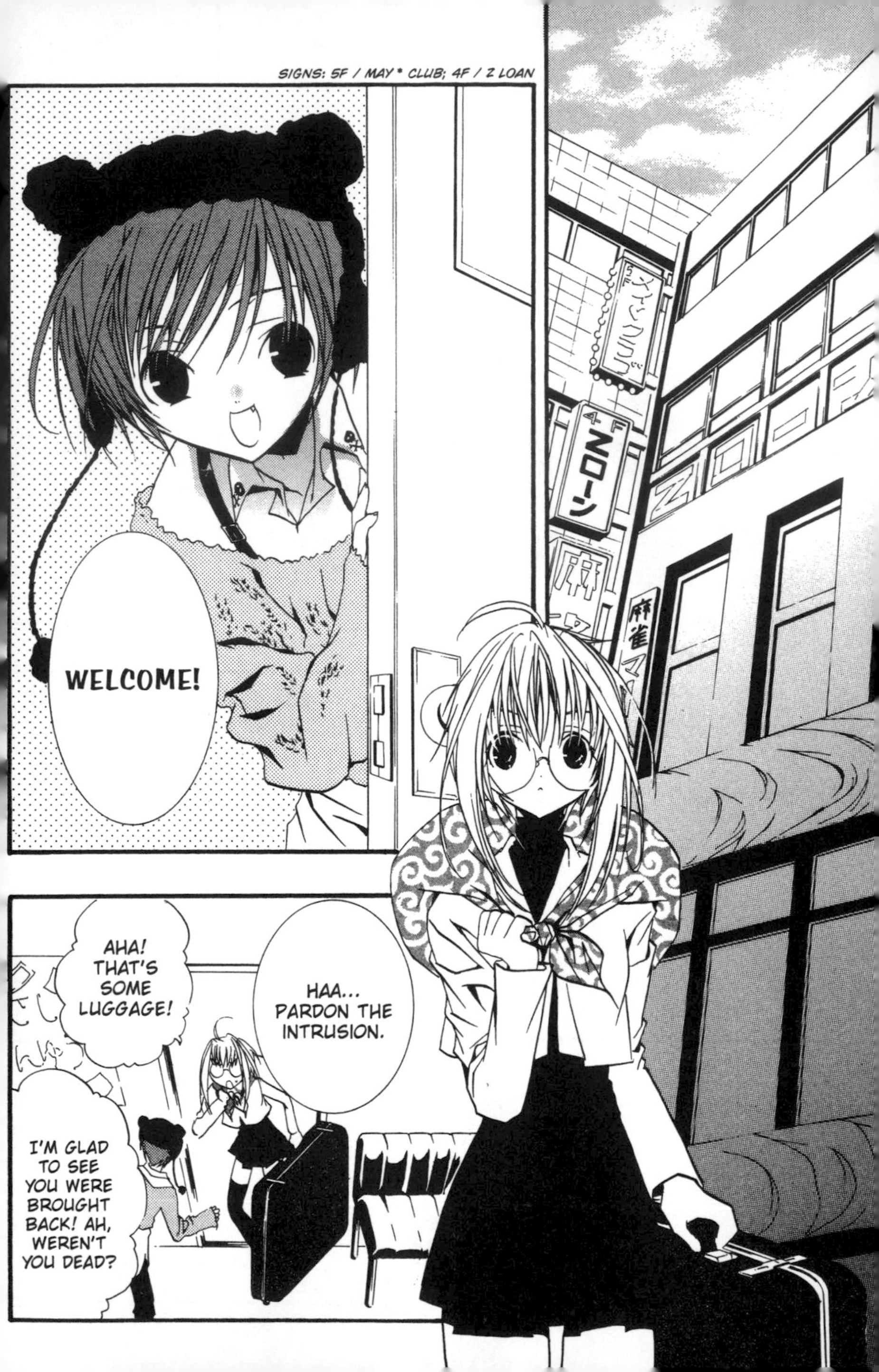
SIGNS: 5F / MAY * CLUB; 4F / Z LOAN
WELCOME!
HAA... PARDON THE INTRUSION.
AHA! THAT'S SOME LUGGAGE!
I'M GLAD TO SEE YOU WERE BROUGHT BACK! AH, WEREN'T YOU DEAD?

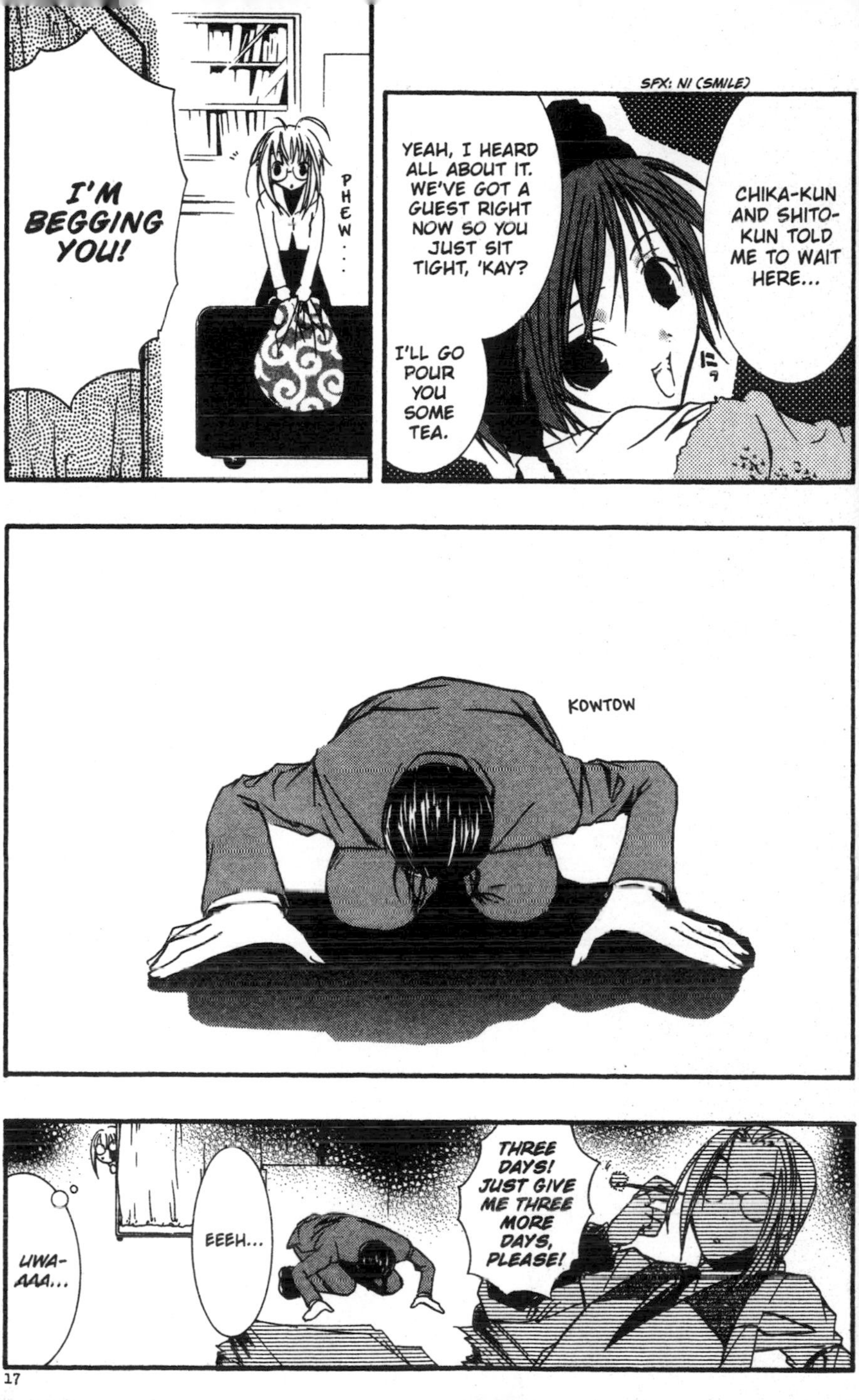
SFX: NI (SMILE)
CHIKA-KUN AND SHITO-KUN TOLD ME TO WAIT HERE...
YEAH, I HEARD ALL ABOUT IT. WE'VE GOT A GUEST RIGHT NOW SO YOU JUST SIT TIGHT, 'KAY?
I'LL GO POUR YOU SOME TEA.
PHEW...
I'M BEGGING YOU!
KOWTOW
THREE DAYS! JUST GIVE ME THREE MORE DAYS, PLEASE!
EEEH...
UWA-AAA...

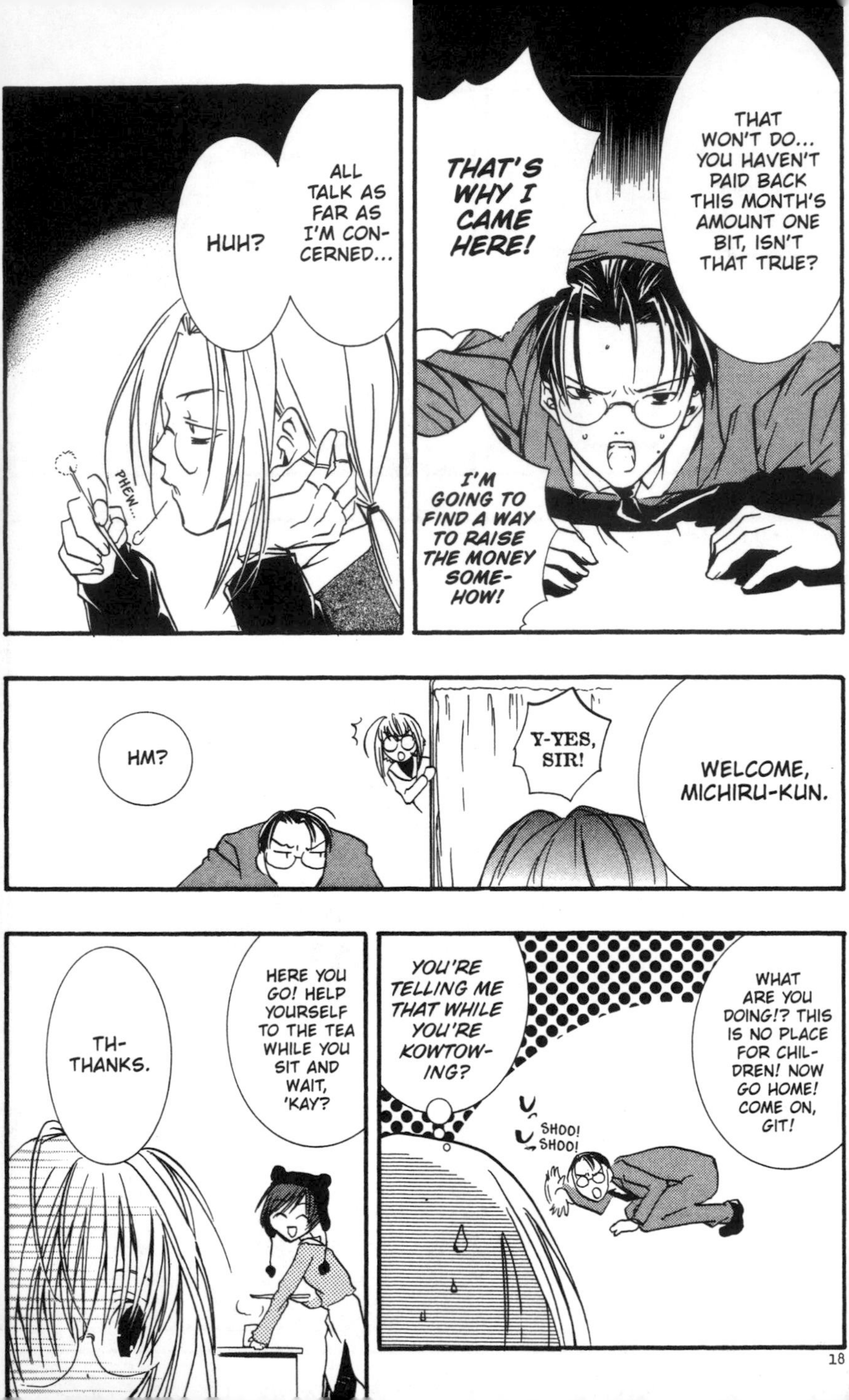
THAT WON'T DO... YOU HAVEN'T PAID BACK THIS MONTH'S AMOUNT ONE BIT, ISN'T THAT TRUE?
THAT'S WHY I CAME HERE!
I'M GOING TO FIND A WAY TO RAISE THE MONEY SOME-HOW!
ALL TALK AS FAR AS I'M CON-CERNED...
HUH?
PHEW...
WELCOME, MICHIRU-KUN.
Y-YES, SIR!
HM?
WHAT ARE YOU DOING!? THIS IS NO PLACE FOR CHIL-DREN! NOW GO HOME! COME ON, GIT!
SHOO! SHOO!
YOU'RE TELLING ME THAT WHILE YOU'RE KOWTOW-ING?
HERE YOU GO! HELP YOURSELF TO THE TEA WHILE YOU SIT AND WAIT, 'KAY?
TH-THANKS.

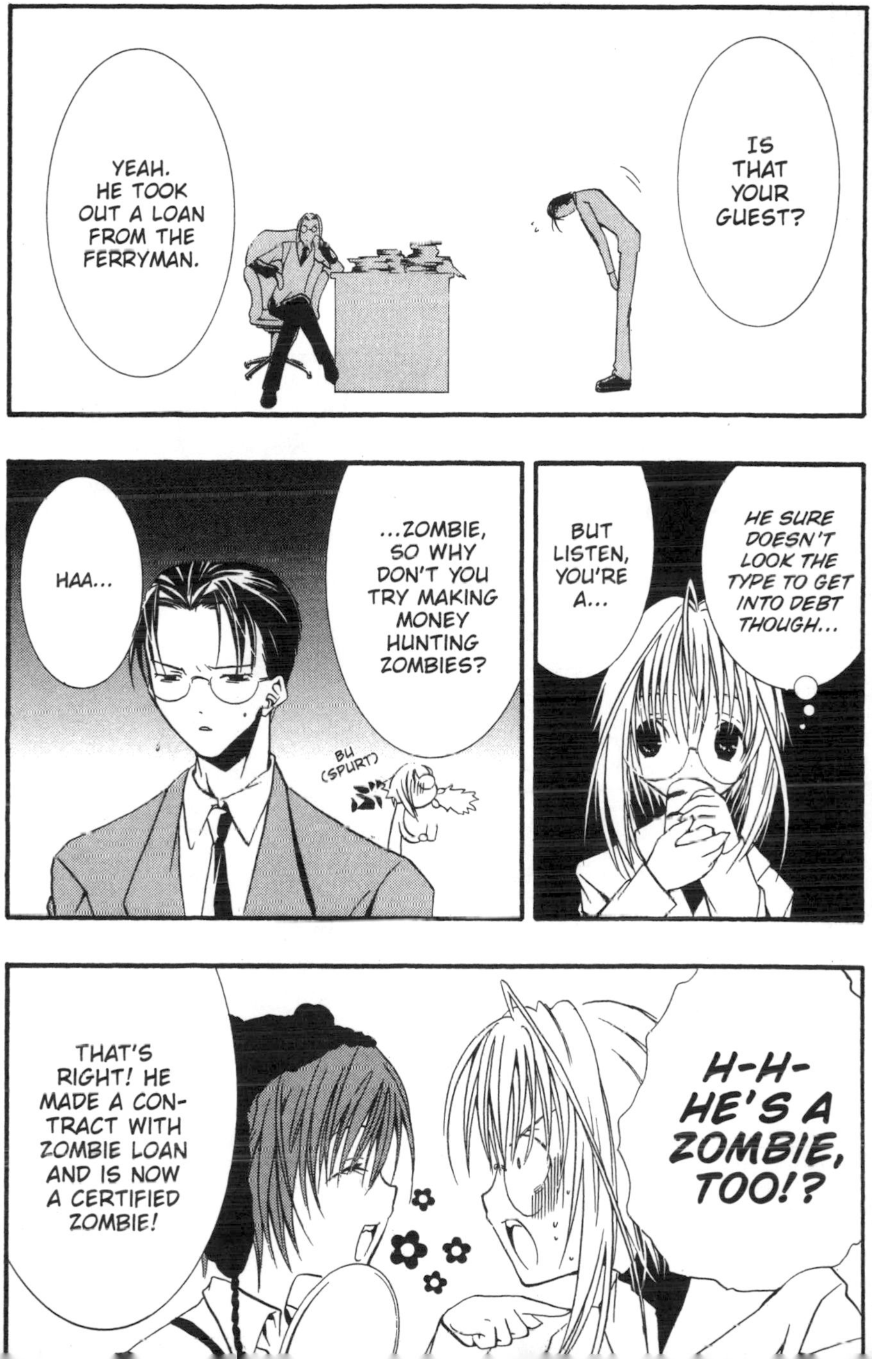
IS THAT YOUR GUEST?
YEAH. HE TOOK OUT A LOAN FROM THE FERRYMAN.
HE SURE DOESN'T LOOK THE TYPE TO GET INTO DEBT THOUGH...
BUT LISTEN, YOU'RE A...
...ZOMBIE, SO WHY DON'T YOU TRY MAKING MONEY HUNTING ZOMBIES?
BU (SPURT)
HAA...
H-H-HE'S A ZOMBIE, TOO!?
THAT'S RIGHT! HE MADE A CON-TRACT WITH ZOMBIE LOAN AND IS NOW A CERTIFIED ZOMBIE!

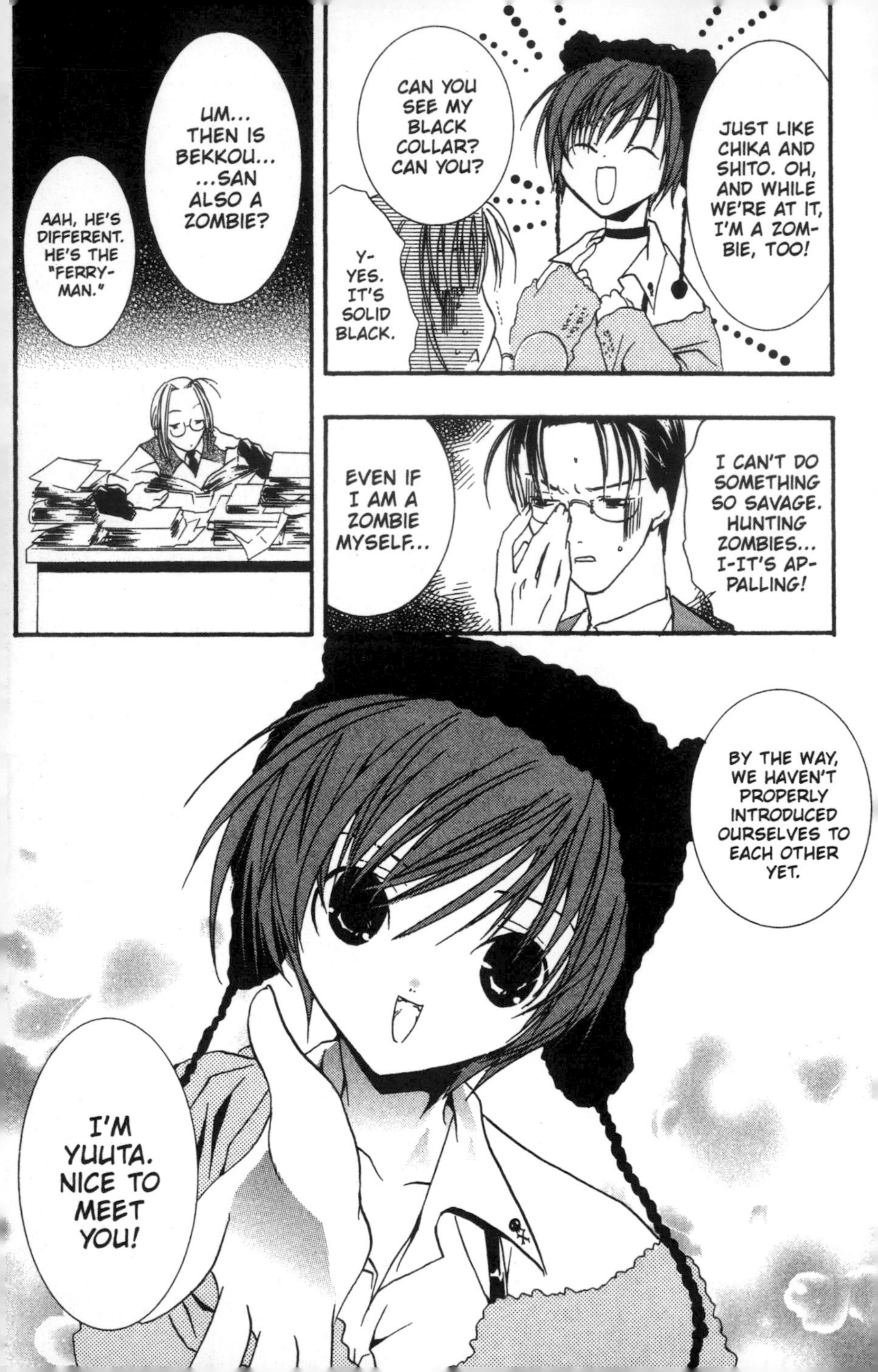
JUST LIKE CHIKA AND SHITO. OH, AND WHILE WE'RE AT IT, I'M A ZOM-BIE, TOO!
CAN YOU SEE MY BLACK COLLAR? CAN YOU?
Y-YES. IT'S SOLID BLACK.
I CAN'T DO SOMETHING SO SAVAGE. HUNTING ZOMBIES... I-IT'S AP-PALLING!
EVEN IF I AM A ZOMBIE MYSELF...
UM... THEN IS BEKKOU... ...SAN ALSO A ZOMBIE?
AAH, HE'S DIFFERENT. HE'S THE "FERRY-MAN."
BY THE WAY, WE HAVEN'T PROPERLY INTRODUCED OURSELVES TO EACH OTHER YET.
I'M YUUTA. NICE TO MEET YOU!

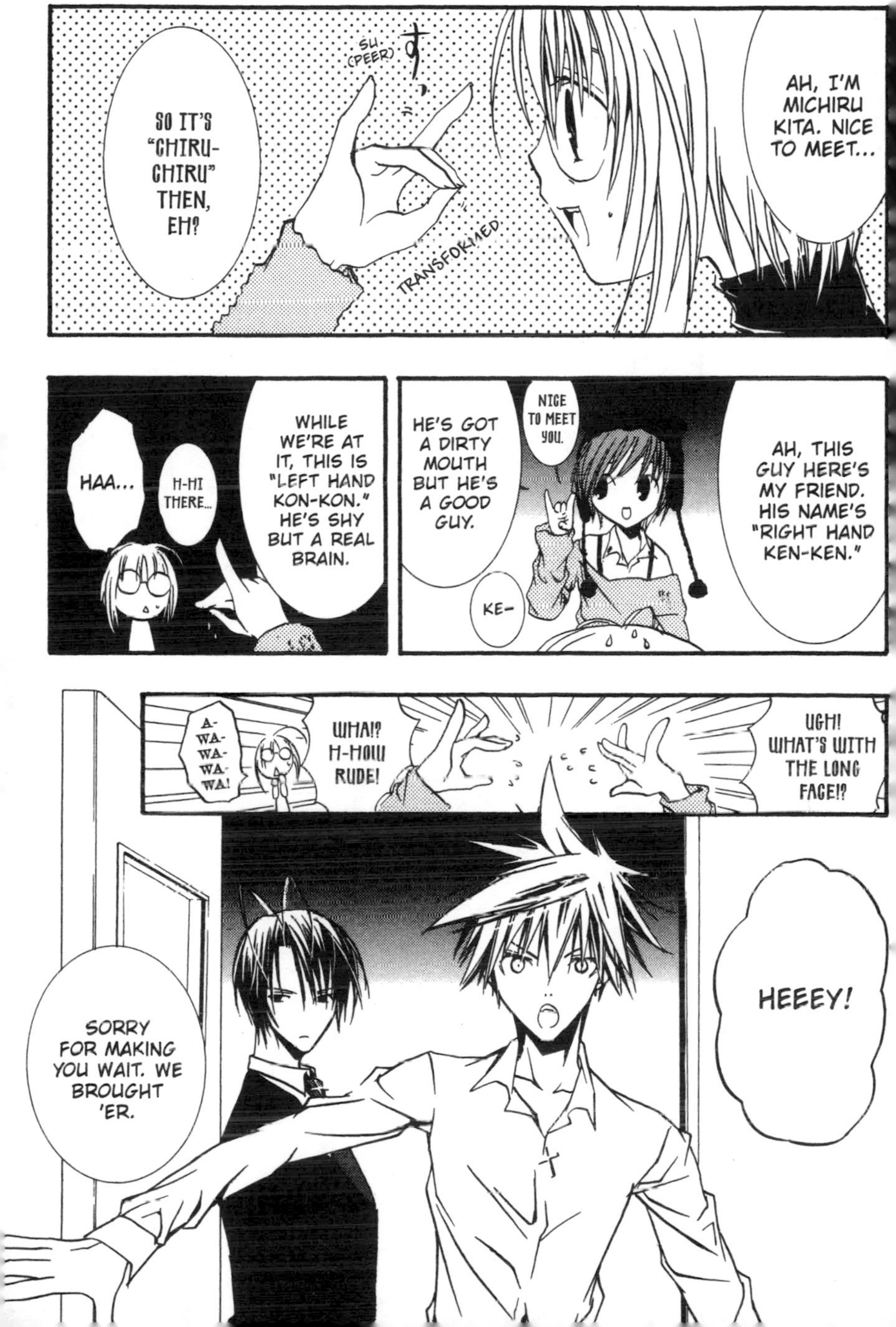
AH, I'M MICHIRU KITA. NICE TO MEET...
SU (PEER)
TRANSFORMED
SO IT'S "CHIRU-CHIRU" THEN, EH?
AH, THIS GUY HERE'S MY FRIEND. HIS NAME'S "RIGHT HAND KEN-KEN."
NICE TO MEET YOU.
HE'S GOT A DIRTY MOUTH BUT HE'S A GOOD GUY.
KE-
WHILE WE'RE AT IT, THIS IS "LEFT HAND KON-KON." HE'S SHY BUT A REAL BRAIN.
H-HI THERE...
HAA...
UGH! WHAT'S WITH THE LONG FACE!?
WHA!? H-HOW RUDE!
A-WA-WA-WA-WA!
HEEEY!
SORRY FOR MAKING YOU WAIT. WE BROUGHT 'ER.

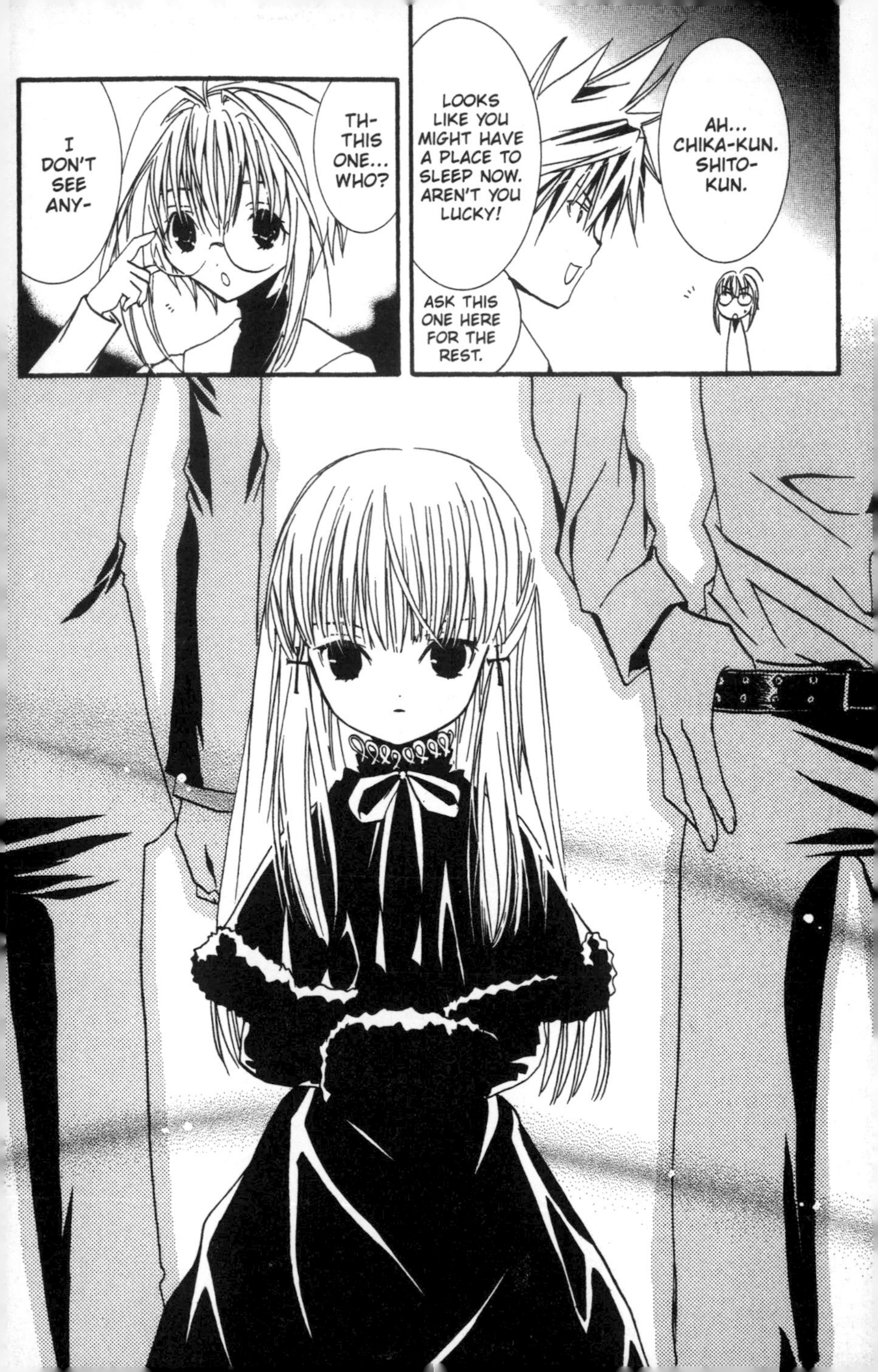
AH... CHIKA-KUN. SHITO-KUN.
LOOKS LIKE YOU MIGHT HAVE A PLACE TO SLEEP NOW. AREN'T YOU LUCKY!
ASK THIS ONE HERE FOR THE REST.
TH- THIS ONE... WHO?
I DON'T SEE ANY-

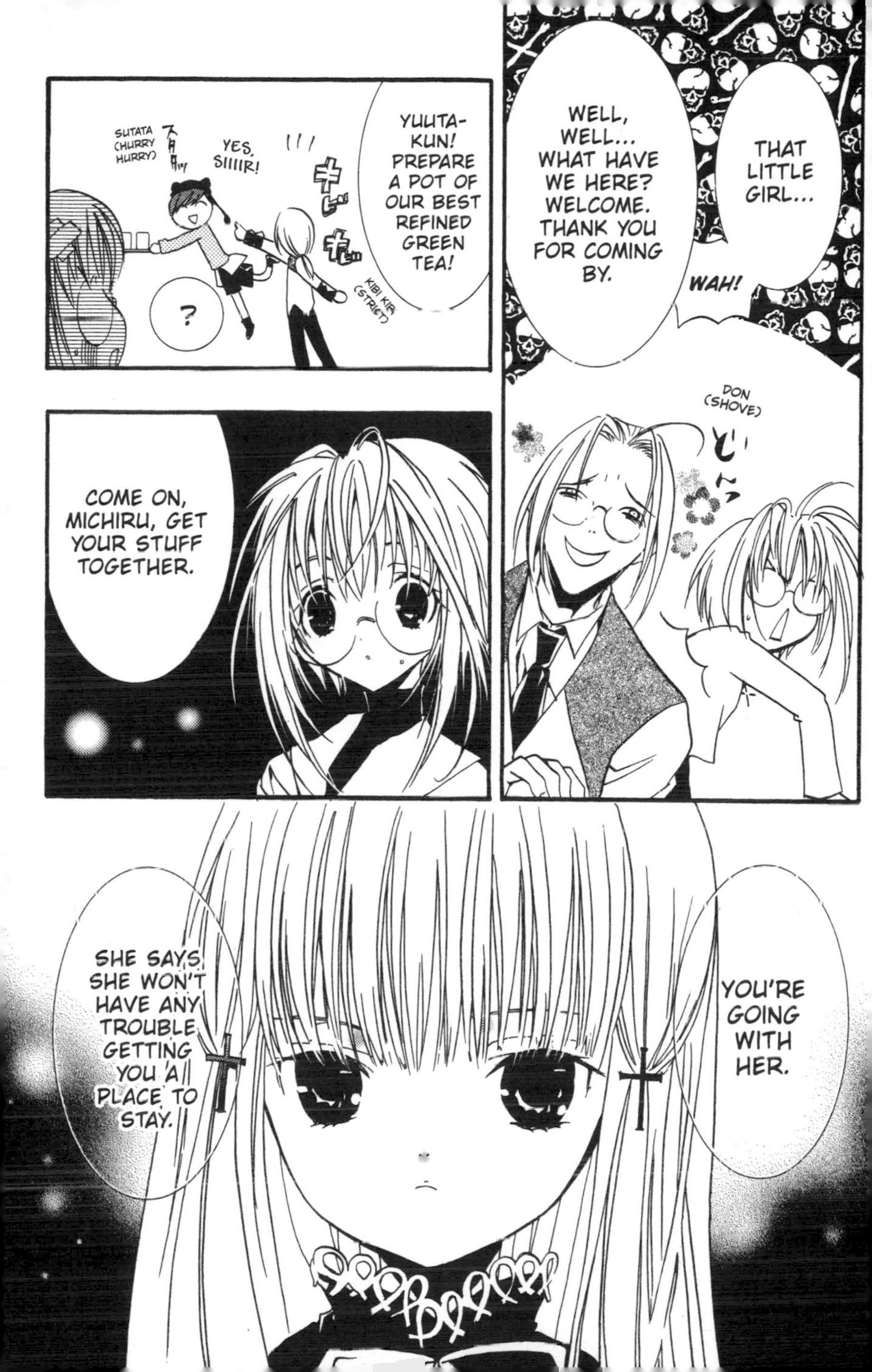
THAT LITTLE GIRL...
WELL, WELL... WHAT HAVE WE HERE? WELCOME. THANK YOU FOR COMING BY.
WAH!
YUUTA-KUN! PREPARE A POT OF OUR BEST REFINED GREEN TEA!
YES, SIIIIR!
SUTATA (HURRY HURRY)
KIBI KIBI (STRICT)
?
DON (SHOVE)
COME ON, MICHIRU, GET YOUR STUFF TOGETHER.
YOU'RE GOING WITH HER.
SHE SAYS SHE WON'T HAVE ANY TROUBLE GETTING YOU A PLACE TO STAY.

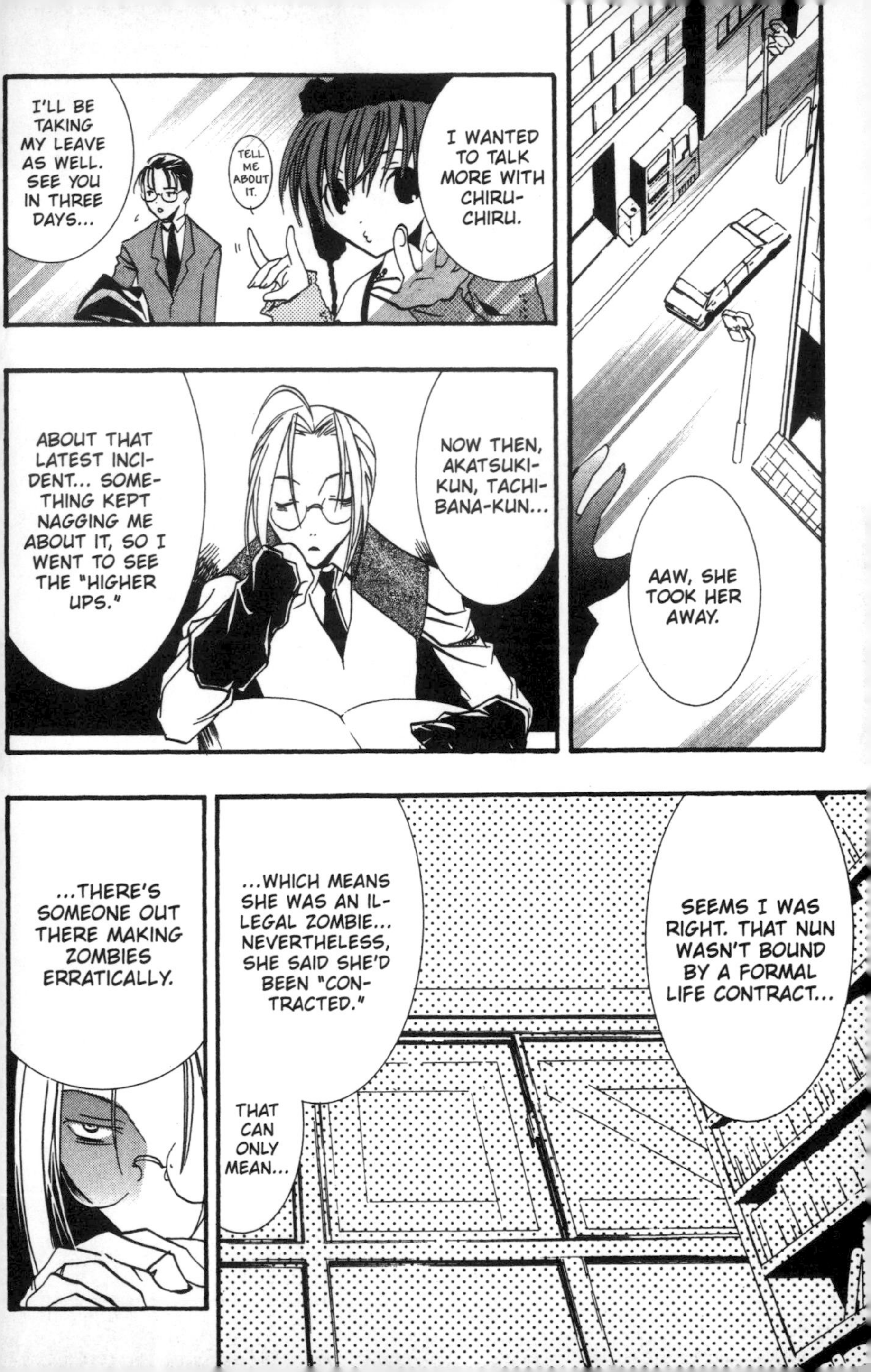
AAW, SHE TOOK HER AWAY.
I WANTED TO TALK MORE WITH CHIRU-CHIRU.
TELL ME ABOUT IT.
I'LL BE TAKING MY LEAVE AS WELL. SEE YOU IN THREE DAYS...
NOW THEN, AKATSUKI-KUN, TACHIBANA-KUN...
ABOUT THAT LATEST INCIDENT... SOMETHING KEPT NAGGING ME ABOUT IT, SO I WENT TO SEE THE "HIGHER UPS."
SEEMS I WAS RIGHT. THAT NUN WASN'T BOUND BY A FORMAL LIFE CONTRACT...
...WHICH MEANS SHE WAS AN ILLEGAL ZOMBIE... NEVERTHELESS, SHE SAID SHE'D BEEN "CONTRACTED."
THAT CAN ONLY MEAN...
...THERE'S SOMEONE OUT THERE MAKING ZOMBIES ERRATICALLY.

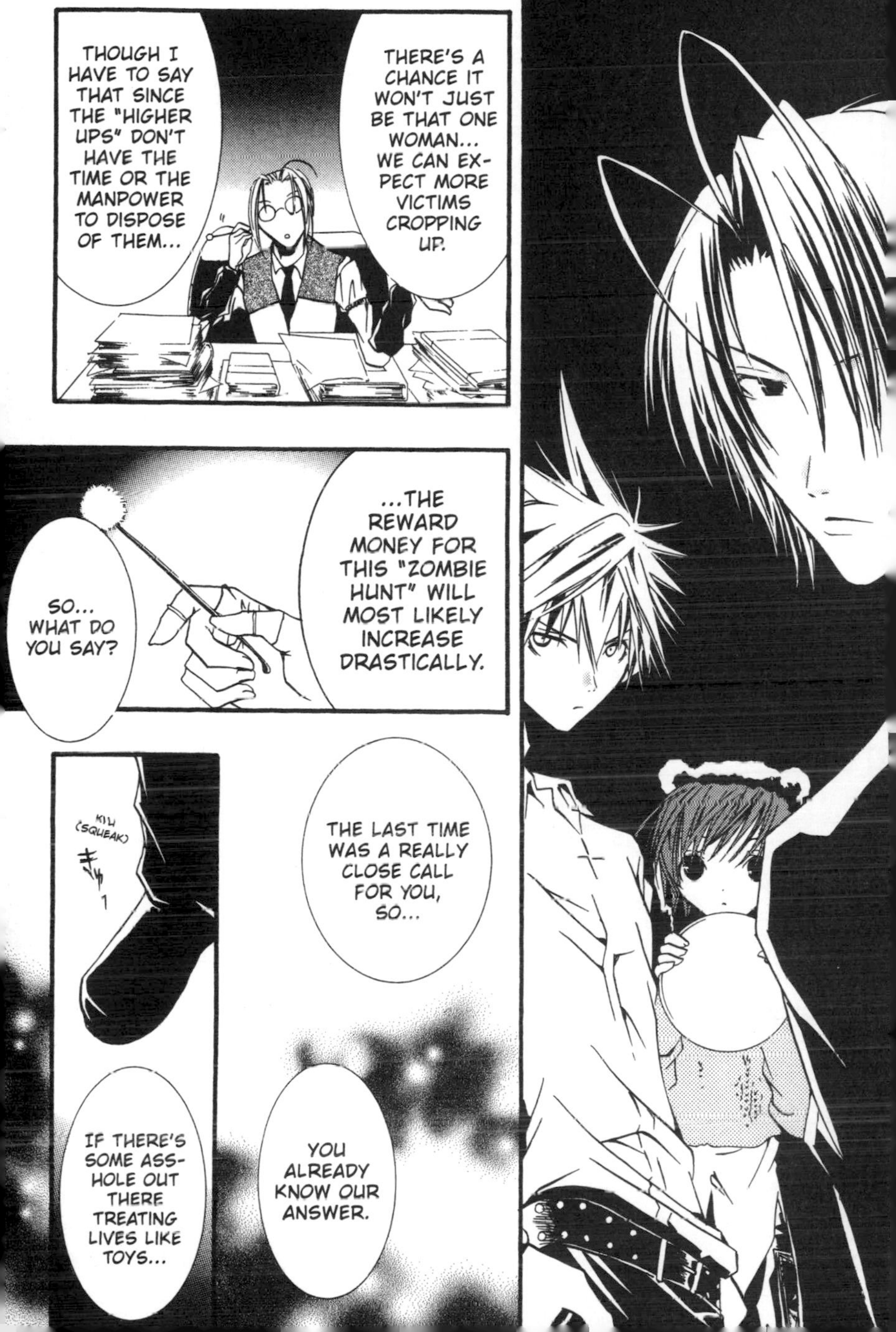
THERE'S A CHANCE IT WON'T JUST BE THAT ONE WOMAN... WE CAN EX-PECT MORE VICTIMS CROPPING UP.
THOUGH I HAVE TO SAY THAT SINCE THE "HIGHER UPS" DON'T HAVE THE TIME OR THE MANPOWER TO DISPOSE OF THEM...
...THE REWARD MONEY FOR THIS "ZOMBIE HUNT" WILL MOST LIKELY INCREASE DRASTICALLY.
SO... WHAT DO YOU SAY?
THE LAST TIME WAS A REALLY CLOSE CALL FOR YOU, SO...
KYU (SQUEAK)
YOU ALREADY KNOW OUR ANSWER.
IF THERE'S SOME ASS-HOLE OUT THERE TREATING LIVES LIKE TOYS...

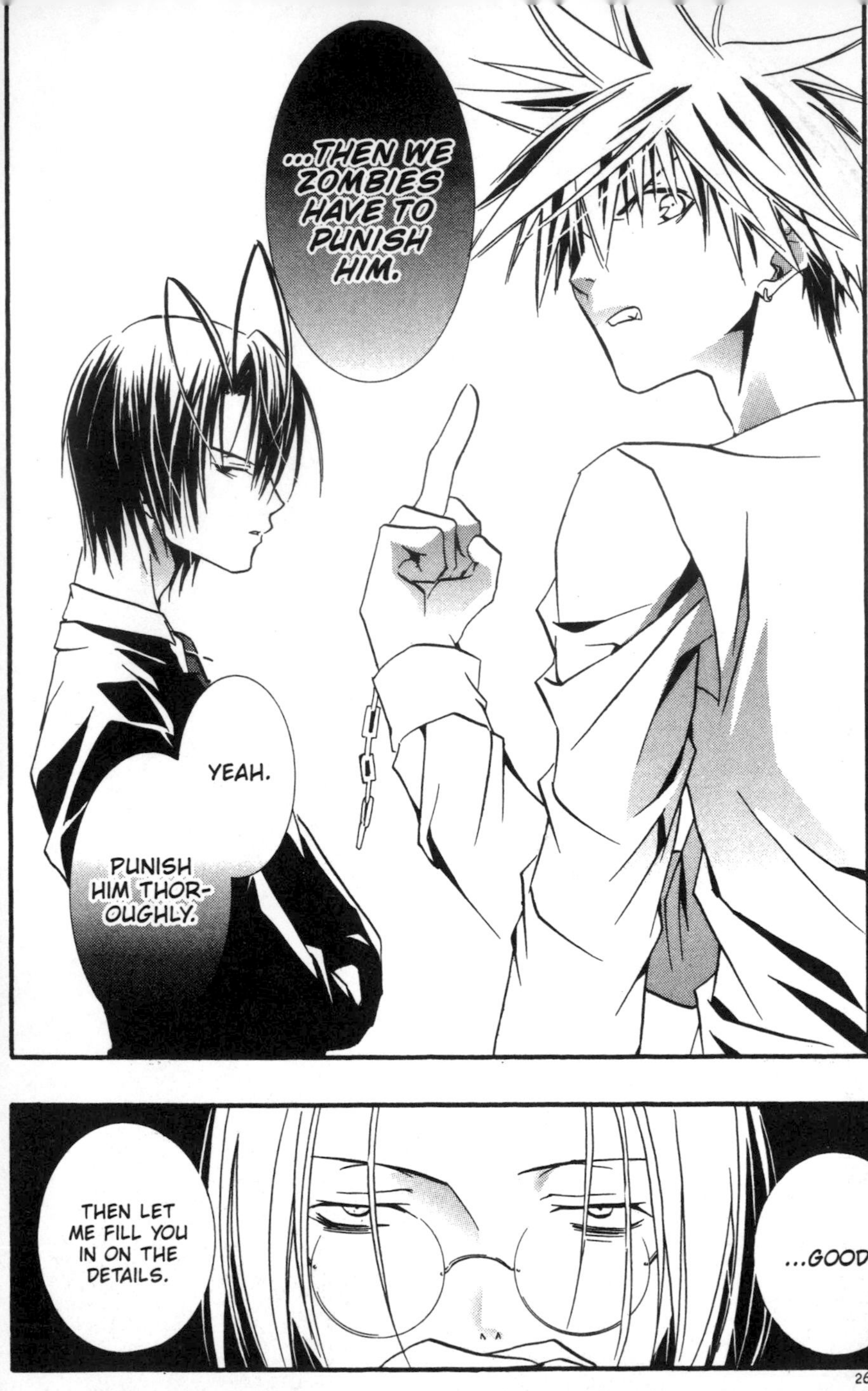
...THEN WE ZOMBIES HAVE TO PUNISH HIM.
YEAH.
PUNISH HIM THOROUGHLY.
...GOOD.
THEN LET ME FILL YOU IN ON THE DETAILS.

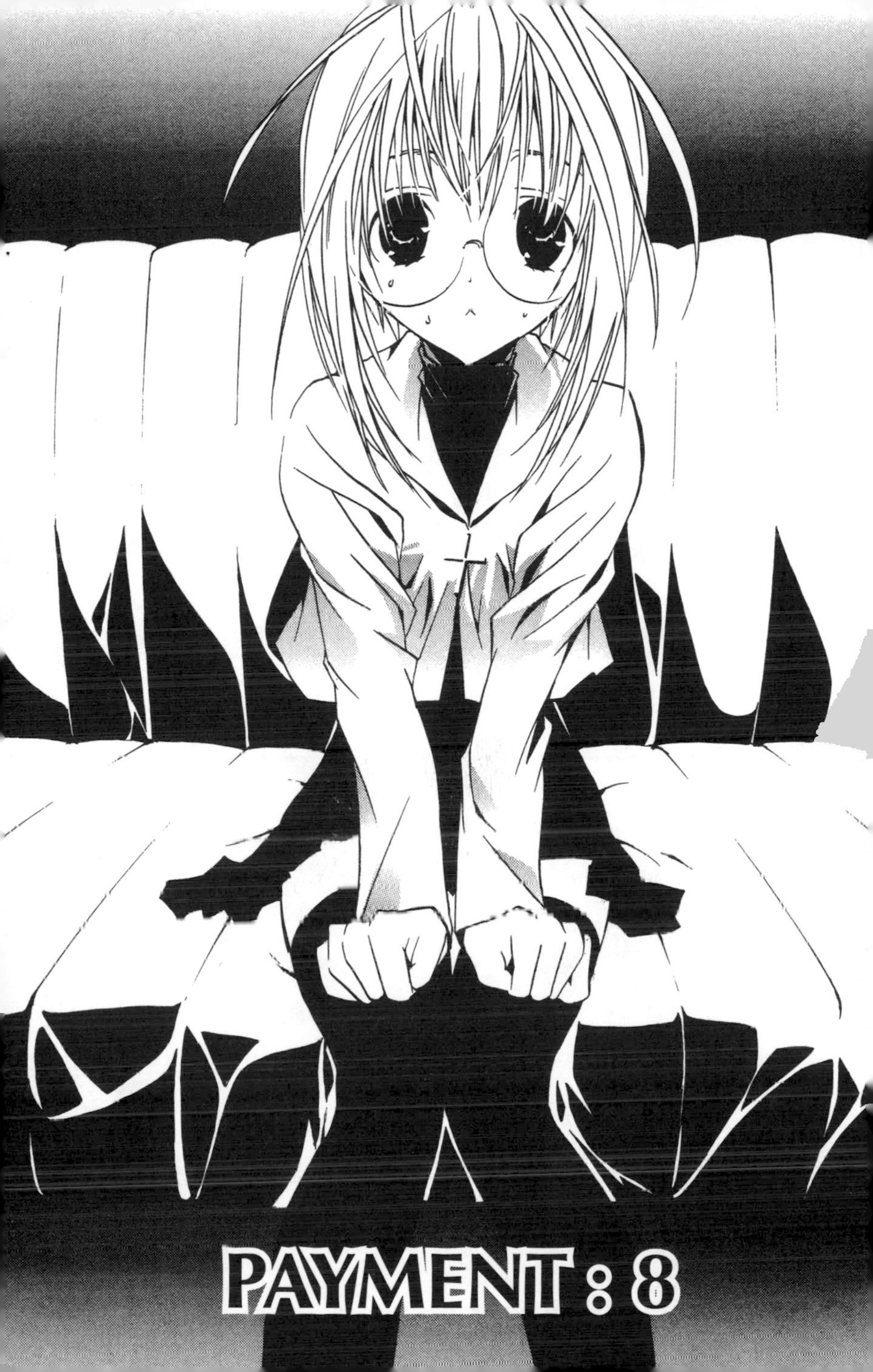
PAYMENT : 8

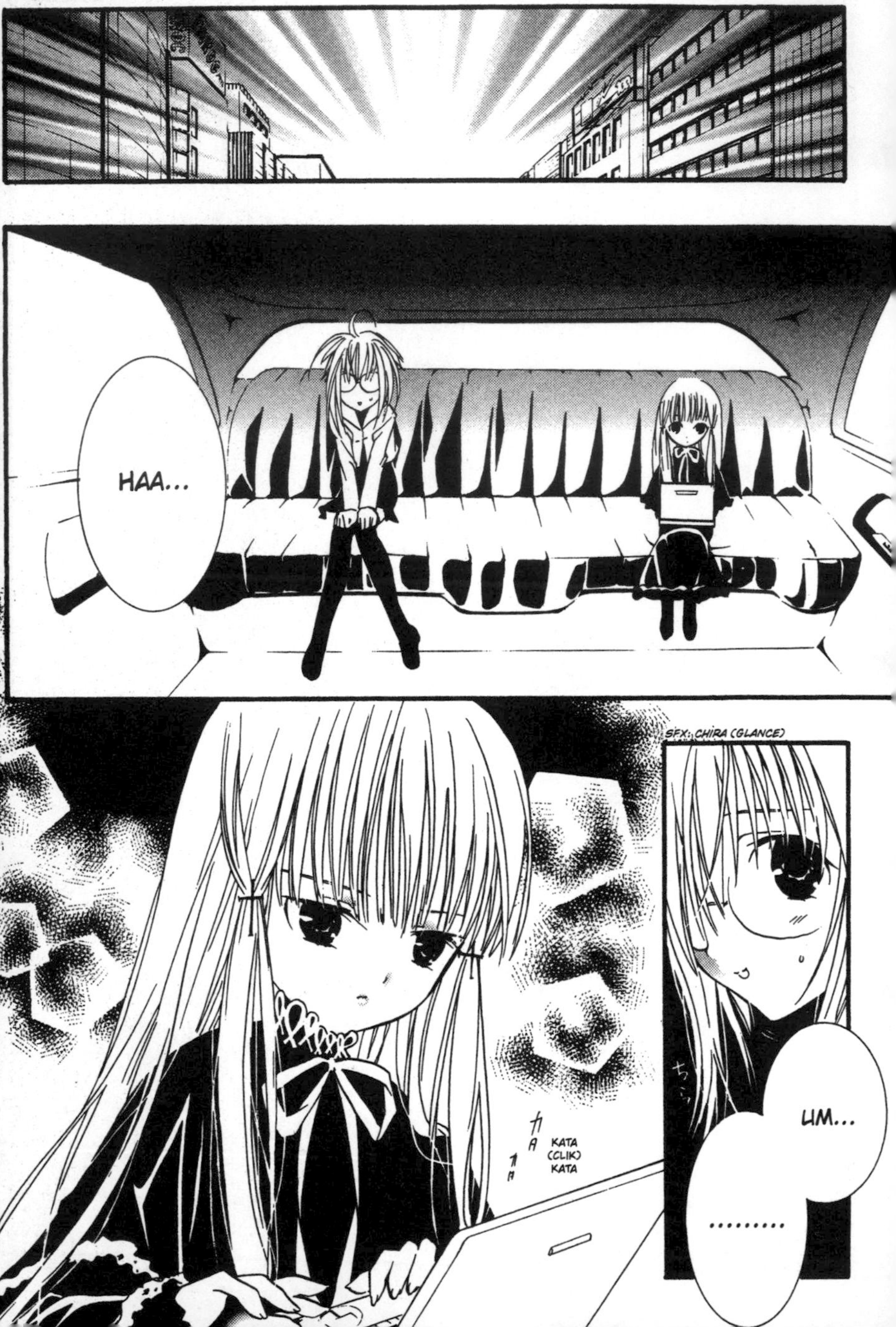
HAA...
SFX: CHIRA (GLANCE)
UM...
....
KATA
(CLIK)
KATA

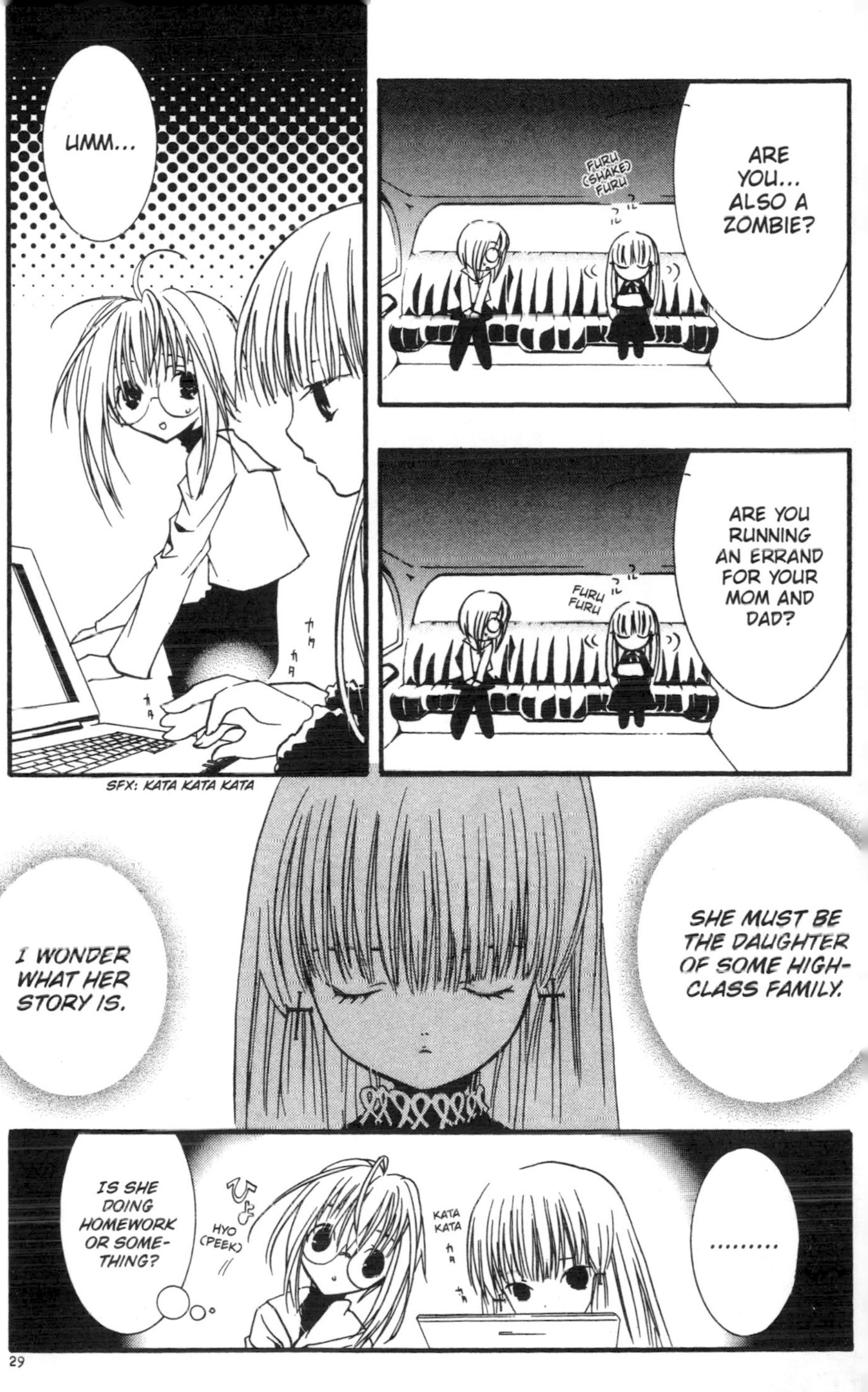
FURU (SHAKE) FURU
ARE YOU... ALSO A ZOMBIE?
FURU FURU
ARE YOU RUNNING AN ERRAND FOR YOUR MOM AND DAD?
UMM...
SFX: KATA KATA KATA
SHE MUST BE THE DAUGHTER OF SOME HIGH-CLASS FAMILY.
I WONDER WHAT HER STORY IS.
....
KATA KATA
HYO (PEEK)
IS SHE DOING HOMEWORK OR SOME-THING?

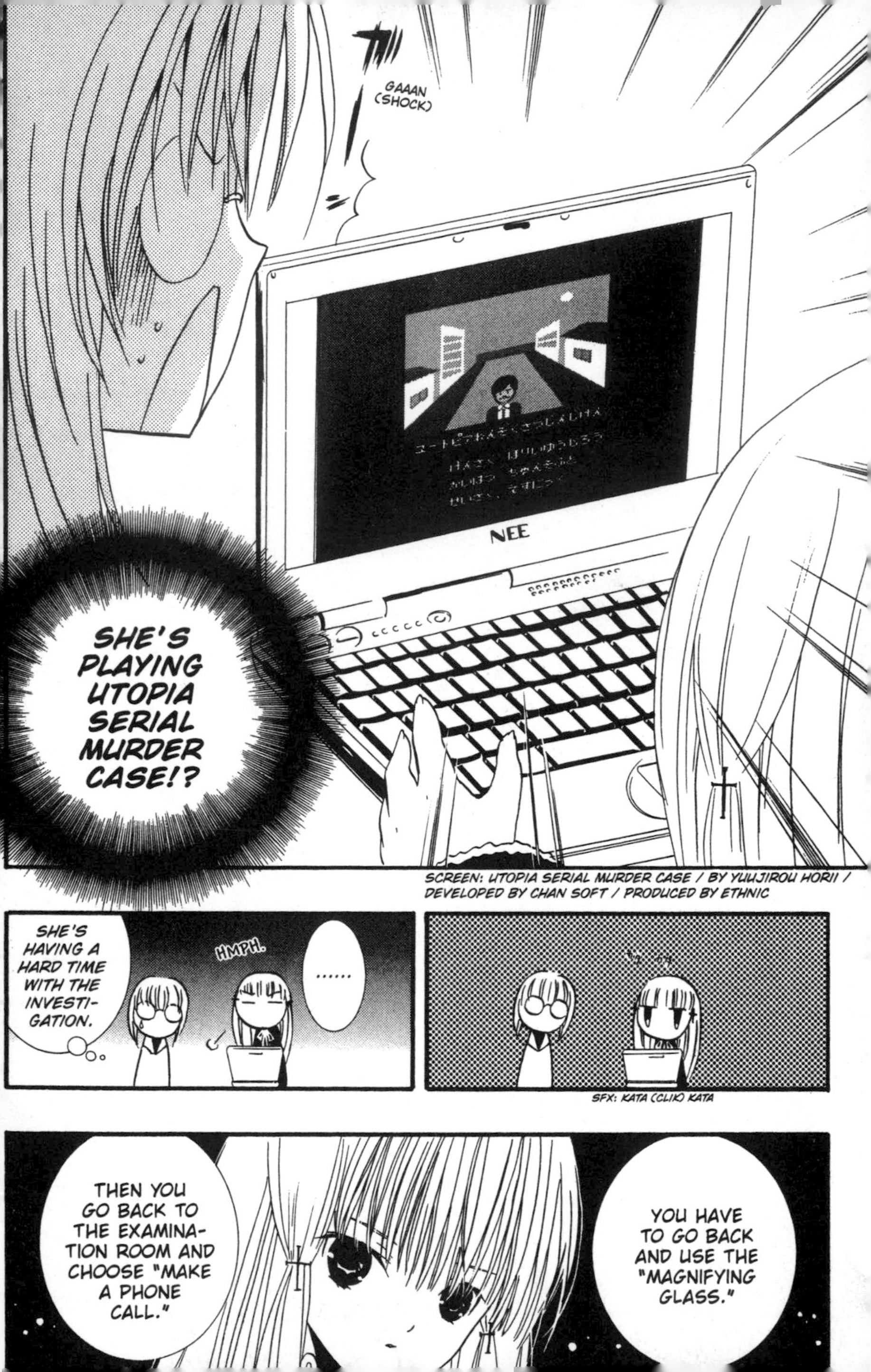
GAAAN (SHOCK)
SHE'S PLAYING UTOPIA SERIAL MURDER CASE!?
NEE
SCREEN: UTOPIA SERIAL MURDER CASE / BY YUUJIROU HORII / DEVELOPED BY CHAN SOFT / PRODUCED BY ETHNIC
SFX: KATA (CLIK) KATA
......
HMPH.
SHE'S HAVING A HARD TIME WITH THE INVESTIGATION.
YOU HAVE TO GO BACK AND USE THE "MAGNIFYING GLASS."
THEN YOU GO BACK TO THE EXAMINATION ROOM AND CHOOSE "MAKE A PHONE CALL."

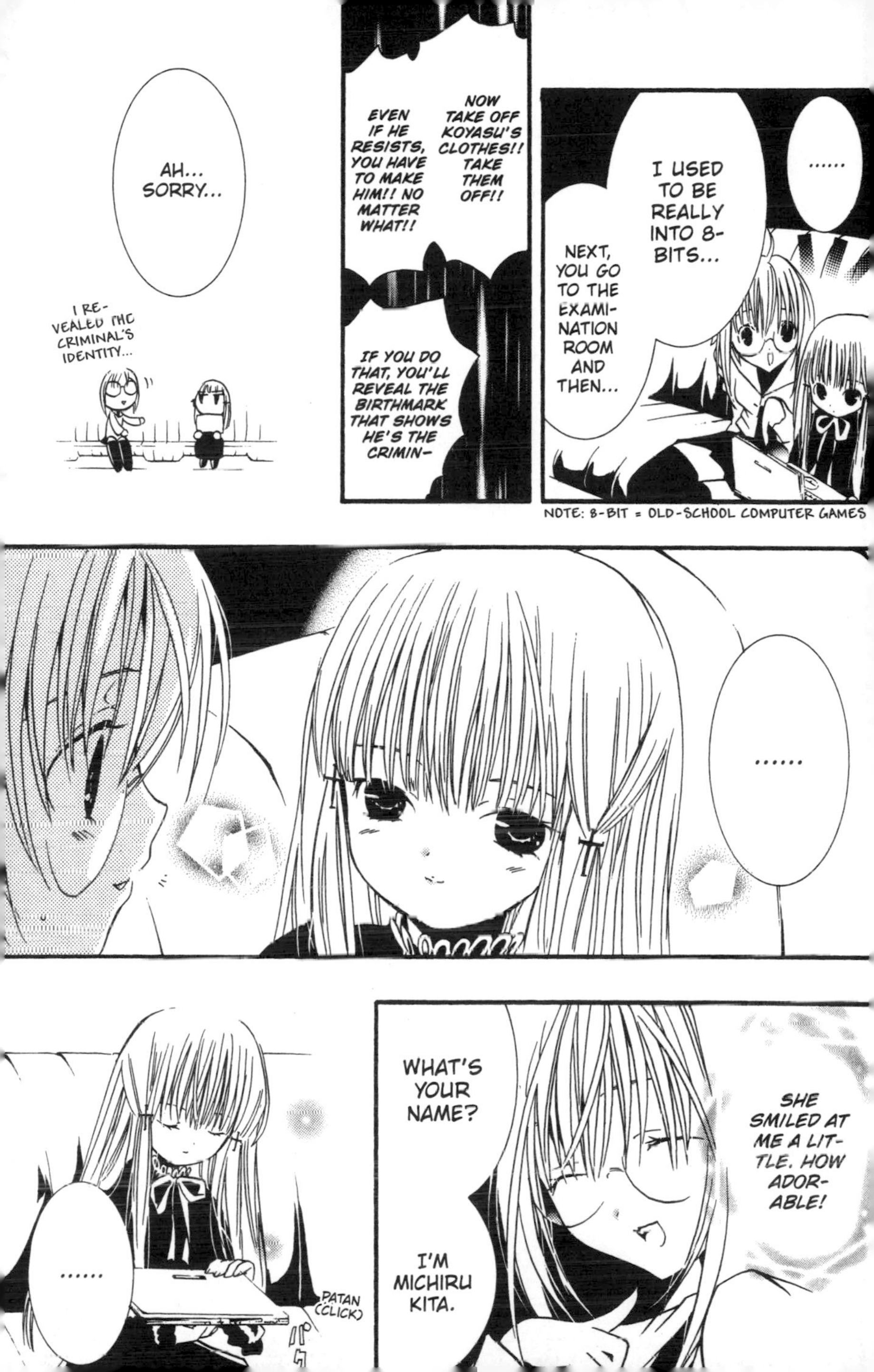
......
I USED TO BE REALLY INTO 8-BITS...
NEXT, YOU GO TO THE EXAMINATION ROOM AND THEN...
NOW TAKE OFF KOYASU'S CLOTHES!! TAKE THEM OFF!!
EVEN IF HE RESISTS, YOU HAVE TO MAKE HIM!! NO MATTER WHAT!!
IF YOU DO THAT, YOU'LL REVEAL THE BIRTHMARK THAT SHOWS HE'S THE CRIMIN-
AH... SORRY...
I REVEALED THE CRIMINAL'S IDENTITY...
NOTE: 8-BIT = OLD-SCHOOL COMPUTER GAMES
......
SHE SMILED AT ME A LITTLE. HOW ADORABLE!
WHAT'S YOUR NAME?
I'M MICHIRU KITA.
......
PATAN (CLICK)

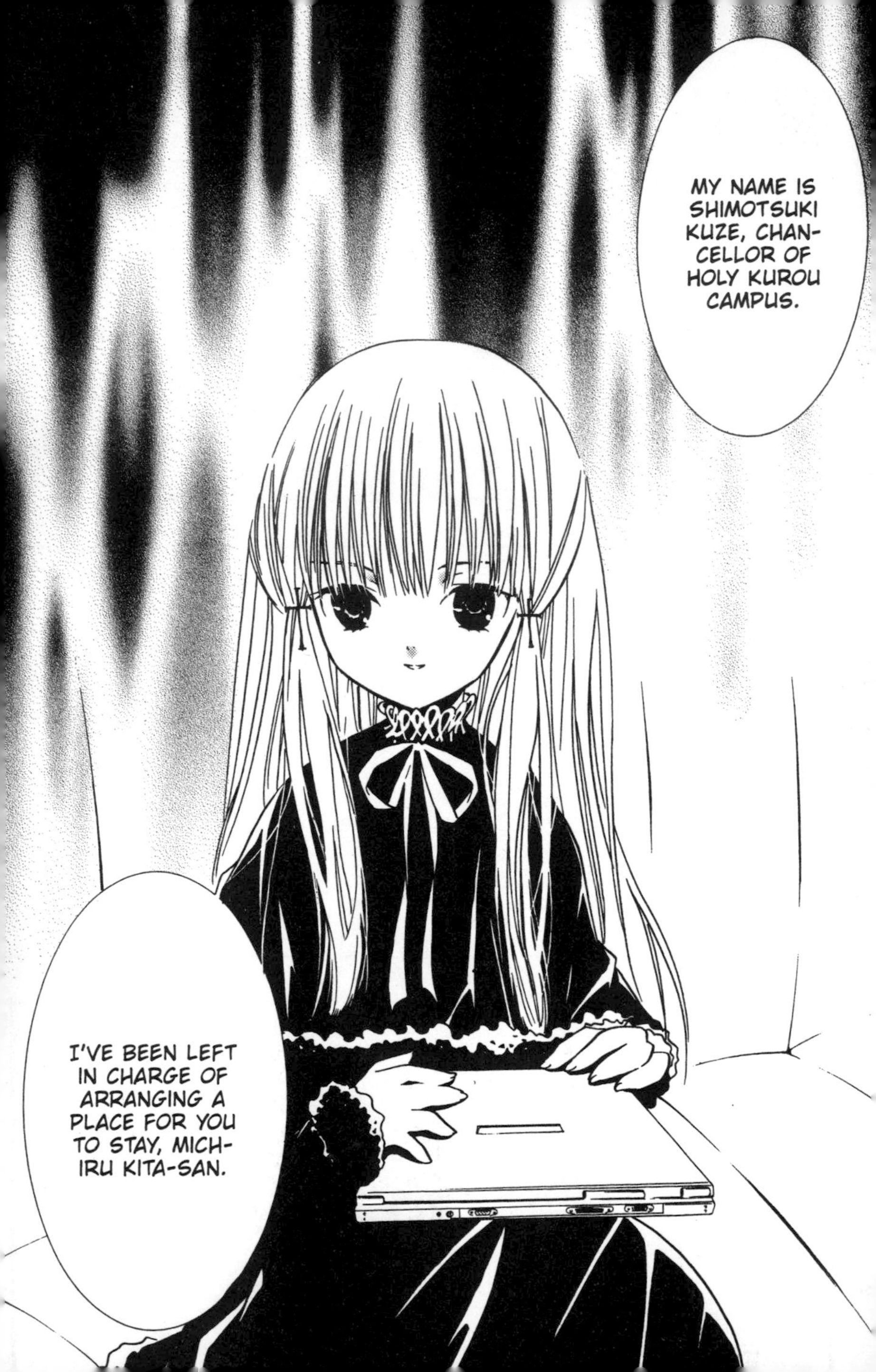
MY NAME IS SHIMOTSUKI KUZE, CHAN-CELLOR OF HOLY KUROU CAMPUS.
I'VE BEEN LEFT IN CHARGE OF ARRANGING A PLACE FOR YOU TO STAY, MICH-IRU KITA-SAN.

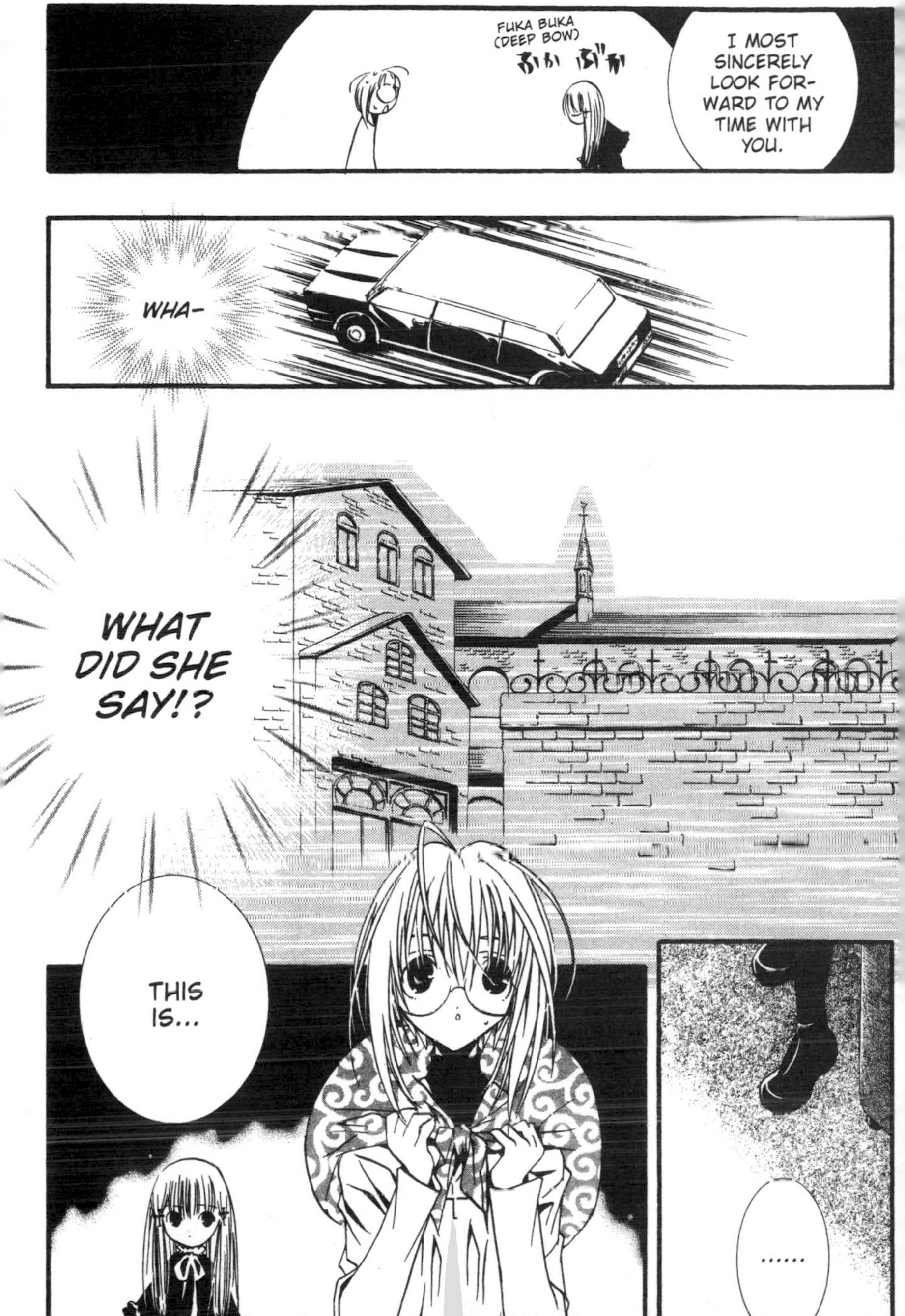
I MOST SINCERELY LOOK FOR-WARD TO MY TIME WITH YOU.
FUKA BUKA (DEEP BOW)
ふか ぶか
WHA-
WHAT DID SHE SAY!?
......
THIS IS...

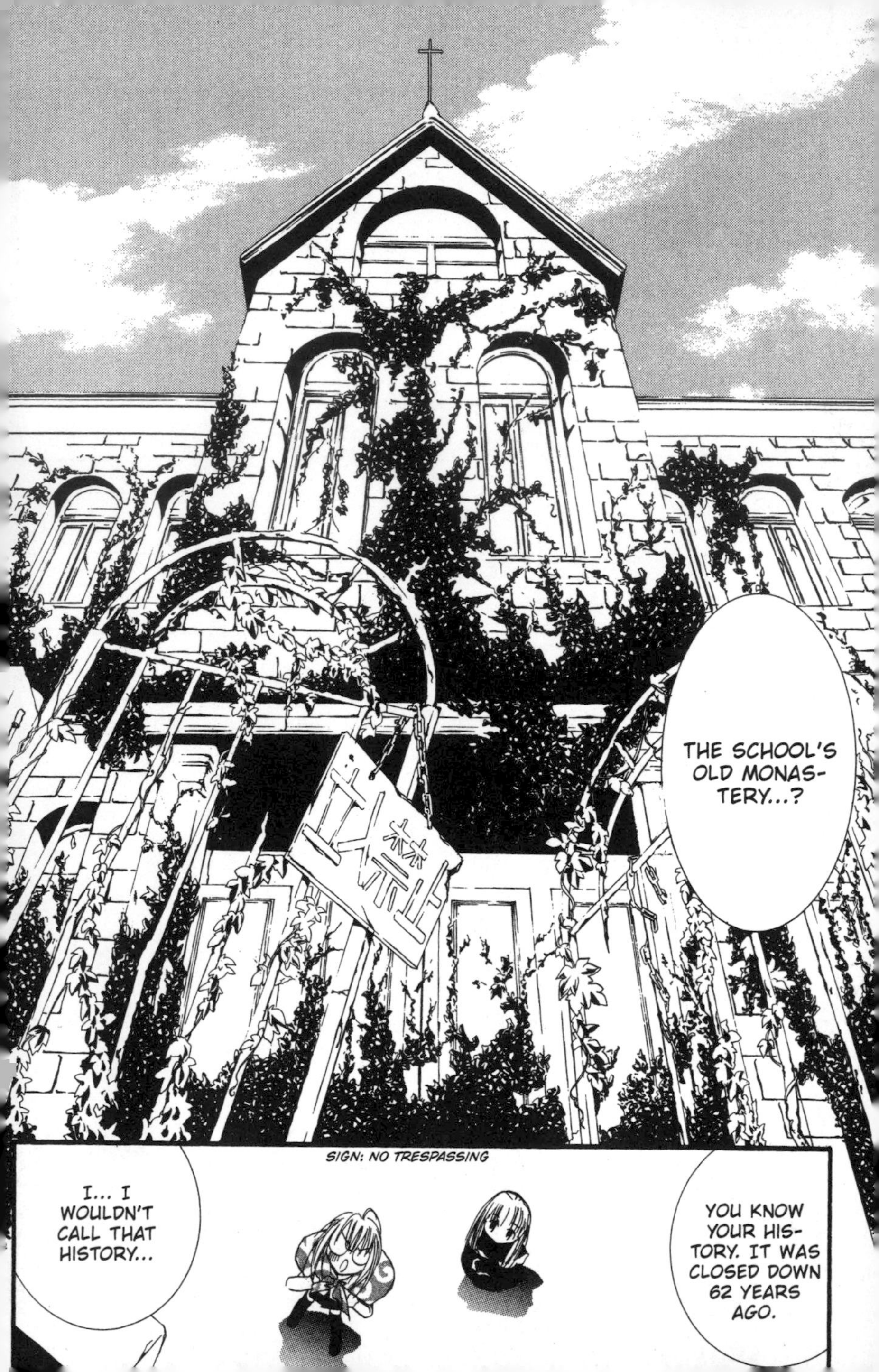
THE SCHOOL'S OLD MONASTERY...?
SIGN: NO TRESPASSING
YOU KNOW YOUR HISTORY. IT WAS CLOSED DOWN 62 YEARS AGO.
I... I WOULDN'T CALL THAT HISTORY...

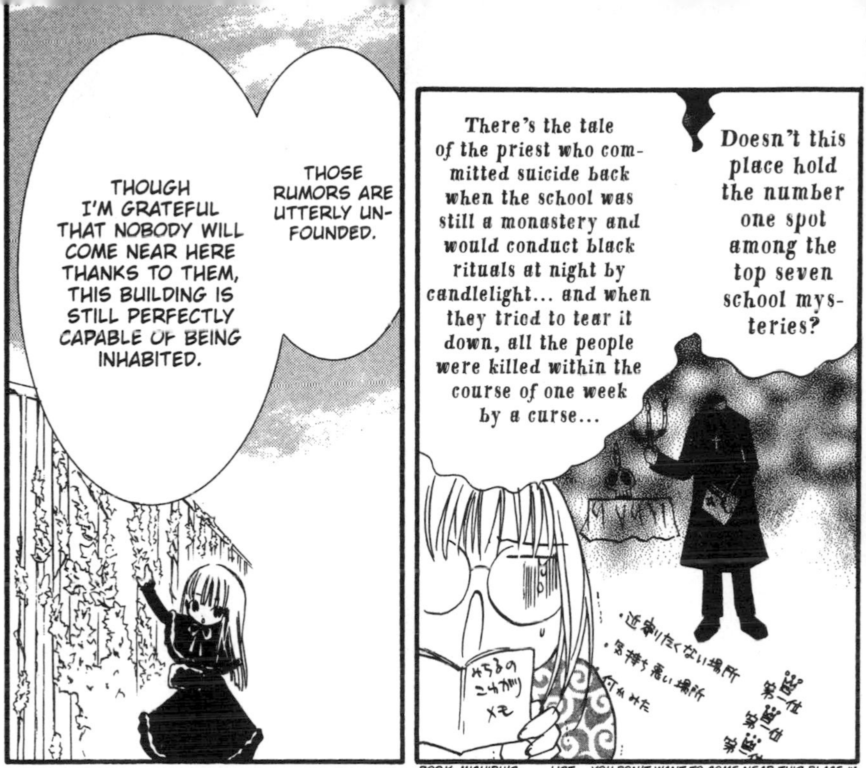
Doesn't this place hold the number one spot among the top seven school mysteries?
There's the tale of the priest who committed suicide back when the school was still a monastery and would conduct black rituals at night by candlelight... and when they tried to tear it down, all the people were killed within the course of one week by a curse...
THOSE RUMORS ARE UTTERLY UNFOUNDED.
THOUGH I'M GRATEFUL THAT NOBODY WILL COME NEAR HERE THANKS TO THEM, THIS BUILDING IS STILL PERFECTLY CAPABLE OF BEING INHABITED.

BOOK: MICHIRU'S FEAR NOTES LIST: - YOU DON'T WANT TO COME NEAR THIS PLACE #1
- IT'S CREEPY AND GROSS #1
- YOU'LL SEE THINGS #1

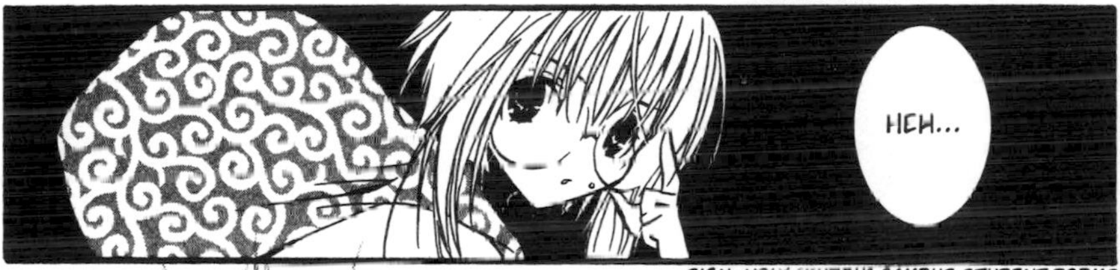
HEH...

SIGN: HOLY [KUROU] CAMPUS STUDENT DORMS

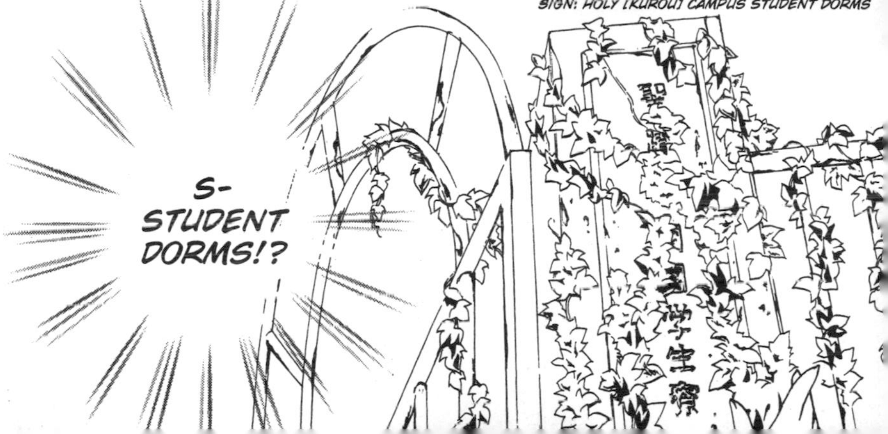
S-STUDENT DORMS!?

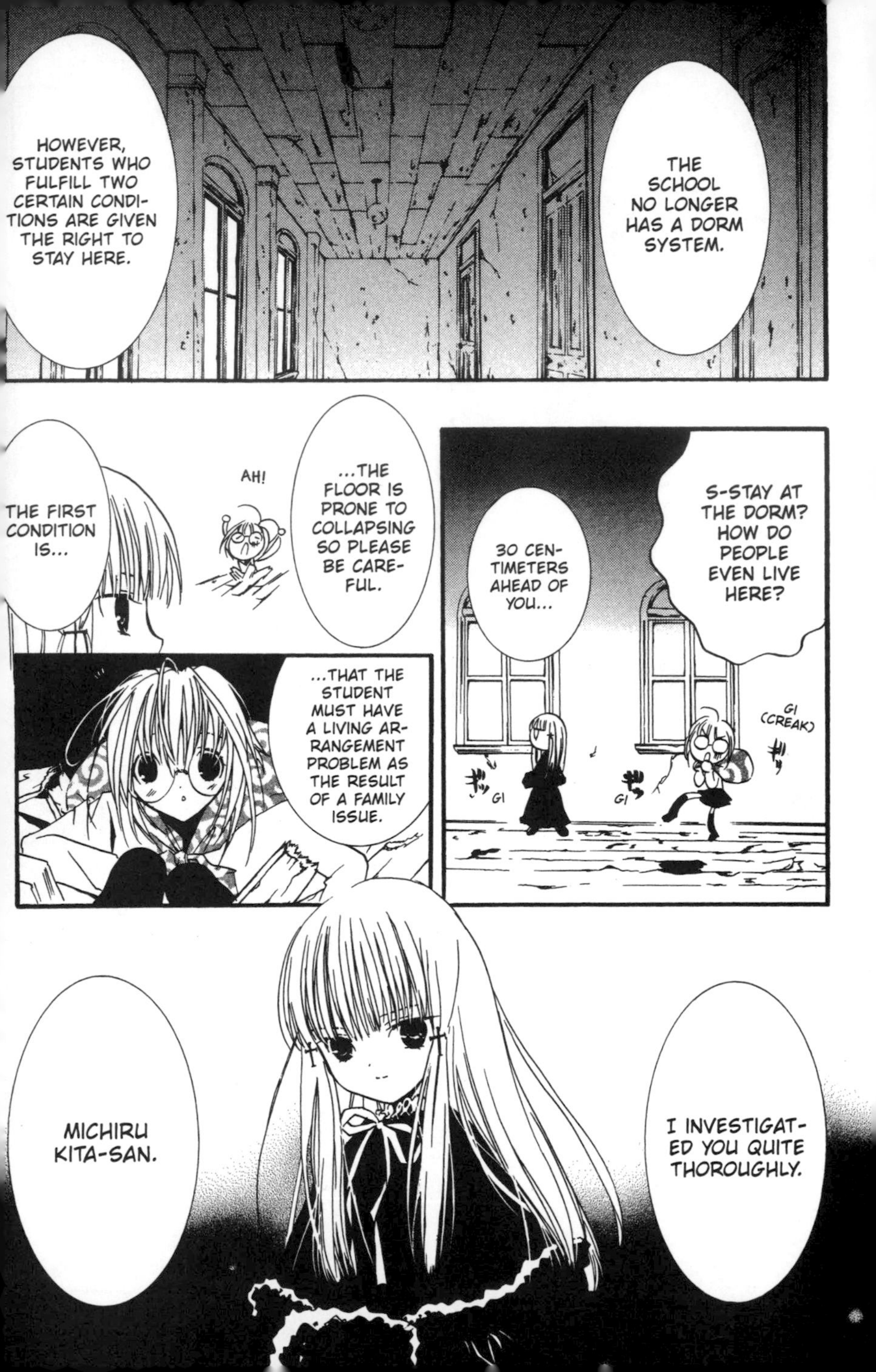
THE SCHOOL NO LONGER HAS A DORM SYSTEM.
HOWEVER, STUDENTS WHO FULFILL TWO CERTAIN CONDITIONS ARE GIVEN THE RIGHT TO STAY HERE.
S-STAY AT THE DORM? HOW DO PEOPLE EVEN LIVE HERE?
30 CENTIMETERS AHEAD OF YOU...
GI (CREAK)
GI
GI
...THE FLOOR IS PRONE TO COLLAPSING SO PLEASE BE CAREFUL.
AH!
THE FIRST CONDITION IS...
...THAT THE STUDENT MUST HAVE A LIVING ARRANGEMENT PROBLEM AS THE RESULT OF A FAMILY ISSUE.
I INVESTIGATED YOU QUITE THOROUGHLY.
MICHIRU KITA-SAN.

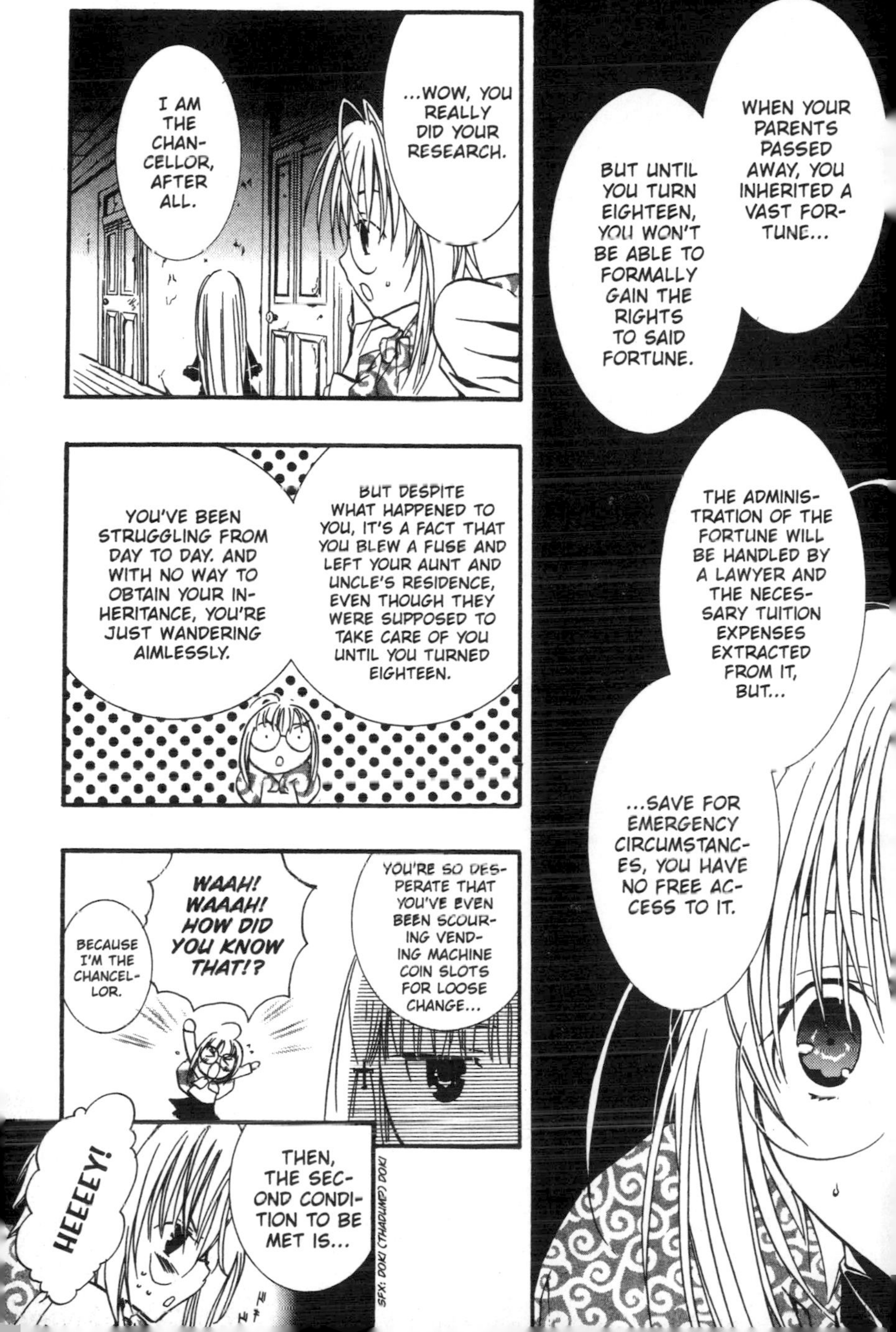
WHEN YOUR PARENTS PASSED AWAY, YOU INHERITED A VAST FOR-TUNE...
BUT UNTIL YOU TURN EIGHTEEN, YOU WON'T BE ABLE TO FORMALLY GAIN THE RIGHTS TO SAID FORTUNE.
THE ADMINIS-TRATION OF THE FORTUNE WILL BE HANDLED BY A LAWYER AND THE NECES-SARY TUITION EXPENSES EXTRACTED FROM IT, BUT...
...SAVE FOR EMERGENCY CIRCUMSTANC-ES, YOU HAVE NO FREE AC-CESS TO IT.
...WOW, YOU REALLY DID YOUR RESEARCH.
I AM THE CHAN-CELLOR, AFTER ALL.
BUT DESPITE WHAT HAPPENED TO YOU, IT'S A FACT THAT YOU BLEW A FUSE AND LEFT YOUR AUNT AND UNCLE'S RESIDENCE, EVEN THOUGH THEY WERE SUPPOSED TO TAKE CARE OF YOU UNTIL YOU TURNED EIGHTEEN.
YOU'VE BEEN STRUGGLING FROM DAY TO DAY. AND WITH NO WAY TO OBTAIN YOUR IN-HERITANCE, YOU'RE JUST WANDERING AIMLESSLY.
YOU'RE SO DES-PERATE THAT YOU'VE EVEN BEEN SCOUR-ING VEND-ING MACHINE COIN SLOTS FOR LOOSE CHANGE...
WAAH! WAAAH! HOW DID YOU KNOW THAT!?
BECAUSE I'M THE CHANCEL-LOR.
THEN, THE SEC-OND CONDI-TION TO BE MET IS...
SFX: DOKI (THADUMP) DOKI
HEEEEY!

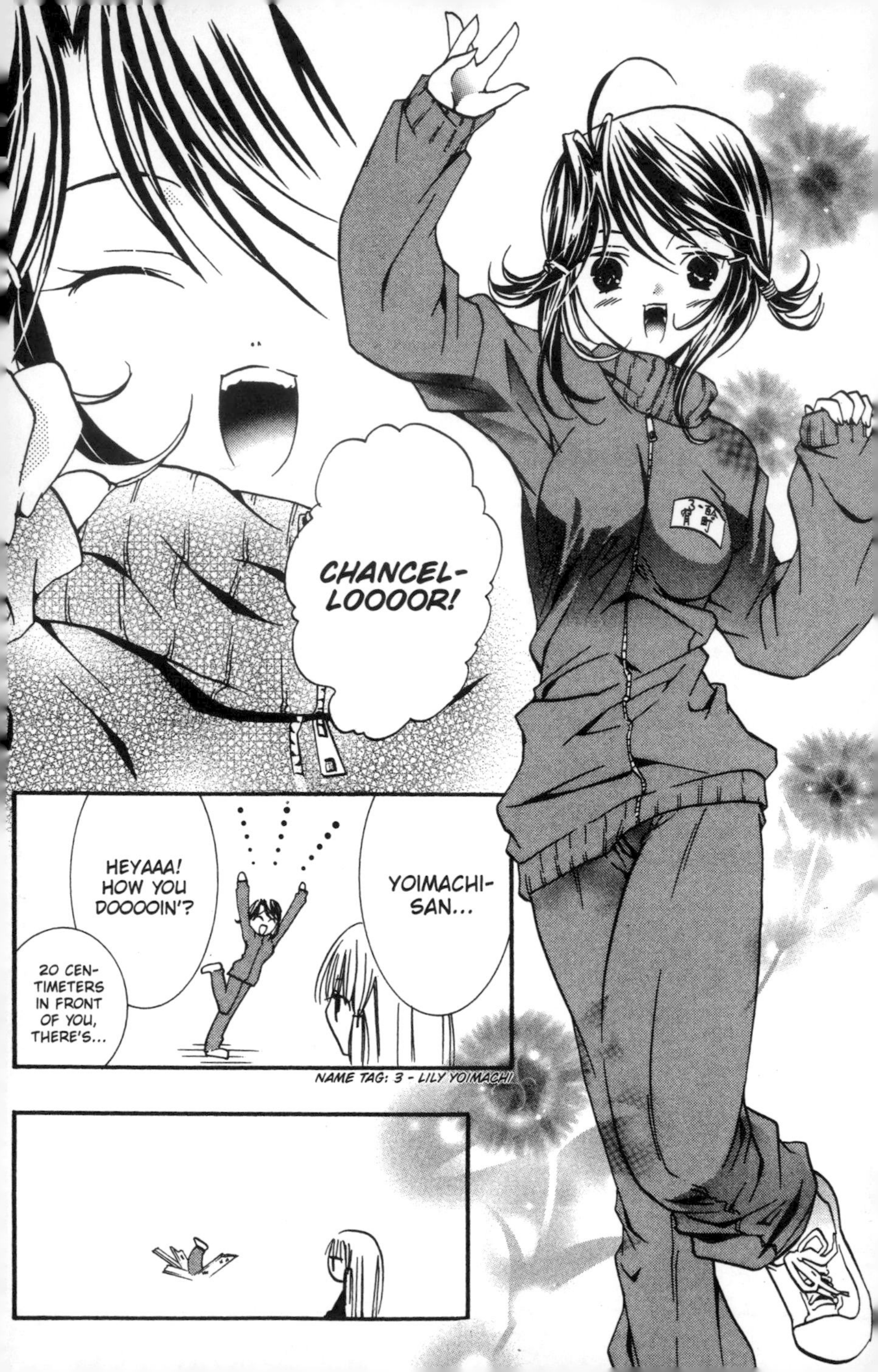

CHANCEL-LOOOOR!
YOIMACHI-SAN...
HEYAAA! HOW YOU DOOOOIN'?
20 CEN-TIMETERS IN FRONT OF YOU, THERE'S...
NAME TAG: 3 - LILY YOIMACHI

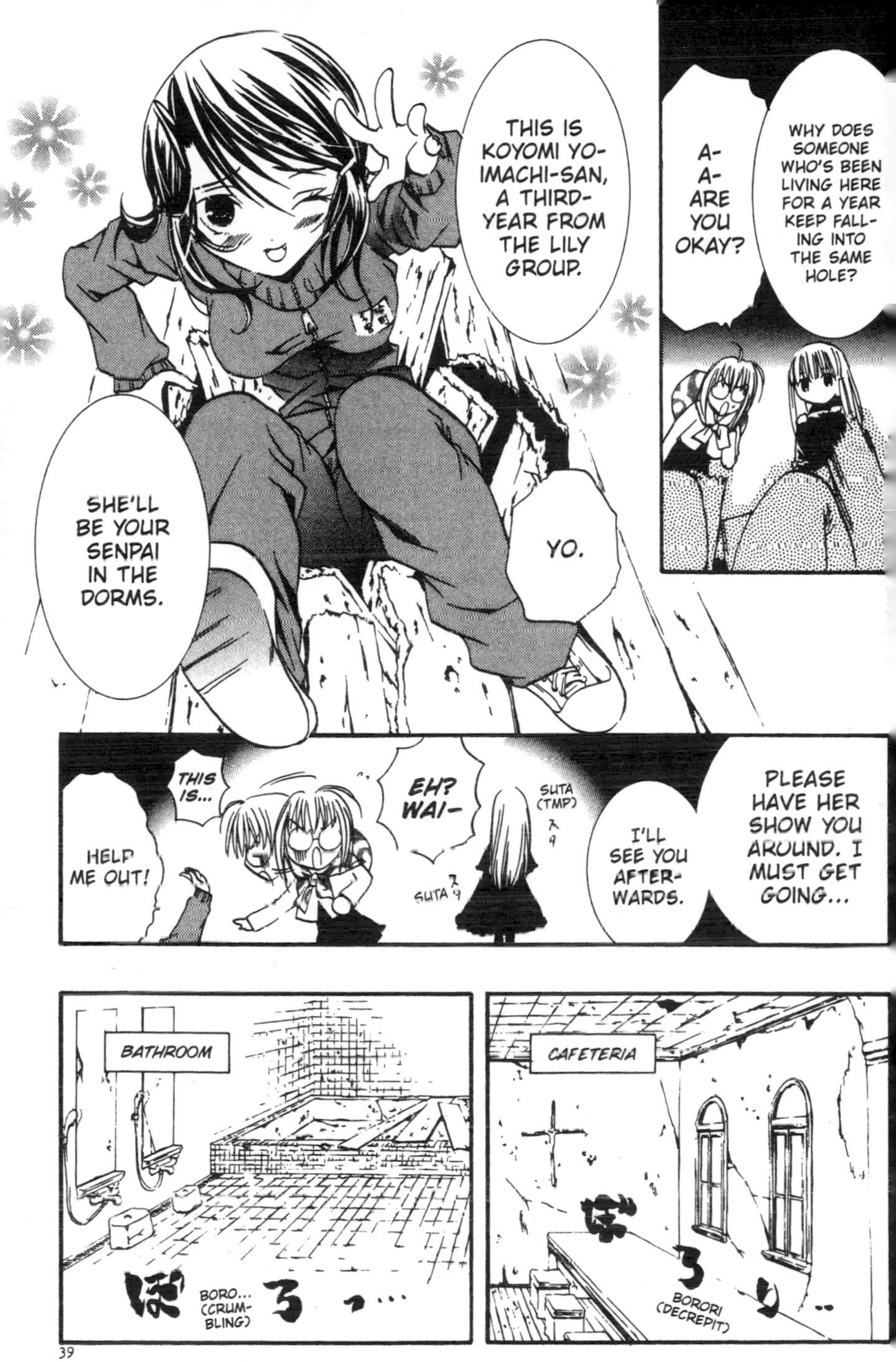
WHY DOES SOMEONE WHO'S BEEN LIVING HERE FOR A YEAR KEEP FALLING INTO THE SAME HOLE?
A-A-ARE YOU OKAY?
THIS IS KOYOMI YOIMACHI-SAN, A THIRD-YEAR FROM THE LILY GROUP.
YO.
SHE'LL BE YOUR SENPAI IN THE DORMS.
PLEASE HAVE HER SHOW YOU AROUND. I MUST GET GOING...
I'LL SEE YOU AFTERWARDS.
SUTA (TMP)
EH? WAI-
THIS IS...
SUTA
HELP ME OUT!
CAFETERIA
BORORI (DECREPIT)
BATHROOM
BORO... (CRUMBLING)

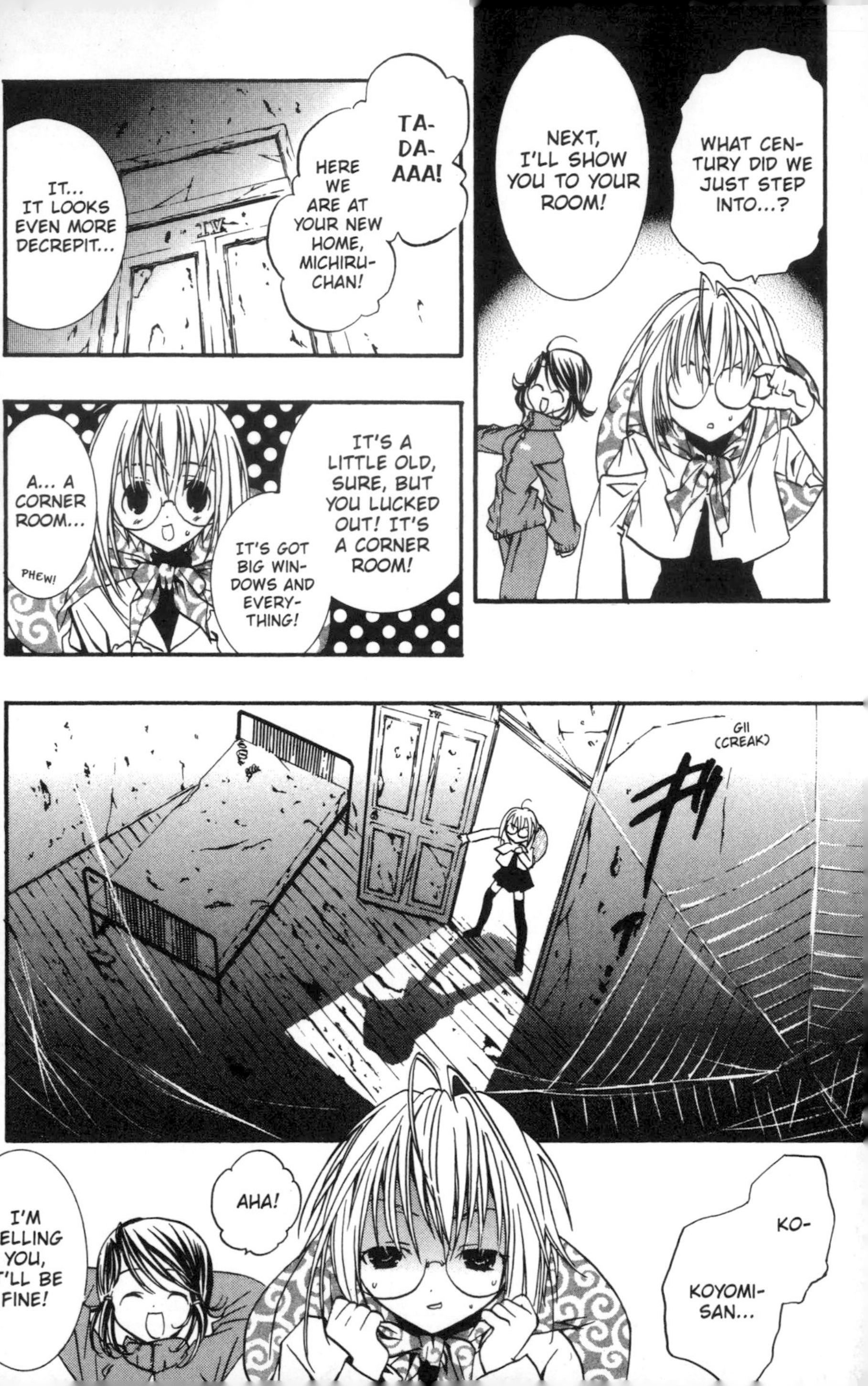
WHAT CENTURY DID WE JUST STEP INTO...?
NEXT, I'LL SHOW YOU TO YOUR ROOM!
TA-DA-AAA!
HERE WE ARE AT YOUR NEW HOME, MICHIRU-CHAN!
IT... IT LOOKS EVEN MORE DECREPIT...
IT'S A LITTLE OLD, SURE, BUT YOU LUCKED OUT! IT'S A CORNER ROOM!
IT'S GOT BIG WINDOWS AND EVERYTHING!
A... A CORNER ROOM...
PHEW!
GII (CREAK)
KO- KOYOMI-SAN...
AHA!
I'M TELLING YOU, T'LL BE FINE!

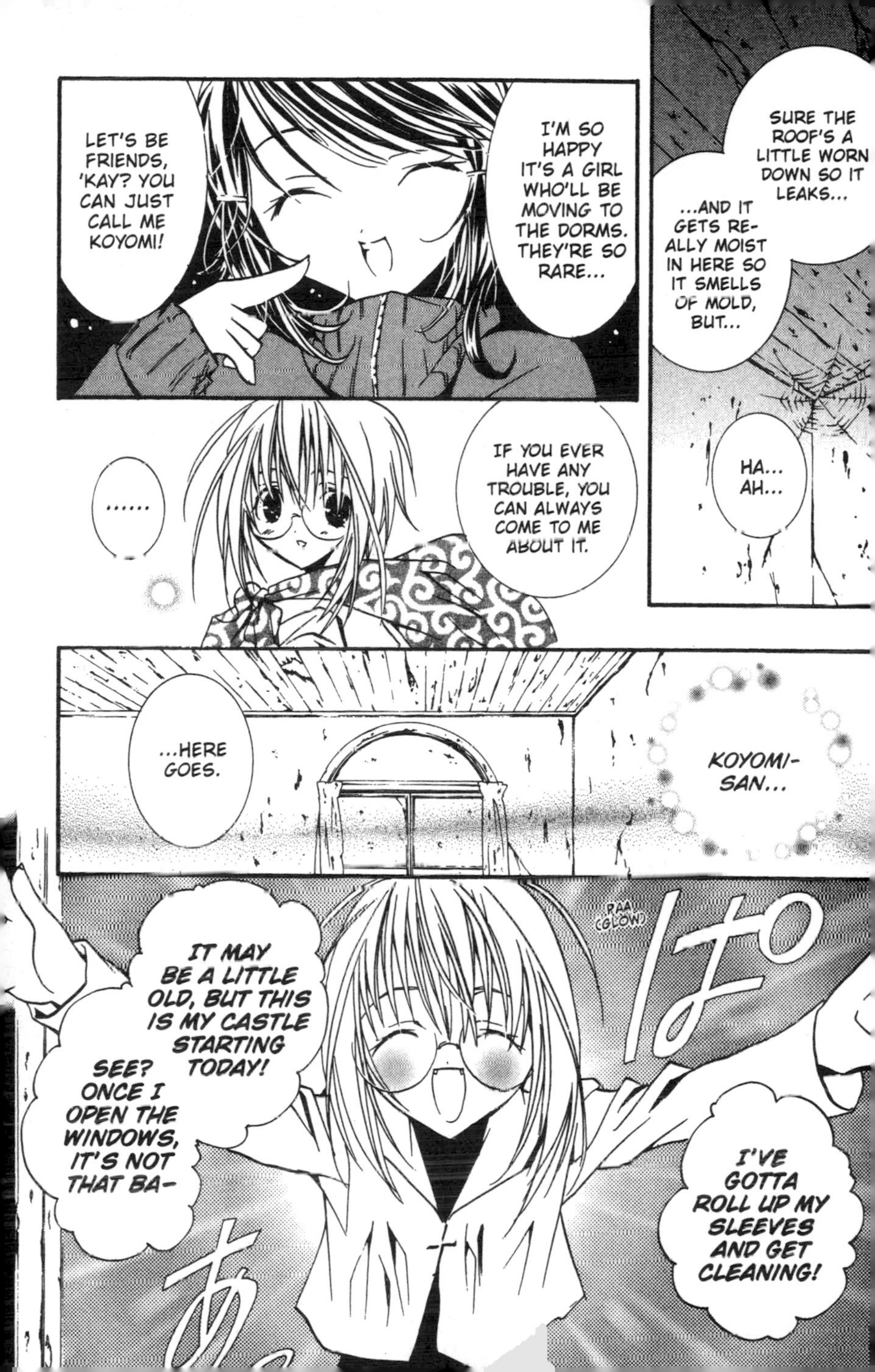
SURE THE ROOF'S A LITTLE WORN DOWN SO IT LEAKS...
...AND IT GETS REALLY MOIST IN HERE SO IT SMELLS OF MOLD, BUT...
HA... AH...
I'M SO HAPPY IT'S A GIRL WHO'LL BE MOVING TO THE DORMS. THEY'RE SO RARE...
LET'S BE FRIENDS, 'KAY? YOU CAN JUST CALL ME KOYOMI!
IF YOU EVER HAVE ANY TROUBLE, YOU CAN ALWAYS COME TO ME ABOUT IT.
......
KOYOMI-SAN...
...HERE GOES.
RAA (GLOW)
ぱ
IT MAY BE A LITTLE OLD, BUT THIS IS MY CASTLE STARTING TODAY!
I'VE GOTTA ROLL UP MY SLEEVES AND GET CLEANING!
SEE? ONCE I OPEN THE WINDOWS, IT'S NOT THAT BA-
あ

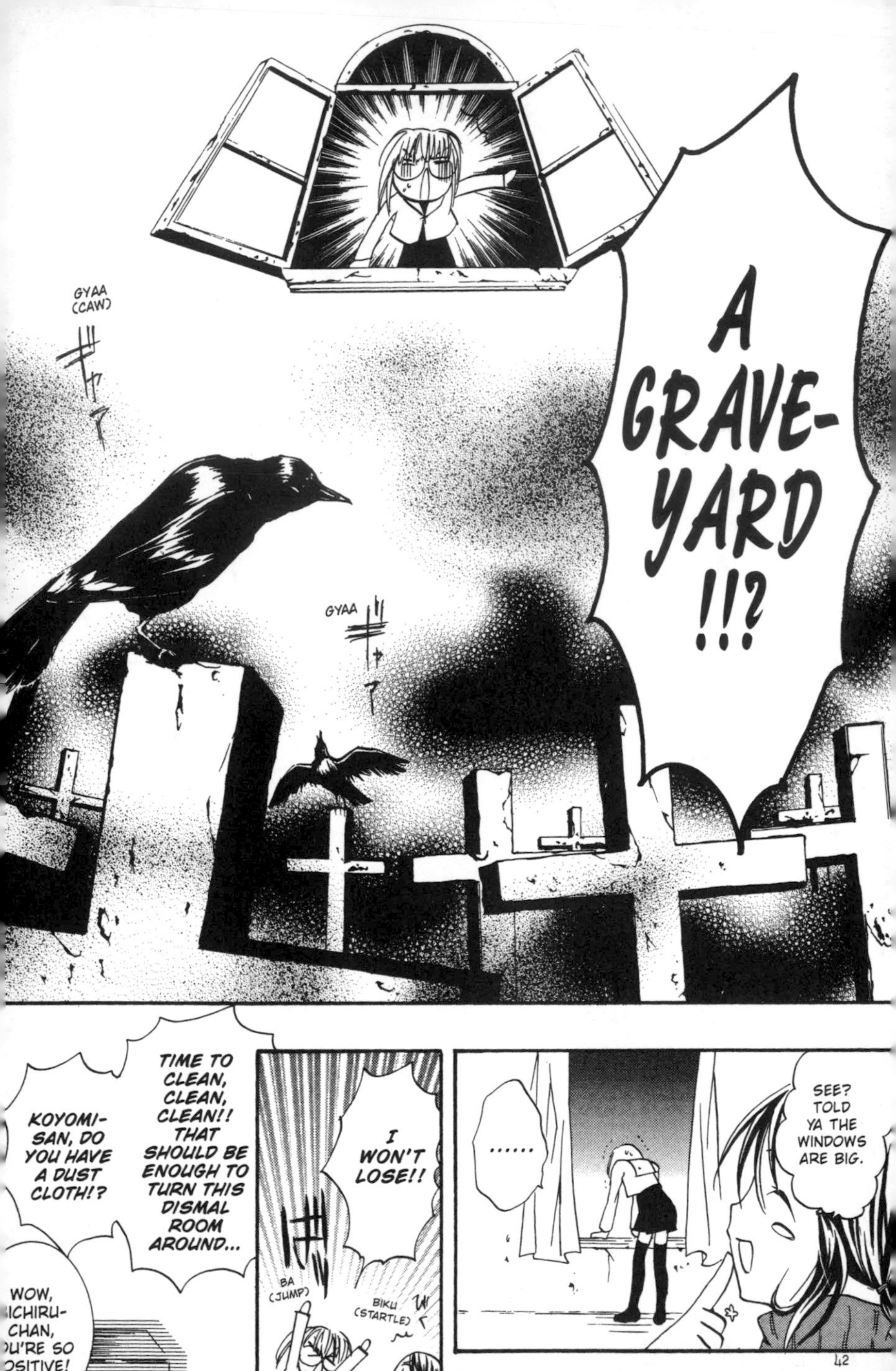
A GRAVE-YARD !!?
GYAA (CAW)
GYAA
SEE? TOLD YA THE WINDOWS ARE BIG.
......
I WON'T LOSE!!
BA (JUMP)
BIKU (STARTLE)
TIME TO CLEAN, CLEAN, CLEAN!! THAT SHOULD BE ENOUGH TO TURN THIS DISMAL ROOM AROUND...
KOYOMI-SAN, DO YOU HAVE A DUST CLOTH!?
WOW, ICHIRU-CHAN, U'RE SO OSITIVE!

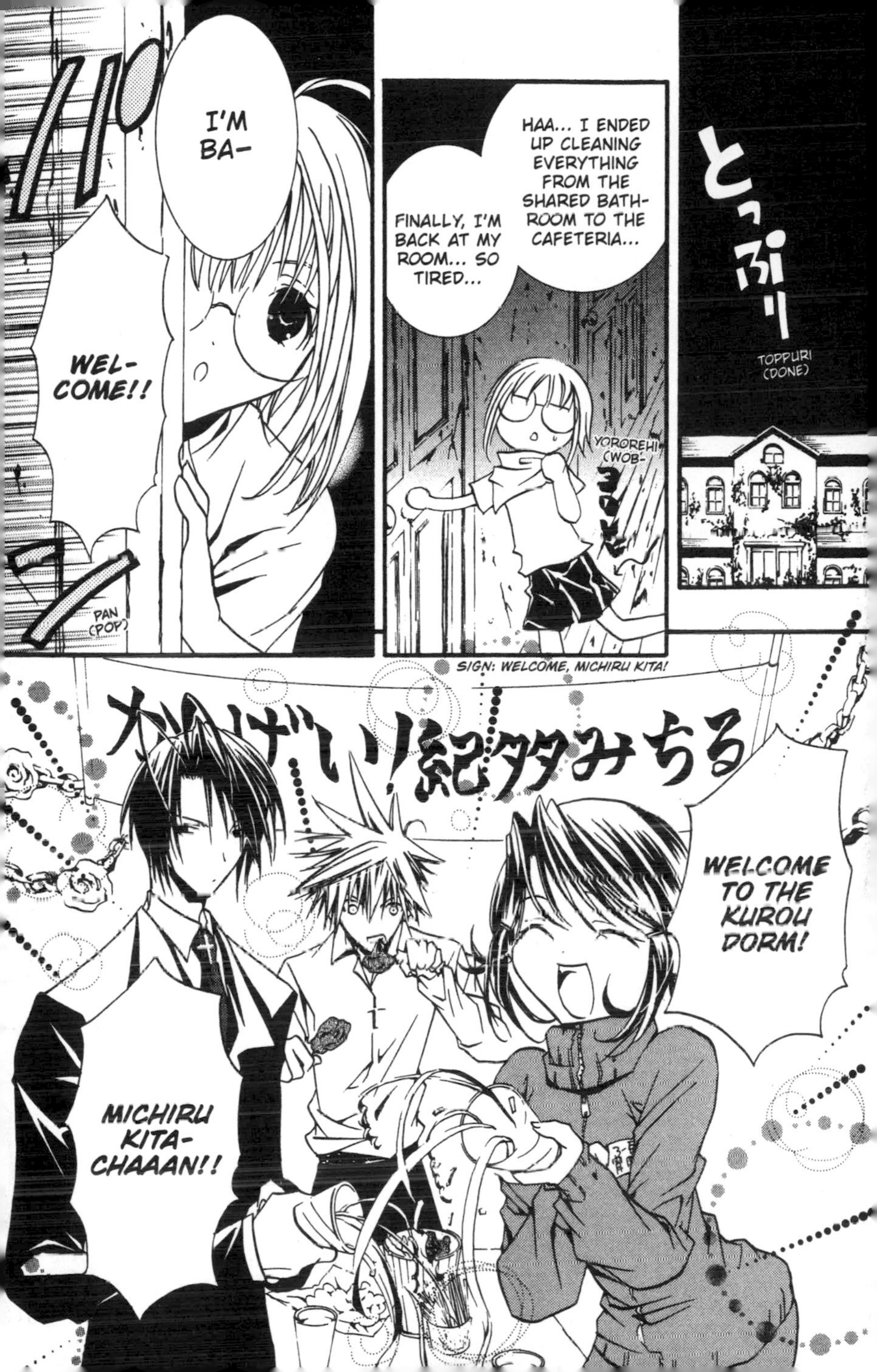

とっぷり
TOPPURI (DONE)
HAA... I ENDED UP CLEANING EVERYTHING FROM THE SHARED BATH-ROOM TO THE CAFETERIA...
FINALLY, I'M BACK AT MY ROOM... SO TIRED...
YOROREHI (WOB-
I'M BA-
WEL-COME!!
PAN (POP)
SIGN: WELCOME, MICHIRU KITA!
WELCOME TO THE KUROU DORM!
MICHIRU KITA-CHAAAN!!

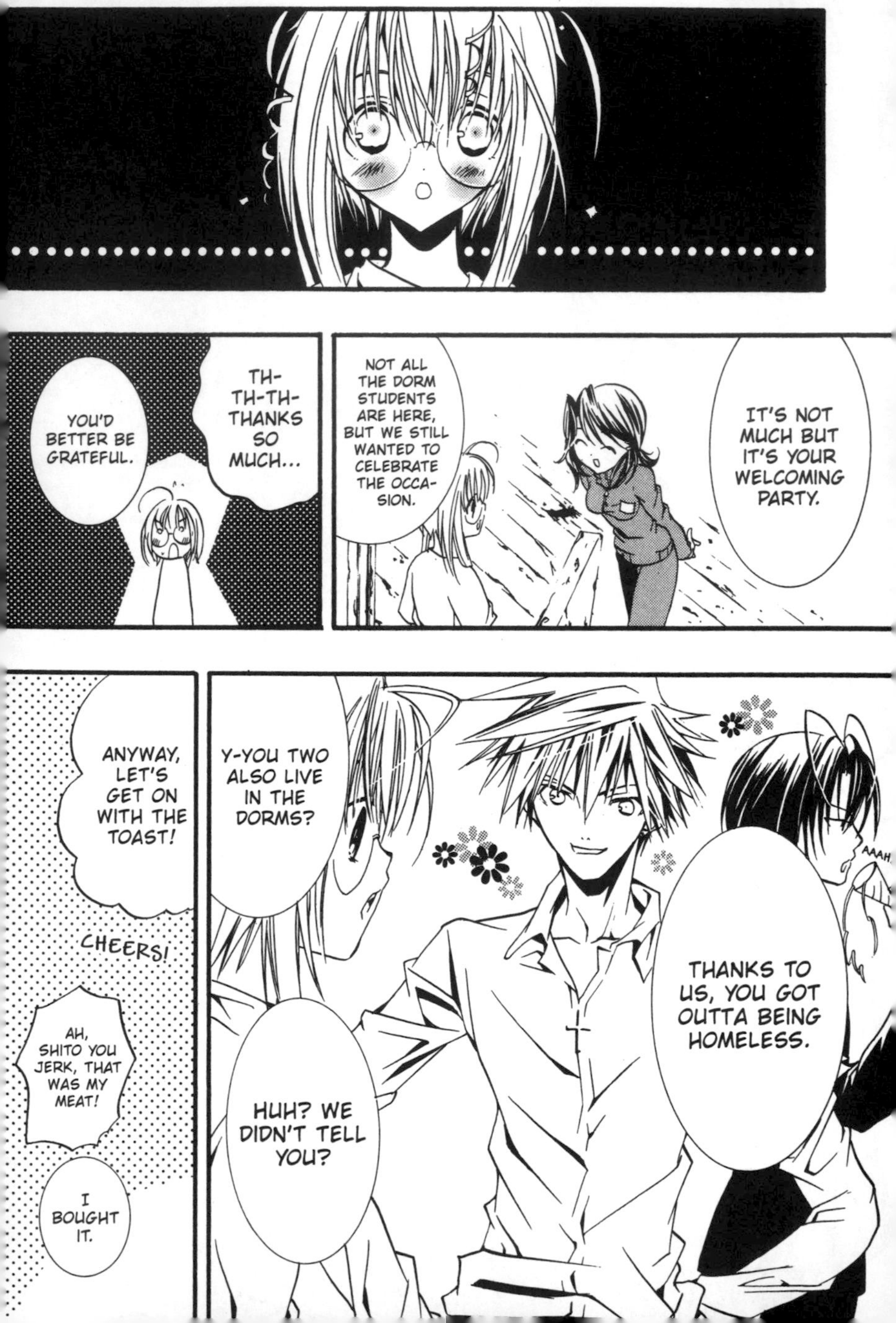
IT'S NOT MUCH BUT IT'S YOUR WELCOMING PARTY.
NOT ALL THE DORM STUDENTS ARE HERE, BUT WE STILL WANTED TO CELEBRATE THE OCCASION.
TH-TH-TH-THANKS SO MUCH...
YOU'D BETTER BE GRATEFUL.
Y-YOU TWO ALSO LIVE IN THE DORMS?
AAAH
THANKS TO US, YOU GOT OUTTA BEING HOMELESS.
HUH? WE DIDN'T TELL YOU?
ANYWAY, LET'S GET ON WITH THE TOAST!
CHEERS!
AH, SHITO YOU JERK, THAT WAS MY MEAT!
I BOUGHT IT.

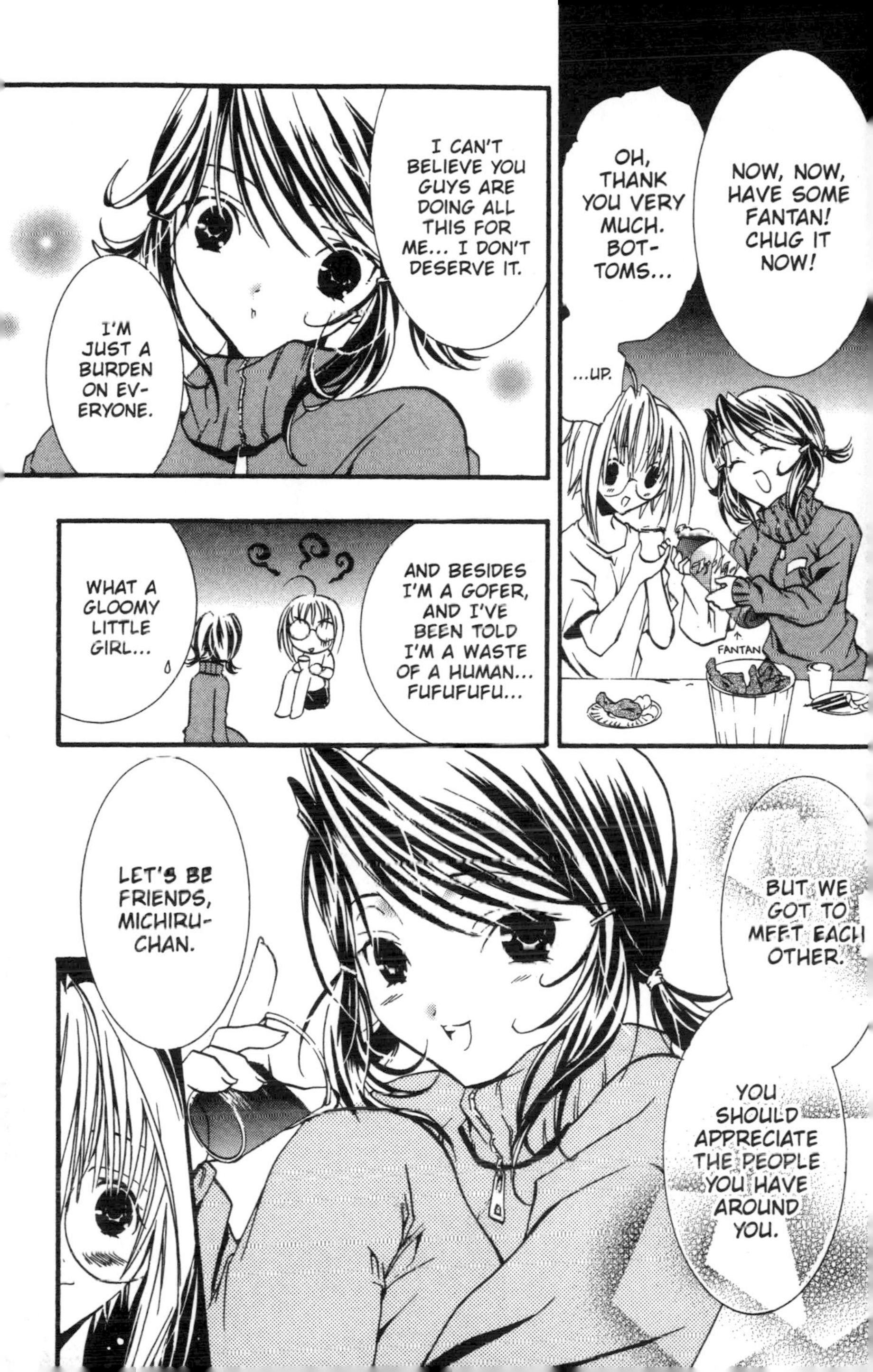
NOW, NOW, HAVE SOME FANTAN! CHUG IT NOW!
OH, THANK YOU VERY MUCH. BOT-TOMS...
...UP.
FANTAN
I CAN'T BELIEVE YOU GUYS ARE DOING ALL THIS FOR ME... I DON'T DESERVE IT.
I'M JUST A BURDEN ON EV-ERYONE.
AND BESIDES I'M A GOFER, AND I'VE BEEN TOLD I'M A WASTE OF A HUMAN... FUFUFUFU...
WHAT A GLOOMY LITTLE GIRL...
BUT WE GOT TO MEET EACH OTHER.
YOU SHOULD APPRECIATE THE PEOPLE YOU HAVE AROUND YOU.
LET'S BE FRIENDS, MICHIRU-CHAN.

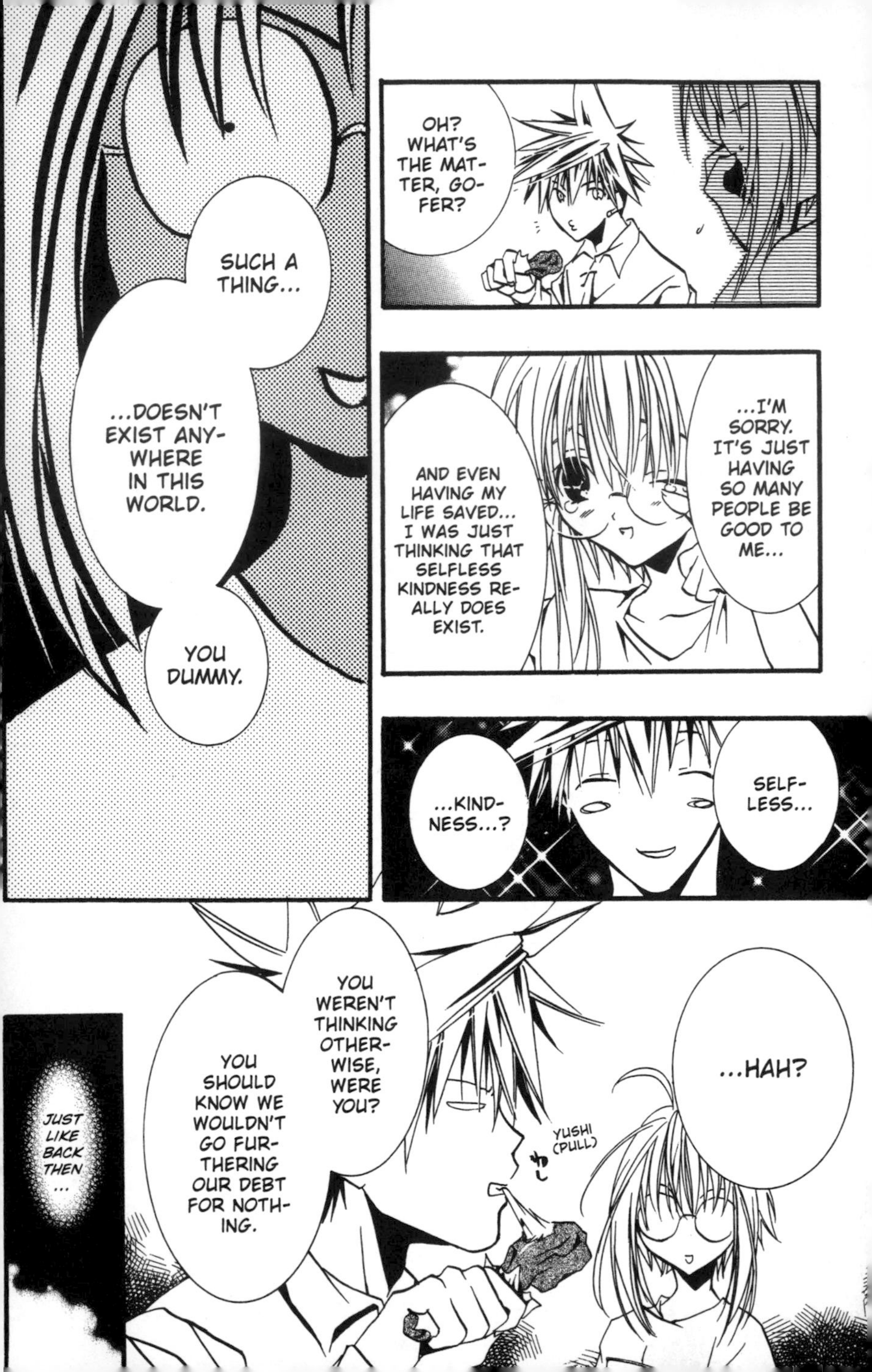
OH? WHAT'S THE MATTER, GOFER?
...I'M SORRY. IT'S JUST HAVING SO MANY PEOPLE BE GOOD TO ME...
AND EVEN HAVING MY LIFE SAVED... I WAS JUST THINKING THAT SELFLESS KINDNESS REALLY DOES EXIST.
SELF-LESS...
...KIND-NESS...?
SUCH A THING...
...DOESN'T EXIST ANYWHERE IN THIS WORLD.
YOU DUMMY.
...HAH?
YUSHI (PULL)
YOU WEREN'T THINKING OTHERWISE, WERE YOU?
YOU SHOULD KNOW WE WOULDN'T GO FURTHERING OUR DEBT FOR NOTHING.
JUST LIKE BACK THEN...

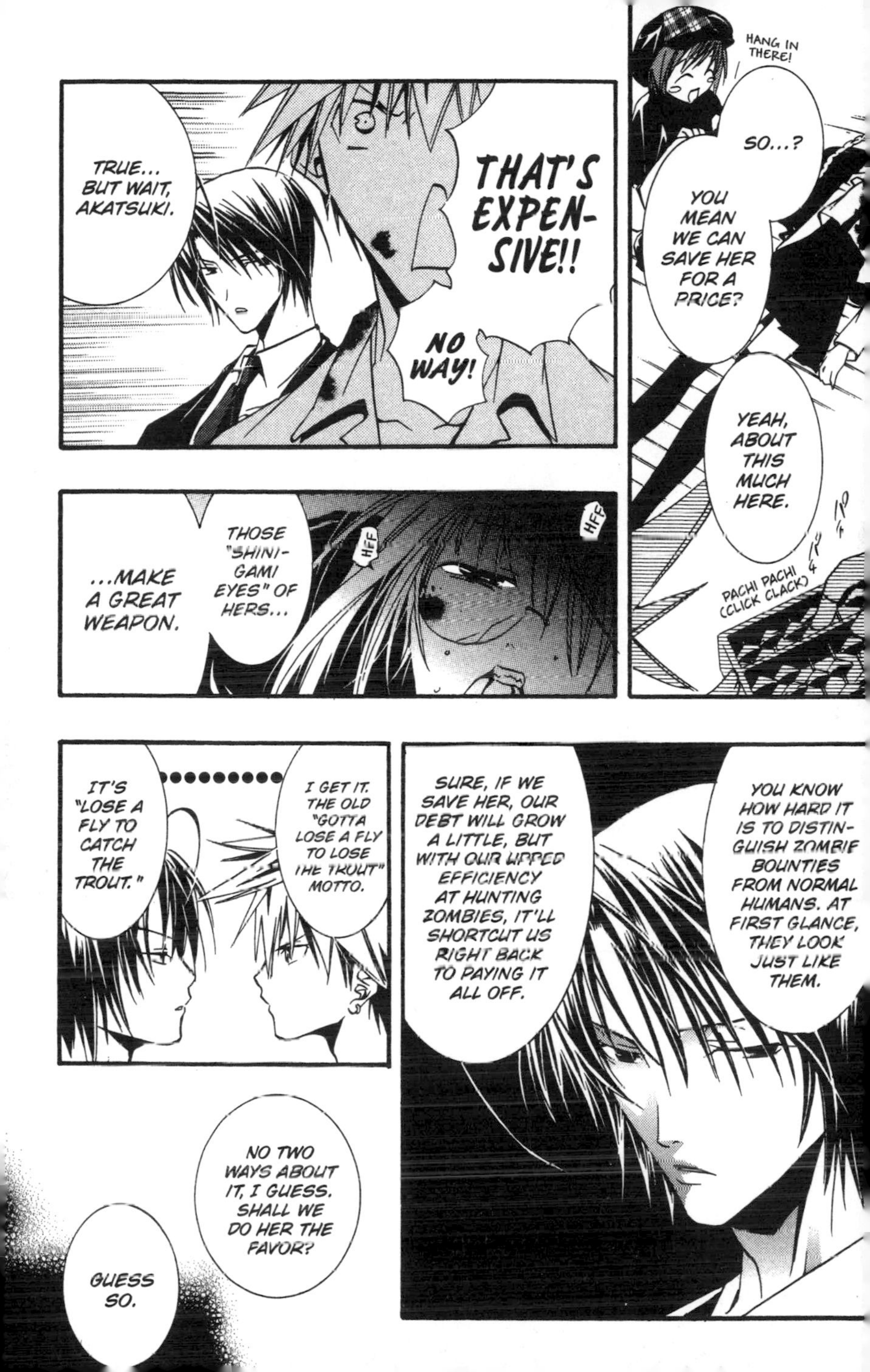
HANG IN THERE!
SO...?
YOU MEAN WE CAN SAVE HER FOR A PRICE?
YEAH, ABOUT THIS MUCH HERE.
PACHI PACHI (CLICK CLACK)
THAT'S EXPEN-SIVE!!
NO WAY!
TRUE... BUT WAIT, AKATSUKI.
HFF
HFF
THOSE "SHINI-GAMI EYES" OF HERS...
...MAKE A GREAT WEAPON.
YOU KNOW HOW HARD IT IS TO DISTIN-GUISH ZOMBIE BOUNTIES FROM NORMAL HUMANS. AT FIRST GLANCE, THEY LOOK JUST LIKE THEM.
SURE, IF WE SAVE HER, OUR DEBT WILL GROW A LITTLE, BUT WITH OUR UPPED EFFICIENCY AT HUNTING ZOMBIES, IT'LL SHORTCUT US RIGHT BACK TO PAYING IT ALL OFF.
I GET IT. THE OLD "GOTTA LOSE A FLY TO LOSE THE TROUT" MOTTO.
IT'S "LOSE A FLY TO CATCH THE TROUT."
NO TWO WAYS ABOUT IT, I GUESS. SHALL WE DO HER THE FAVOR?
GUESS SO.

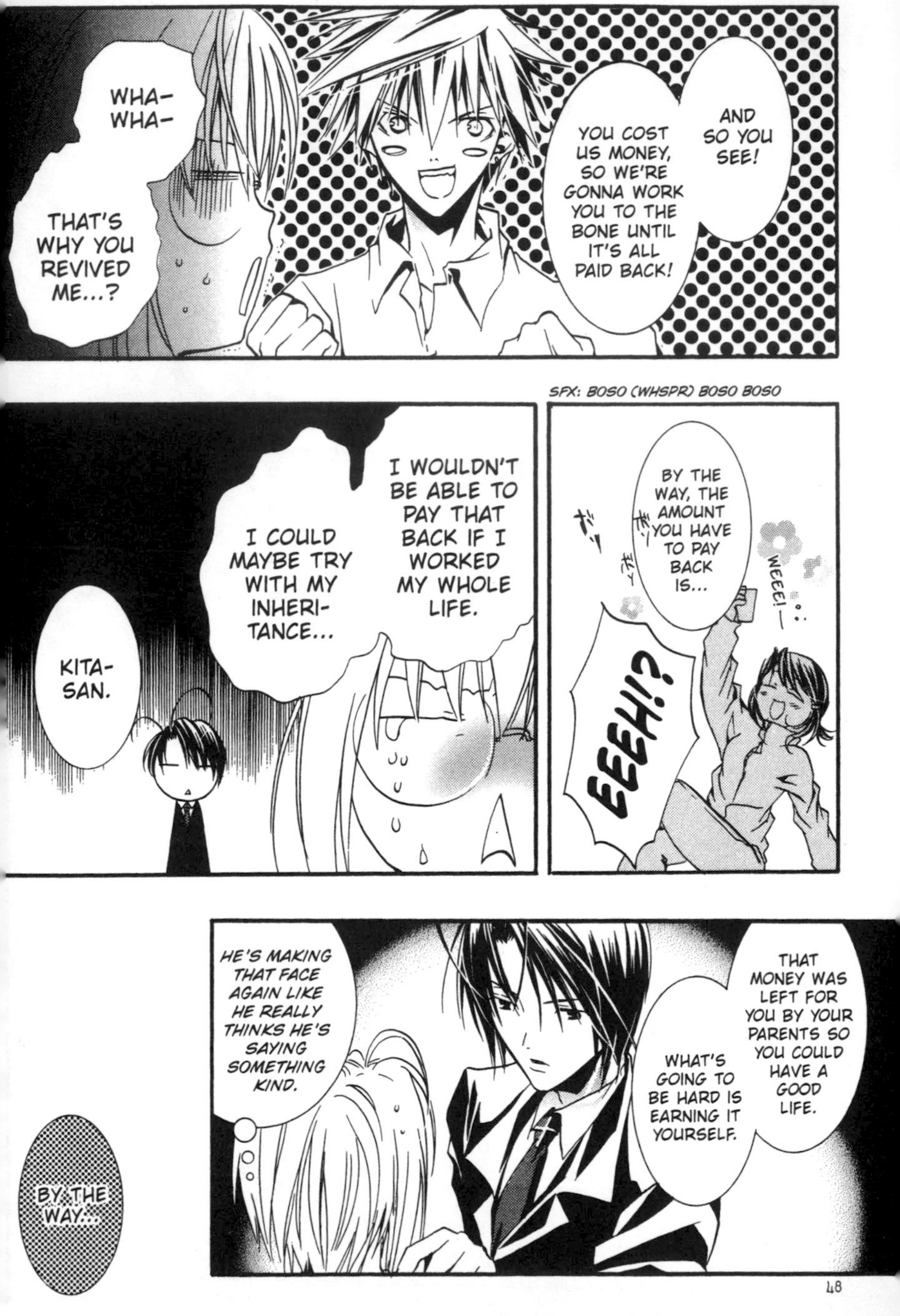
AND SO YOU SEE!
YOU COST US MONEY, SO WE'RE GONNA WORK YOU TO THE BONE UNTIL IT'S ALL PAID BACK!
WHA-WHA-
THAT'S WHY YOU REVIVED ME...?
SFX: BOSO (WHSPR) BOSO BOSO
BY THE WAY, THE AMOUNT YOU HAVE TO PAY BACK IS...
WEEE!
EEEH!?
I WOULDN'T BE ABLE TO PAY THAT BACK IF I WORKED MY WHOLE LIFE.
I COULD MAYBE TRY WITH MY INHERITANCE...
KITA-SAN.
THAT MONEY WAS LEFT FOR YOU BY YOUR PARENTS SO YOU COULD HAVE A GOOD LIFE.
WHAT'S GOING TO BE HARD IS EARNING IT YOURSELF.
HE'S MAKING THAT FACE AGAIN LIKE HE REALLY THINKS HE'S SAYING SOMETHING KIND.
BY THE WAY...

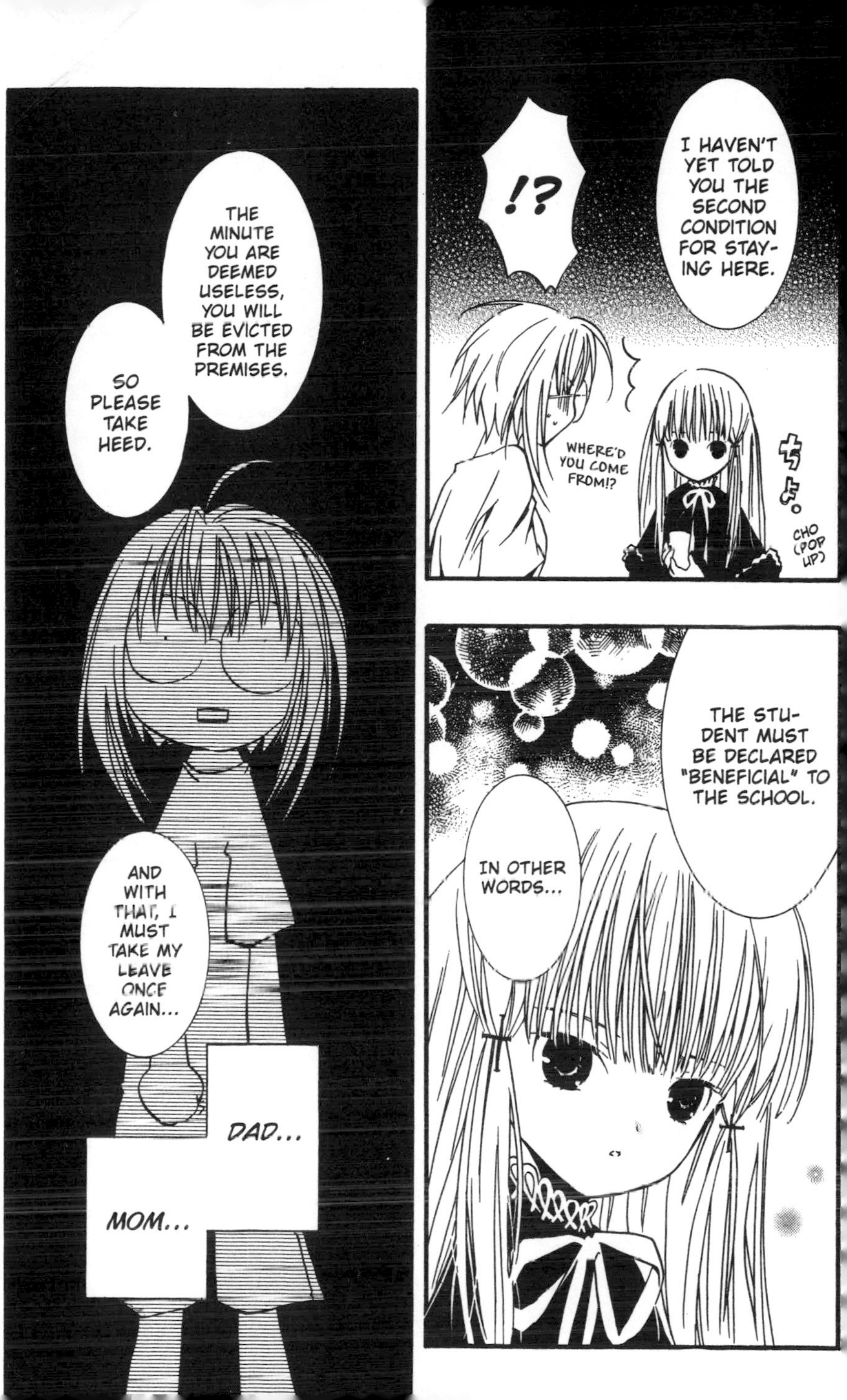
I HAVEN'T YET TOLD YOU THE SECOND CONDITION FOR STAYING HERE.
!?
WHERE'D YOU COME FROM!?
CHO (POP UP)
THE STUDENT MUST BE DECLARED "BENEFICIAL" TO THE SCHOOL.
IN OTHER WORDS...
THE MINUTE YOU ARE DEEMED USELESS, YOU WILL BE EVICTED FROM THE PREMISES.
SO PLEASE TAKE HEED.
AND WITH THAT, I MUST TAKE MY LEAVE ONCE AGAIN...
DAD...
MOM...

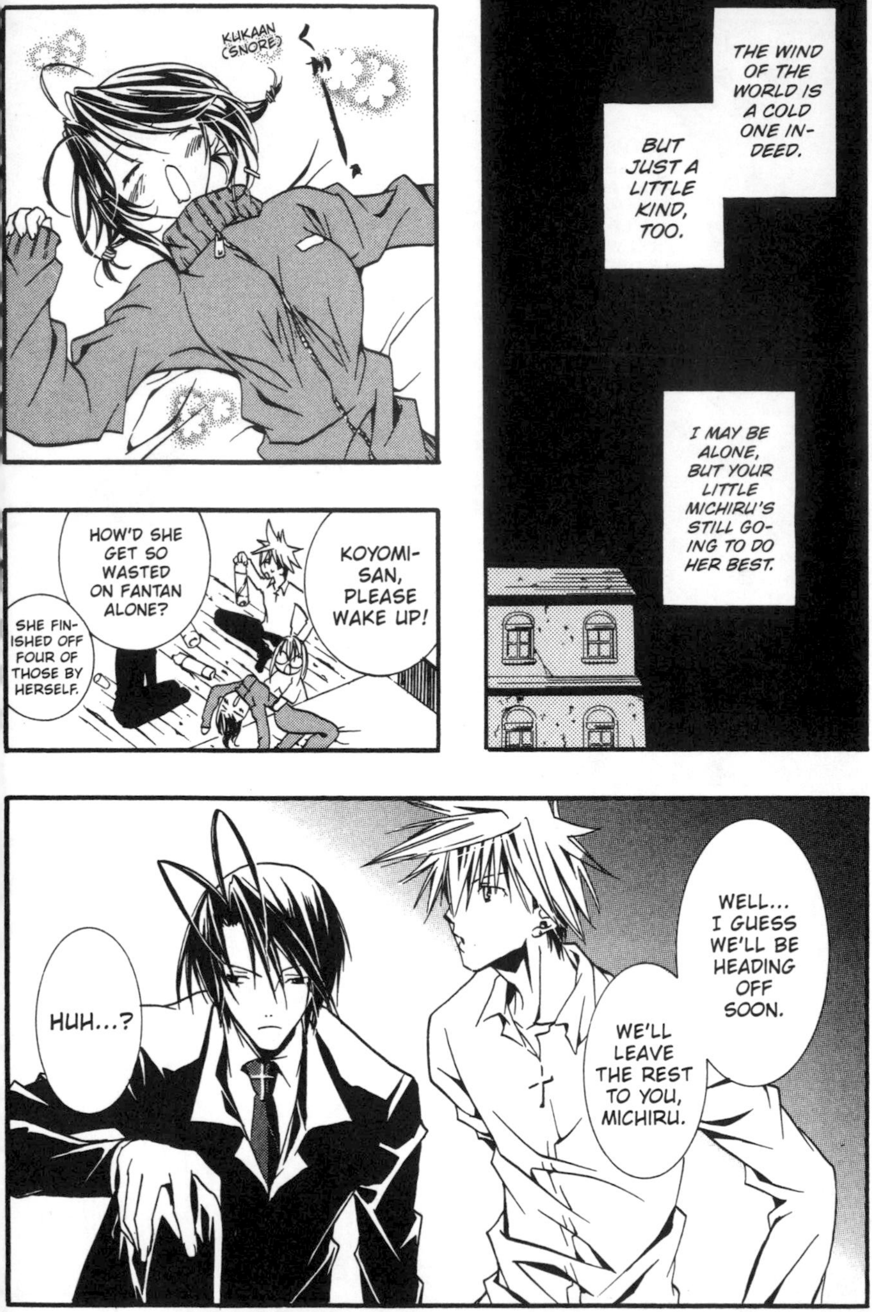
THE WIND OF THE WORLD IS A COLD ONE IN-DEED.
BUT JUST A LITTLE KIND, TOO.
I MAY BE ALONE, BUT YOUR LITTLE MICHIRU'S STILL GO-ING TO DO HER BEST.
KUKAAN (SNORE)
KOYOMI-SAN, PLEASE WAKE UP!
HOW'D SHE GET SO WASTED ON FANTAN ALONE?
SHE FIN-ISHED OFF FOUR OF THOSE BY HERSELF.
WELL... I GUESS WE'LL BE HEADING OFF SOON.
WE'LL LEAVE THE REST TO YOU, MICHIRU.
HUH...?

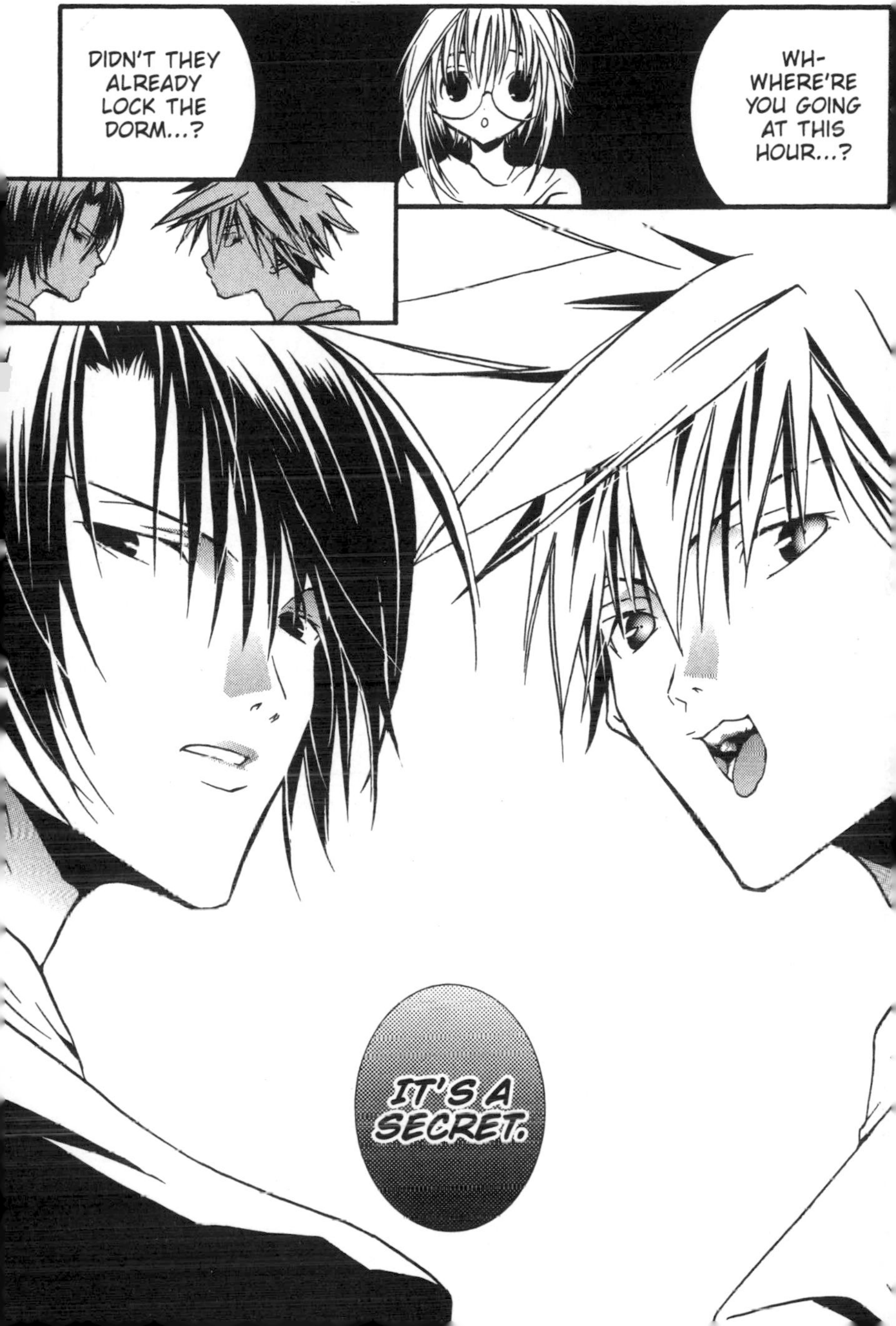
WH- WHERE'RE YOU GOING AT THIS HOUR...?
DIDN'T THEY ALREADY LOCK THE DORM...?
IT'S A SECRET.

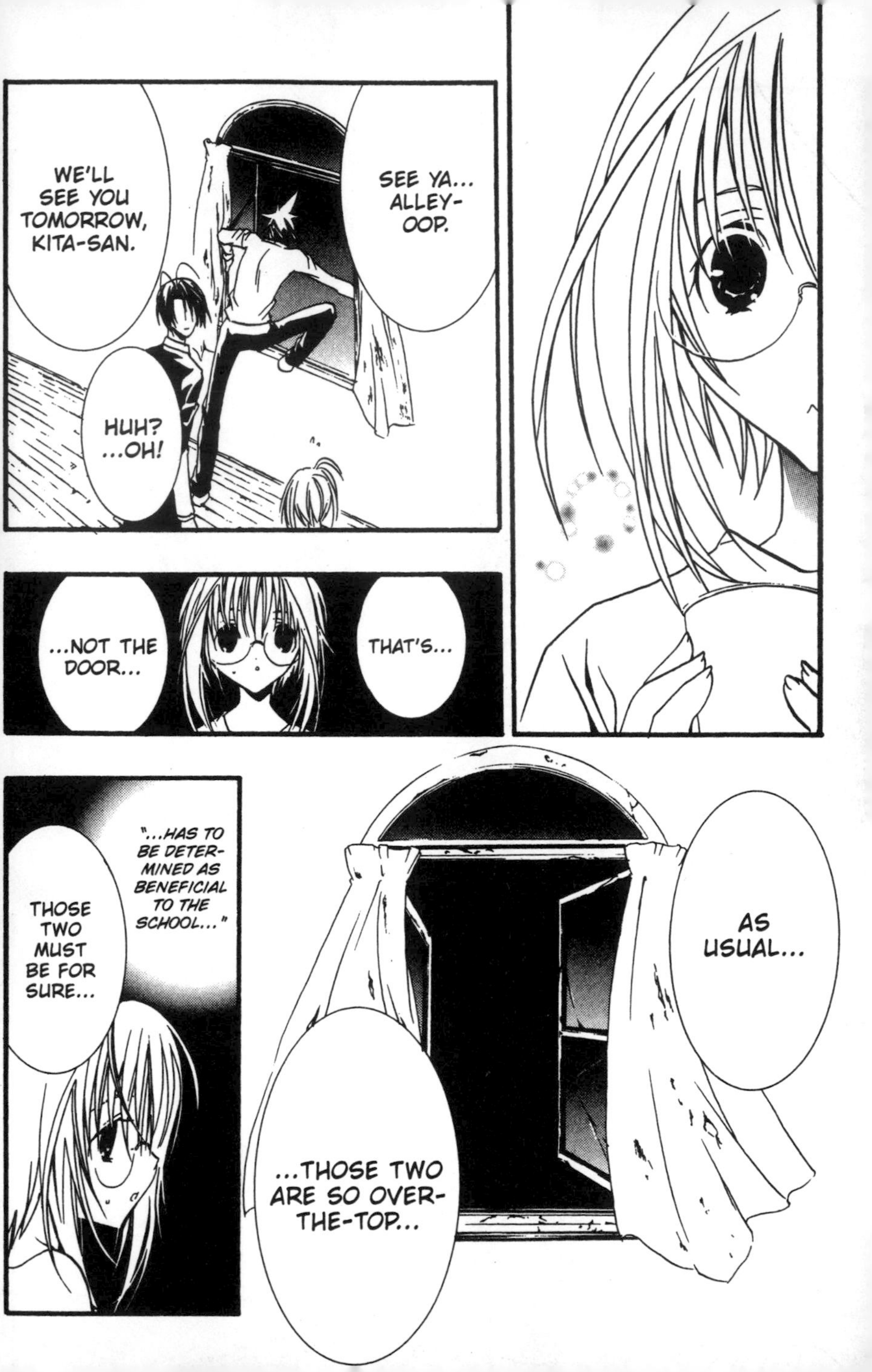
SEE YA... ALLEY-OOP.
WE'LL SEE YOU TOMORROW, KITA-SAN.
HUH? ...OH!
THAT'S...
...NOT THE DOOR...
AS USUAL...
...THOSE TWO ARE SO OVER-THE-TOP...
"...HAS TO BE DETERMINED AS BENEFICIAL TO THE SCHOOL..."
THOSE TWO MUST BE FOR SURE...

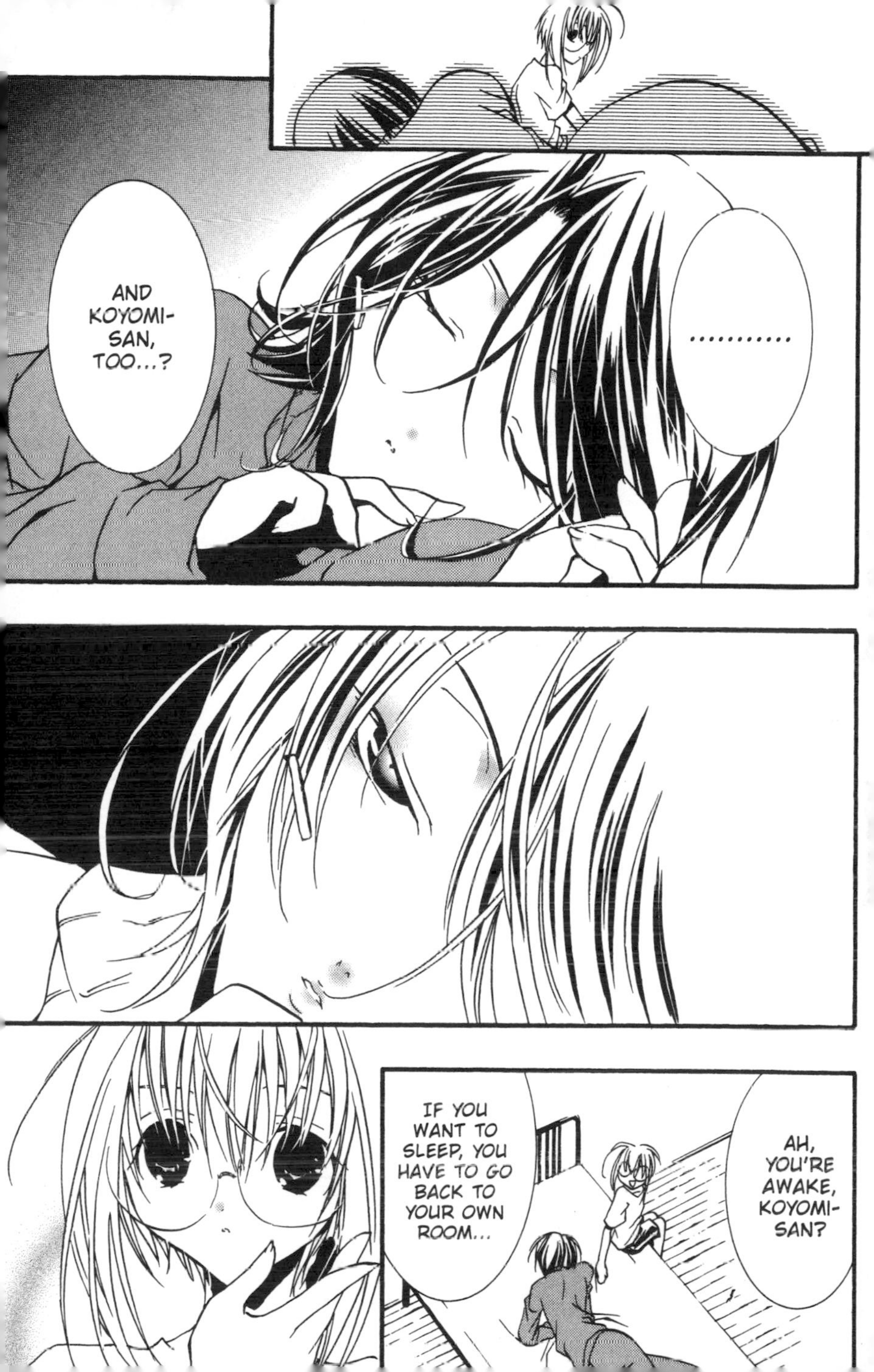
....
AND KOYOMI-SAN, TOO...?
AH, YOU'RE AWAKE, KOYOMI-SAN?
IF YOU WANT TO SLEEP, YOU HAVE TO GO BACK TO YOUR OWN ROOM...

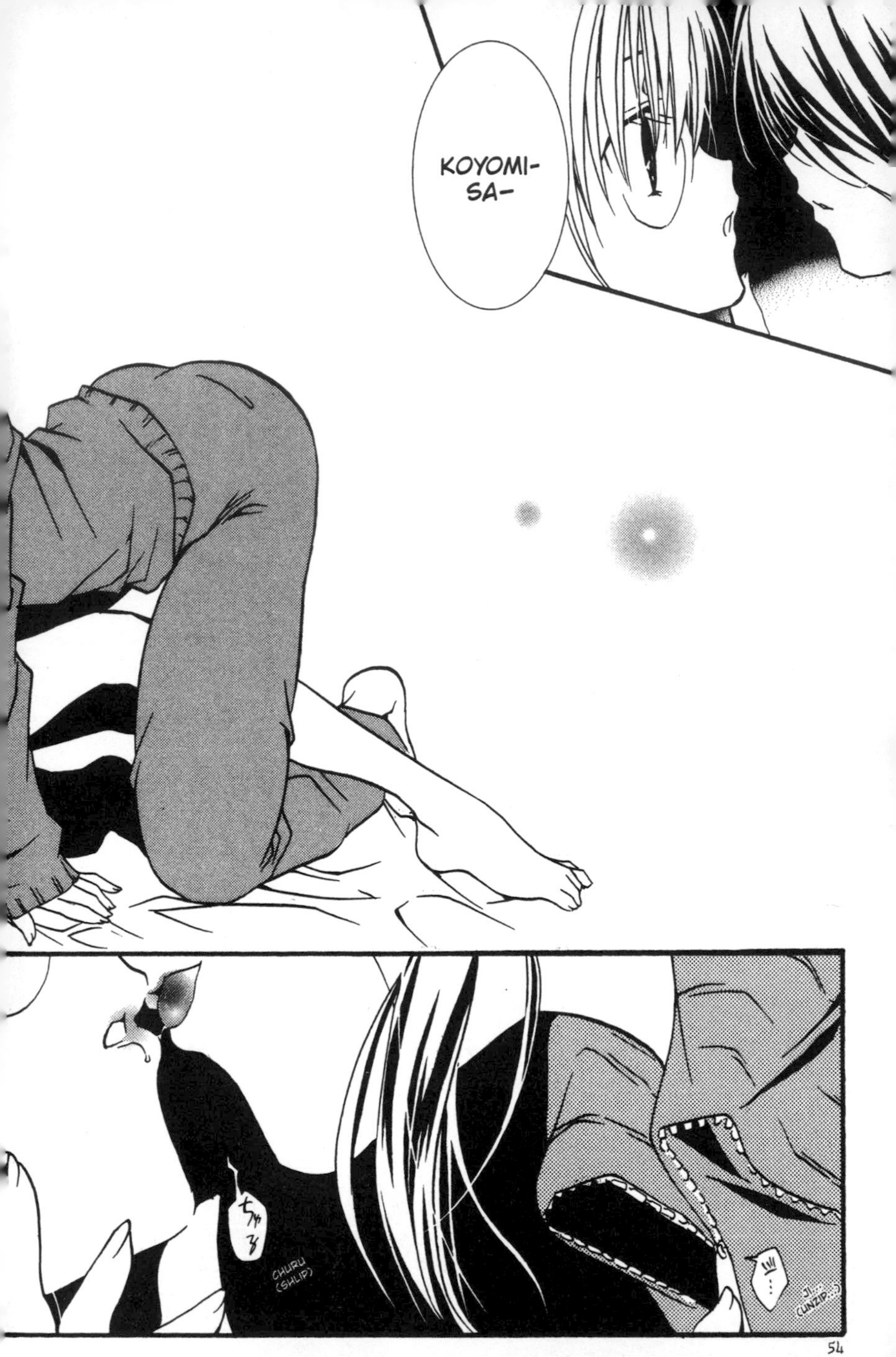
KOYOMI-SA-
ジ…
JI... (UNZIP...)
ちゅる
CHURU (SHLIP)

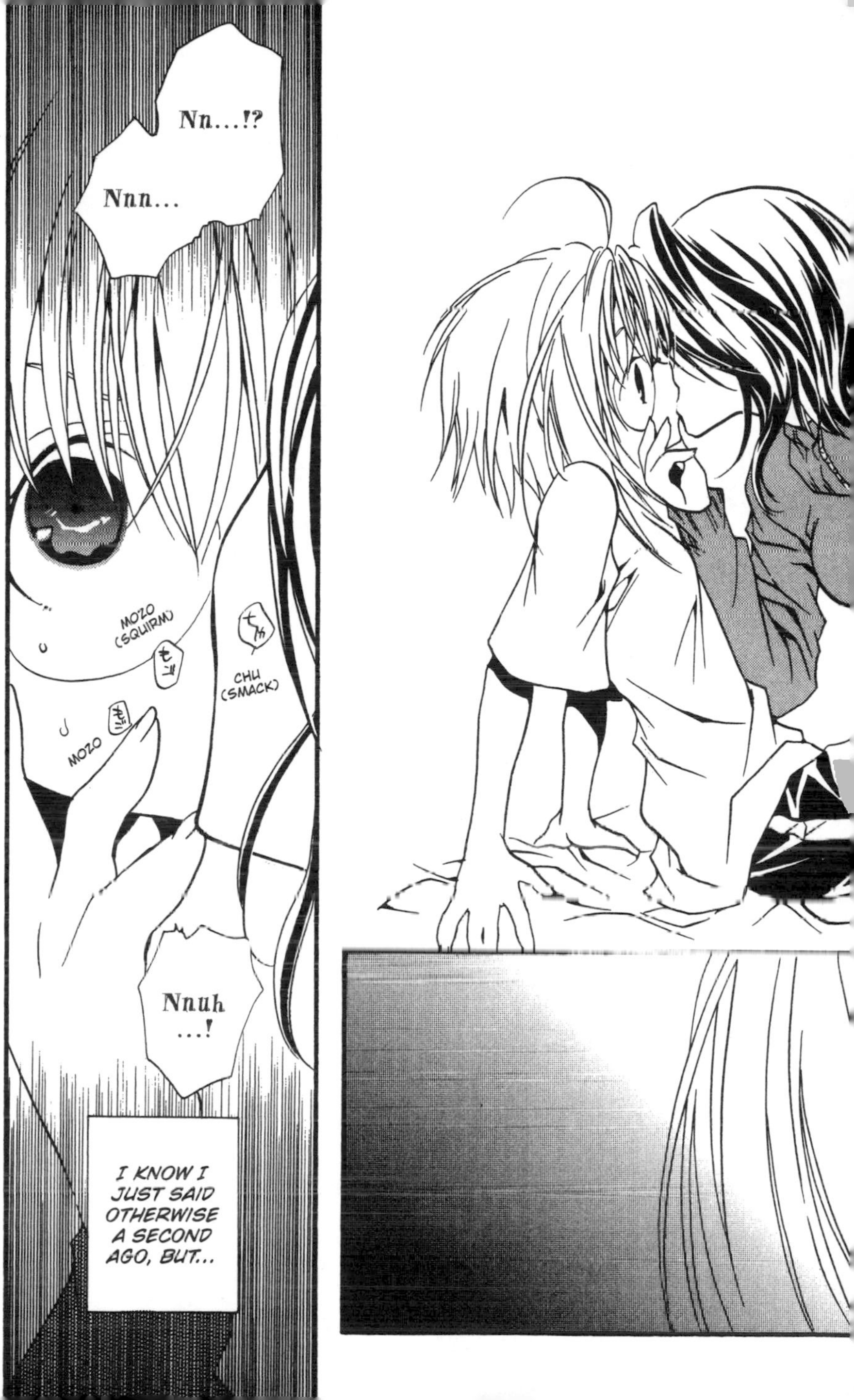
Nn...!?
Nnn...
CHU (SMACK)
MOZO (SQUIRM)
MOZO
Nnuh ...!
I KNOW I JUST SAID OTHERWISE A SECOND AGO, BUT...

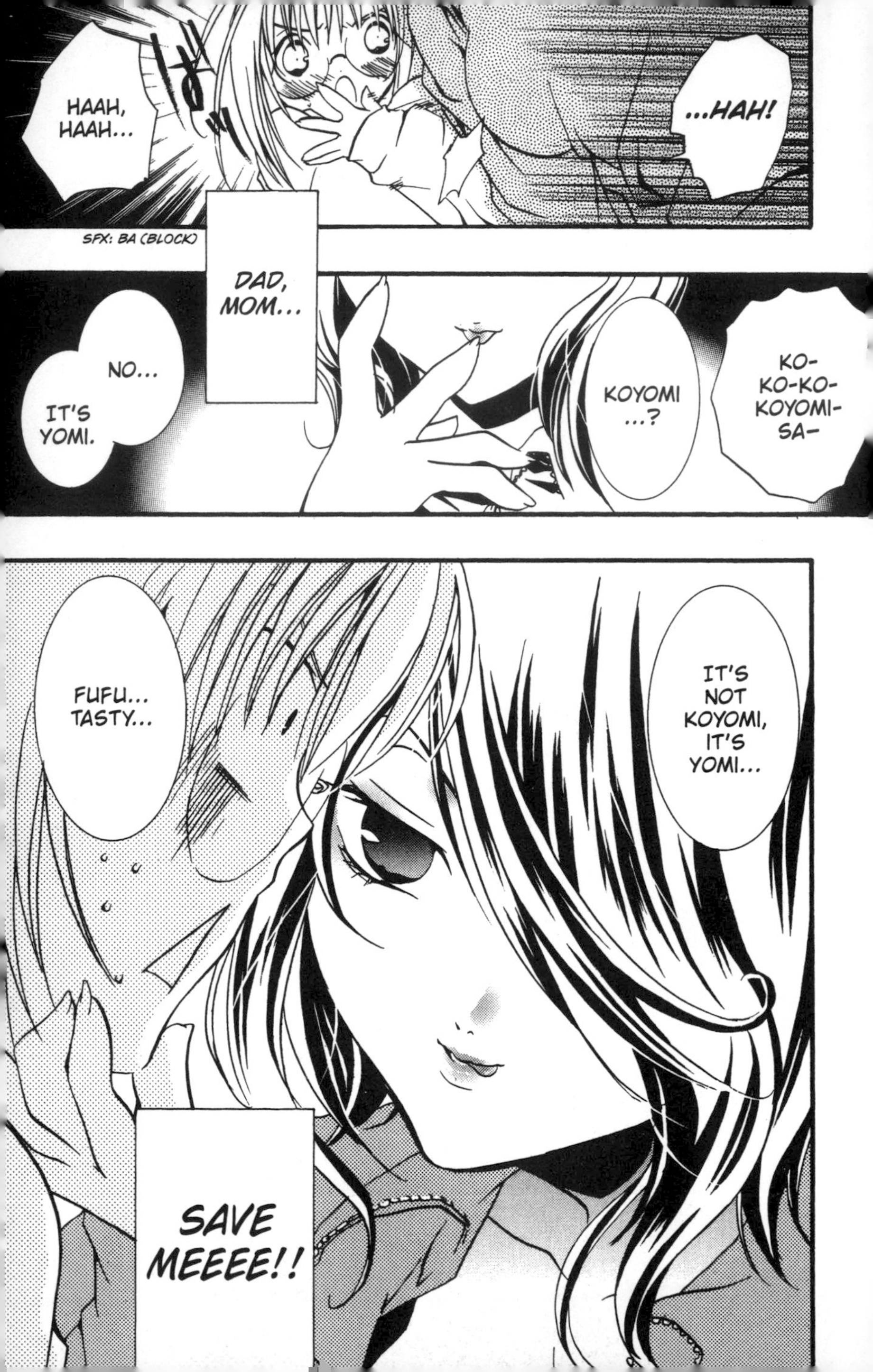
...HAH!
HAAH, HAAH...
SFX: BA (BLOCK)
DAD, MOM...
KO-KO-KO-KOYOMI-SA-
KOYOMI ...?
NO... IT'S YOMI.
IT'S NOT KOYOMI, IT'S YOMI...
FUFU... TASTY...
SAVE MEEEE!!

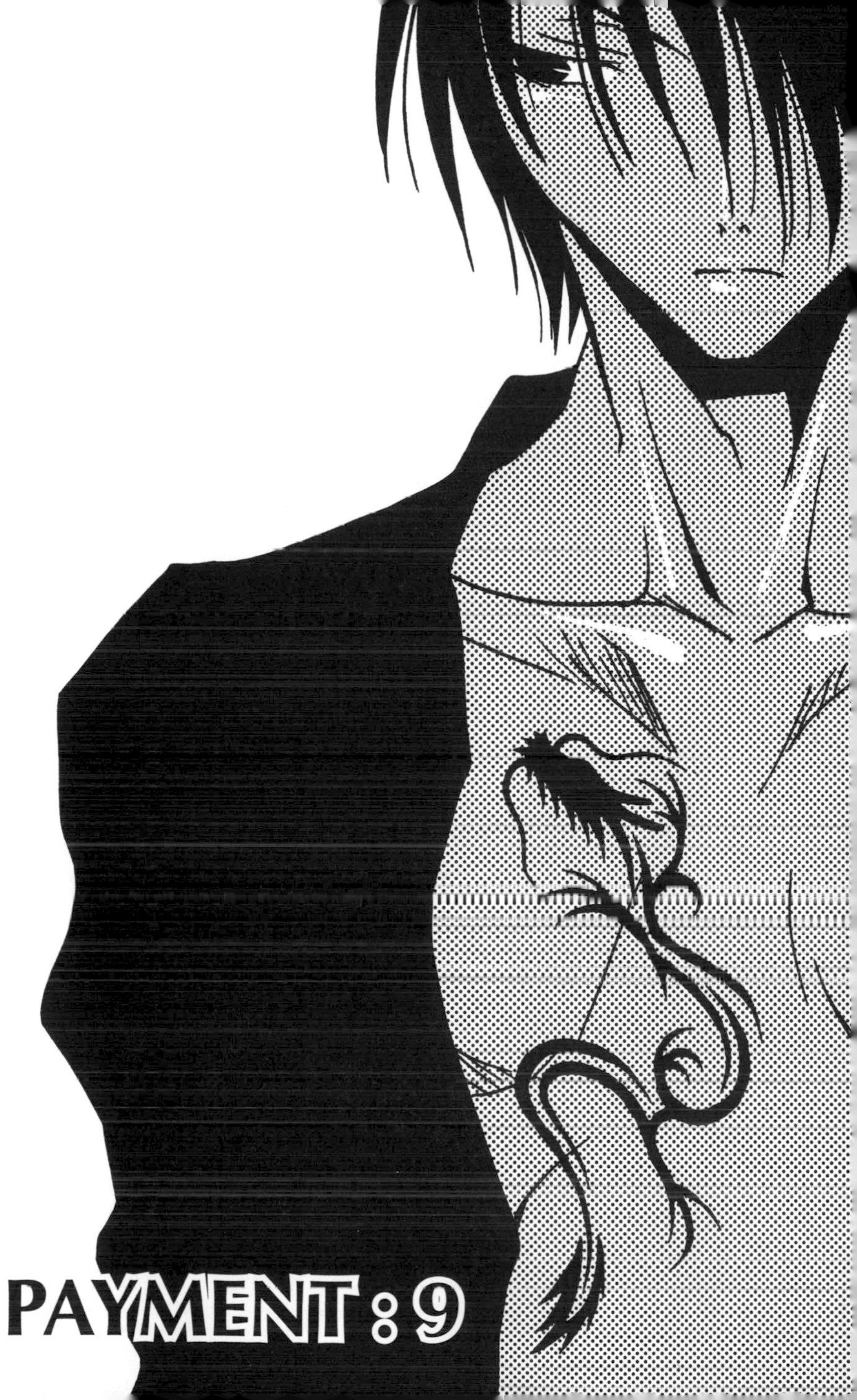
PAYMENT : 9

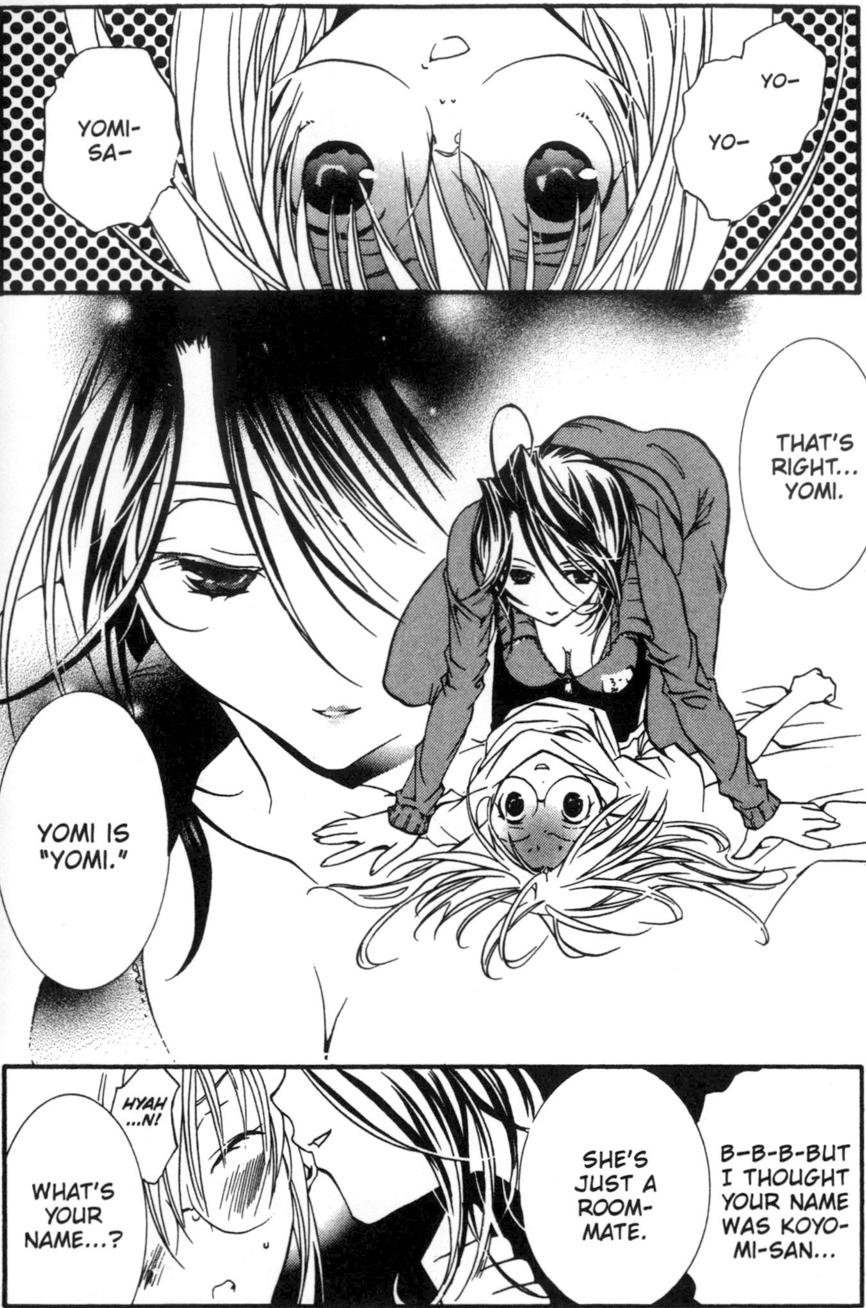
YO- YO-
YOMI-SA-
THAT'S RIGHT... YOMI.
YOMI IS "YOMI."
B-B-B-BUT I THOUGHT YOUR NAME WAS KOYO-MI-SAN...
SHE'S JUST A ROOM-MATE.
HYAH ...N!
WHAT'S YOUR NAME...?

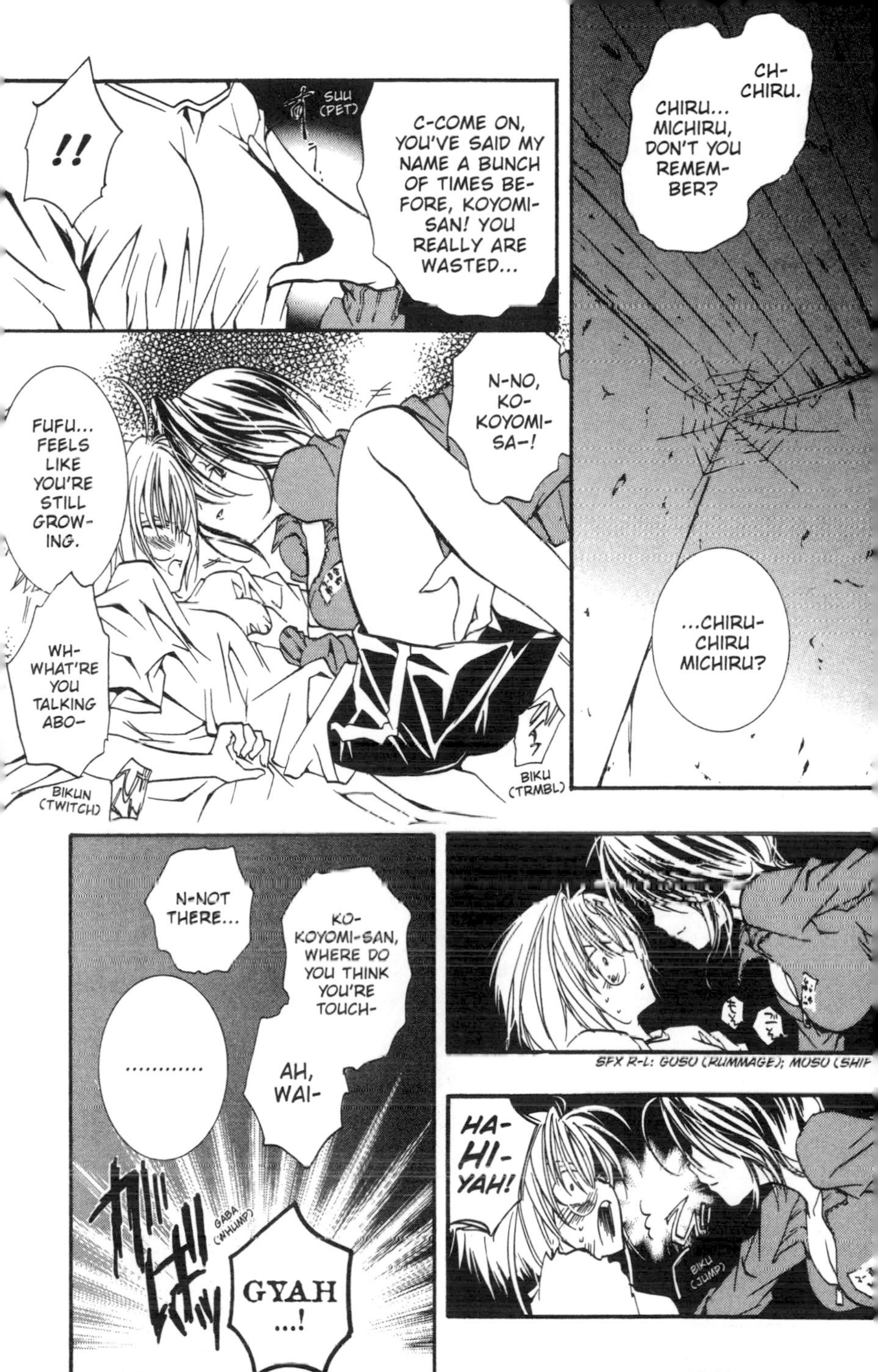
CH-CHIRU.
CHIRU... MICHIRU, DON'T YOU REMEMBER?
...CHIRU-CHIRU MICHIRU?
C-COME ON, YOU'VE SAID MY NAME A BUNCH OF TIMES BEFORE, KOYOMI-SAN! YOU REALLY ARE WASTED...
SUU (PET)
!!
N-NO, KO-KOYOMI-SA-!
BIKU (TRMBL)
FUFU... FEELS LIKE YOU'RE STILL GROWING.
WH-WHAT'RE YOU TALKING ABO-
BIKUN (TWITCH)
SFX R-L: GUSO (RUMMAGE); MUSO (SHIF
HA-HI-YAH!
BIKU (JUMP)
KO-KOYOMI-SAN, WHERE DO YOU THINK YOU'RE TOUCH-
N-NOT THERE...
AH, WAI-
....
GABA (WHUMP)
GYAH ...!

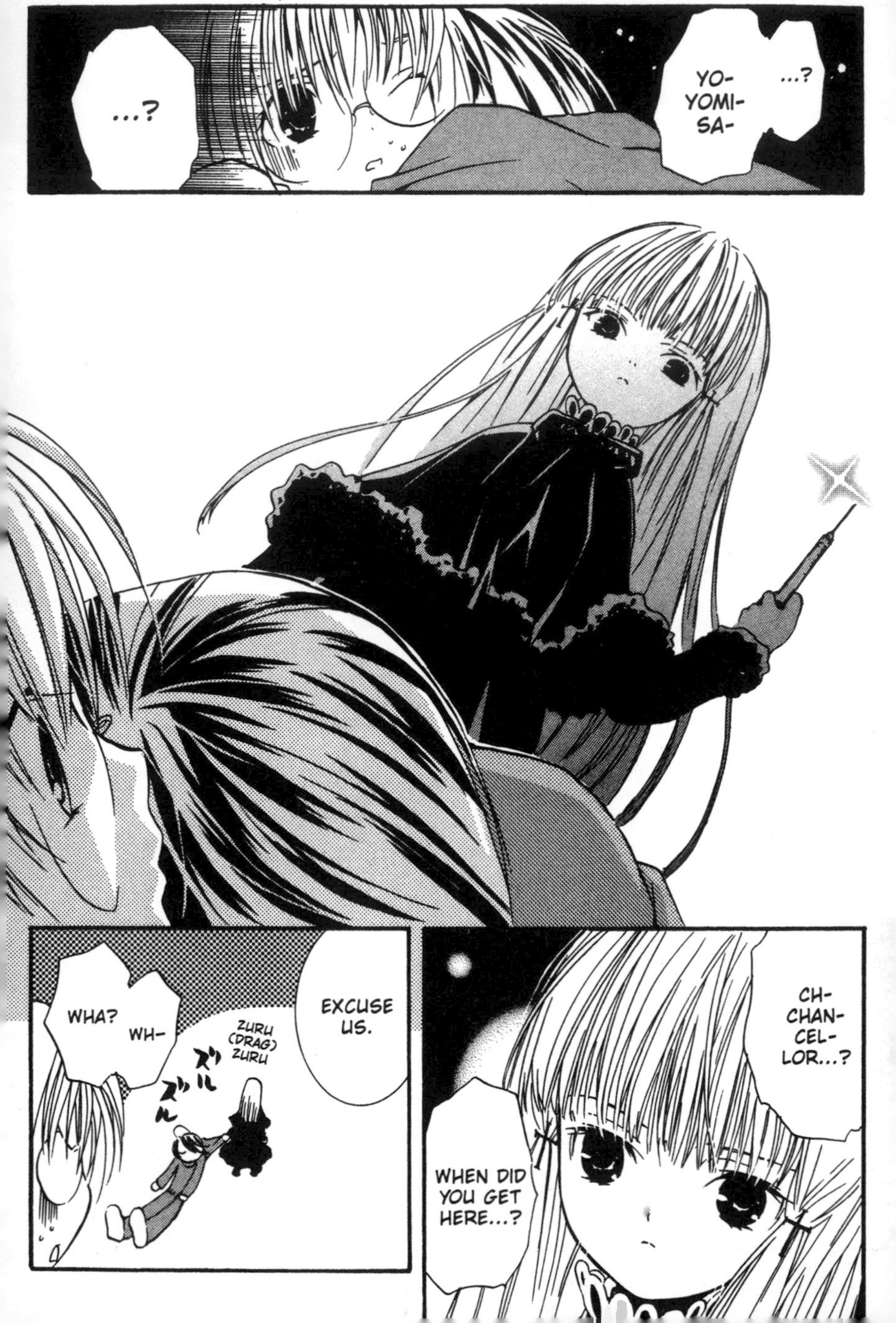
YO-YOMI-SA- ...?
...?
CH-CHAN-CEL-LOR...?
WHEN DID YOU GET HERE...?
EXCUSE US.
ZURU (DRAG) ZURU
WH- WHA?

...MICHIRU-SAN.

IT'S RATHER RARE THAT YOMI-SAN "COMES FORTH" OF HER OWN WILL...

SHE'S REALLY TAKEN A LIKING TO YOU.

HA-HEH...?

WHAA!?

THIS IS WHERE I SAY GOOD-BYE.

WAIT A MIN-UTE...!

SIGN: NO TRESPASSING

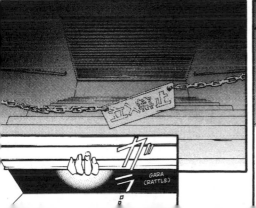

GARA
(RATTLE)

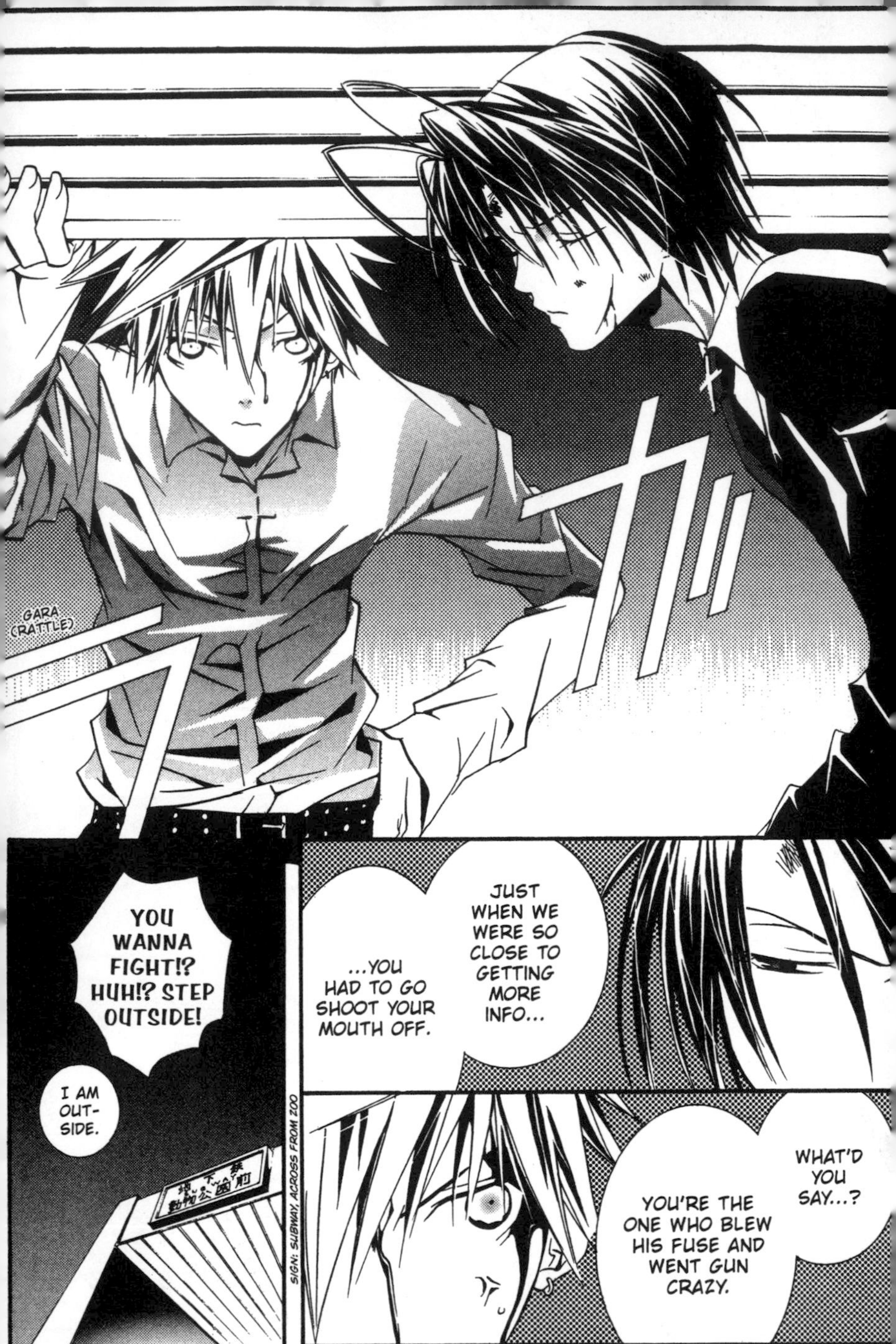
GARA (RATTLE)
JUST WHEN WE WERE SO CLOSE TO GETTING MORE INFO...
...YOU HAD TO GO SHOOT YOUR MOUTH OFF.
WHAT'D YOU SAY...?
YOU'RE THE ONE WHO BLEW HIS FUSE AND WENT GUN CRAZY.
YOU WANNA FIGHT!? HUH!? STEP OUTSIDE!
I AM OUTSIDE.
地下鉄
動物公園前
SIGN: SUBWAY, ACROSS FROM ZOO

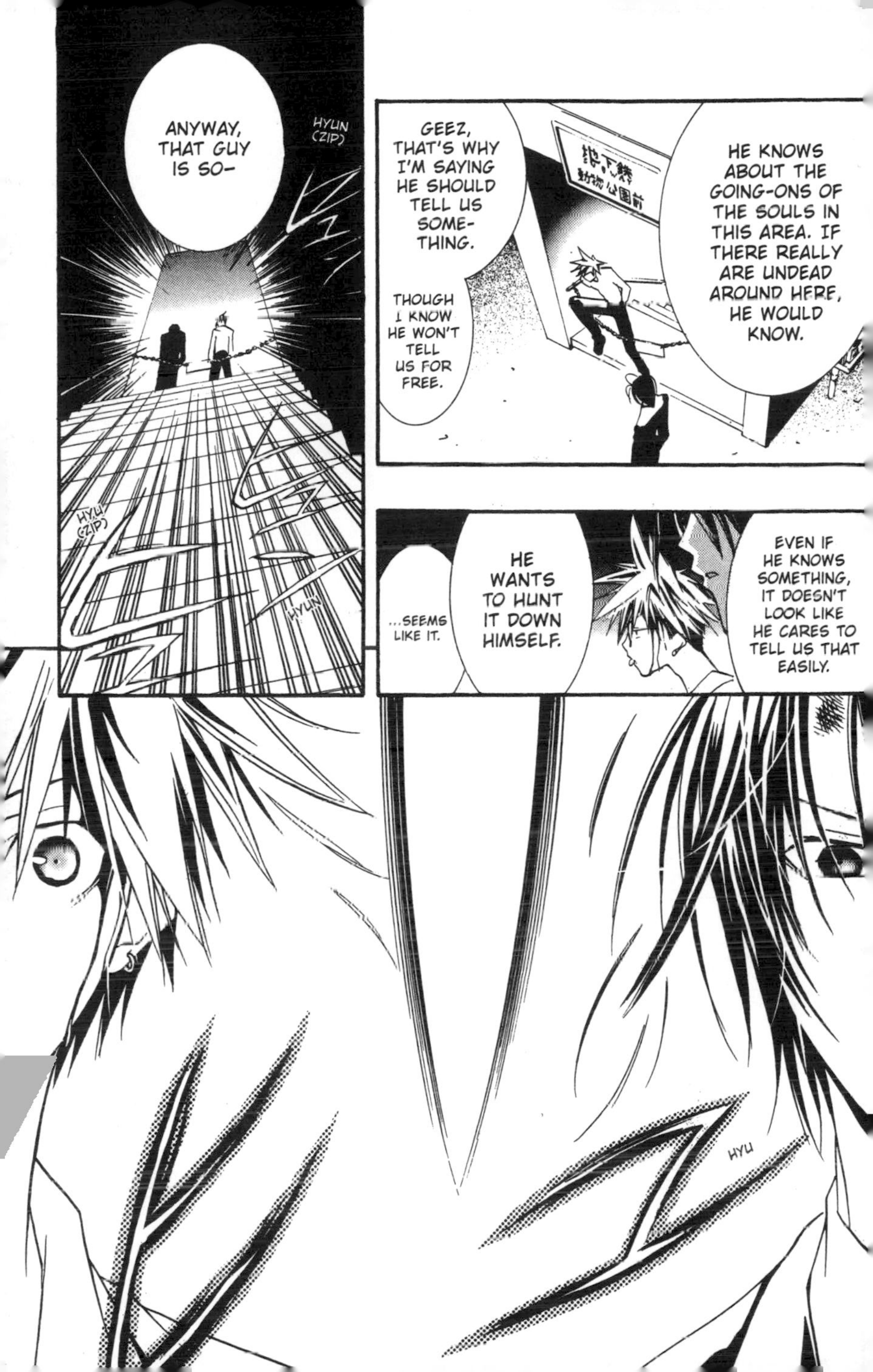
地下鉄
動物公園前
HE KNOWS ABOUT THE GOING-ONS OF THE SOULS IN THIS AREA. IF THERE REALLY ARE UNDEAD AROUND HERE, HE WOULD KNOW.
GEEZ, THAT'S WHY I'M SAYING HE SHOULD TELL US SOME-THING.
THOUGH I KNOW HE WON'T TELL US FOR FREE.
EVEN IF HE KNOWS SOMETHING, IT DOESN'T LOOK LIKE HE CARES TO TELL US THAT EASILY.
HE WANTS TO HUNT IT DOWN HIMSELF.
...SEEMS LIKE IT.
ANYWAY, THAT GUY IS SO-
HYUN (ZIP)
HYU (ZIP)
HYUN
HYU

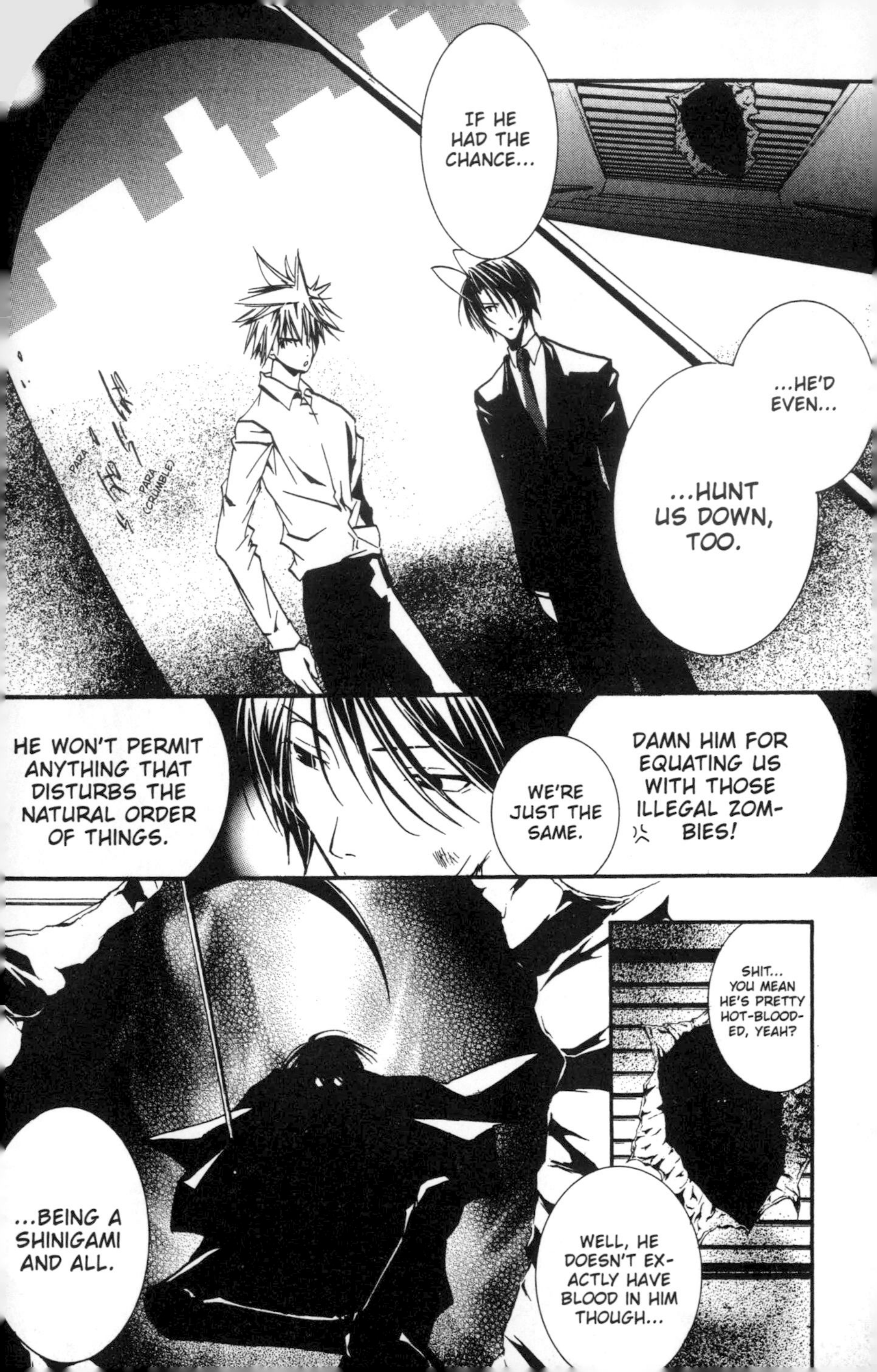
IF HE HAD THE CHANCE...
...HE'D EVEN...
...HUNT US DOWN, TOO.
PARA PARA (CRUMBLE)
DAMN HIM FOR EQUATING US WITH THOSE ILLEGAL ZOM-BIES!
WE'RE JUST THE SAME.
HE WON'T PERMIT ANYTHING THAT DISTURBS THE NATURAL ORDER OF THINGS.
SHIT... YOU MEAN HE'S PRETTY HOT-BLOOD-ED, YEAH?
WELL, HE DOESN'T EX-ACTLY HAVE BLOOD IN HIM THOUGH...
...BEING A SHINIGAMI AND ALL.

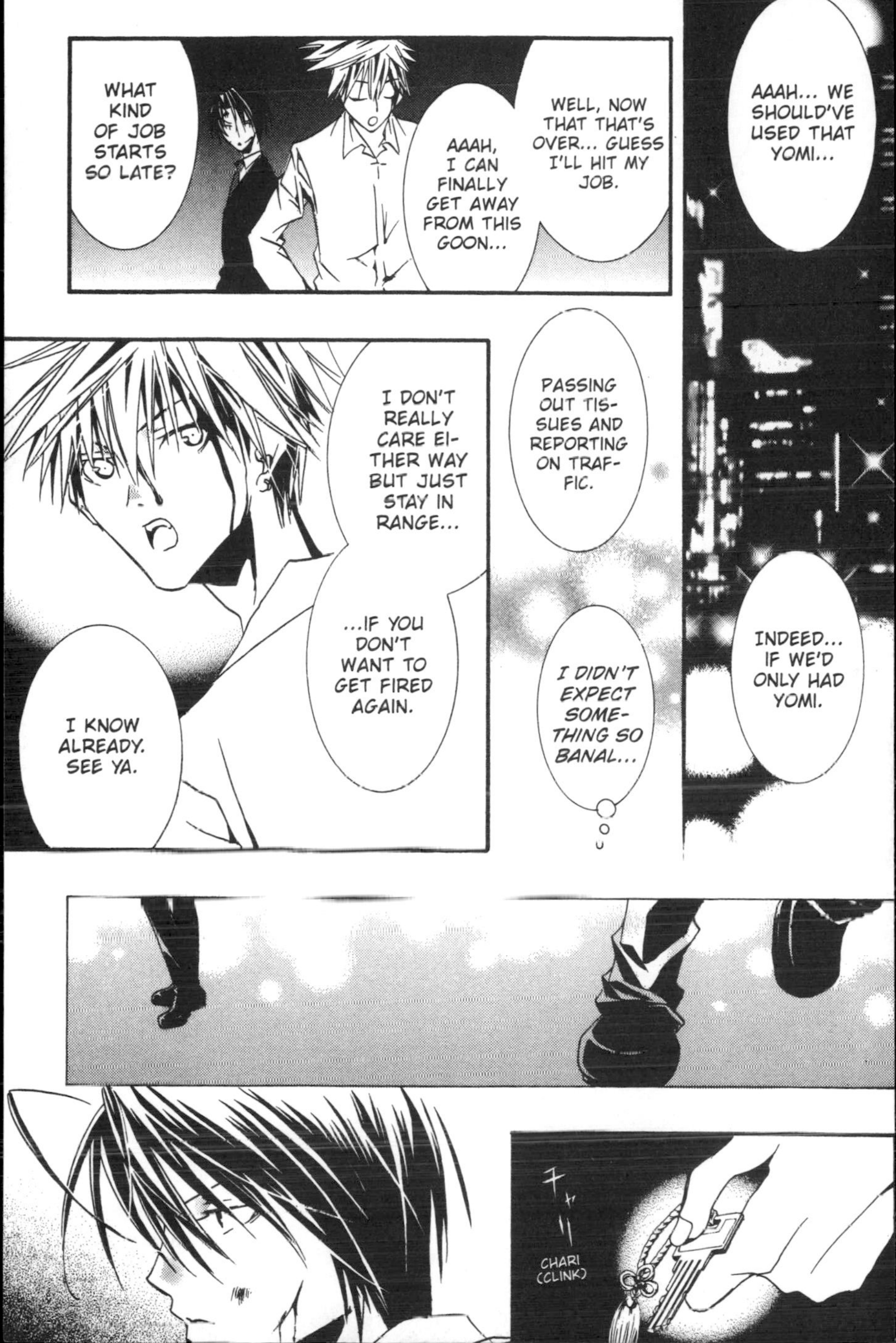
AAAH... WE SHOULD'VE USED THAT YOMI...
INDEED... IF WE'D ONLY HAD YOMI.
WELL, NOW THAT THAT'S OVER... GUESS I'LL HIT MY JOB.
AAAH, I CAN FINALLY GET AWAY FROM THIS GOON...
WHAT KIND OF JOB STARTS SO LATE?
PASSING OUT TISSUES AND REPORTING ON TRAFFIC.
I DON'T REALLY CARE EITHER WAY BUT JUST STAY IN RANGE...
...IF YOU DON'T WANT TO GET FIRED AGAIN.
I KNOW ALREADY. SEE YA.
I DIDN'T EXPECT SOMETHING SO BANAL...
チャリ
CHARI (CLINK)

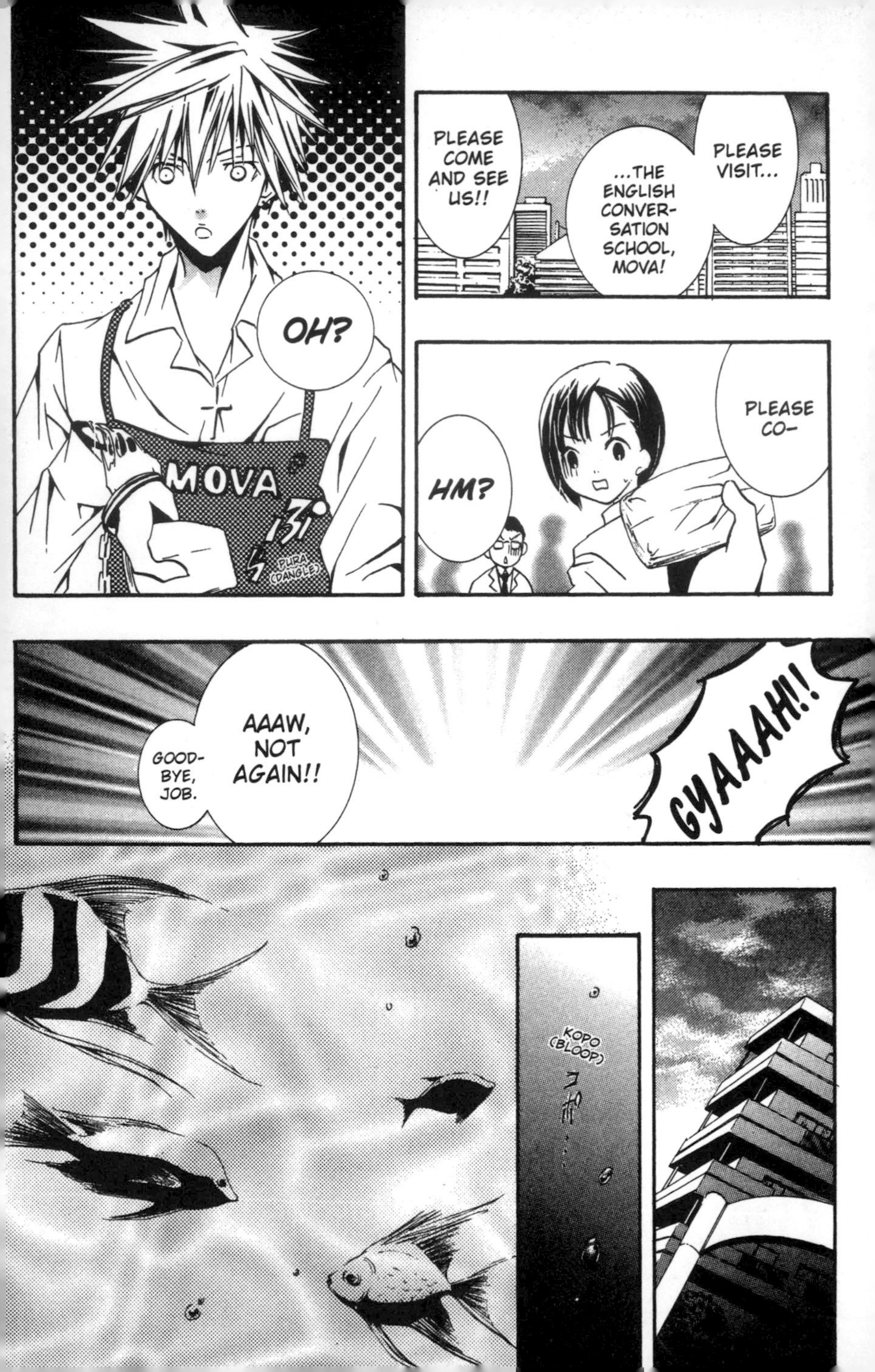
PLEASE VISIT...
...THE ENGLISH CONVER-SATION SCHOOL, MOVA!
PLEASE COME AND SEE US!!
PLEASE CO-
HM?
OH?
MOVA
PURA (DANGLE)
GYAAAH!!
AAAW, NOT AGAIN!!
GOOD-BYE, JOB.
KOPO (BLOOP)

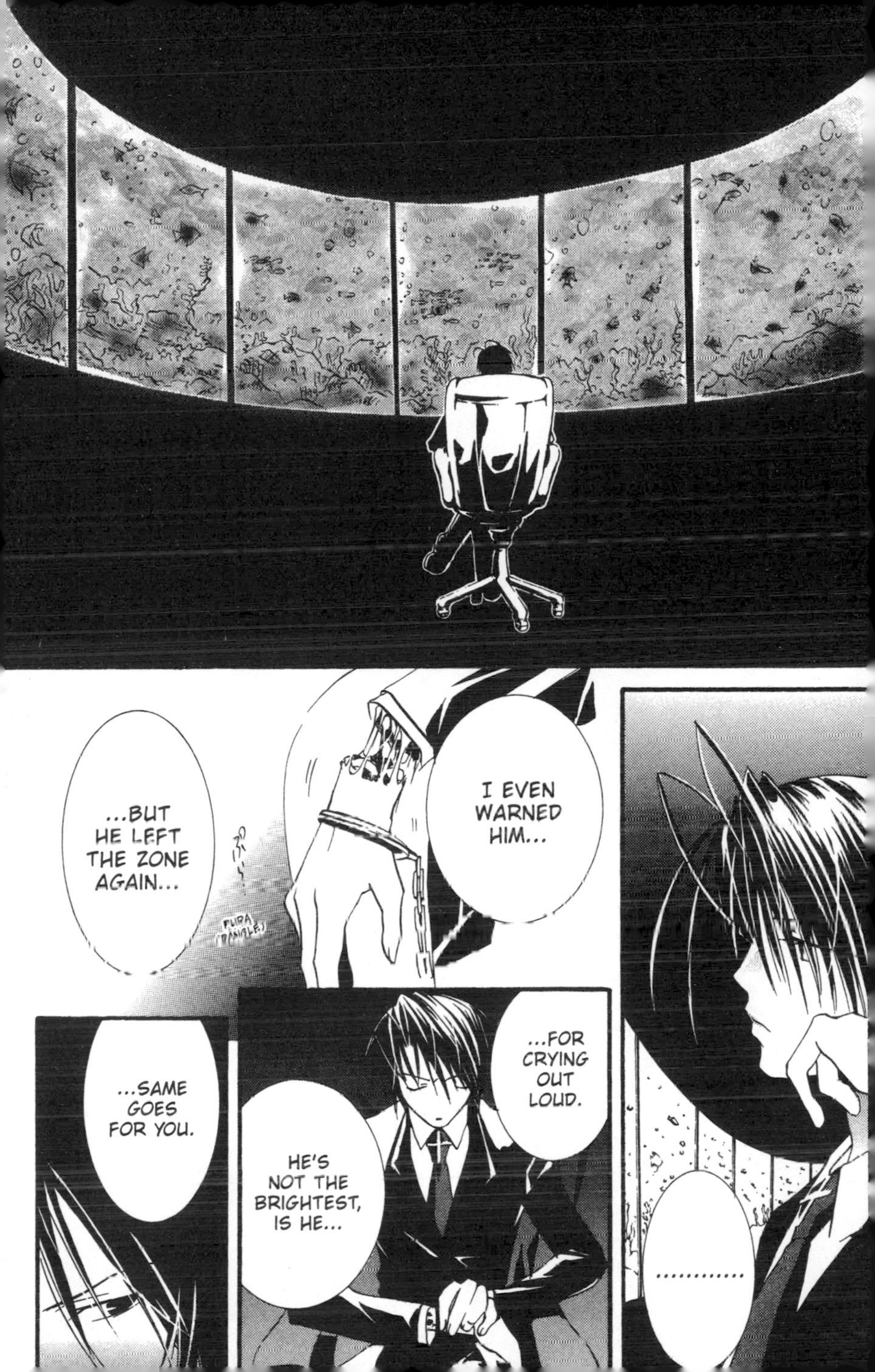
I EVEN WARNED HIM...
...BUT HE LEFT THE ZONE AGAIN...
FURA (DANGLE)
...FOR CRYING OUT LOUD.
HE'S NOT THE BRIGHTEST, IS HE...
...SAME GOES FOR YOU.
....

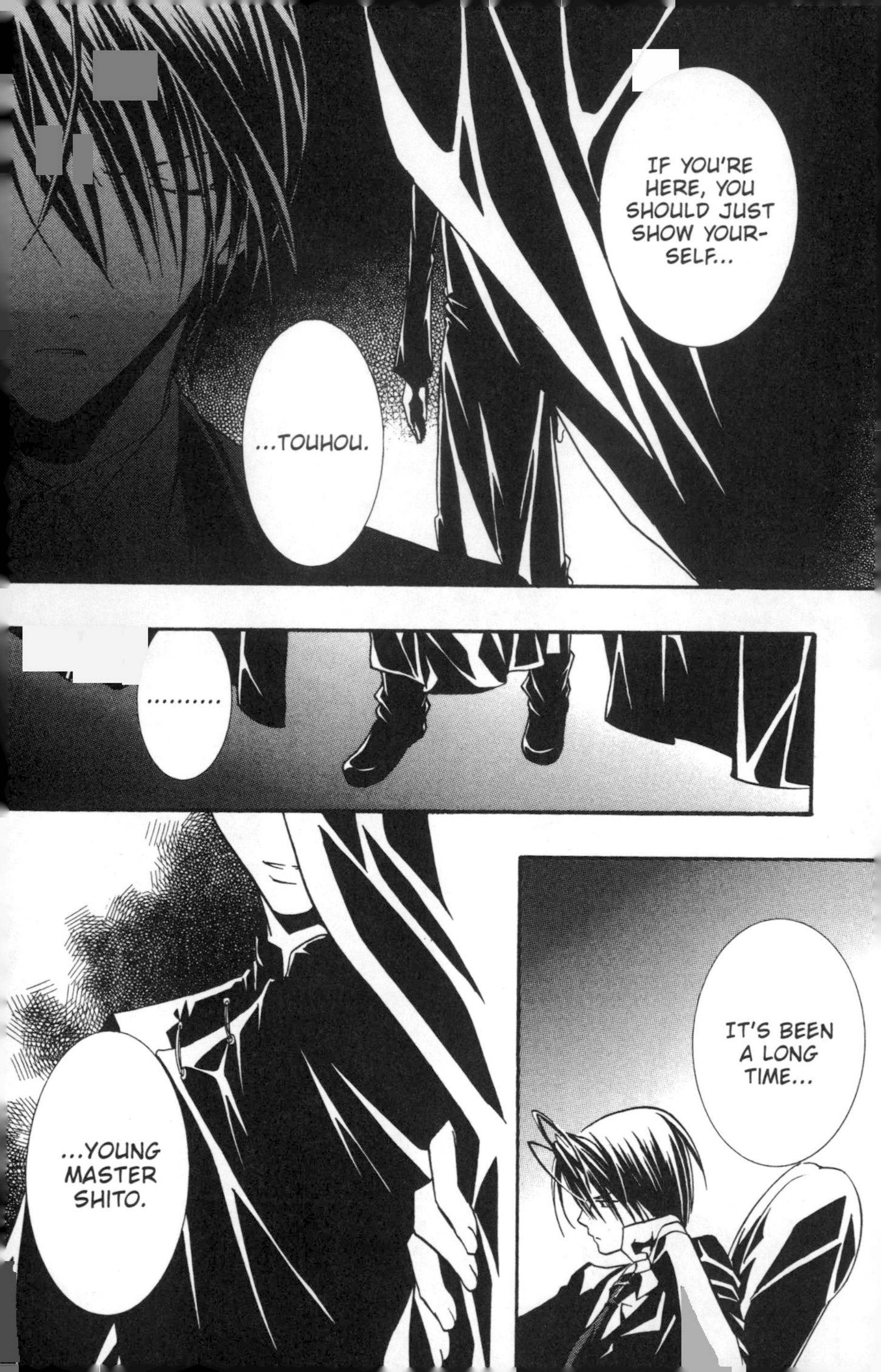
IF YOU'RE HERE, YOU SHOULD JUST SHOW YOUR-SELF...
...TOUHOU.
....
IT'S BEEN A LONG TIME...
...YOUNG MASTER SHITO.

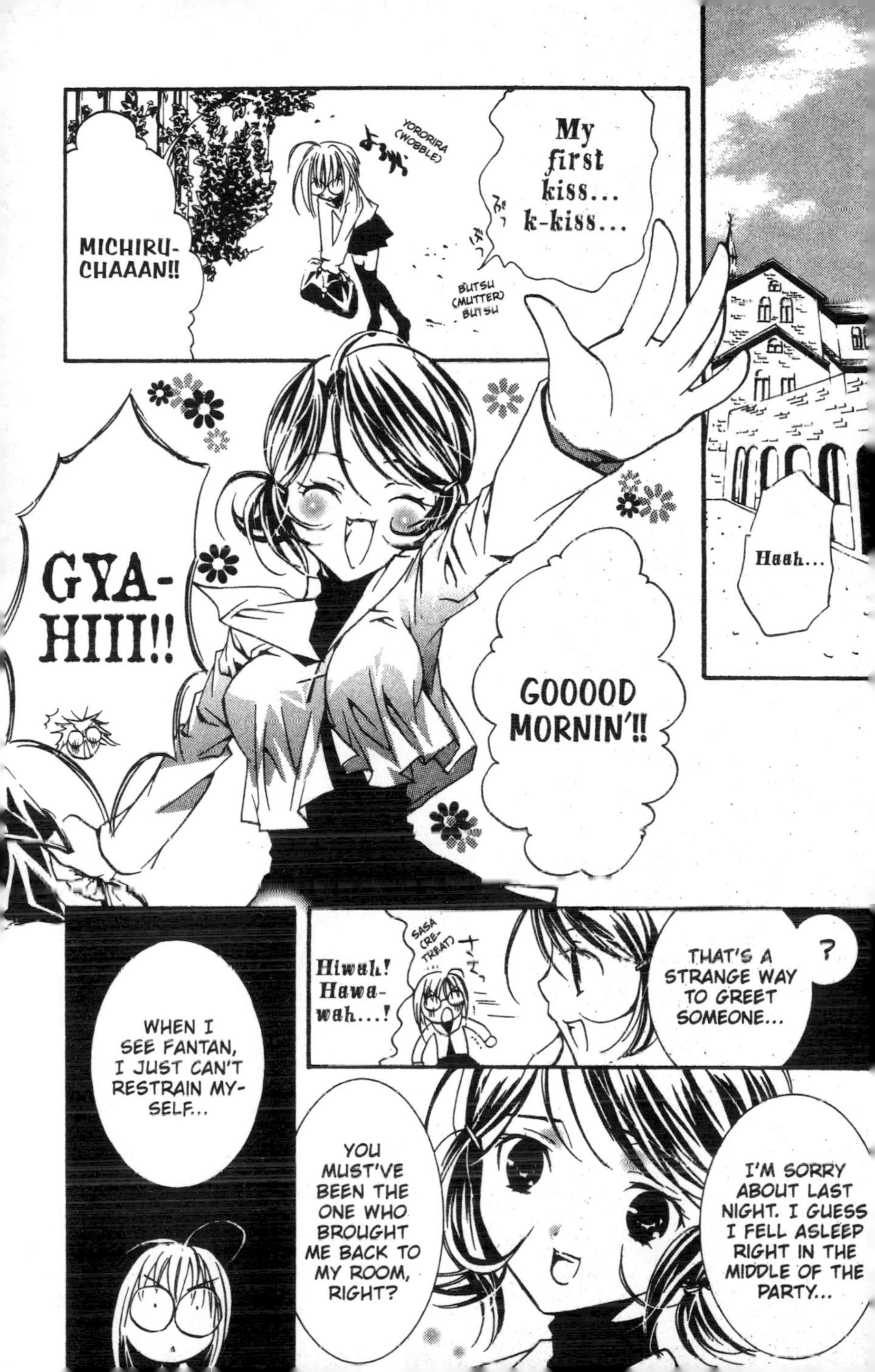
Haah...
YORORIRA (WOBBLE)
My first kiss... k-kiss...
BUTSU (MUTTER) BUTSU
MICHIRU-CHAAAN!!
GOOOOD MORNIN'!!
GYA-HIII!!
?
THAT'S A STRANGE WAY TO GREET SOMEONE...
SASA (RE-TREAT)
Hiwah! Hawa-wah...!
I'M SORRY ABOUT LAST NIGHT. I GUESS I FELL ASLEEP RIGHT IN THE MIDDLE OF THE PARTY...
YOU MUST'VE BEEN THE ONE WHO BROUGHT ME BACK TO MY ROOM, RIGHT?
WHEN I SEE FANTAN, I JUST CAN'T RESTRAIN MY-SELF...

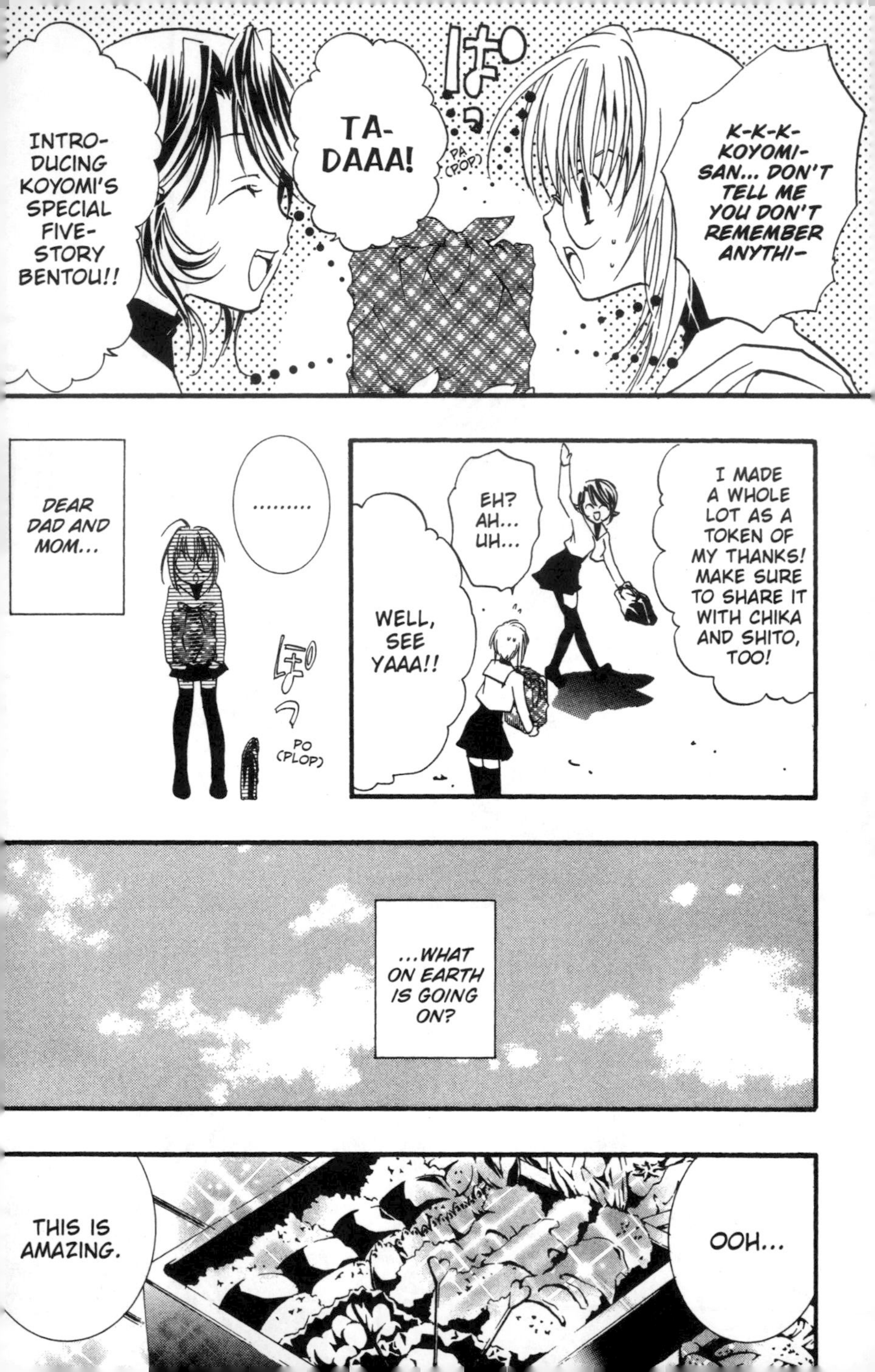
K-K-K-KOYOMI-SAN... DON'T TELL ME YOU DON'T REMEMBER ANYTHI-
ぱっ
PA (POP)
TA-DAAA!
INTRO-DUCING KOYOMI'S SPECIAL FIVE-STORY BENTOU!!
I MADE A WHOLE LOT AS A TOKEN OF MY THANKS! MAKE SURE TO SHARE IT WITH CHIKA AND SHITO, TOO!
EH? AH... UH...
WELL, SEE YAAA!!
....
ぽっ
PO (PLOP)
DEAR DAD AND MOM...
...WHAT ON EARTH IS GOING ON?
OOH...
THIS IS AMAZING.

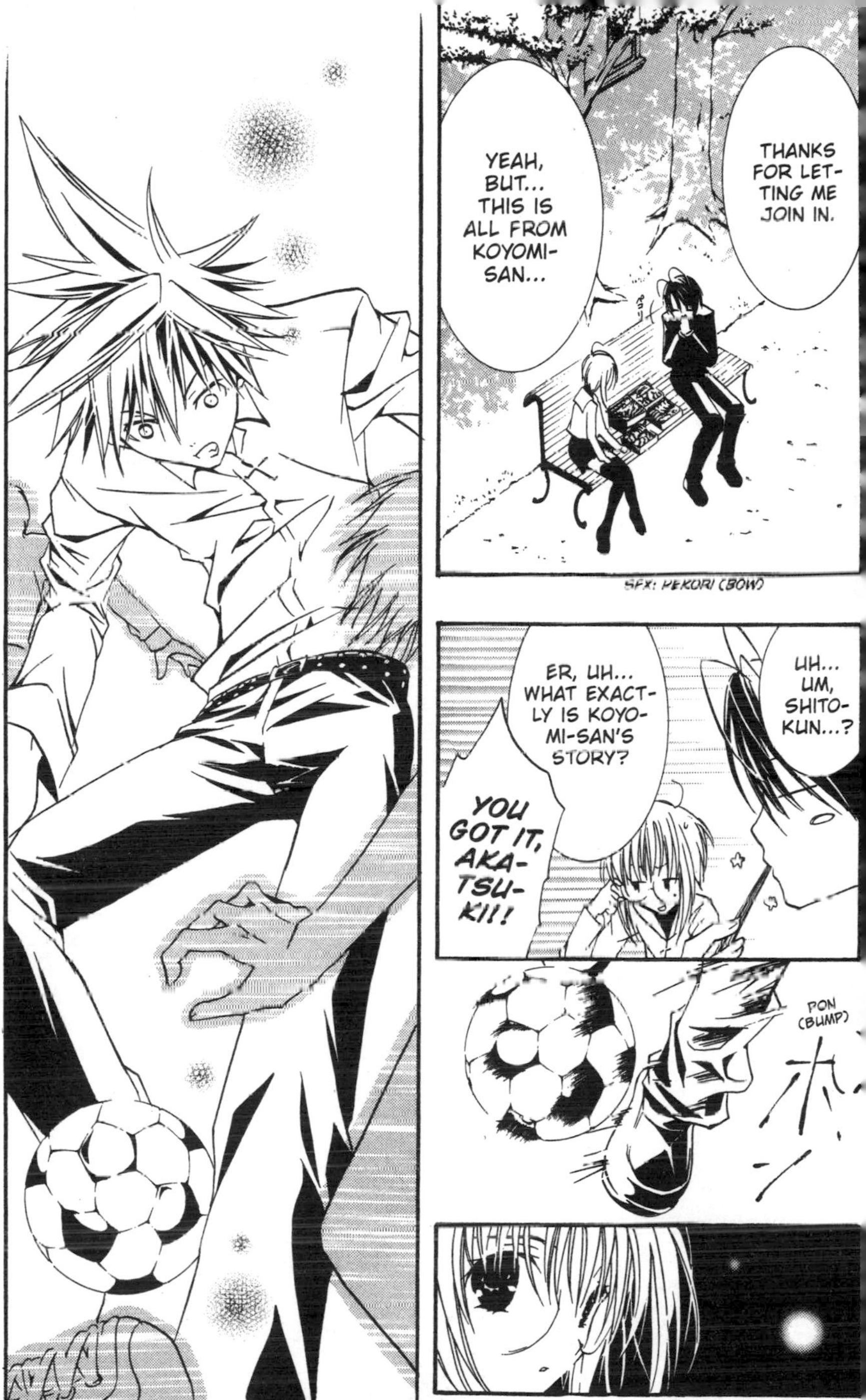
THANKS FOR LET-TING ME JOIN IN.
YEAH, BUT... THIS IS ALL FROM KOYOMI-SAN...
SFX: PEKORI (BOW)
UH... UM, SHITO-KUN...?
ER, UH... WHAT EXACT-LY IS KOYO-MI-SAN'S STORY?
YOU GOT IT, AKA-TSU-KI!!
PON (BUMP)

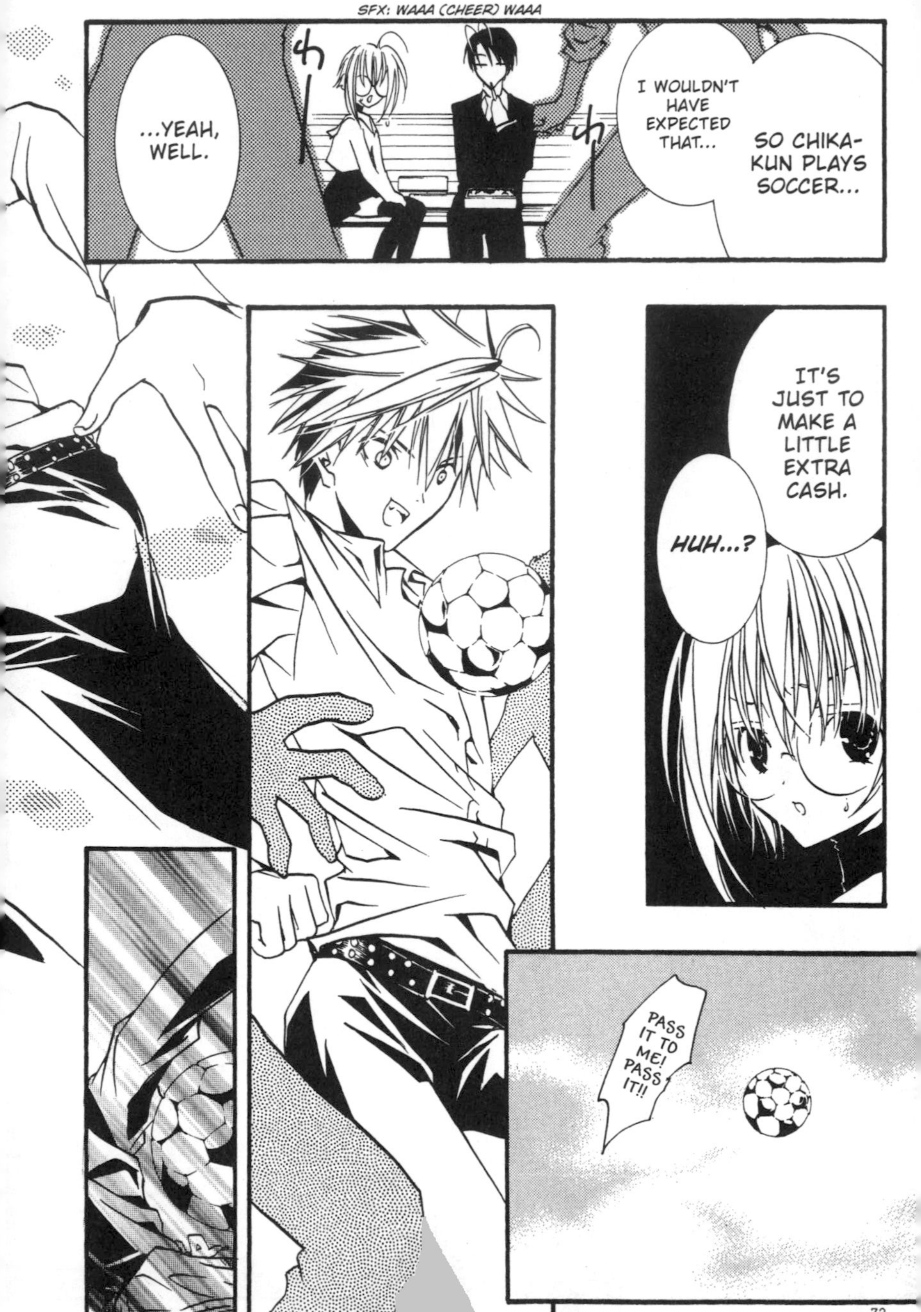
SFX: WAAA (CHEER) WAAA
SO CHIKA-KUN PLAYS SOCCER...
I WOULDN'T HAVE EXPECTED THAT...
...YEAH, WELL.
IT'S JUST TO MAKE A LITTLE EXTRA CASH.
HUH...?
PASS IT TO ME! PASS IT!!

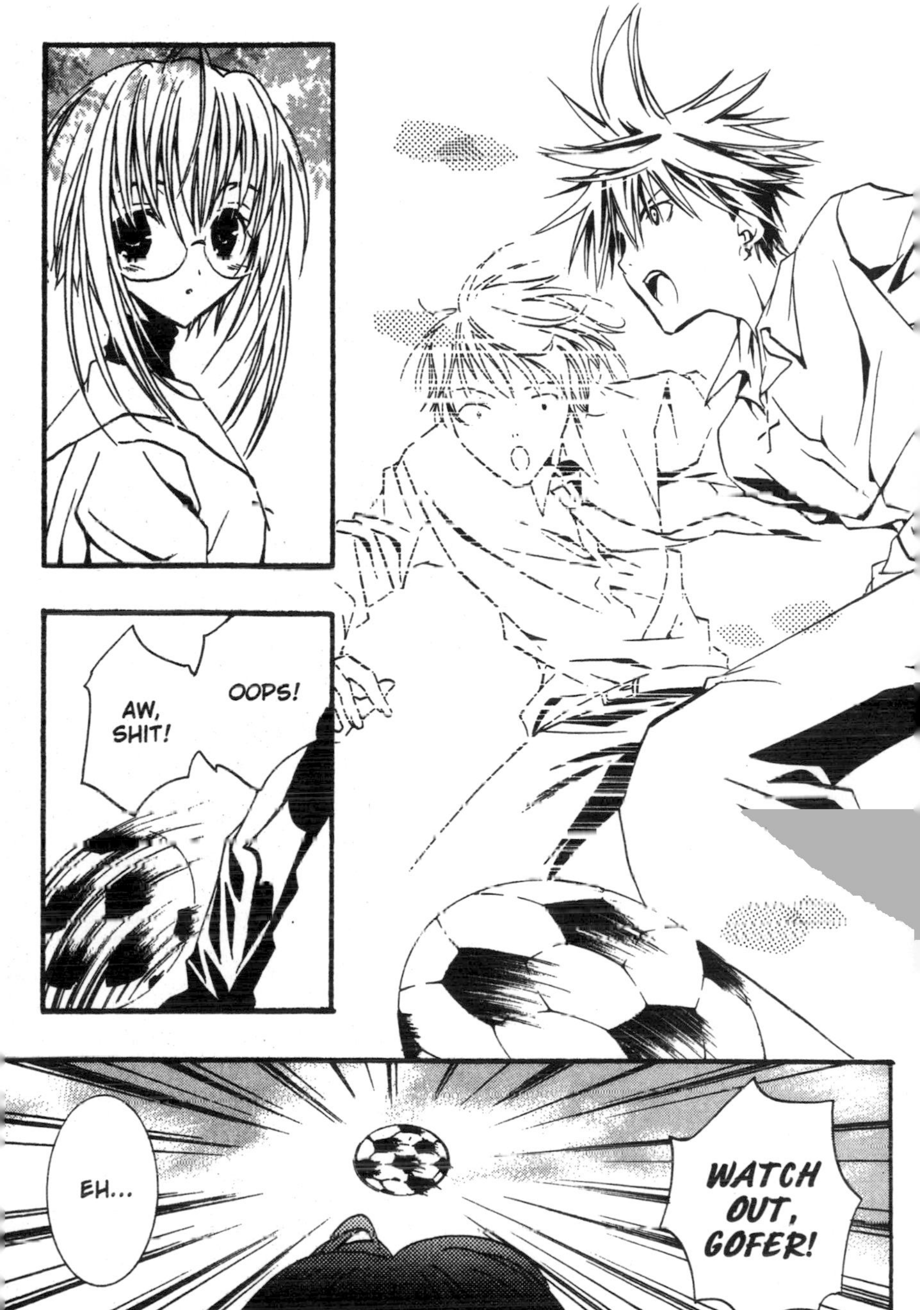
OOPS!
AW, SHIT!
WATCH OUT, GOFER!
EH...

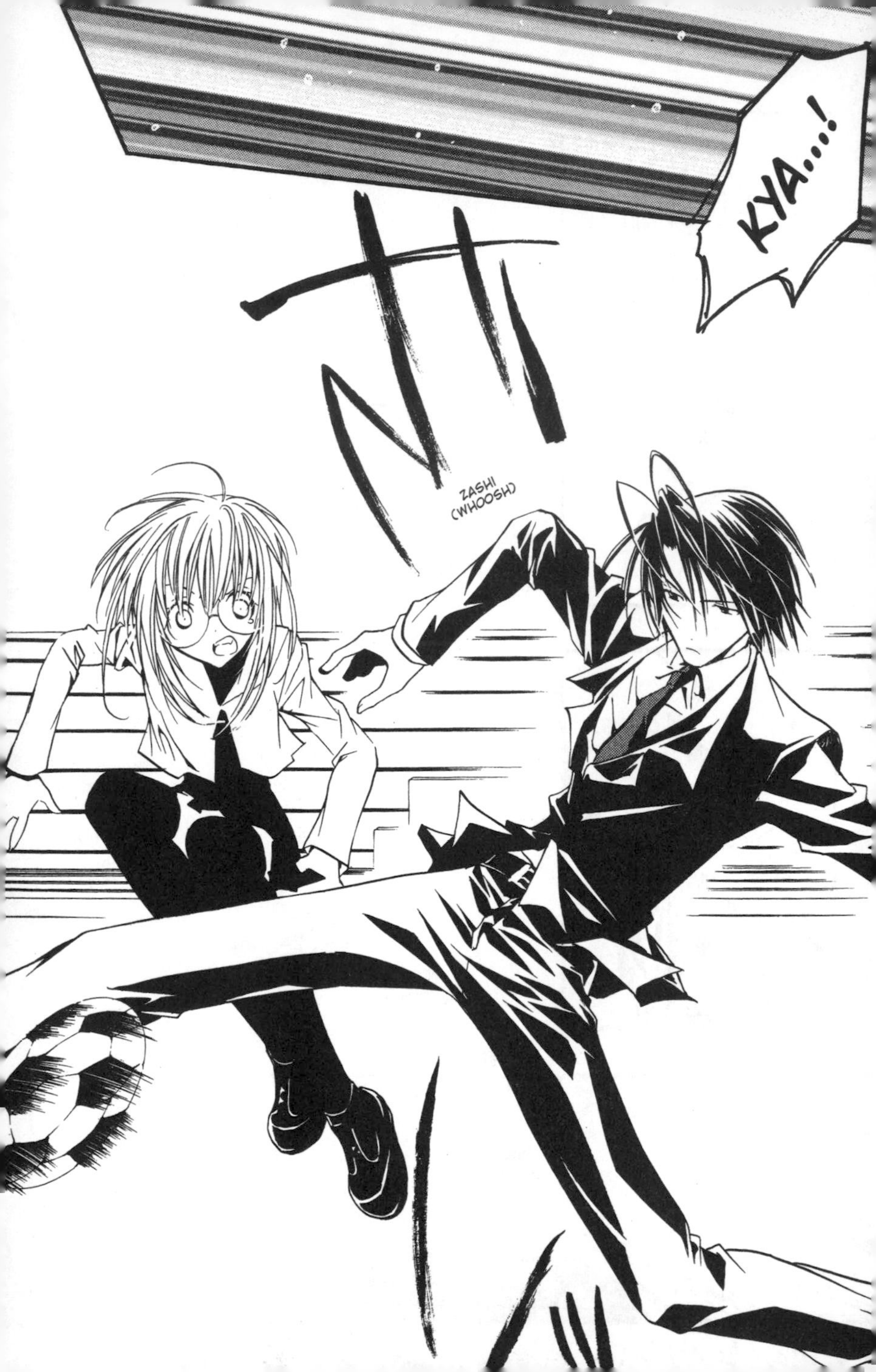

KYA...!
ZASHI (WHOOSH)

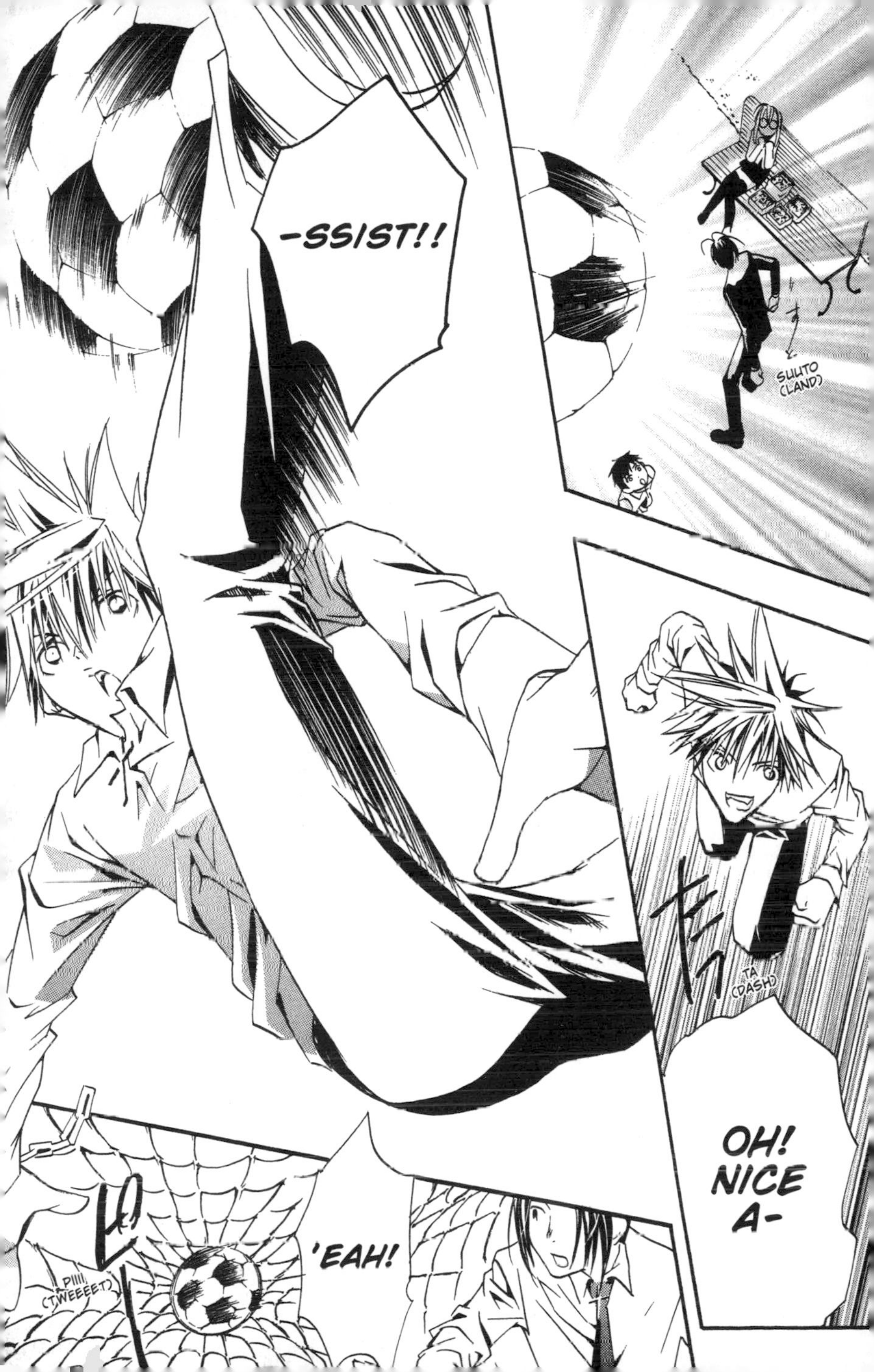
SUUTO (LAND)
TA (DASH)
OH! NICE A-
-SSIST!!
'EAH!
PIIII (TWEEEEET)

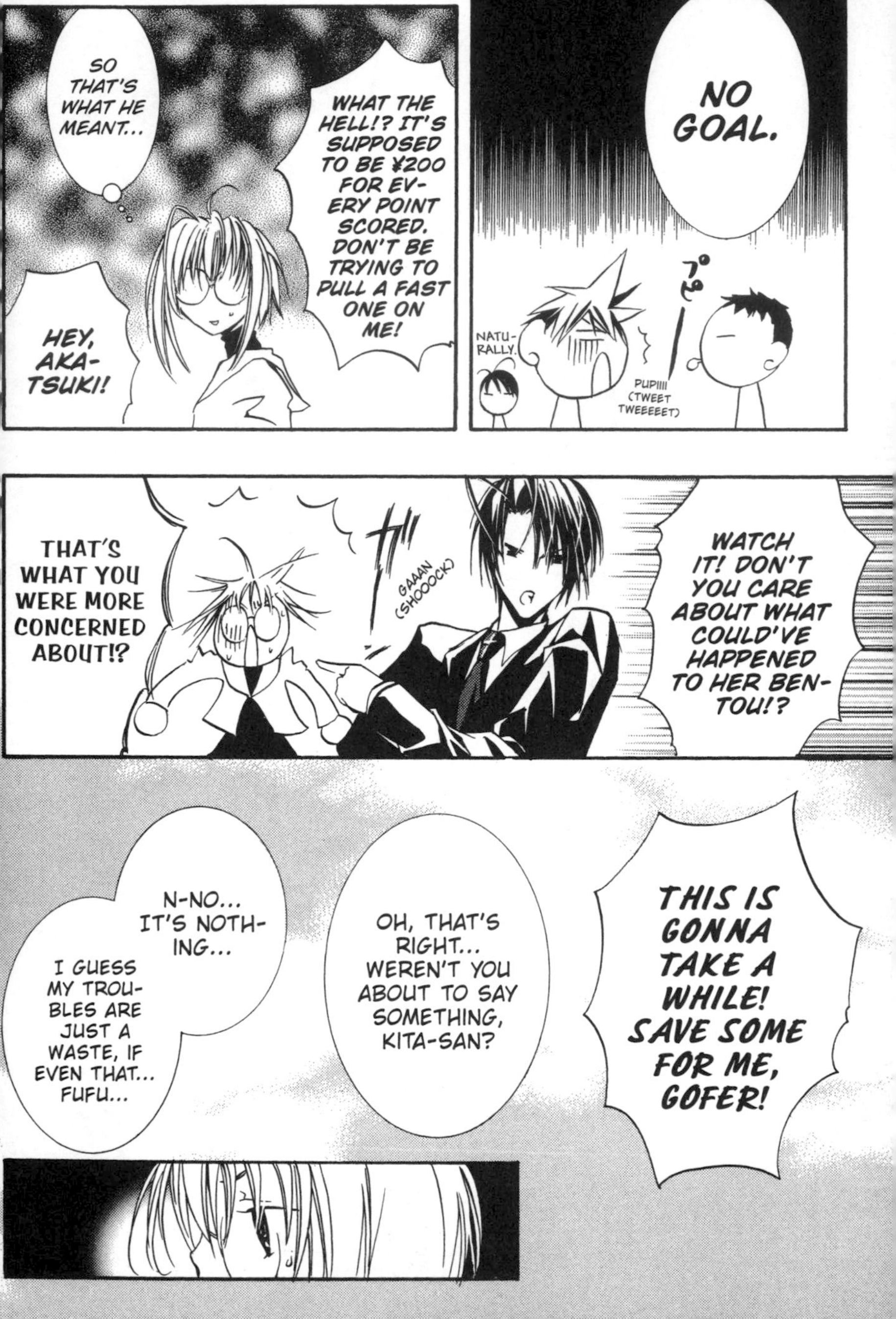
NO GOAL.
PUPIIII (TWEET TWEEEEET)
NATU-RALLY.
WHAT THE HELL!? IT'S SUPPOSED TO BE ¥200 FOR EV-ERY POINT SCORED. DON'T BE TRYING TO PULL A FAST ONE ON ME!
SO THAT'S WHAT HE MEANT...
HEY, AKA-TSUKI!
WATCH IT! DON'T YOU CARE ABOUT WHAT COULD'VE HAPPENED TO HER BEN-TOU!?
GAAAN (SHOOOCK)
THAT'S WHAT YOU WERE MORE CONCERNED ABOUT!?
THIS IS GONNA TAKE A WHILE! SAVE SOME FOR ME, GOFER!
OH, THAT'S RIGHT... WEREN'T YOU ABOUT TO SAY SOMETHING, KITA-SAN?
N-NO... IT'S NOTH-ING...
I GUESS MY TROU-BLES ARE JUST A WASTE, IF EVEN THAT... FUFU...

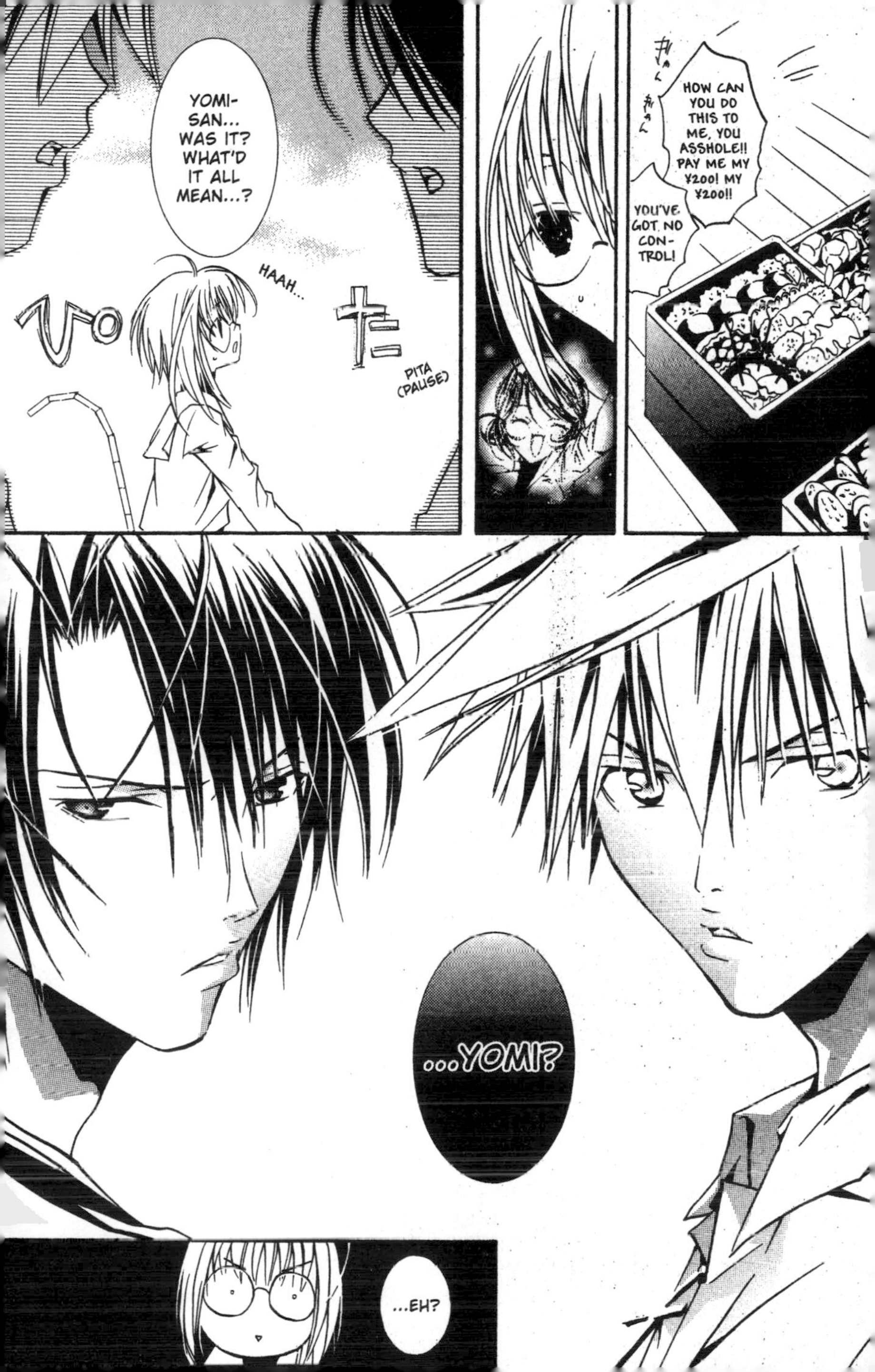
HOW CAN YOU DO THIS TO ME, YOU ASSHOLE!! PAY ME MY ¥200! MY ¥200!!
YOU'VE GOT NO CON-TROL!
YOMI-SAN... WAS IT? WHAT'D IT ALL MEAN...?
HAAH...
PITA (PAUSE)
...YOMI?
...EH?

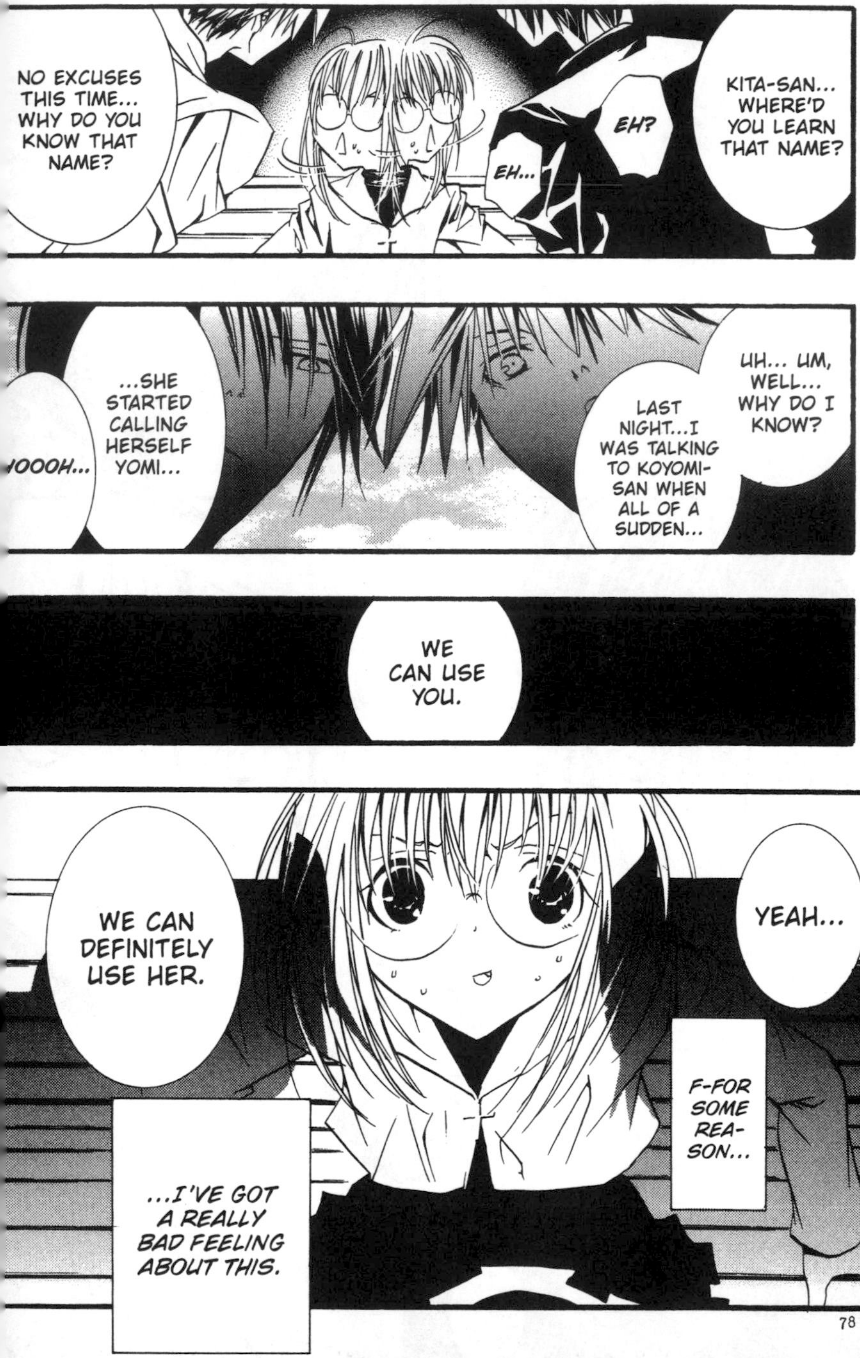
KITA-SAN... WHERE'D YOU LEARN THAT NAME?
EH?
EH...
NO EXCUSES THIS TIME... WHY DO YOU KNOW THAT NAME?
UH... UM, WELL... WHY DO I KNOW?
LAST NIGHT...I WAS TALKING TO KOYOMI-SAN WHEN ALL OF A SUDDEN...
...SHE STARTED CALLING HERSELF YOMI...
OOOH...
WE CAN USE YOU.
YEAH...
WE CAN DEFINITELY USE HER.
F-FOR SOME REA-SON...
...I'VE GOT A REALLY BAD FEELING ABOUT THIS.

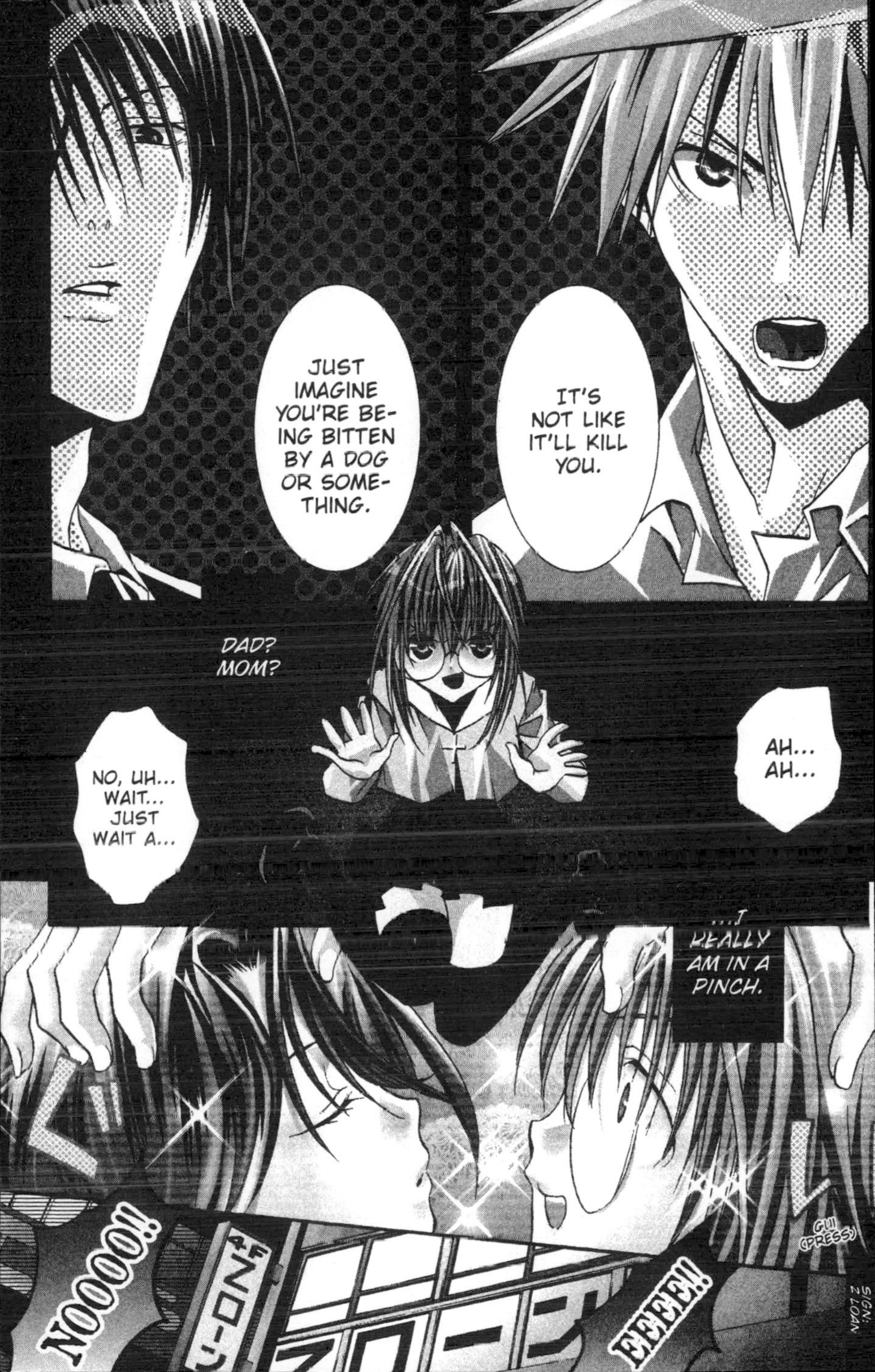
IT'S NOT LIKE IT'LL KILL YOU.
JUST IMAGINE YOU'RE BE-ING BITTEN BY A DOG OR SOME-THING.
DAD? MOM?
AH... AH...
NO, UH... WAIT... JUST WAIT A...
...I REALLY AM IN A PINCH.
GUI (PRESS)
EEEE!!
NOOOON!!
4-F
SIGN: Z LOAN

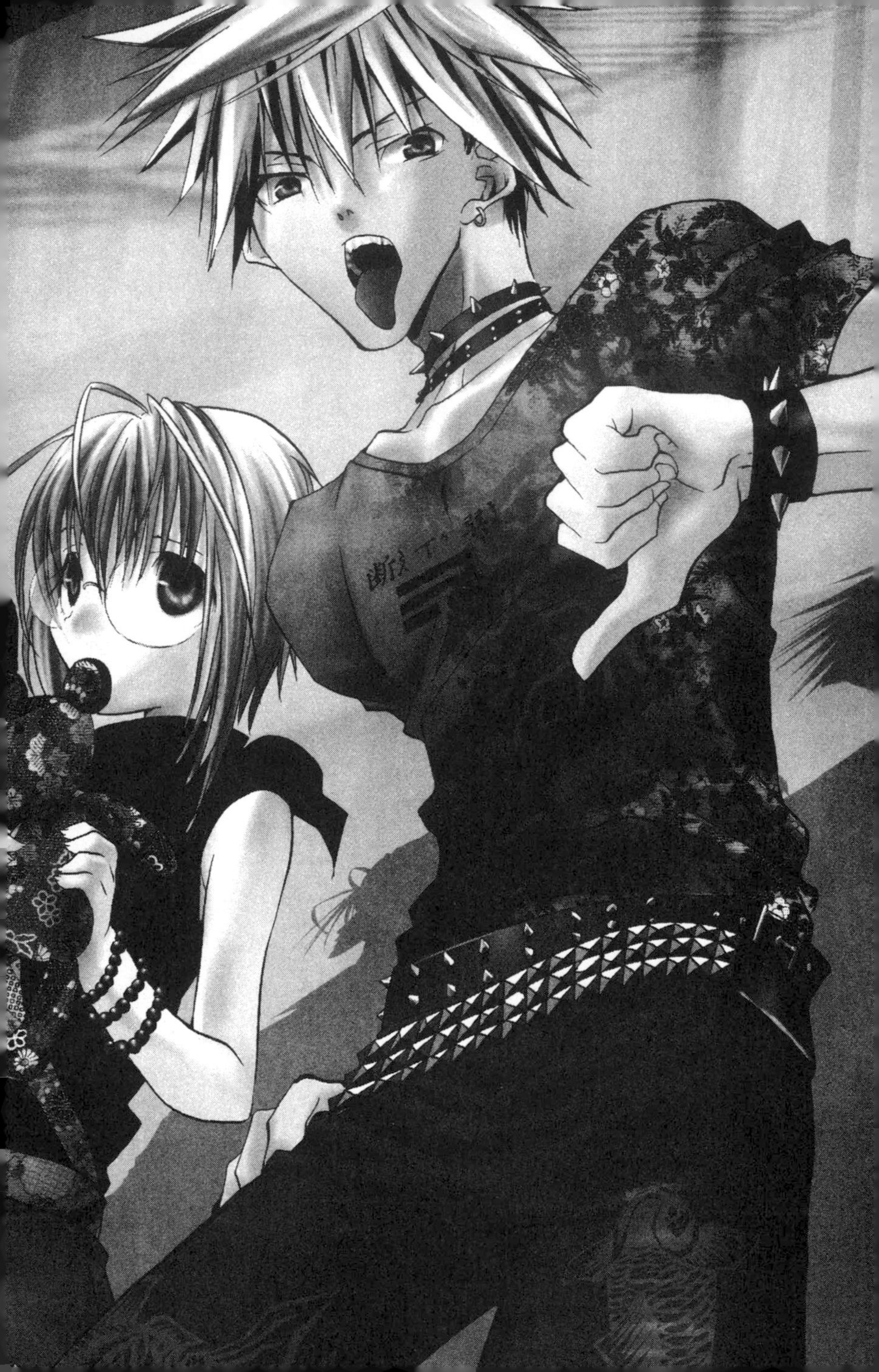

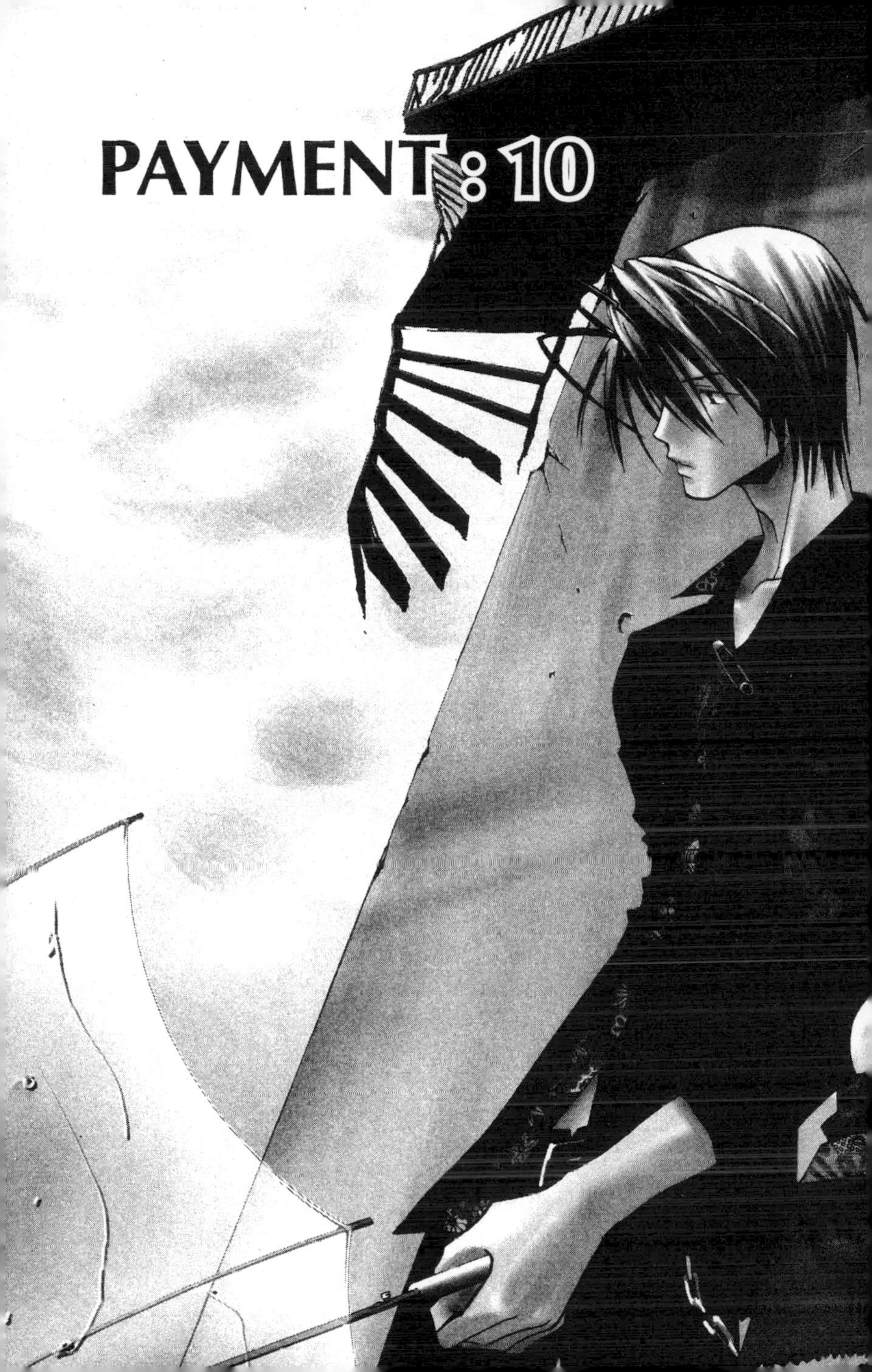
PAYMENT : 10

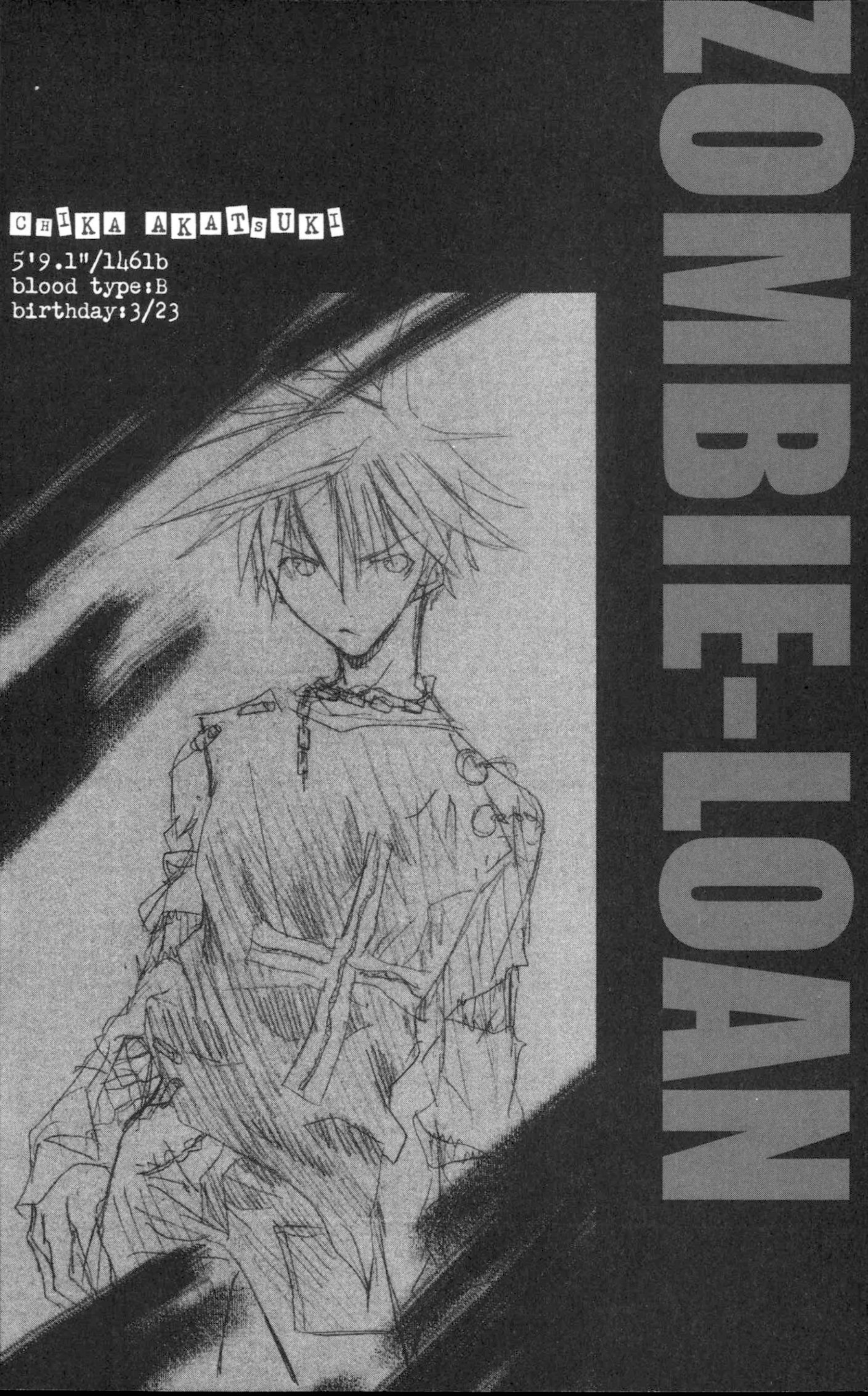
CHIKA AKATSUKI
5'9.1"/146lb
blood type:B
birthday:3/23
ZOMBIE-LOAN

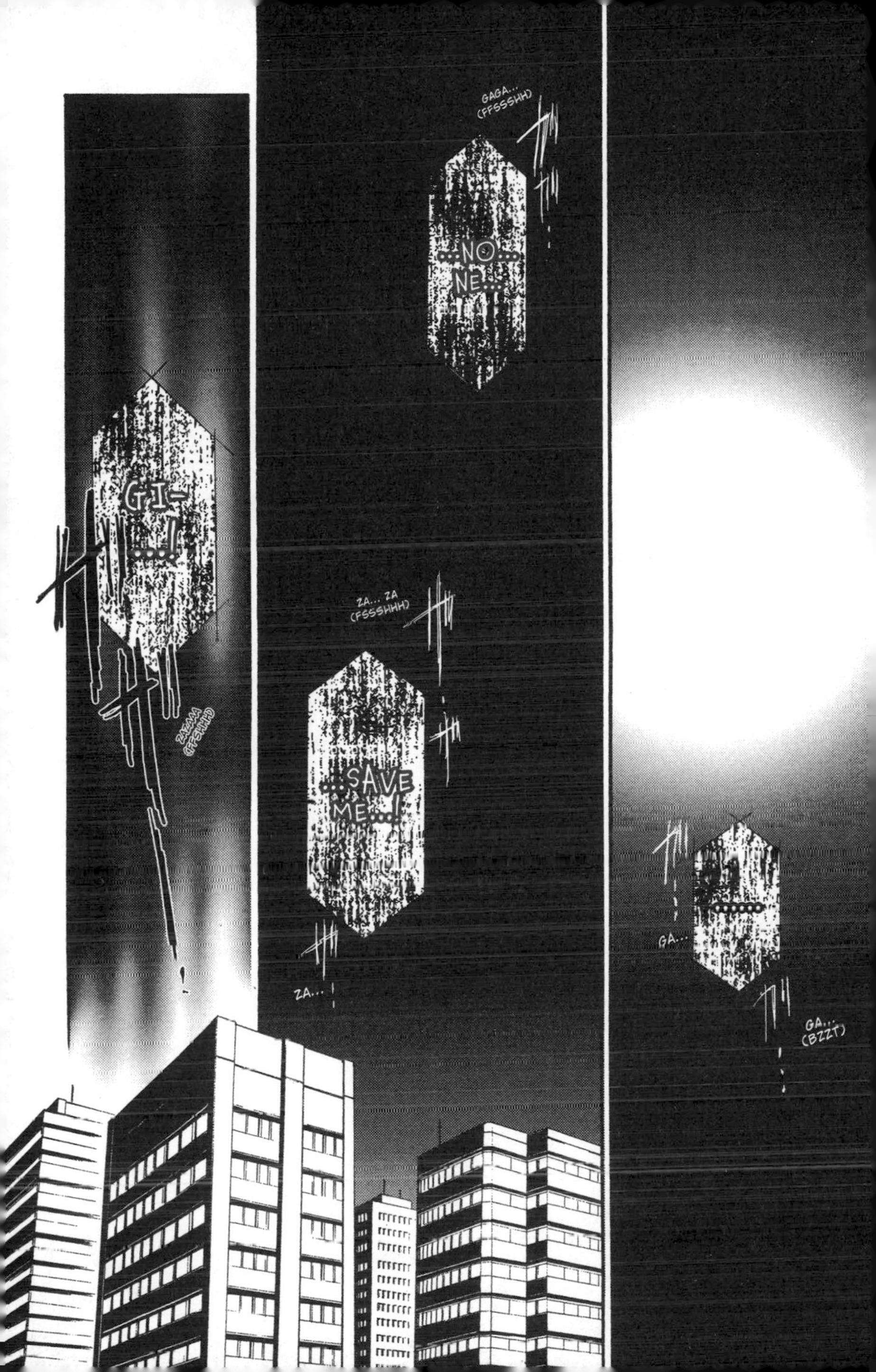
....
GA...
GA... (BZZT)
GAGA... (FFSSSHH)
...NO... NE...
ZA... ZA (FSSSHHH)
...SAVE ME...!
ZA... !
GI-...!
ZAZAAA (FFSHHH)

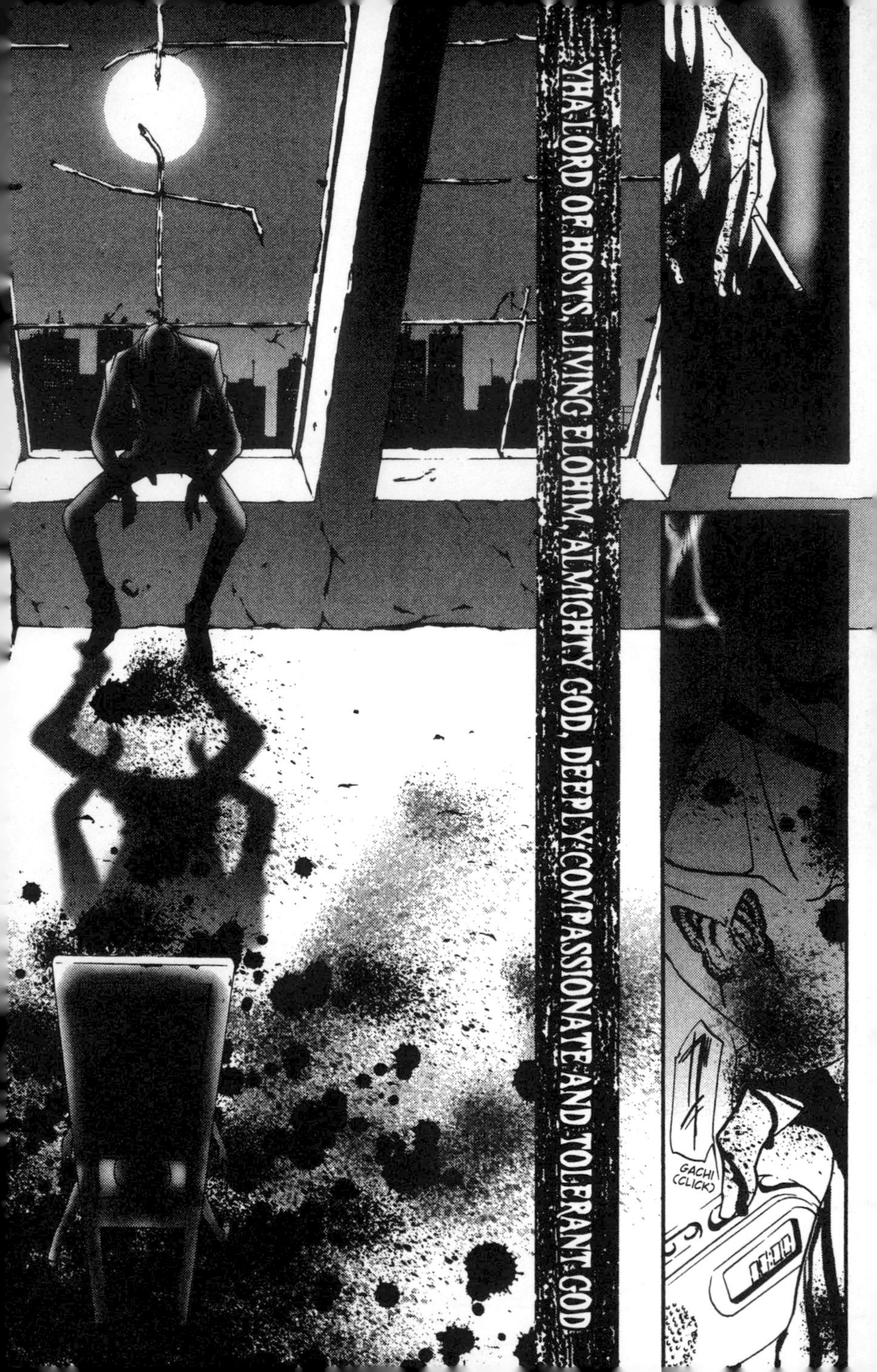
GACHI
(CLICK)
YHA LORD OF HOSTS, LIVING ELOHIM, ALMIGHTY GOD, DEEPLY COMPASSIONATE AND TOLERANT GOD

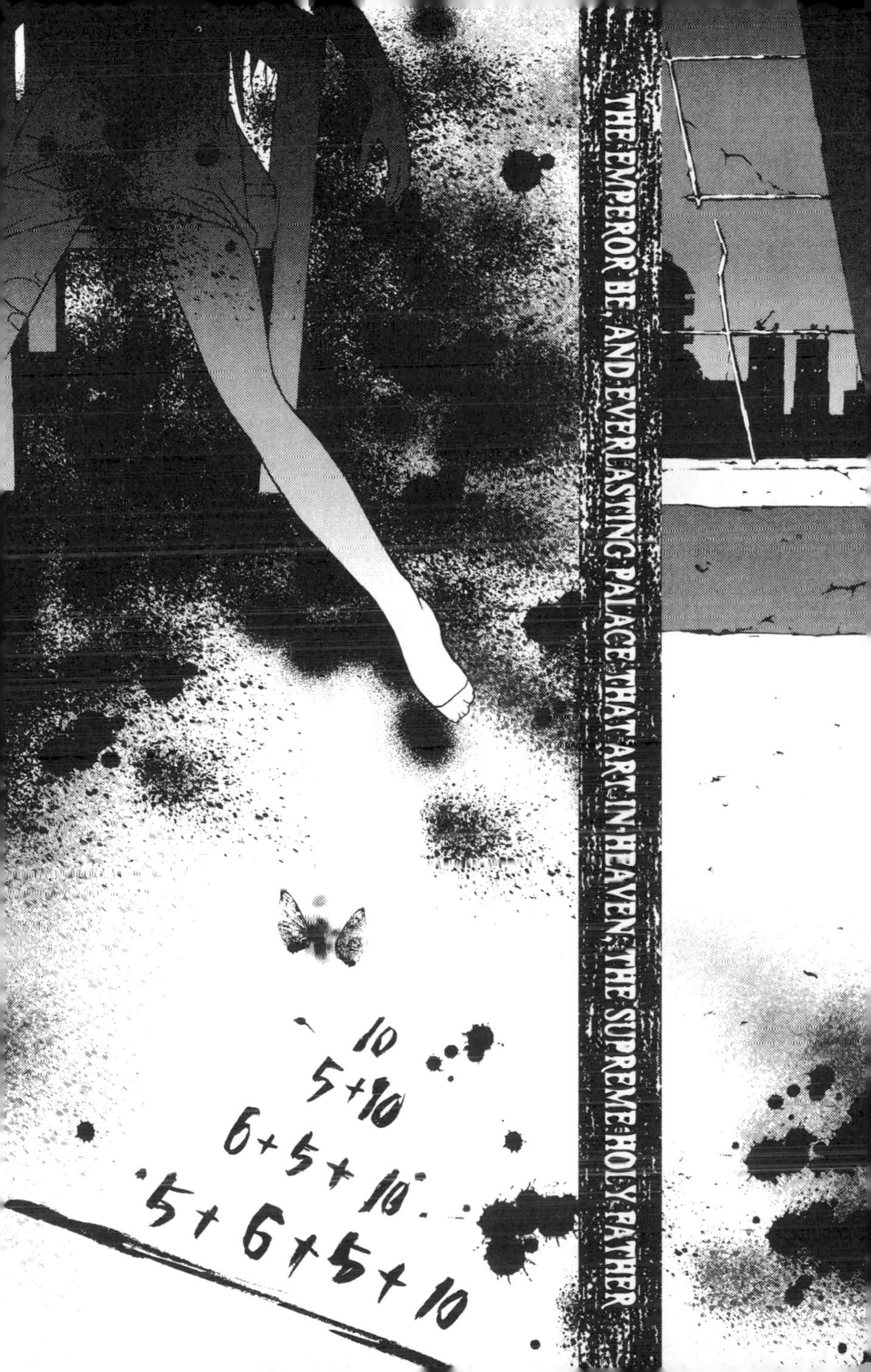
THE EMPEROR BE, AND EVERLASTING PALACE THAT ART IN HEAVEN, THE SUPREME HOLY FATHER
10
5+10
6+5+10
5+6+5+10

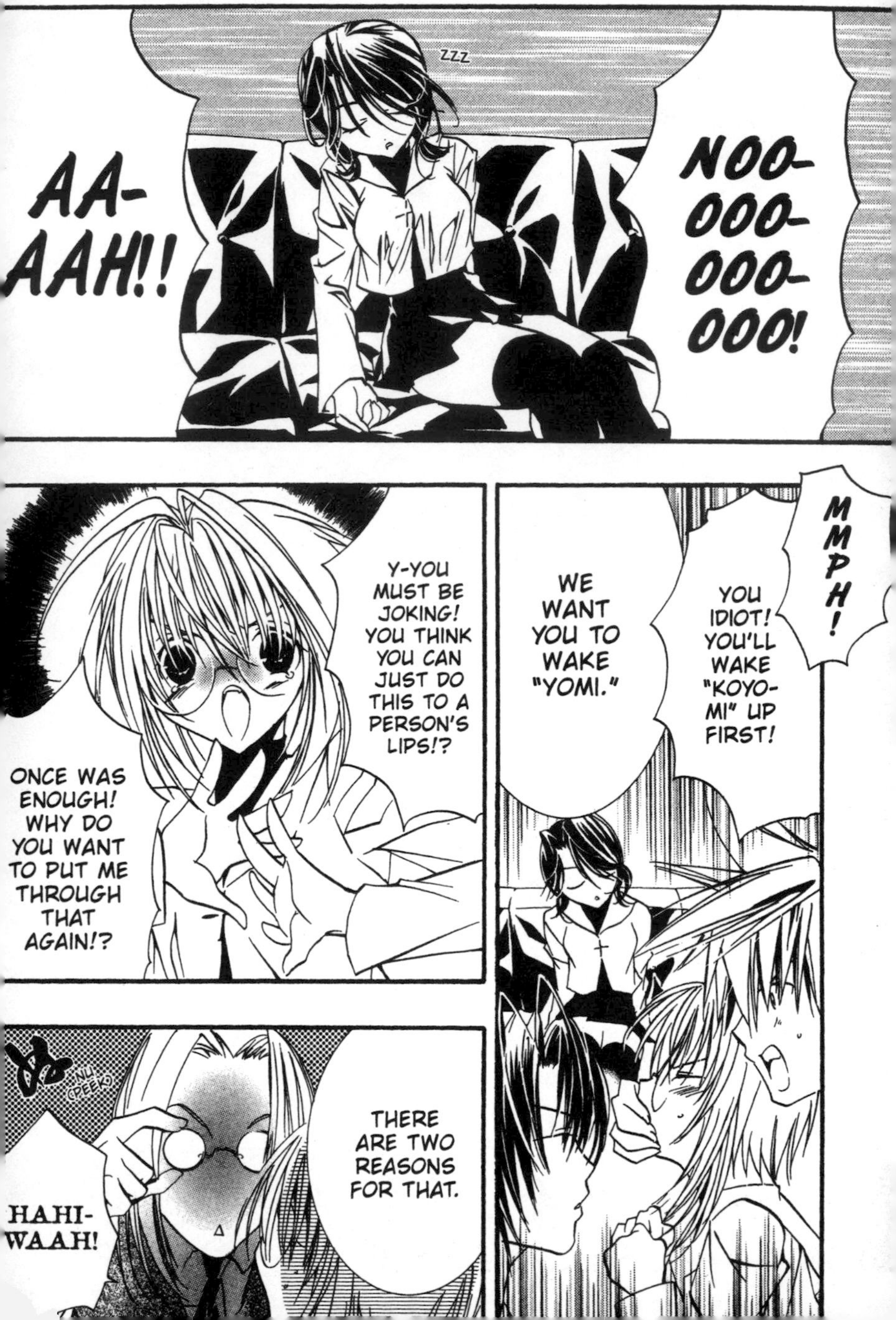
NOO-OOO-OOO-OOO!
ZZZ
AA-AAAH!!
MMPH!
YOU IDIOT! YOU'LL WAKE "KOYO-MI" UP FIRST!
WE WANT YOU TO WAKE "YOMI."
Y-YOU MUST BE JOKING! YOU THINK YOU CAN JUST DO THIS TO A PERSON'S LIPS!?
ONCE WAS ENOUGH! WHY DO YOU WANT TO PUT ME THROUGH THAT AGAIN!?
THERE ARE TWO REASONS FOR THAT.
NU (PEEK)
HAHI-WAAH!

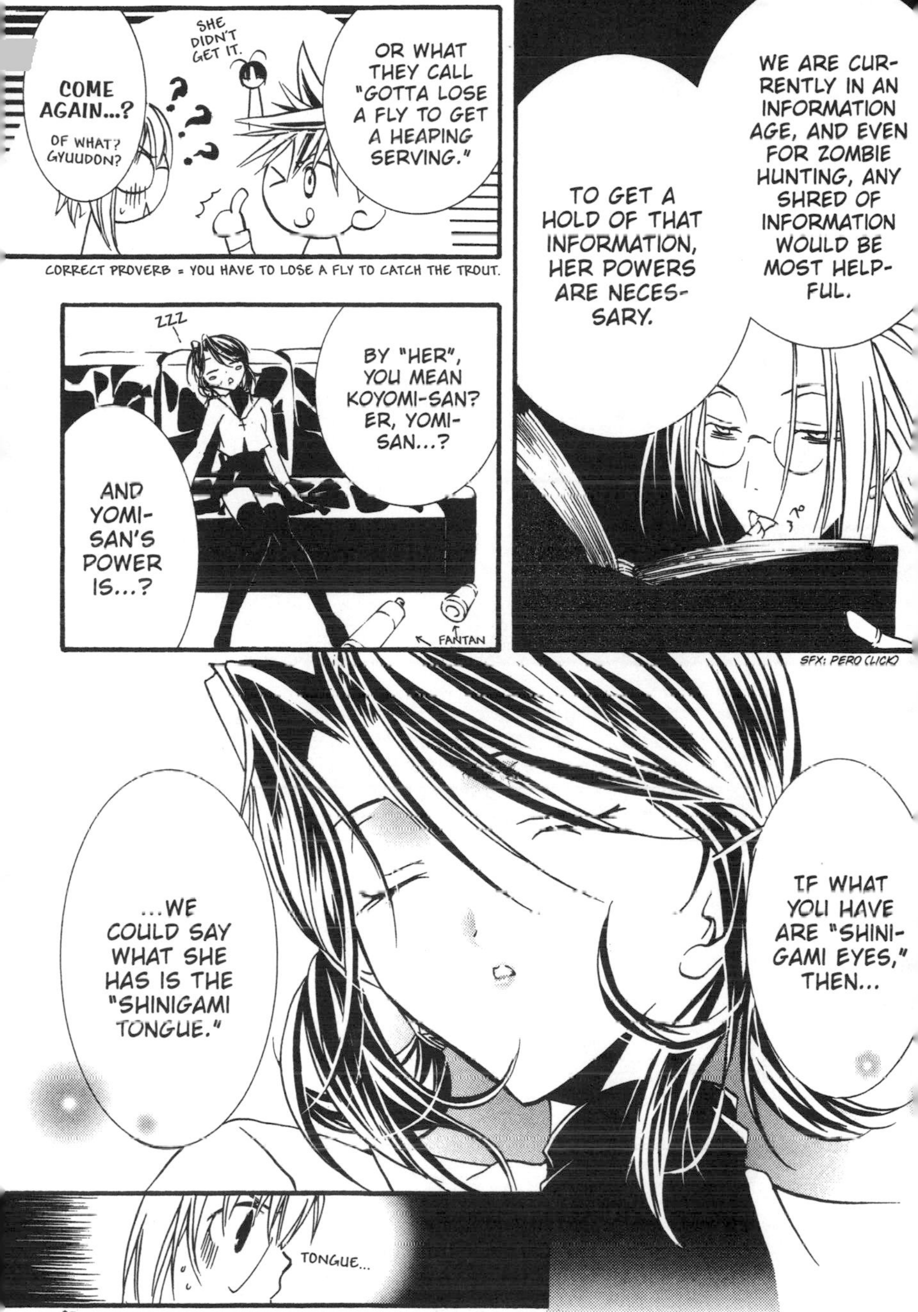
WE ARE CURRENTLY IN AN INFORMATION AGE, AND EVEN FOR ZOMBIE HUNTING, ANY SHRED OF INFORMATION WOULD BE MOST HELPFUL.
TO GET A HOLD OF THAT INFORMATION, HER POWERS ARE NECESSARY.
SFX: PERO (LICK)
OR WHAT THEY CALL "GOTTA LOSE A FLY TO GET A HEAPING SERVING."
SHE DIDN'T GET IT.
COME AGAIN...?
OF WHAT? GYUUDON?
CORRECT PROVERB = YOU HAVE TO LOSE A FLY TO CATCH THE TROUT.
BY "HER", YOU MEAN KOYOMI-SAN? ER, YOMI-SAN...?
ZZZ
AND YOMI-SAN'S POWER IS...?
FANTAN
IF WHAT YOU HAVE ARE "SHINIGAMI EYES," THEN...
...WE COULD SAY WHAT SHE HAS IS THE "SHINIGAMI TONGUE."
TONGUE...

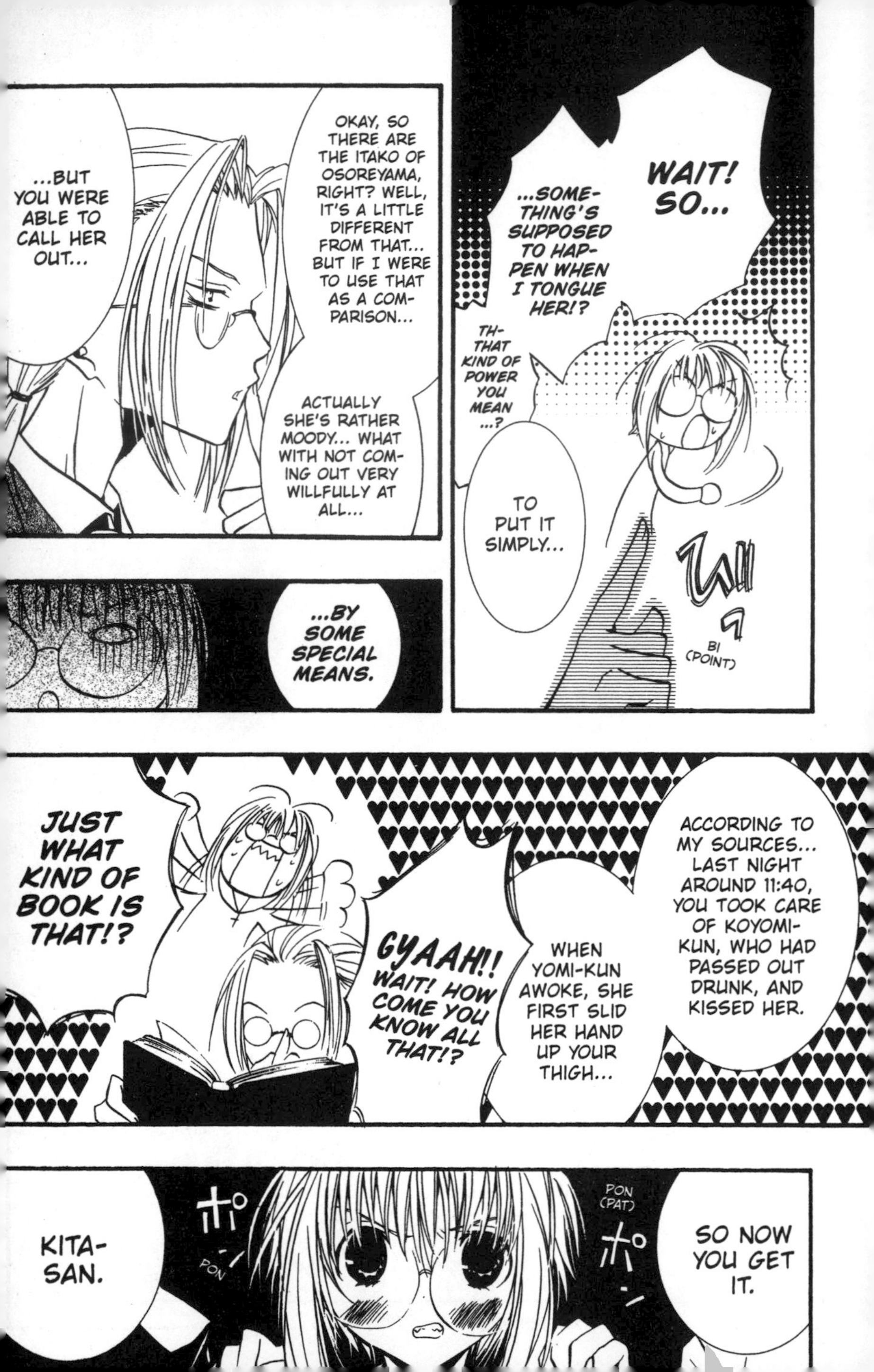
WAIT! SO...
...SOMETHING'S SUPPOSED TO HAPPEN WHEN I TONGUE HER!?
TH-THAT KIND OF POWER YOU MEAN ...?
TO PUT IT SIMPLY...
BI (POINT)
OKAY, SO THERE ARE THE ITAKO OF OSOREYAMA, RIGHT? WELL, IT'S A LITTLE DIFFERENT FROM THAT... BUT IF I WERE TO USE THAT AS A COMPARISON...
ACTUALLY SHE'S RATHER MOODY... WHAT WITH NOT COMING OUT VERY WILLFULLY AT ALL...
...BUT YOU WERE ABLE TO CALL HER OUT...
...BY SOME SPECIAL MEANS.
ACCORDING TO MY SOURCES... LAST NIGHT AROUND 11:40, YOU TOOK CARE OF KOYOMI-KUN, WHO HAD PASSED OUT DRUNK, AND KISSED HER.
WHEN YOMI-KUN AWOKE, SHE FIRST SLID HER HAND UP YOUR THIGH...
GYAAH!! WAIT! HOW COME YOU KNOW ALL THAT!?
JUST WHAT KIND OF BOOK IS THAT!?
SO NOW YOU GET IT.
PON (PAT)
PON
KITA-SAN.

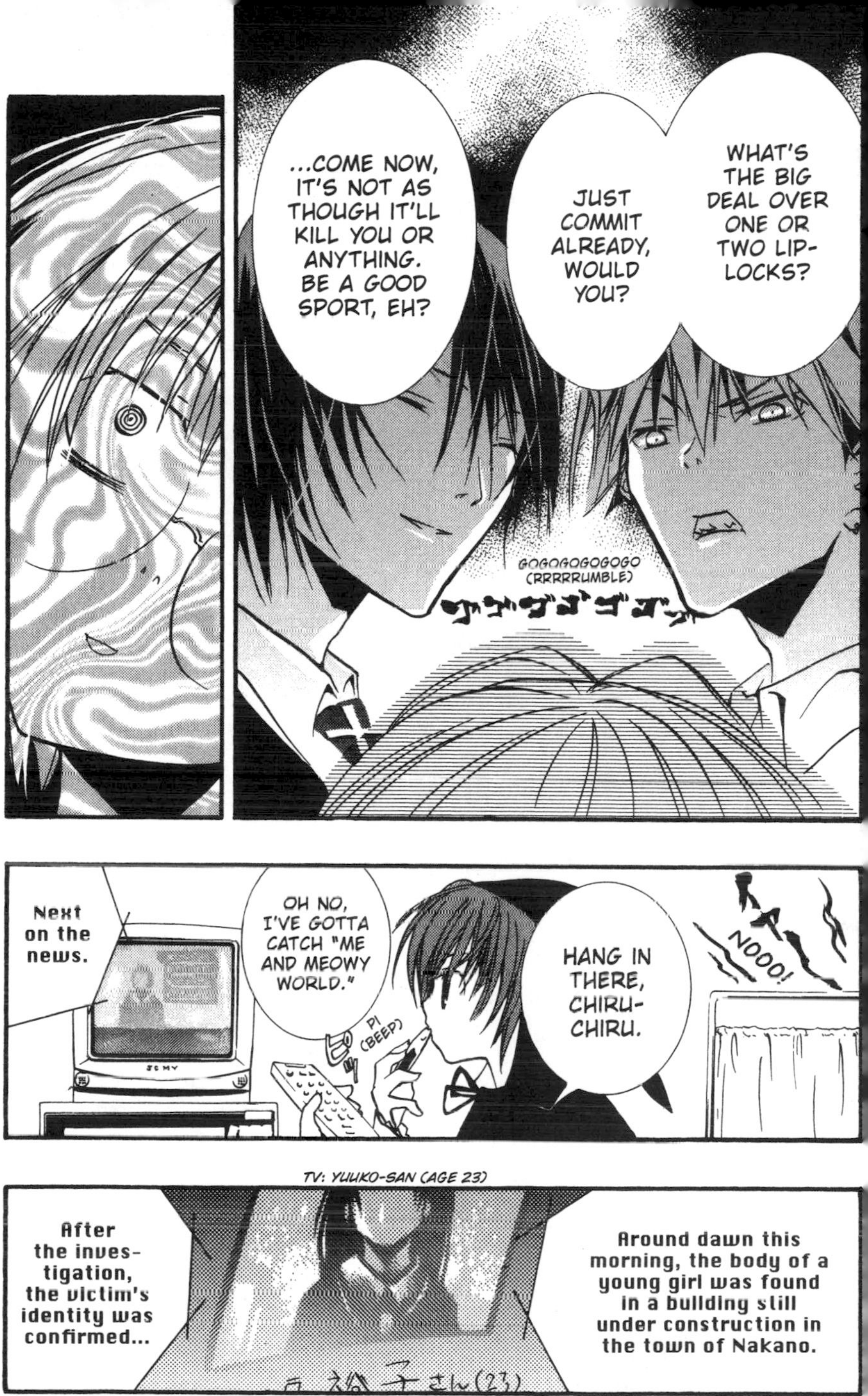
WHAT'S THE BIG DEAL OVER ONE OR TWO LIP-LOCKS?
JUST COMMIT ALREADY, WOULD YOU?
...COME NOW, IT'S NOT AS THOUGH IT'LL KILL YOU OR ANYTHING. BE A GOOD SPORT, EH?
GOGOGOGOGOGO (RRRRRUMBLE)
NOOO!
HANG IN THERE, CHIRU-CHIRU.
OH NO, I'VE GOTTA CATCH "ME AND MEOWY WORLD."
PI (BEEP)
Next on the news.
TV: YUUKO-SAN (AGE 23)
Around dawn this morning, the body of a young girl was found in a building still under construction in the town of Nakano.
After the inves-tigation, the victim's identity was confirmed...

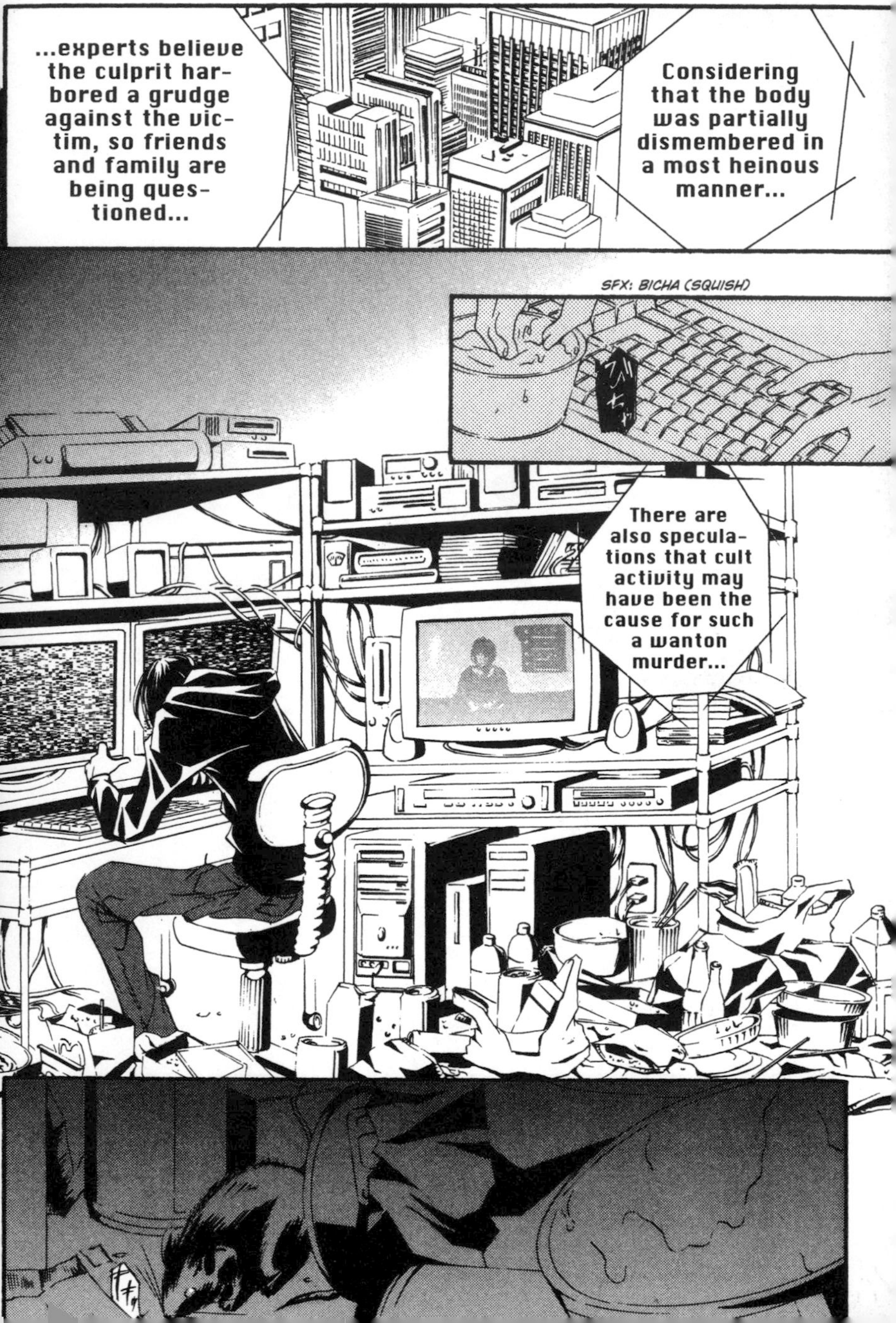
Considering that the body was partially dismembered in a most heinous manner...
...experts believe the culprit harbored a grudge against the victim, so friends and family are being questioned...
SFX: BICHA (SQUISH)
There are also speculations that cult activity may have been the cause for such a wanton murder...

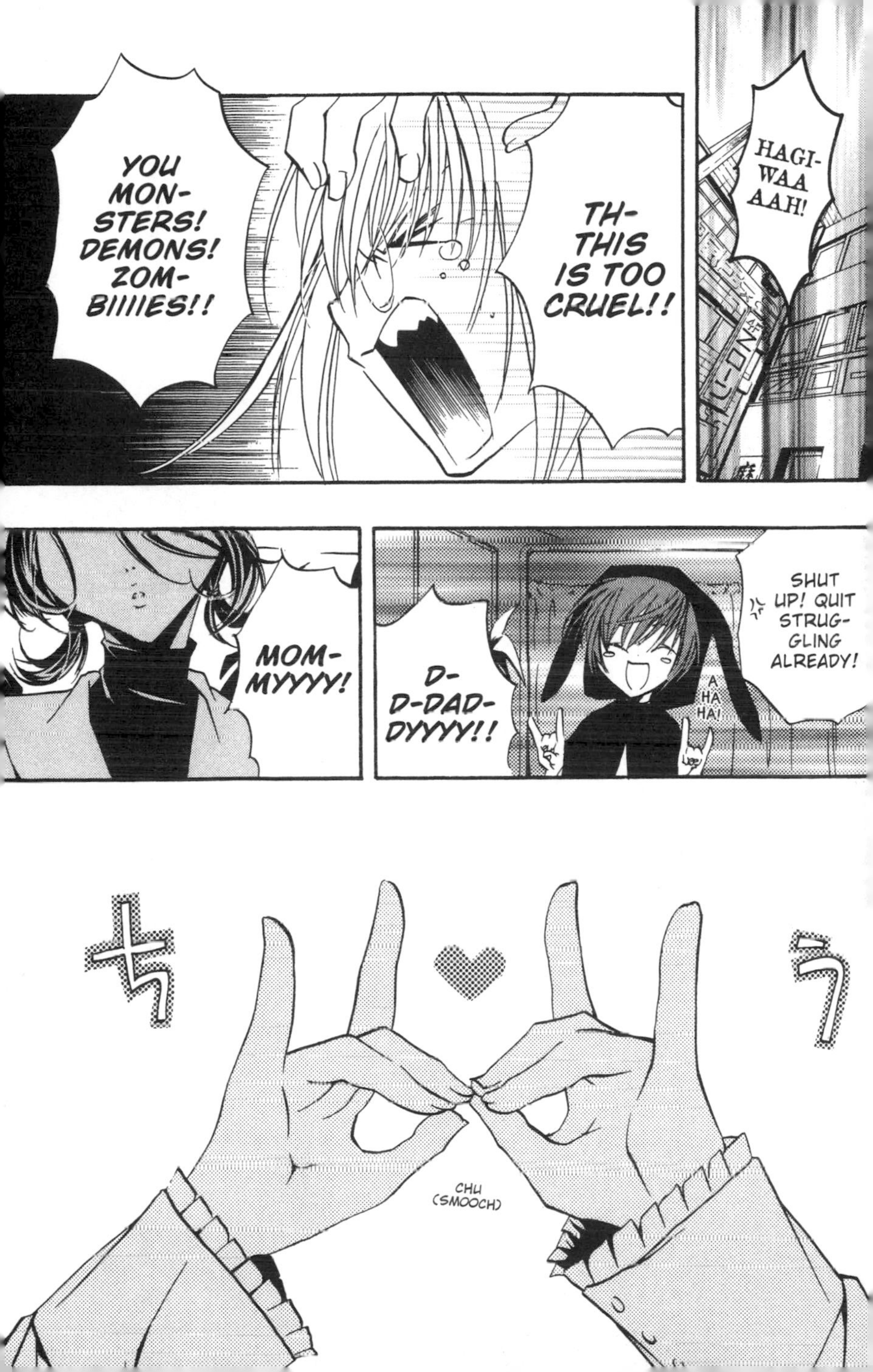
HAGI-WAAAAH!
TH-THIS IS TOO CRUEL!!
YOU MON-STERS! DEMONS! ZOM-BIIIIES!!
SHUT UP! QUIT STRUG-GLING ALREADY!
A HA HA!
D-D-DAD-DYYYY!!
MOM-MYYYY!
う
ち
CHU (SMOOCH)

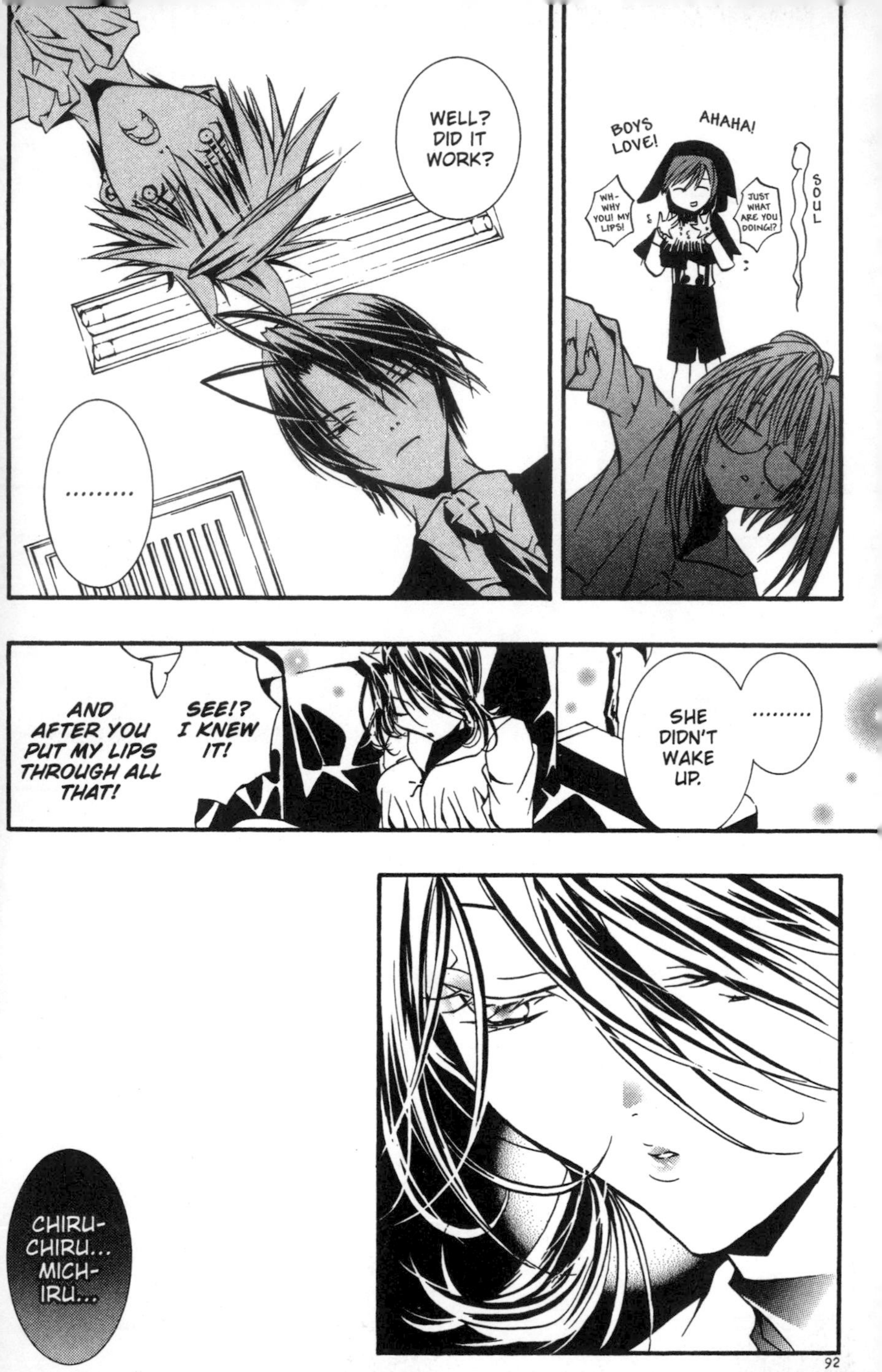
SOUL
AHAHA!
JUST WHAT ARE YOU DOING!?
BOYS LOVE!
WH-WHY YOU! MY LIPS!
WELL? DID IT WORK?
....
....
SHE DIDN'T WAKE UP.
SEE!? I KNEW IT!
AND AFTER YOU PUT MY LIPS THROUGH ALL THAT!
CHIRU-CHIRU... MICH-IRU...

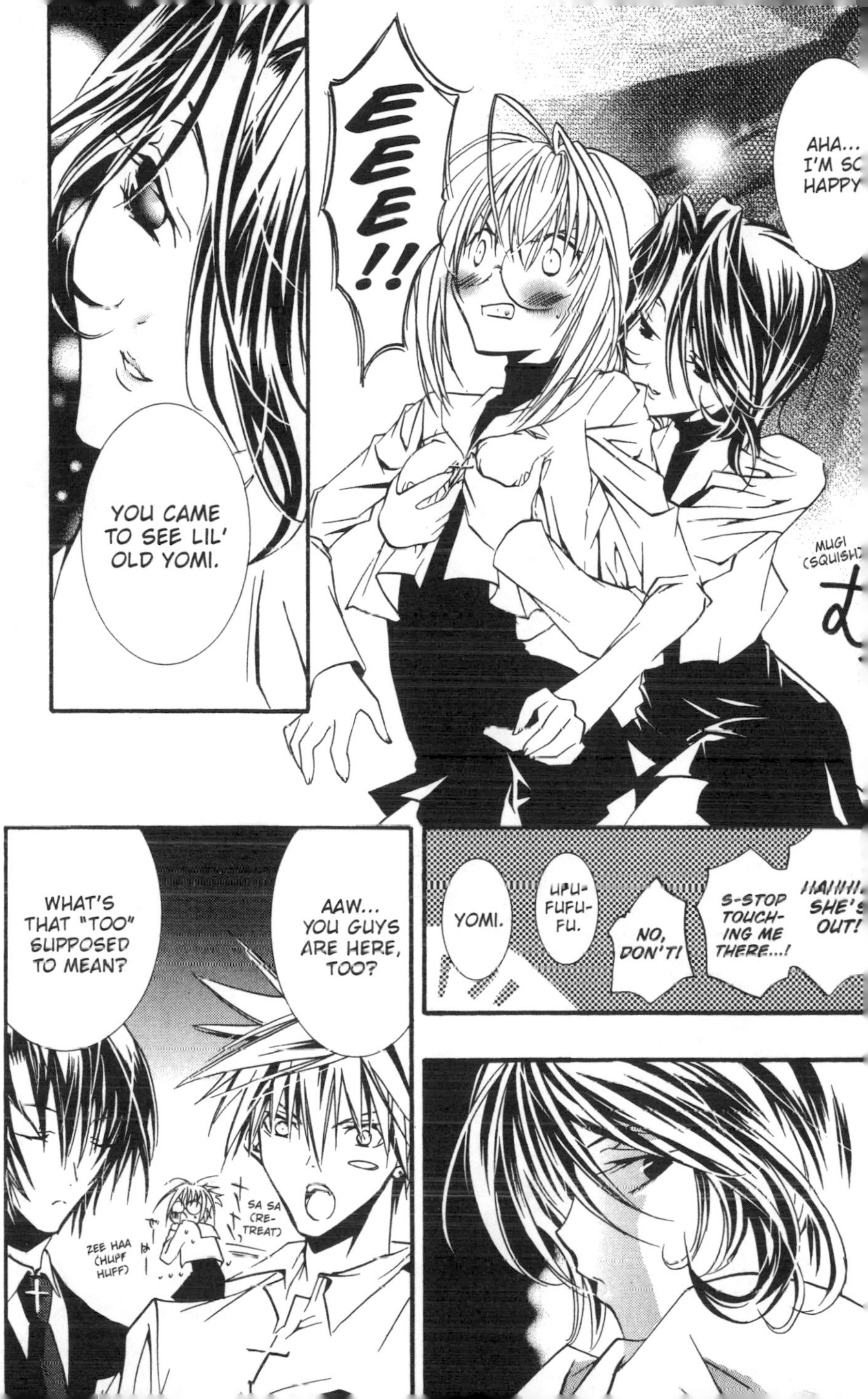
AHA... I'M SO HAPPY
EEE!!
MUGI (SQUISH)
YOU CAME TO SEE LIL' OLD YOMI.
SHE'S OUT!
S-STOP TOUCHING ME THERE...!
NO, DON'T!
UPUFUFUFU.
YOMI.
AAW... YOU GUYS ARE HERE, TOO?
WHAT'S THAT "TOO" SUPPOSED TO MEAN?
SA SA (RETREAT)
ZEE HAA (HUFF HUFF)

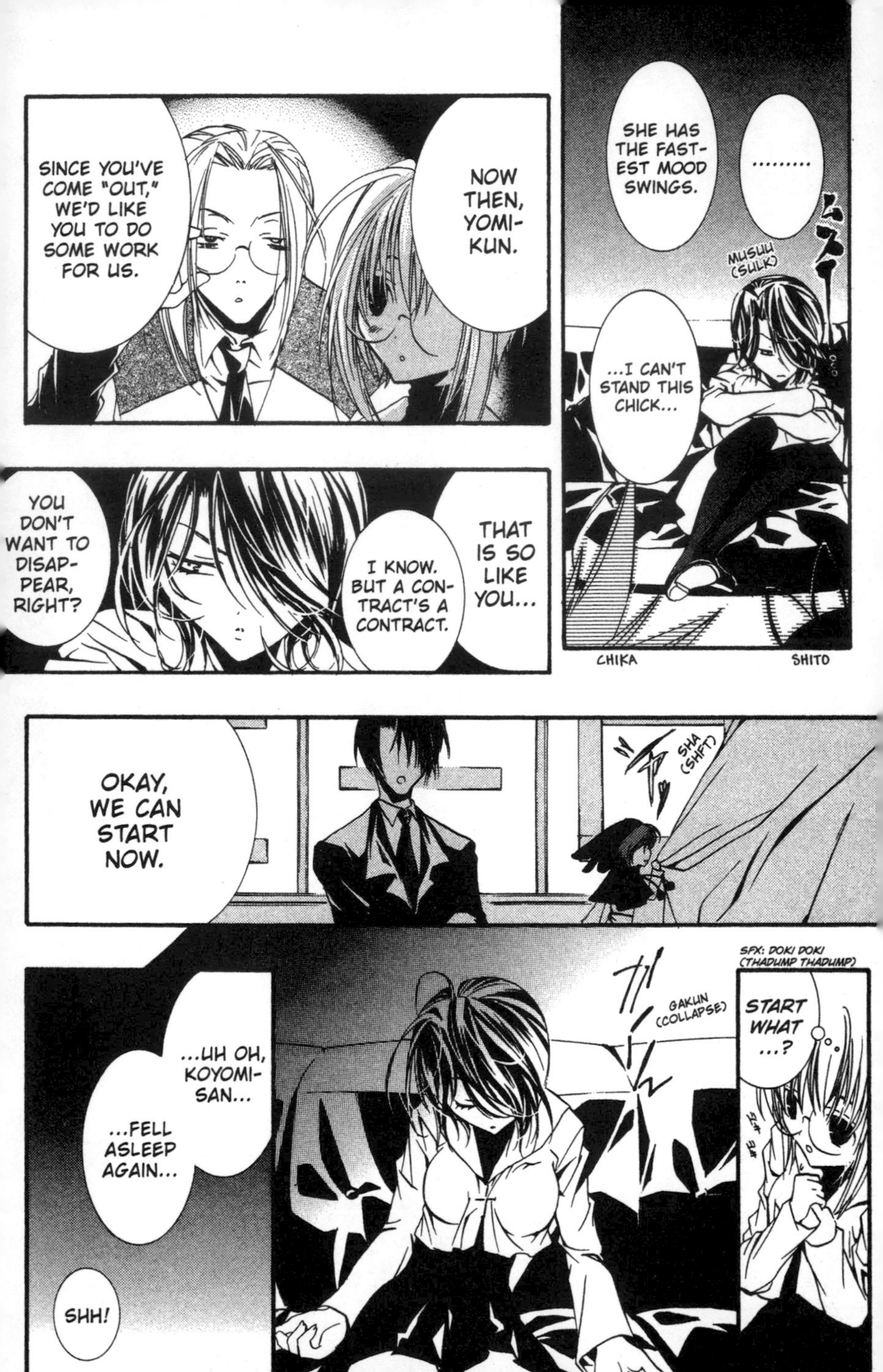
....
SHE HAS THE FAST-EST MOOD SWINGS.
MUSUU (SULK)
...I CAN'T STAND THIS CHICK...
CHIKA
SHITO
NOW THEN, YOMI-KUN.
SINCE YOU'VE COME "OUT," WE'D LIKE YOU TO DO SOME WORK FOR US.
THAT IS SO LIKE YOU...
I KNOW. BUT A CON-TRACT'S A CONTRACT.
YOU DON'T WANT TO DISAP-PEAR, RIGHT?
SHA (SHFT)
OKAY, WE CAN START NOW.
SFX: DOKI DOKI (THADUMP THADUMP)
START WHAT ...?
GAKUN (COLLAPSE)
...UH OH, KOYOMI-SAN...
...FELL ASLEEP AGAIN...
SHH!

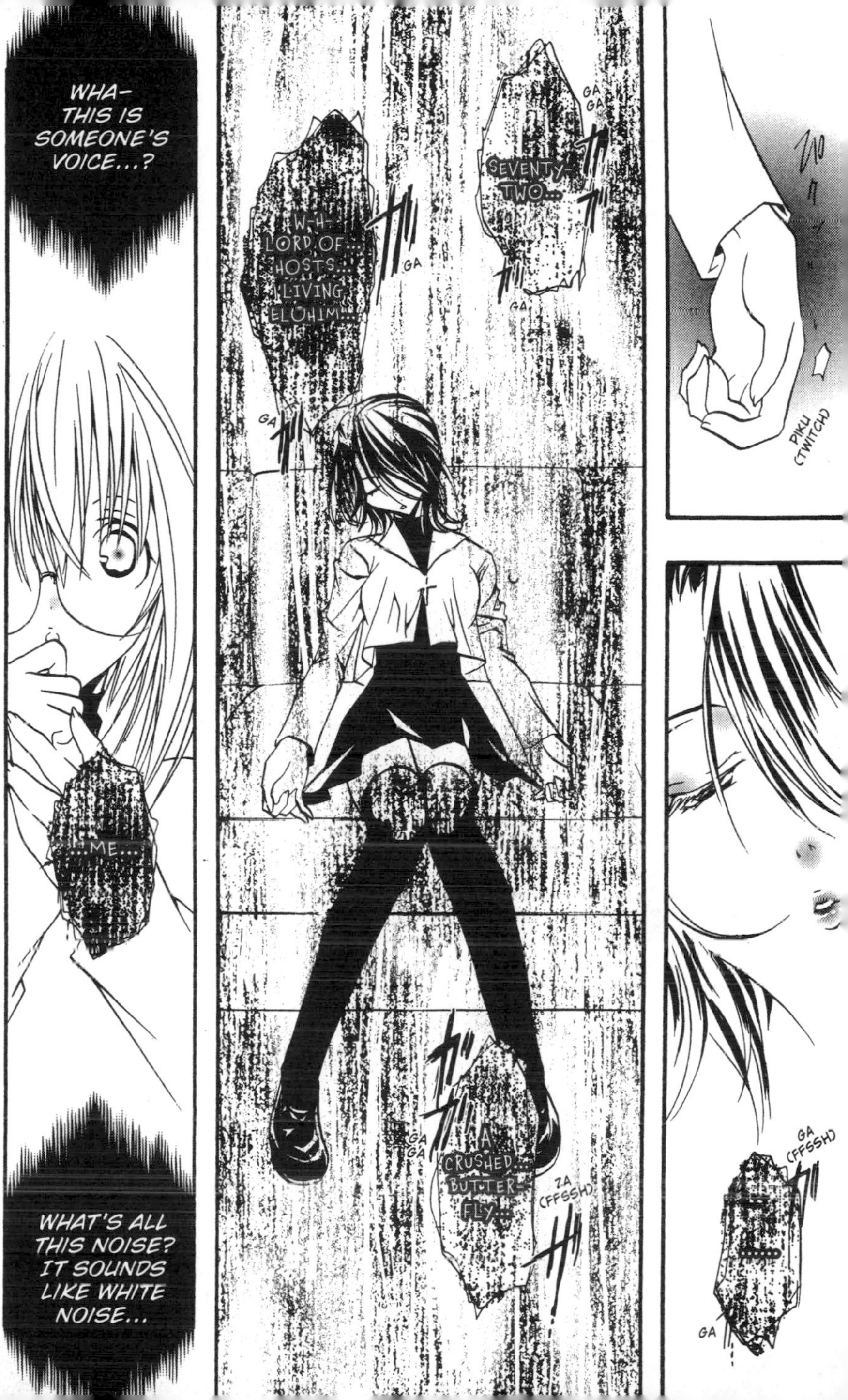
PIKU (TWITCH)
GA (FFSSH)
GA
GA GA
SEVENTY-TWO...
GA
GA
W-H- LORD OF... HOSTS... LIVING ELOHIM...
GA
ZA (FFSSH)
A CRUSHED... BUTTER-FLY...
GA GA
WHA- THIS IS SOMEONE'S VOICE...?
...ME...
WHAT'S ALL THIS NOISE? IT SOUNDS LIKE WHITE NOISE...

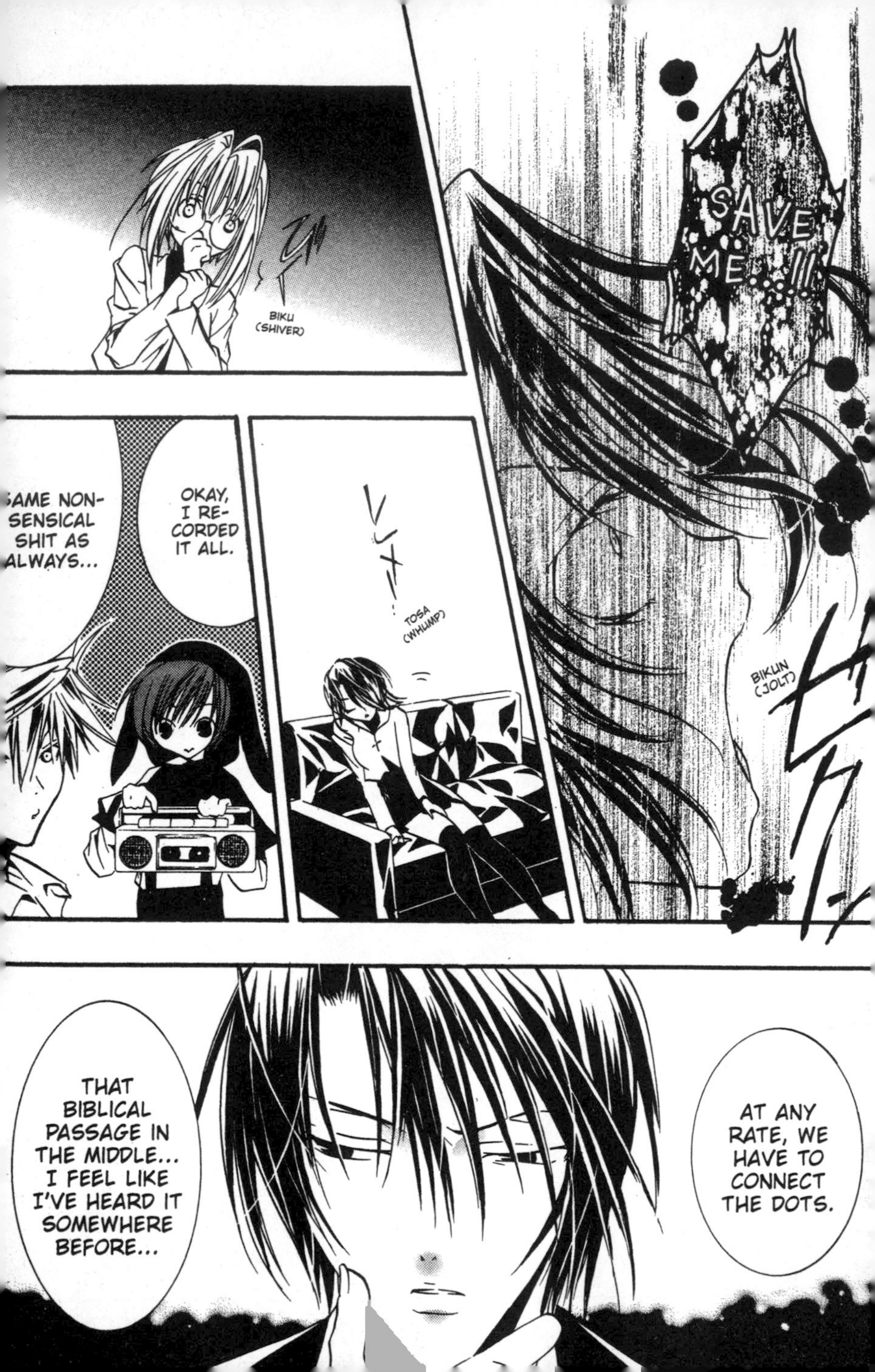
SAVE ME...!!
BIKUN (JOLT)
BIKU (SHIVER)
TOSA (WHUMP)
OKAY, I RE-CORDED IT ALL.
SAME NON-SENSICAL SHIT AS ALWAYS...
AT ANY RATE, WE HAVE TO CONNECT THE DOTS.
THAT BIBLICAL PASSAGE IN THE MIDDLE... I FEEL LIKE I'VE HEARD IT SOMEWHERE BEFORE...

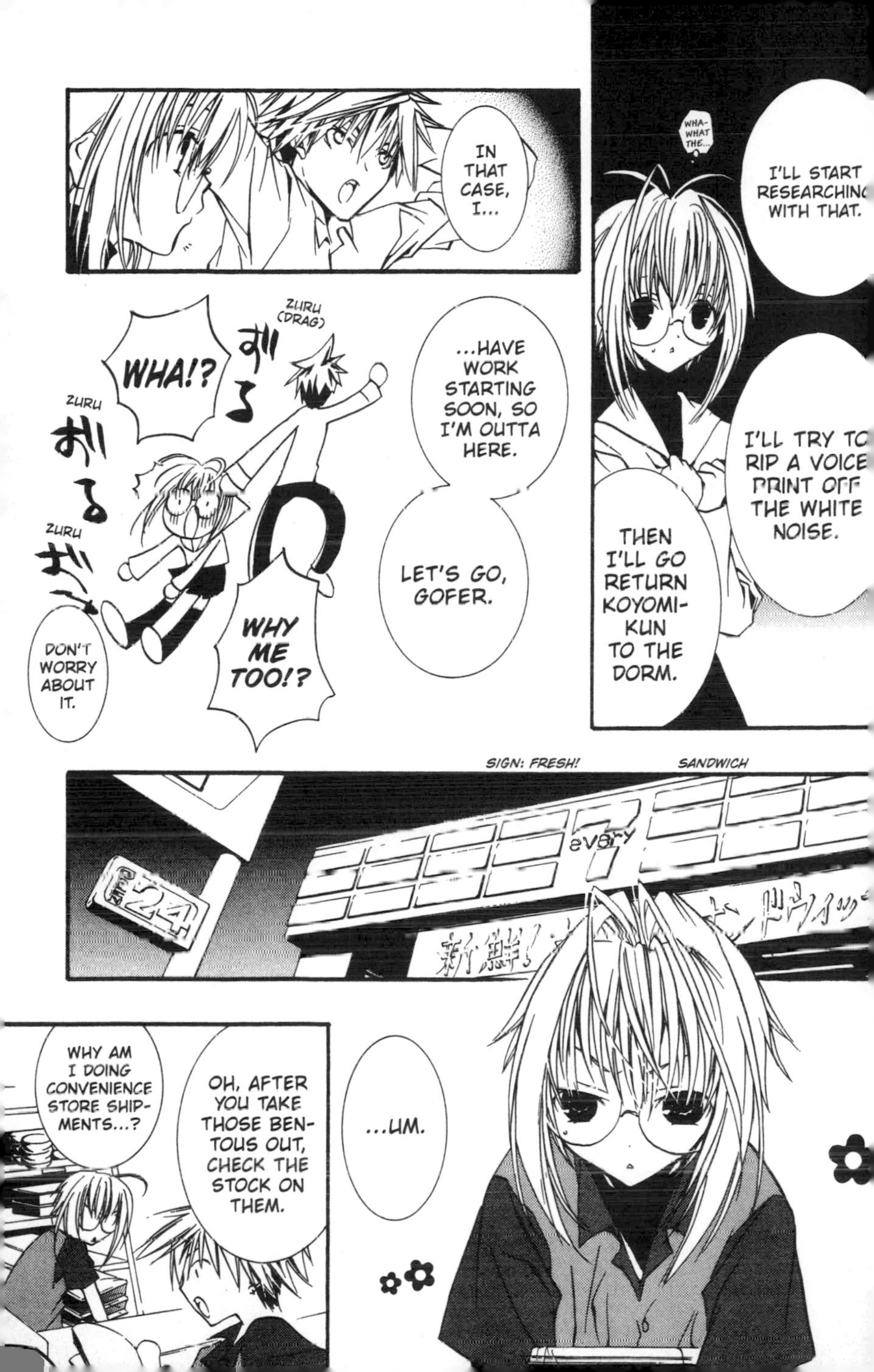
I'LL START RESEARCHING WITH THAT.
WHA-WHAT THE...
I'LL TRY TO RIP A VOICE PRINT OFF THE WHITE NOISE.
THEN I'LL GO RETURN KOYOMI-KUN TO THE DORM.
IN THAT CASE, I...
...HAVE WORK STARTING SOON, SO I'M OUTTA HERE.
LET'S GO, GOFER.
ZURU (DRAG)
WHA!?
ZURU
ZURU
WHY ME TOO!?
DON'T WORRY ABOUT IT.
SIGN: FRESH!
SANDWICH
every 7
24
...UM.
OH, AFTER YOU TAKE THOSE BEN-TOUS OUT, CHECK THE STOCK ON THEM.
WHY AM I DOING CONVENIENCE STORE SHIP-MENTS...?

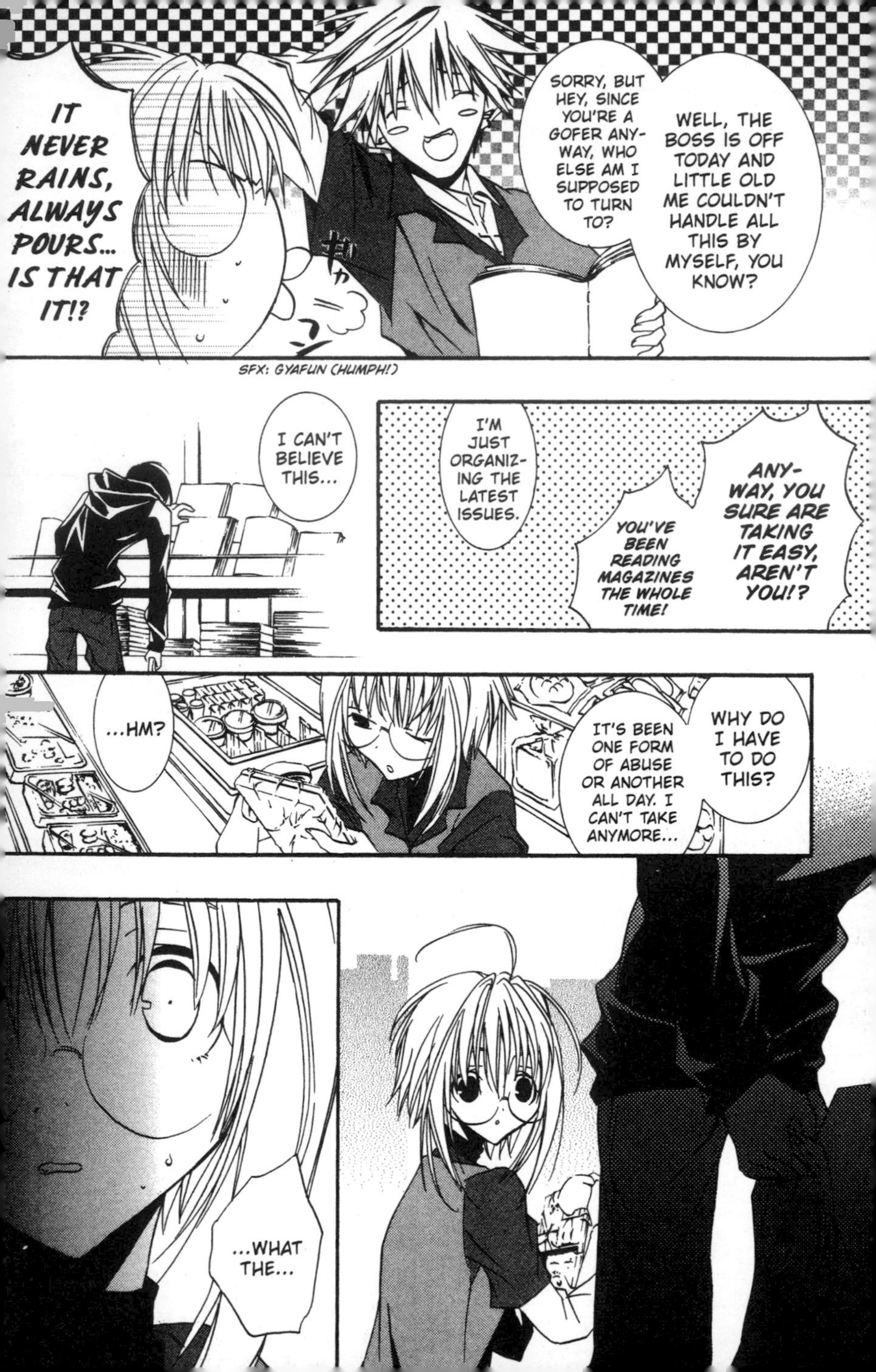
WELL, THE BOSS IS OFF TODAY AND LITTLE OLD ME COULDN'T HANDLE ALL THIS BY MYSELF, YOU KNOW?
SORRY, BUT HEY, SINCE YOU'RE A GOFER ANY-WAY, WHO ELSE AM I SUPPOSED TO TURN TO?
IT NEVER RAINS, ALWAYS POURS... IS THAT IT!?
SFX: GYAFUN (HUMPH!)
ANY-WAY, YOU SURE ARE TAKING IT EASY, AREN'T YOU!?
YOU'VE BEEN READING MAGAZINES THE WHOLE TIME!
I'M JUST ORGANIZ-ING THE LATEST ISSUES.
I CAN'T BELIEVE THIS...
WHY DO I HAVE TO DO THIS?
IT'S BEEN ONE FORM OF ABUSE OR ANOTHER ALL DAY. I CAN'T TAKE ANYMORE...
...HM?
...WHAT THE...

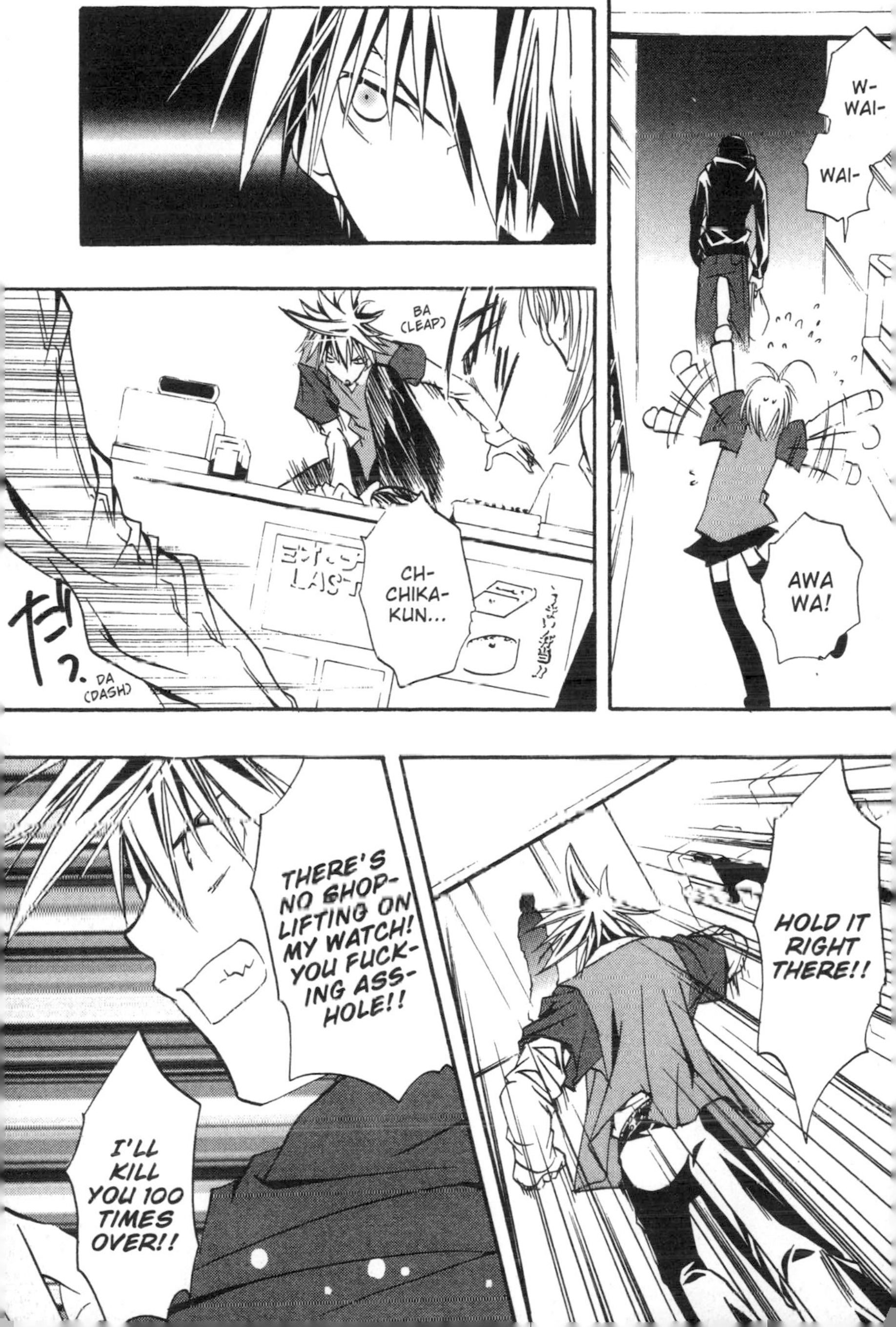
W-WAI-
WAI-
AWA WA!
BA (LEAP)
CH-CHIKA-KUN...
DA (DASH)
HOLD IT RIGHT THERE!!
THERE'S NO SHOP-LIFTING ON MY WATCH! YOU FUCKING ASS-HOLE!!
I'LL KILL YOU 100 TIMES OVER!!

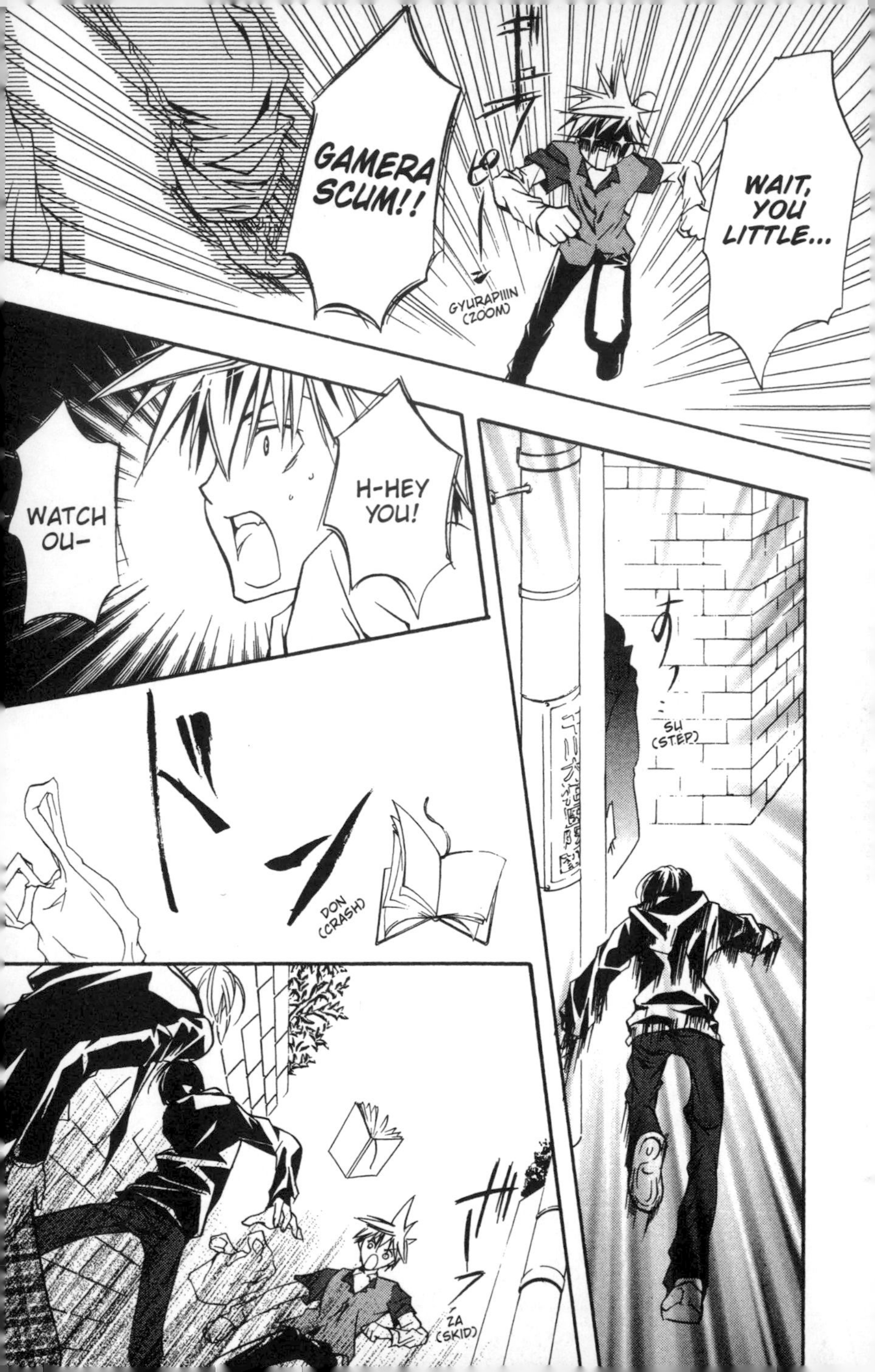
WAIT, YOU LITTLE...
GAMERA SCUM!!
GYURAPIIIN (ZOOM)
SU (STEP)
H-HEY YOU!
WATCH OU-
DON (CRASH)
ZA (SKID)

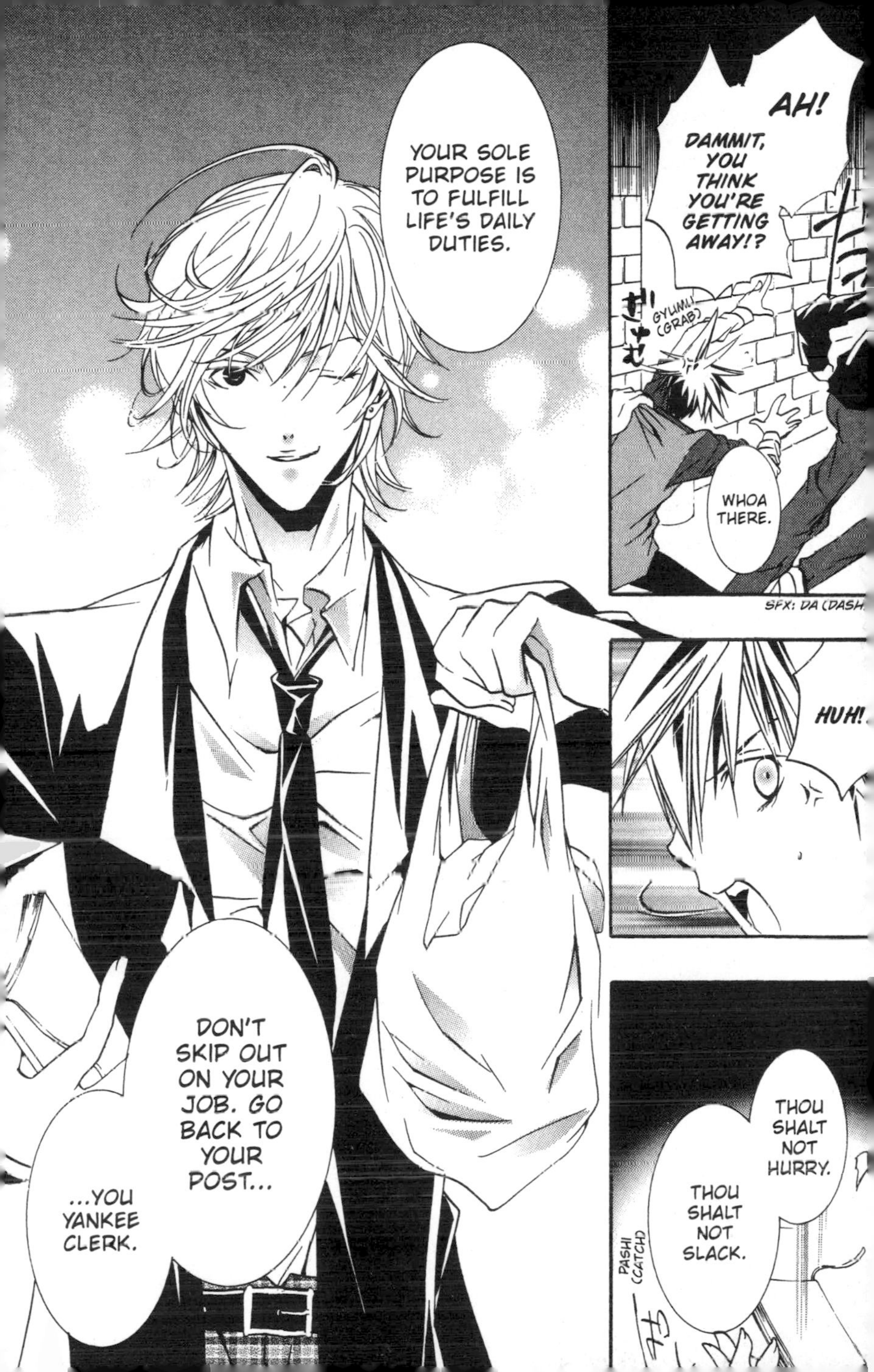
AH!
DAMMIT, YOU THINK YOU'RE GETTING AWAY!?
GYUM!! (GRAB)
WHOA THERE.
SFX: DA (DASH
HUH!
THOU SHALT NOT HURRY.
THOU SHALT NOT SLACK.
PASHI (CATCH)
YOUR SOLE PURPOSE IS TO FULFILL LIFE'S DAILY DUTIES.
DON'T SKIP OUT ON YOUR JOB. GO BACK TO YOUR POST...
...YOU YANKEE CLERK.

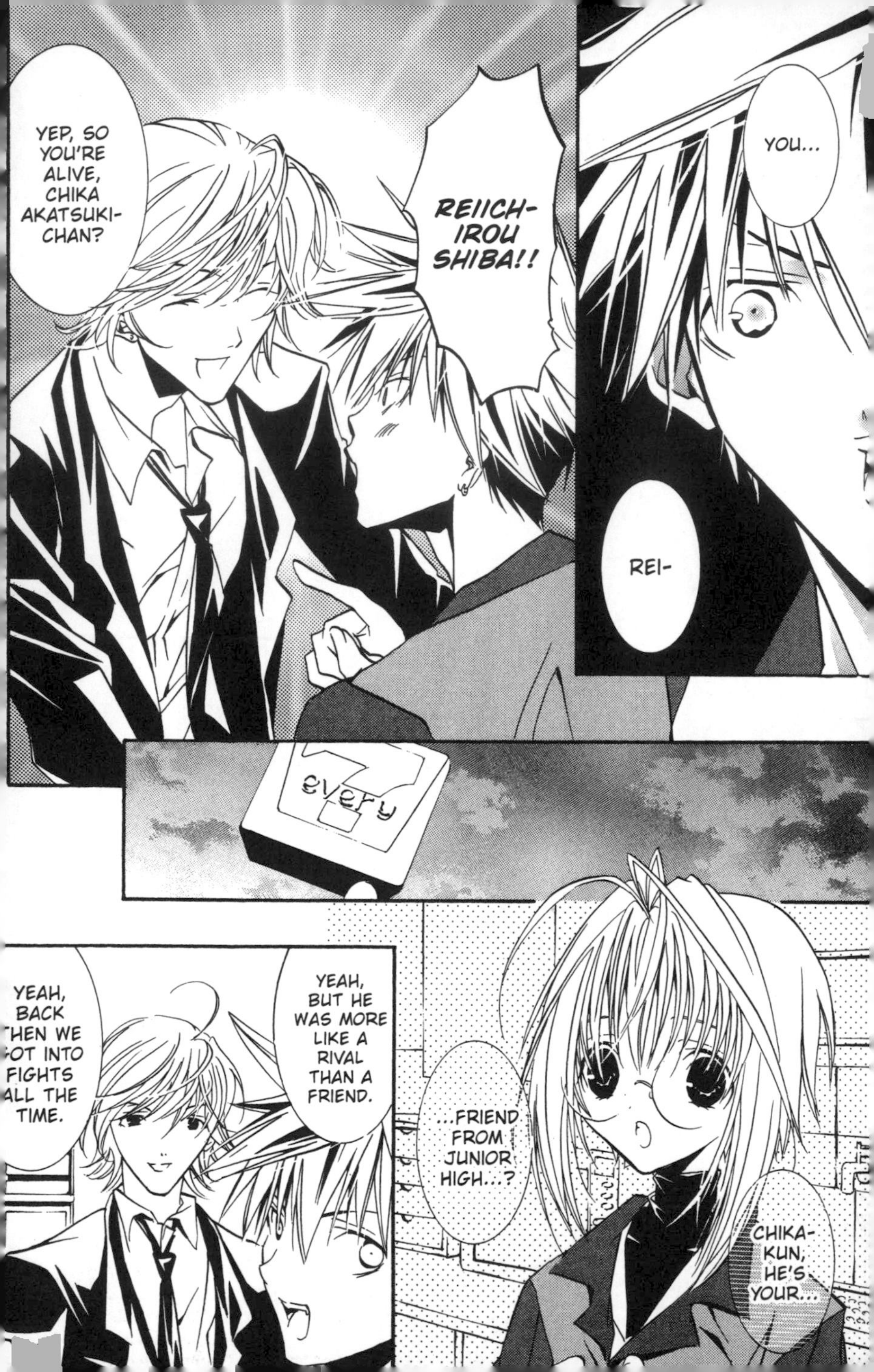
YOU...
REI-
REIICH-IROU SHIBA!!
YEP, SO YOU'RE ALIVE, CHIKA AKATSUKI-CHAN?
every
CHIKA-KUN, HE'S YOUR...
...FRIEND FROM JUNIOR HIGH...?
YEAH, BUT HE WAS MORE LIKE A RIVAL THAN A FRIEND.
YEAH, BACK THEN WE GOT INTO FIGHTS ALL THE TIME.

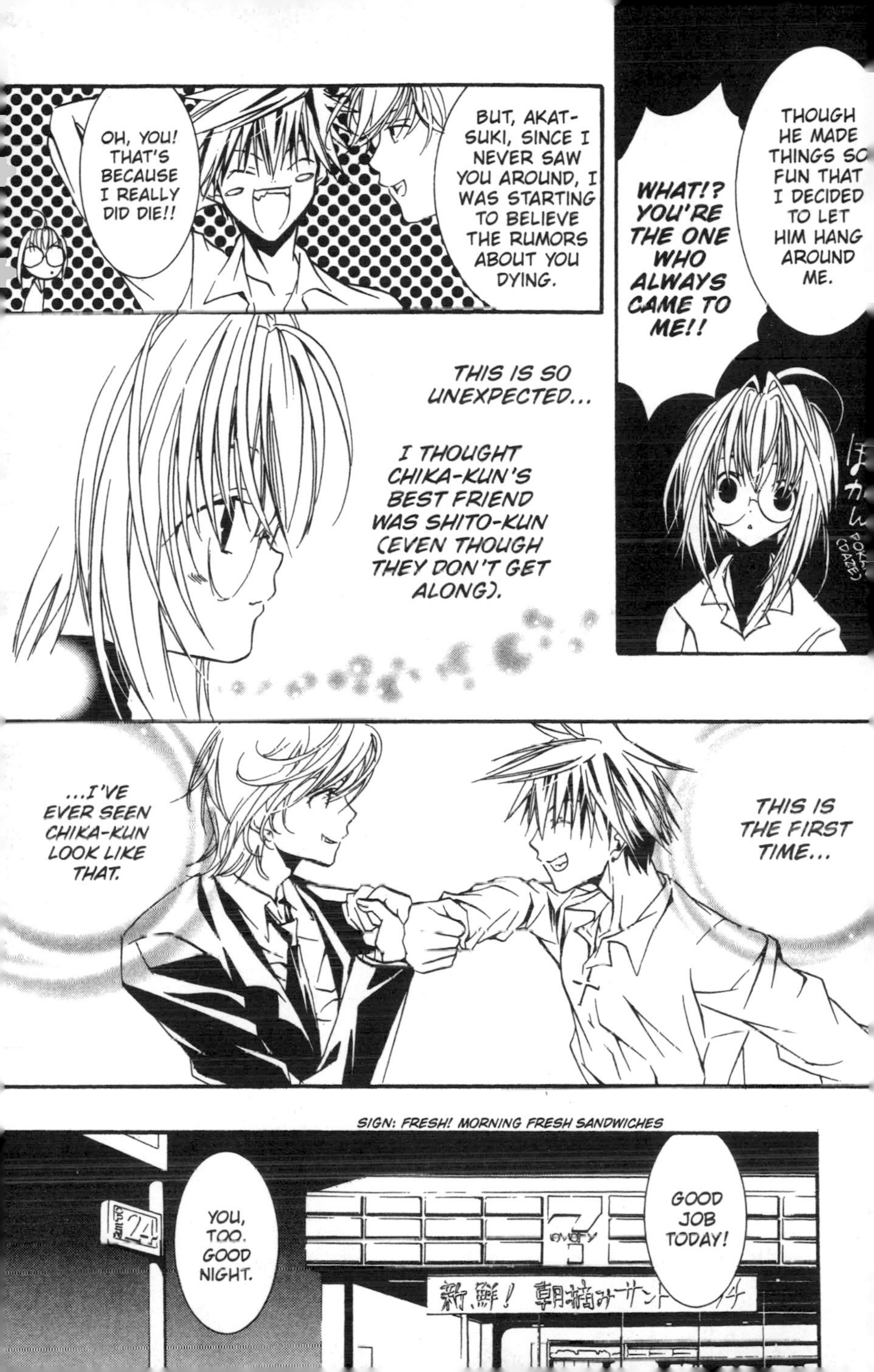
THOUGH HE MADE THINGS SO FUN THAT I DECIDED TO LET HIM HANG AROUND ME.
WHAT!? YOU'RE THE ONE WHO ALWAYS CAME TO ME!!
(DAZE)
BUT, AKATSUKI, SINCE I NEVER SAW YOU AROUND, I WAS STARTING TO BELIEVE THE RUMORS ABOUT YOU DYING.
OH, YOU! THAT'S BECAUSE I REALLY DID DIE!!
THIS IS SO UNEXPECTED...
I THOUGHT CHIKA-KUN'S BEST FRIEND WAS SHITO-KUN (EVEN THOUGH THEY DON'T GET ALONG).
THIS IS THE FIRST TIME...
...I'VE EVER SEEN CHIKA-KUN LOOK LIKE THAT.
SIGN: FRESH! MORNING FRESH SANDWICHES
24
GOOD JOB TODAY!
YOU, TOO. GOOD NIGHT.

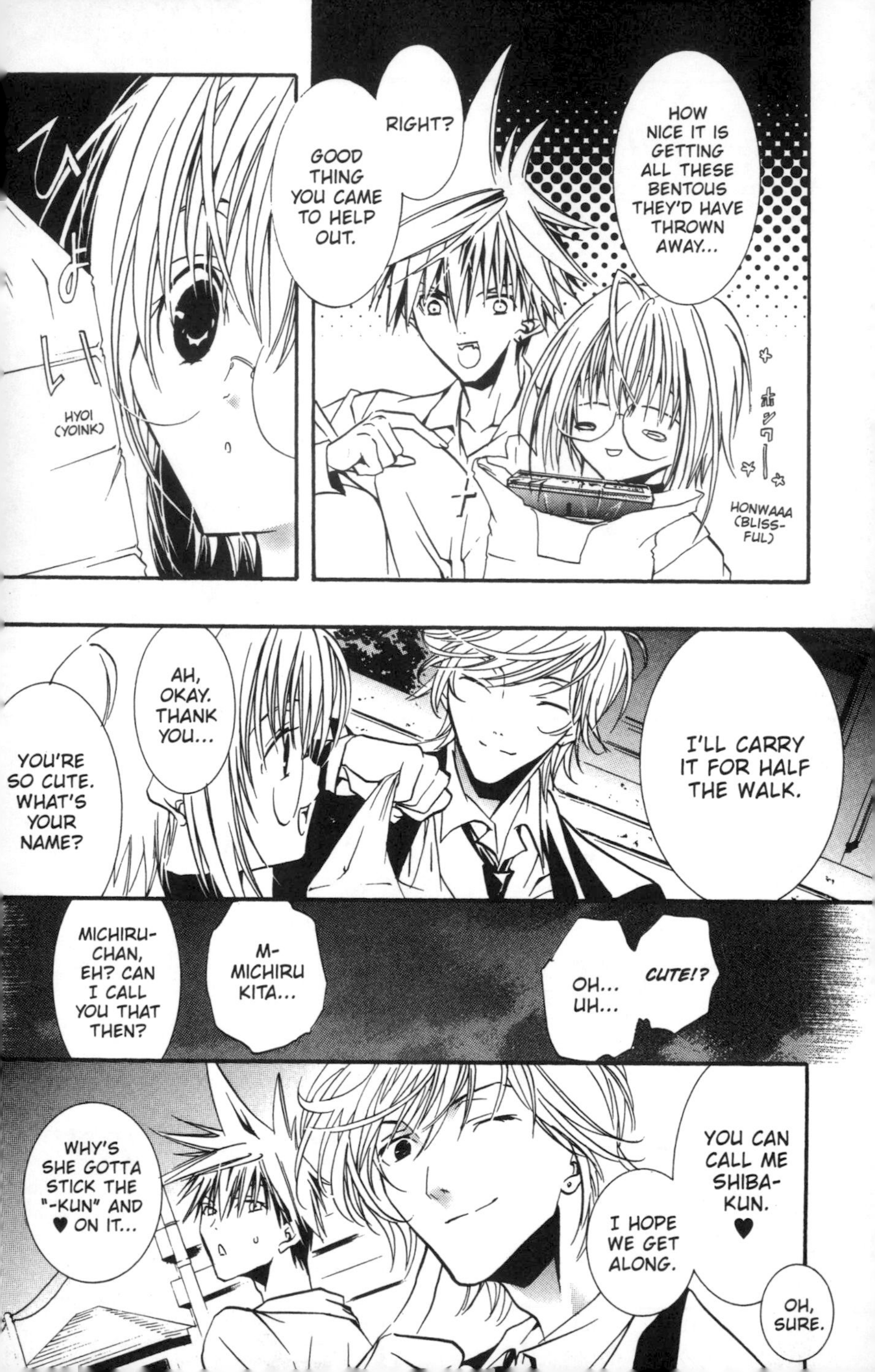
HOW NICE IT IS GETTING ALL THESE BENTOUS THEY'D HAVE THROWN AWAY...
HONWAAA (BLISS-FUL)
RIGHT?
GOOD THING YOU CAME TO HELP OUT.
HYOI (YOINK)
I'LL CARRY IT FOR HALF THE WALK.
AH, OKAY. THANK YOU...
YOU'RE SO CUTE. WHAT'S YOUR NAME?
CUTE!?
OH... UH...
M-MICHIRU KITA...
MICHIRU-CHAN, EH? CAN I CALL YOU THAT THEN?
YOU CAN CALL ME SHIBA-KUN. ♥
I HOPE WE GET ALONG.
OH, SURE.
WHY'S SHE GOTTA STICK THE "-KUN" AND ♥ ON IT...

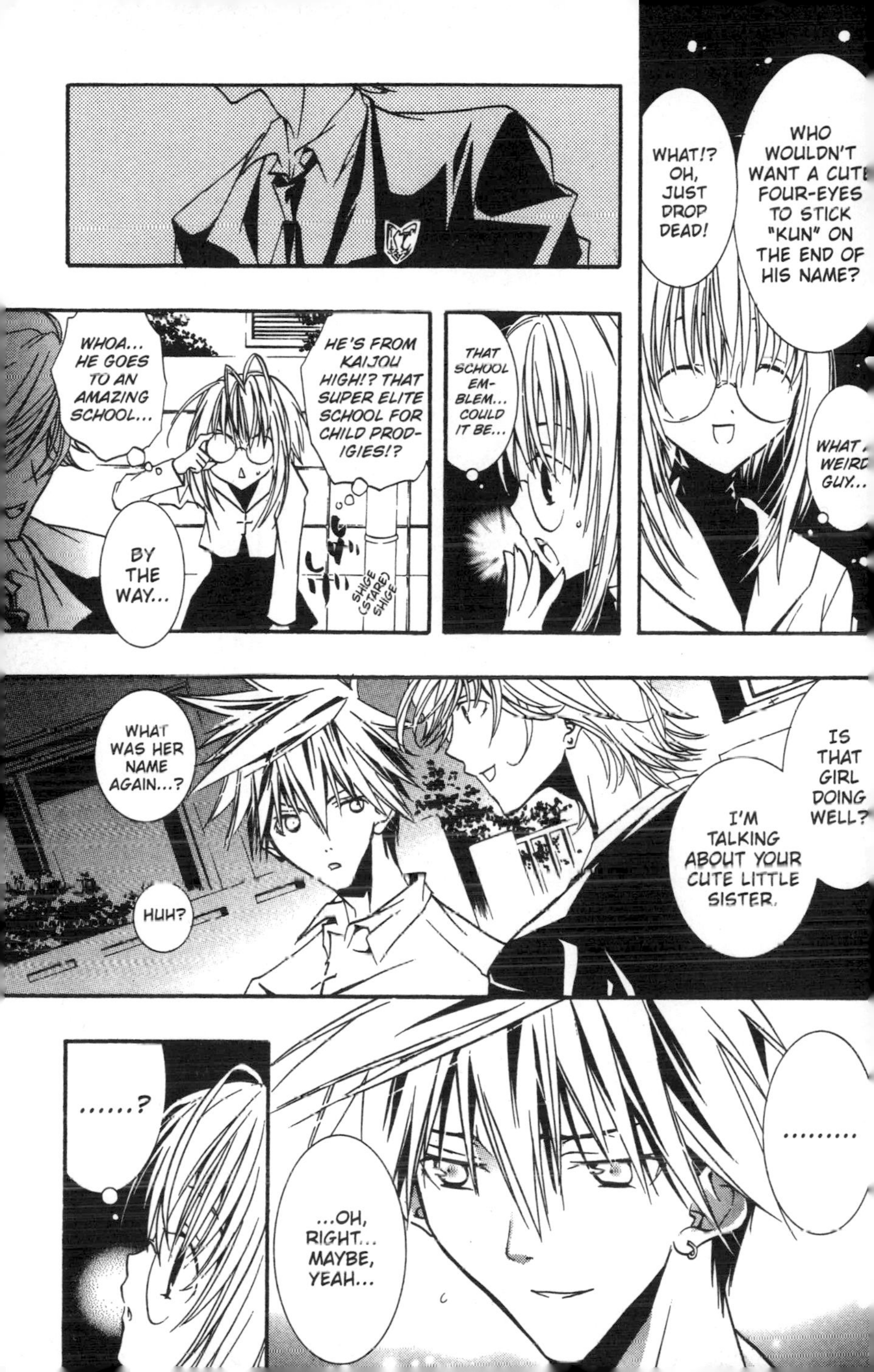
WHO WOULDN'T WANT A CUTE FOUR-EYES TO STICK "KUN" ON THE END OF HIS NAME?
WHAT!? OH, JUST DROP DEAD!
WHAT A WEIRD GUY...
THAT SCHOOL EM-BLEM... COULD IT BE...
HE'S FROM KAIJOU HIGH!? THAT SUPER ELITE SCHOOL FOR CHILD PROD-IGIES!?
WHOA... HE GOES TO AN AMAZING SCHOOL...
SHIGE (STARE) SHIGE
BY THE WAY...
IS THAT GIRL DOING WELL?
I'M TALKING ABOUT YOUR CUTE LITTLE SISTER.
WHAT WAS HER NAME AGAIN...?
HUH?
....
...OH, RIGHT... MAYBE, YEAH...
......?

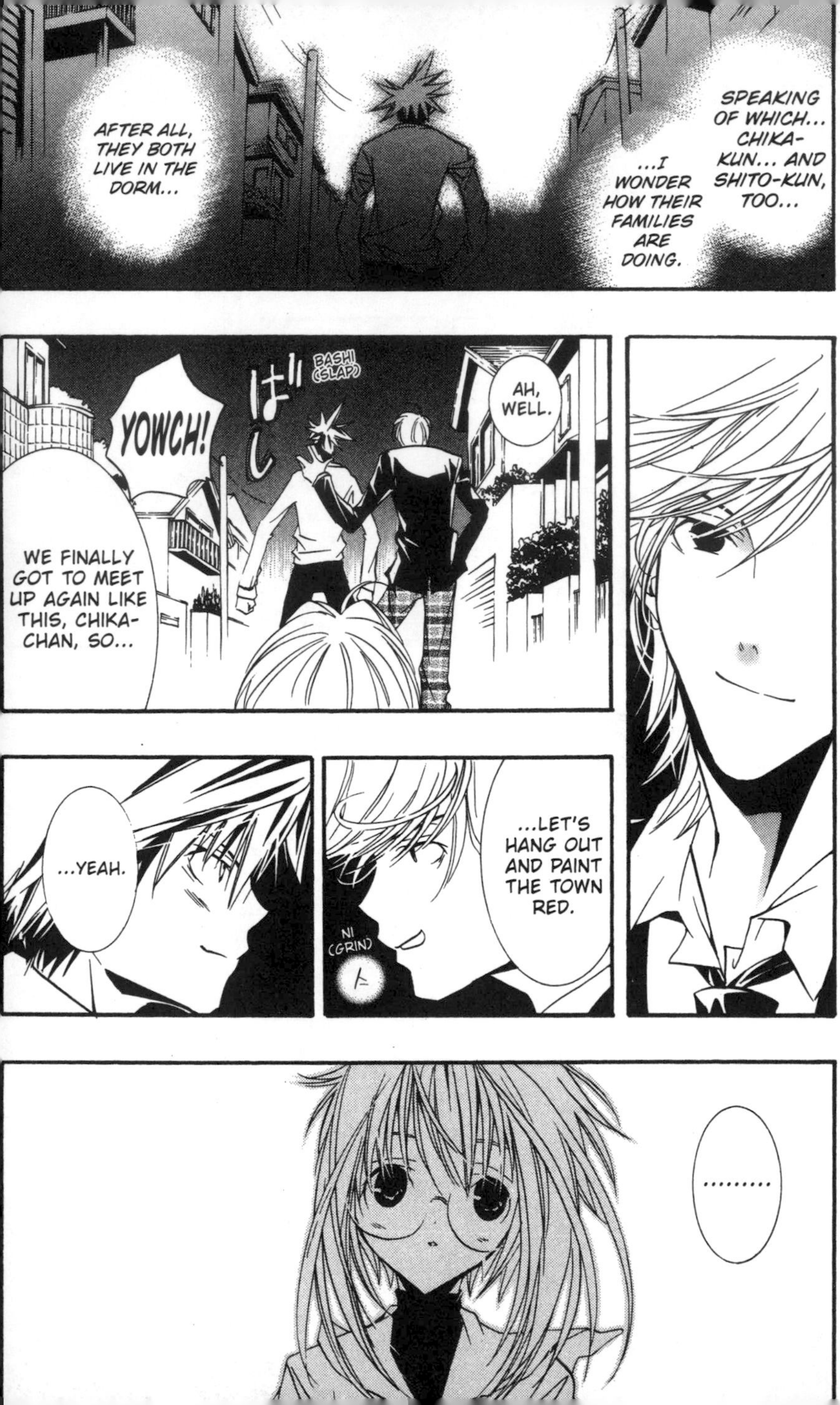
SPEAKING OF WHICH... CHIKA-KUN... AND SHITO-KUN, TOO...
...I WONDER HOW THEIR FAMILIES ARE DOING.
AFTER ALL, THEY BOTH LIVE IN THE DORM...
AH, WELL.
BASHI (SLAP)
YOWCH!
WE FINALLY GOT TO MEET UP AGAIN LIKE THIS, CHIKA-CHAN, SO...
...LET'S HANG OUT AND PAINT THE TOWN RED.
NI (GRIN)
...YEAH.
....

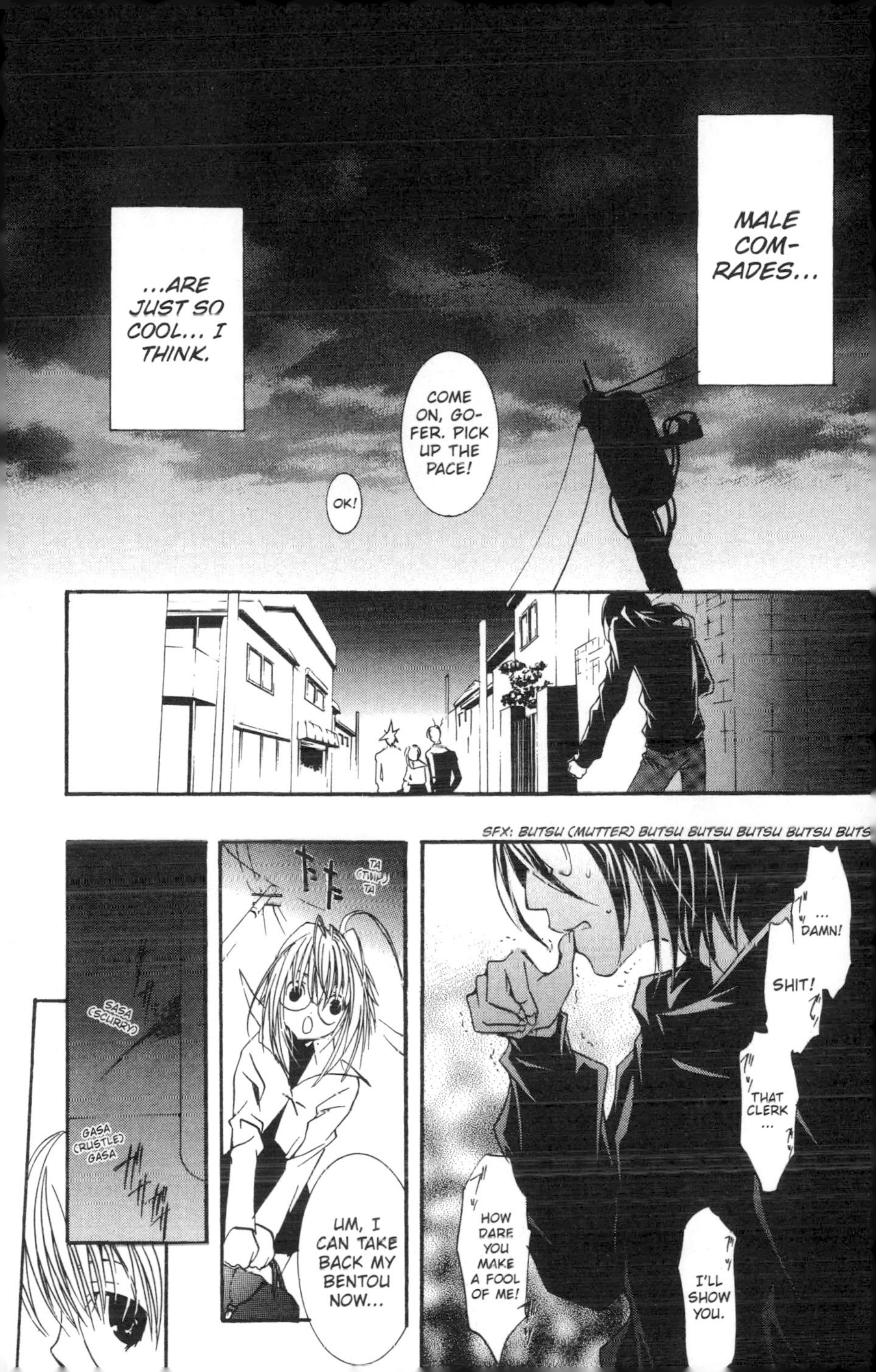
MALE COM-RADES...
...ARE JUST SO COOL... I THINK.
COME ON, GO-FER. PICK UP THE PACE!
OK!
SFX: BUTSU (MUTTER) BUTSU BUTSU BUTSU BUTSU BUTS
...DAMN!
SHIT!
THAT CLERK...
HOW DARE YOU MAKE A FOOL OF ME!
I'LL SHOW YOU.
TA (TMP) TA
UM, I CAN TAKE BACK MY BENTOU NOW...
SASA (SCURRY)
GASA (RUSTLE) GASA

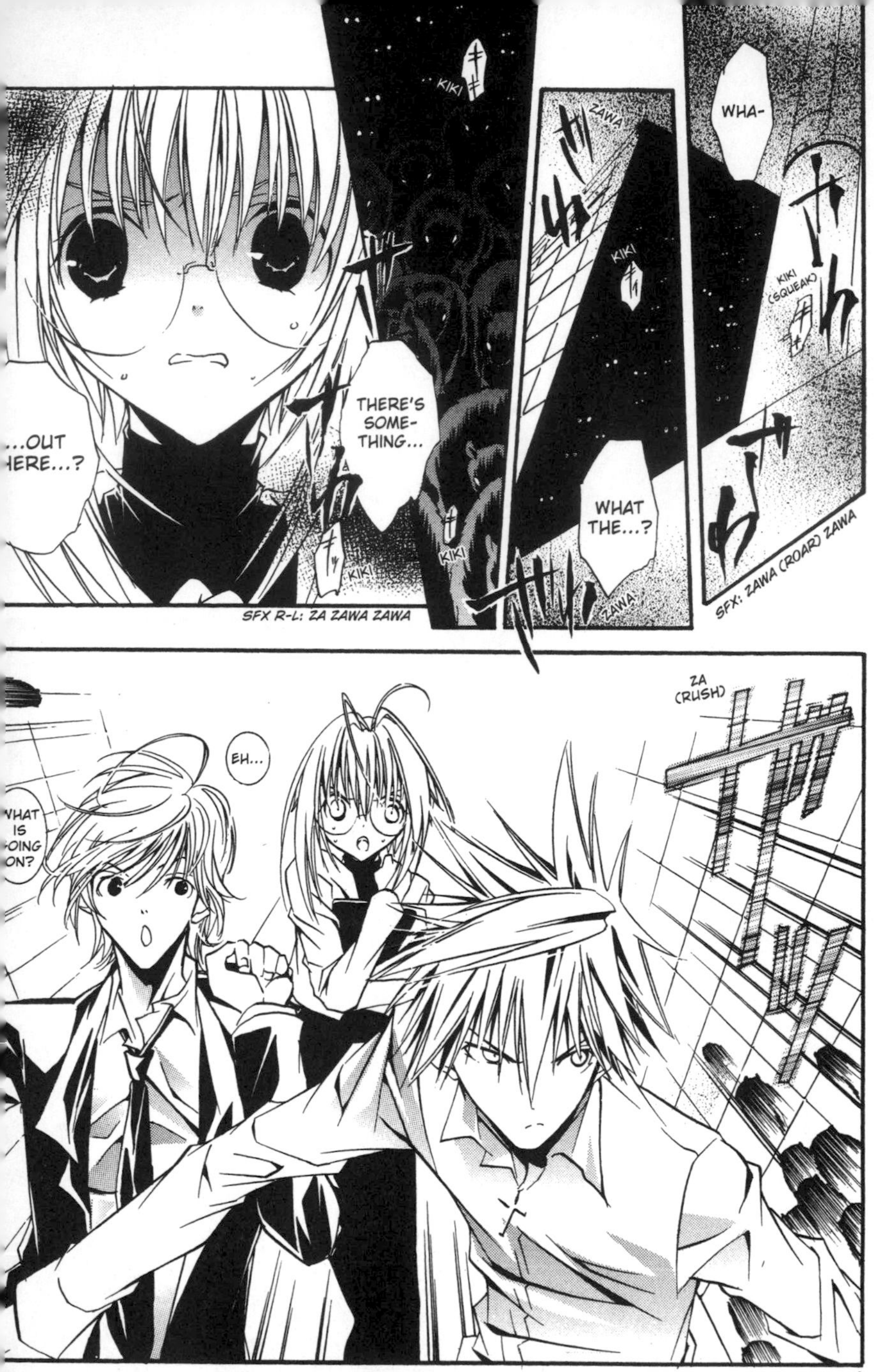
WHA-
KIKI (SQUEAK)
SFX: ZAWA (ROAR) ZAWA
ZAWA
KIKI
WHAT THE...?
ZAWA
KIKI
KIKI
THERE'S SOME-THING...
...OUT HERE...?
KIKI
SFX R-L: ZA ZAWA ZAWA
ZA (RUSH)
EH...
WHAT IS GOING ON?

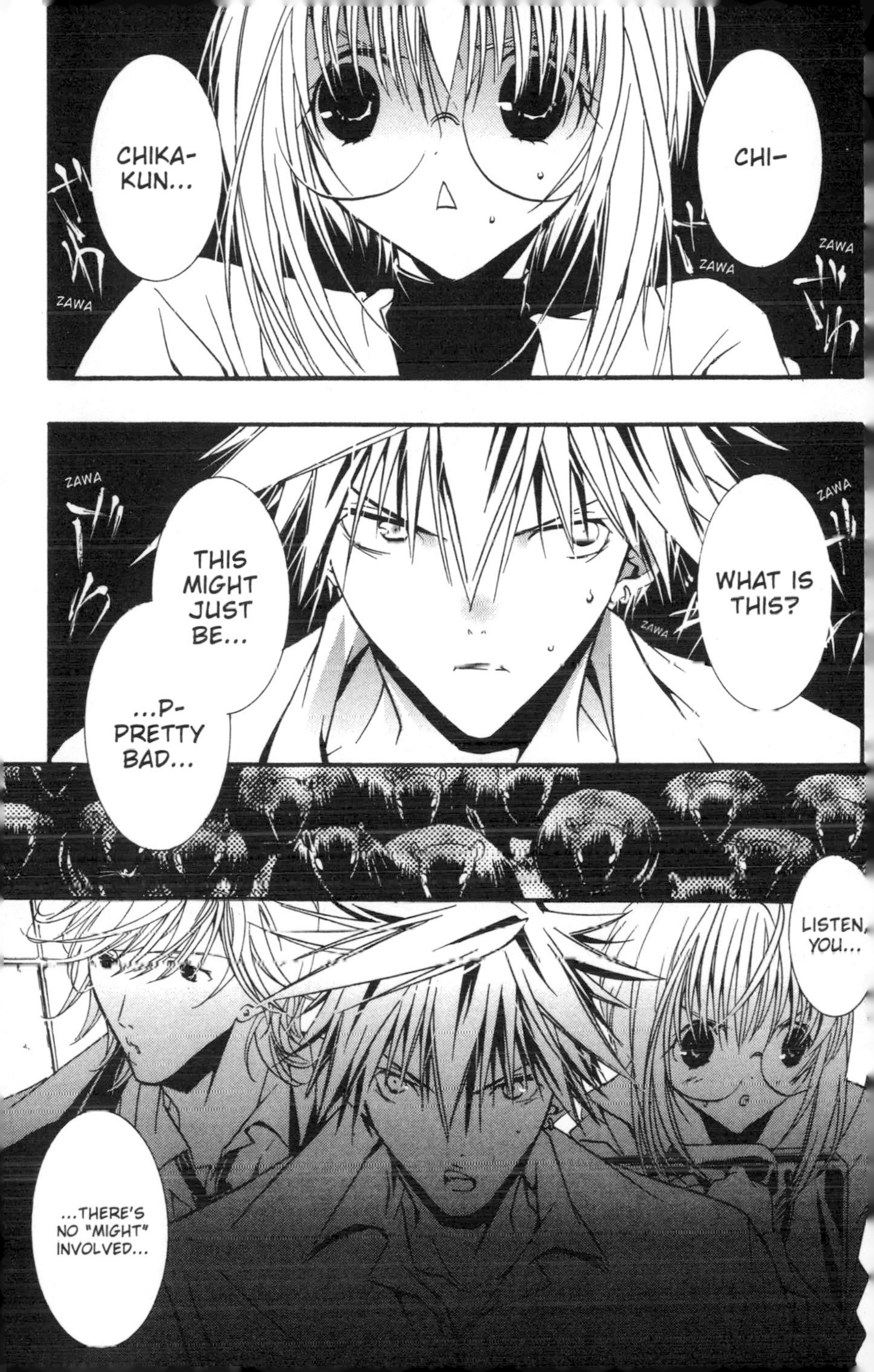
CHI-
ZAWA
ZAWA
CHIKA-KUN...
ZAWA
WHAT IS THIS?
ZAWA
ZAWA
THIS MIGHT JUST BE...
...P-PRETTY BAD...
ZAWA
LISTEN, YOU...
...THERE'S NO "MIGHT" INVOLVED...

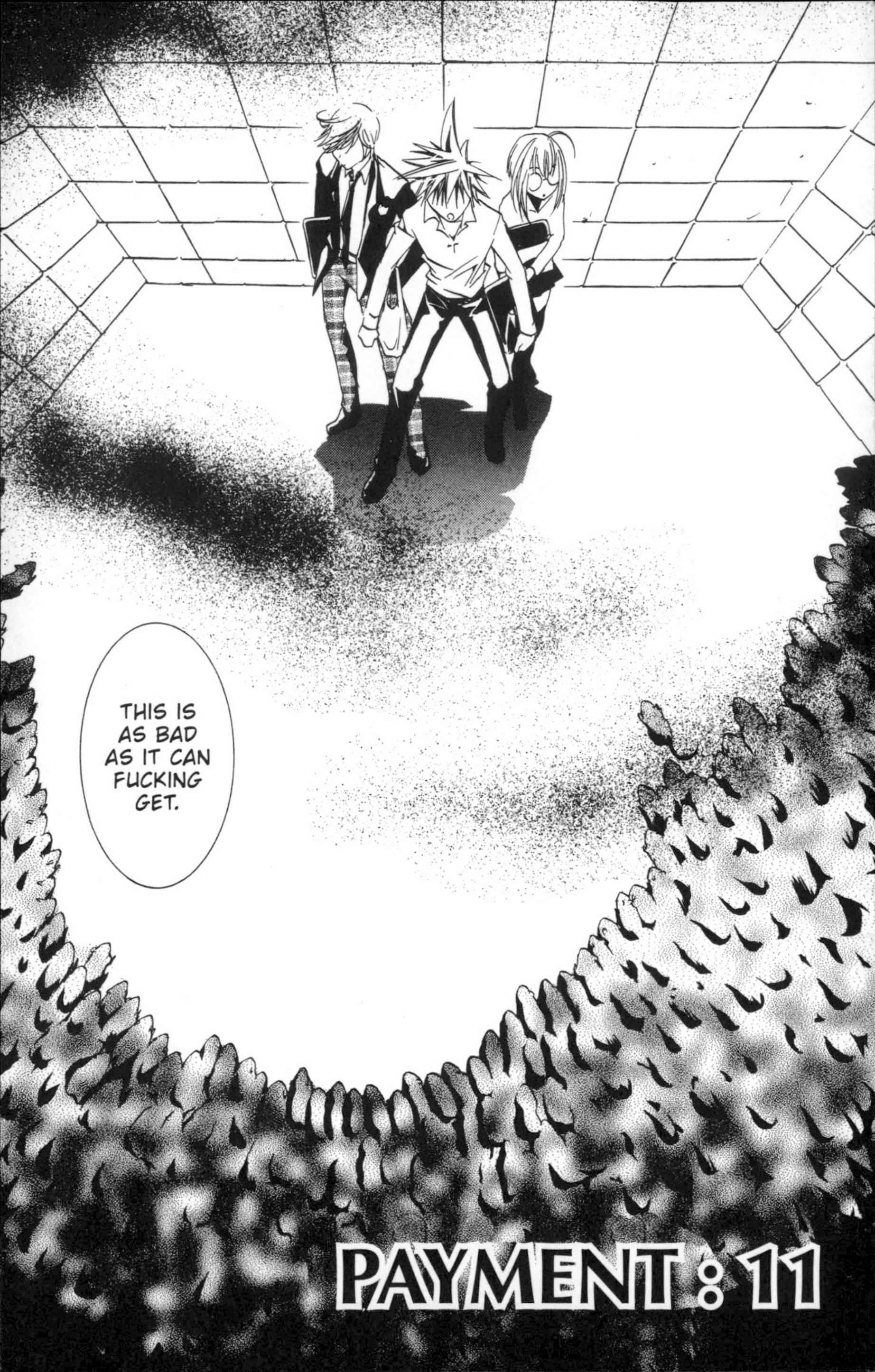
THIS IS AS BAD AS IT CAN FUCKING GET.
PAYMENT : 11

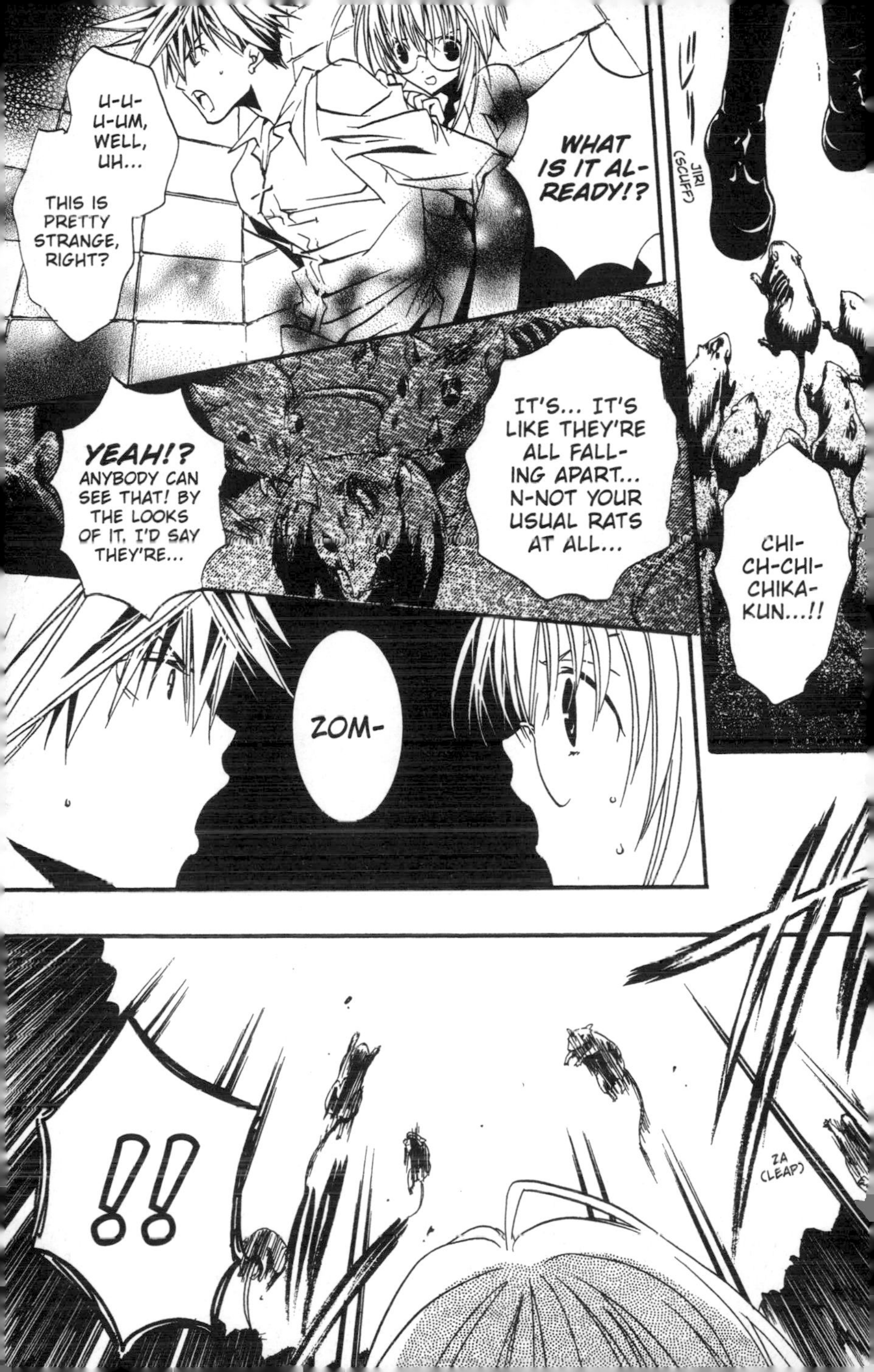
JIRI (SCUFF)
CHI-CH-CHI-CHIKA-KUN...!!
WHAT IS IT ALREADY!?
U-U-U-UM, WELL, UH...
THIS IS PRETTY STRANGE, RIGHT?
IT'S... IT'S LIKE THEY'RE ALL FALLING APART... N-NOT YOUR USUAL RATS AT ALL...
YEAH!? ANYBODY CAN SEE THAT! BY THE LOOKS OF IT, I'D SAY THEY'RE...
ZOM-
ZA (LEAP)
!!

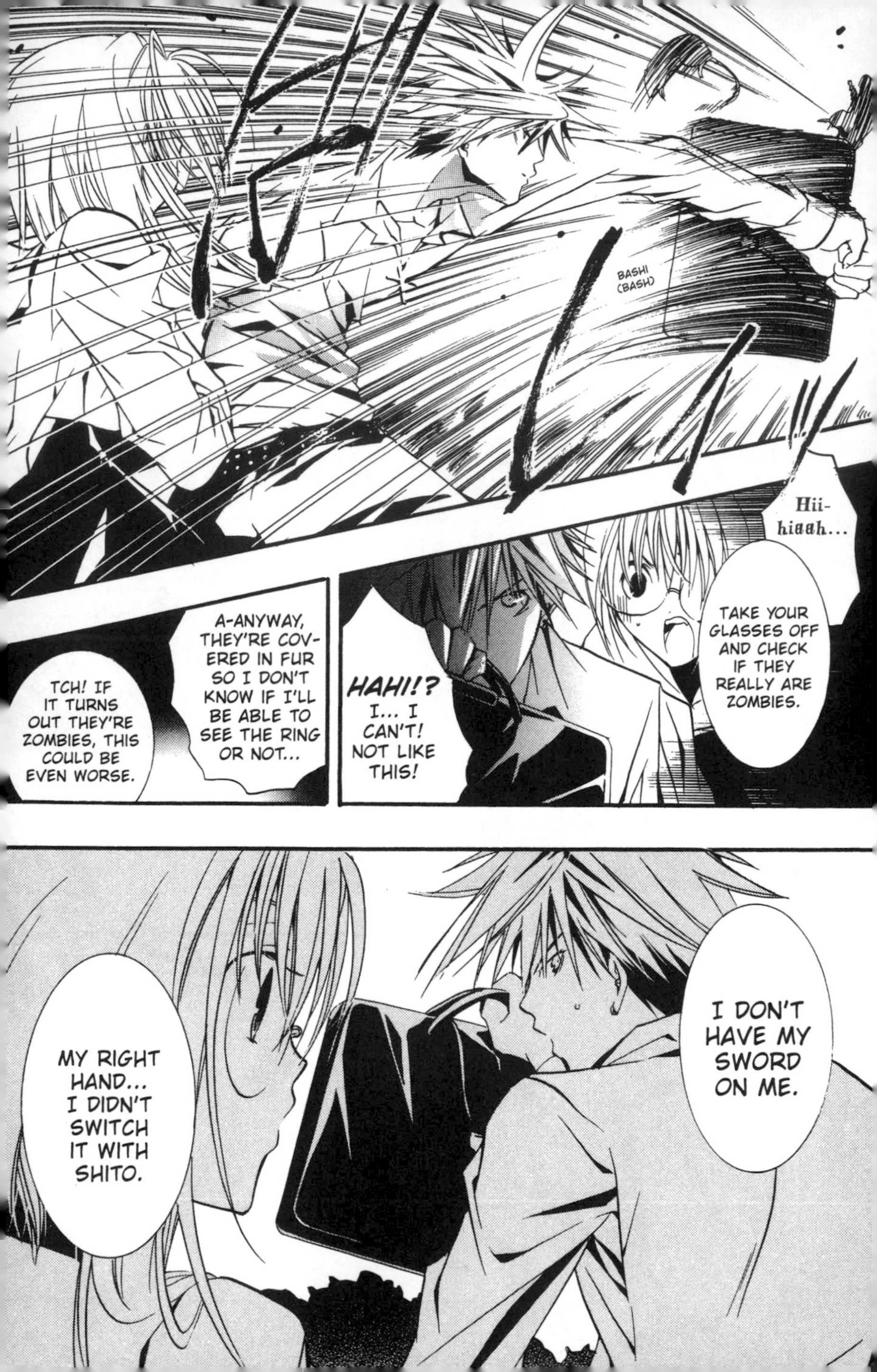
BASHI (BASH)
Hii- hiaah...
TAKE YOUR GLASSES OFF AND CHECK IF THEY REALLY ARE ZOMBIES.
HAHI!? I... I CAN'T! NOT LIKE THIS!
A-ANYWAY, THEY'RE COV- ERED IN FUR SO I DON'T KNOW IF I'LL BE ABLE TO SEE THE RING OR NOT...
TCH! IF IT TURNS OUT THEY'RE ZOMBIES, THIS COULD BE EVEN WORSE.
I DON'T HAVE MY SWORD ON ME.
MY RIGHT HAND... I DIDN'T SWITCH IT WITH SHITO.

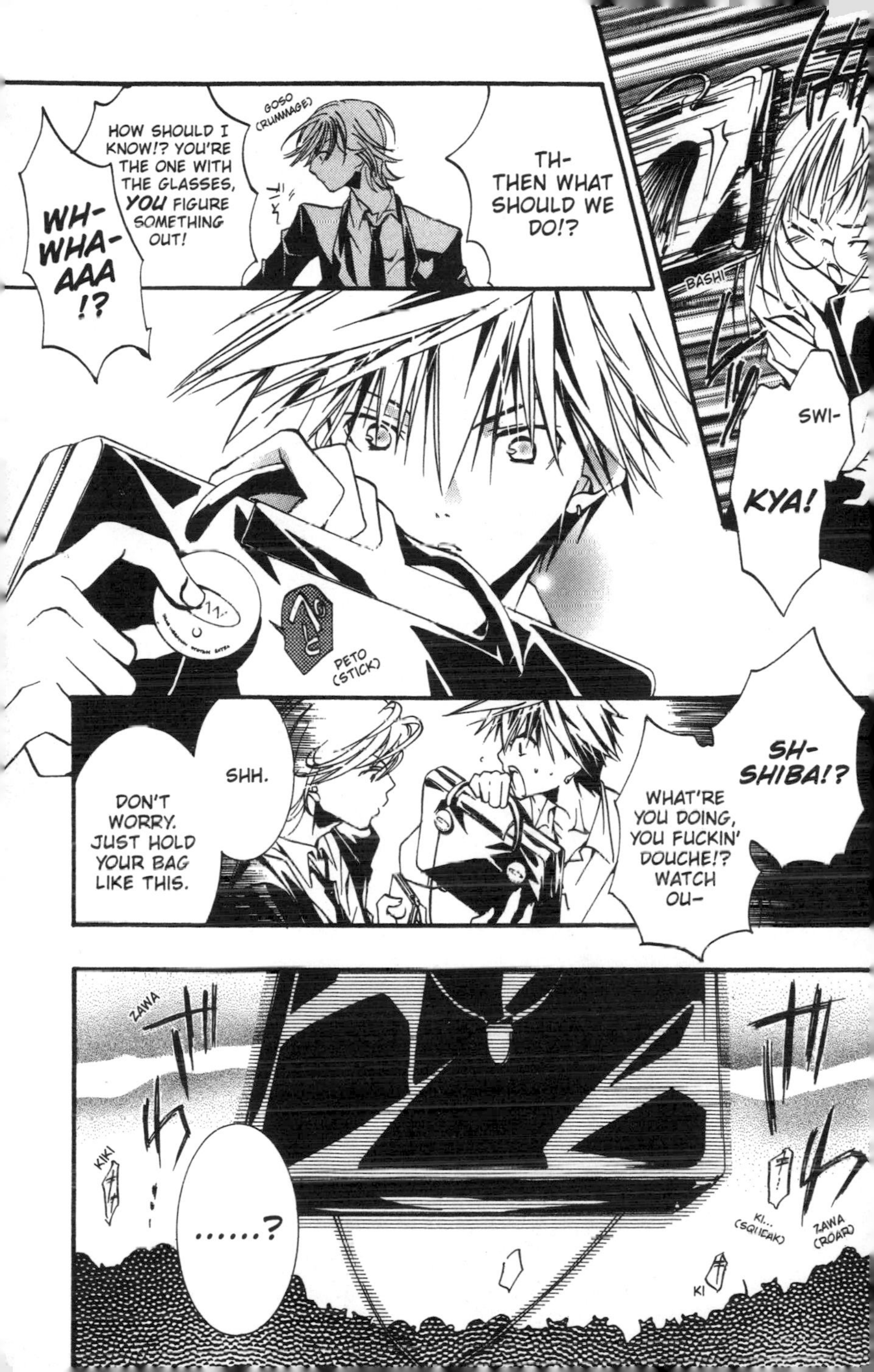
BASHI
SWI-
KYA!
TH-THEN WHAT SHOULD WE DO!?
GOSO (RUMMAGE)
HOW SHOULD I KNOW!? YOU'RE THE ONE WITH THE GLASSES, YOU FIGURE SOMETHING OUT!
WH-WHA-AAA!?
PETO (STICK)
SH-SHIBA!?
WHAT'RE YOU DOING, YOU FUCKIN' DOUCHE!? WATCH OU-
SHH.
DON'T WORRY. JUST HOLD YOUR BAG LIKE THIS.
ZAWA (ROAR)
KI... (SQUEAK)
KI
......?
KIKI
ZAWA

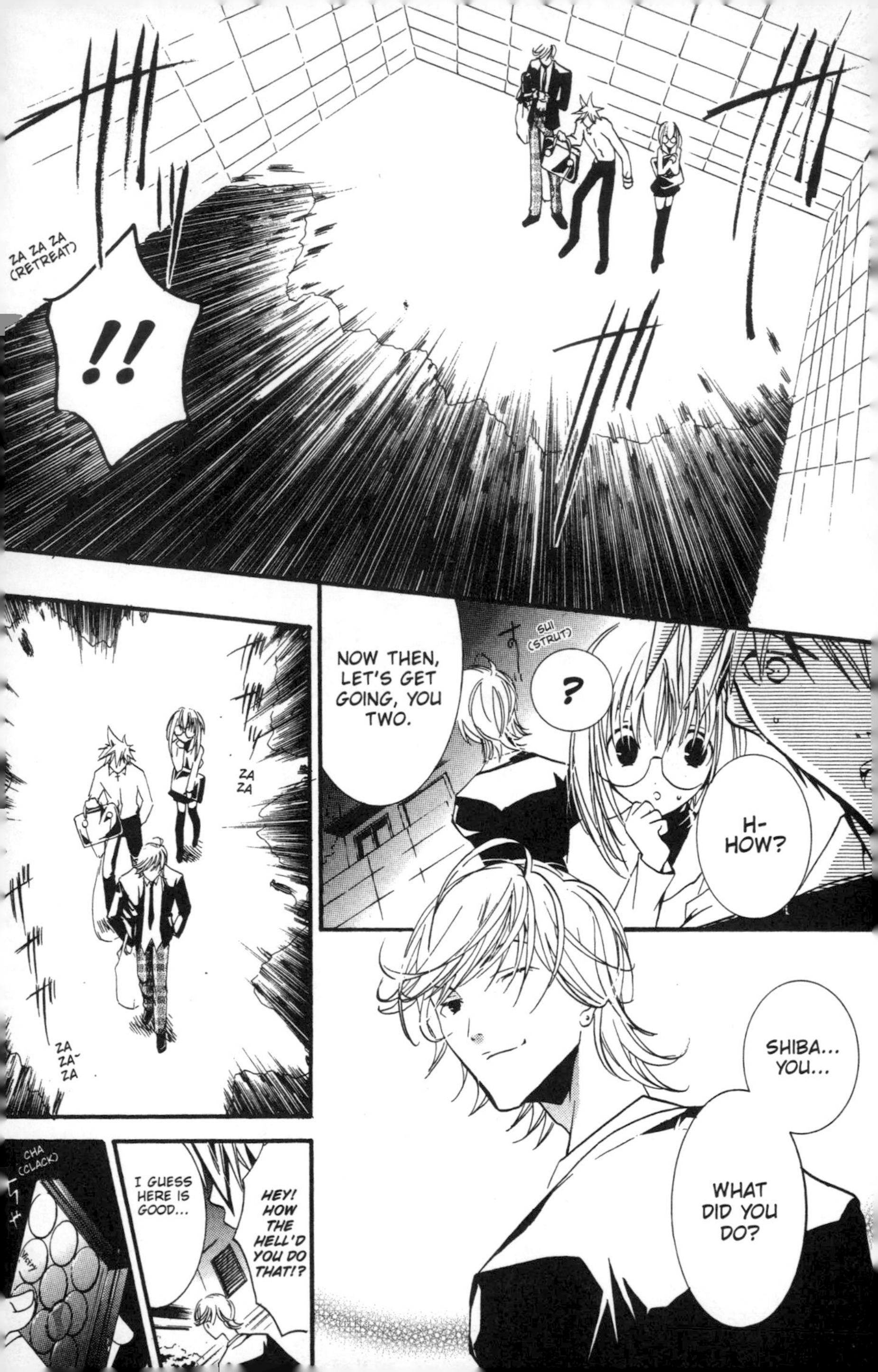
ZA ZA ZA (RETREAT)
!!
SUI (STRUT)
?
NOW THEN, LET'S GET GOING, YOU TWO.
H-HOW?
ZA ZA
ZA ZA- ZA
SHIBA... YOU...
WHAT DID YOU DO?
I GUESS HERE IS GOOD...
HEY! HOW THE HELL'D YOU DO THAT!?
CHA (CLACK)

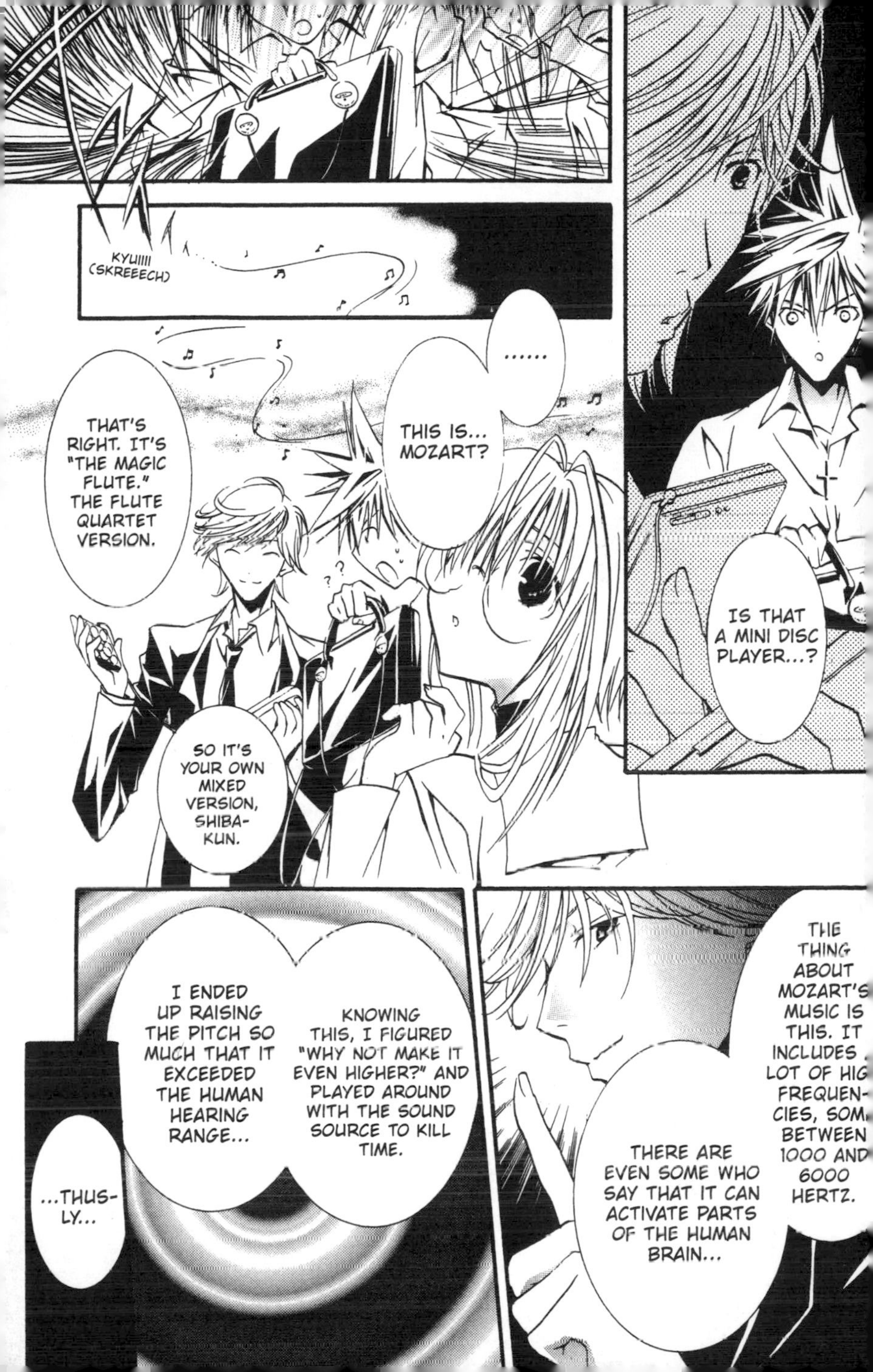
IS THAT A MINI DISC PLAYER...?
KYUIIII (SKREEECH)
......
THIS IS... MOZART?
THAT'S RIGHT. IT'S "THE MAGIC FLUTE." THE FLUTE QUARTET VERSION.
SO IT'S YOUR OWN MIXED VERSION, SHIBA-KUN.
THE THING ABOUT MOZART'S MUSIC IS THIS. IT INCLUDES LOT OF HIG FREQUEN-CIES, SOM BETWEEN 1000 AND 6000 HERTZ.
THERE ARE EVEN SOME WHO SAY THAT IT CAN ACTIVATE PARTS OF THE HUMAN BRAIN...
KNOWING THIS, I FIGURED "WHY NOT MAKE IT EVEN HIGHER?" AND PLAYED AROUND WITH THE SOUND SOURCE TO KILL TIME.
I ENDED UP RAISING THE PITCH SO MUCH THAT IT EXCEEDED THE HUMAN HEARING RANGE...
...THUS-LY...

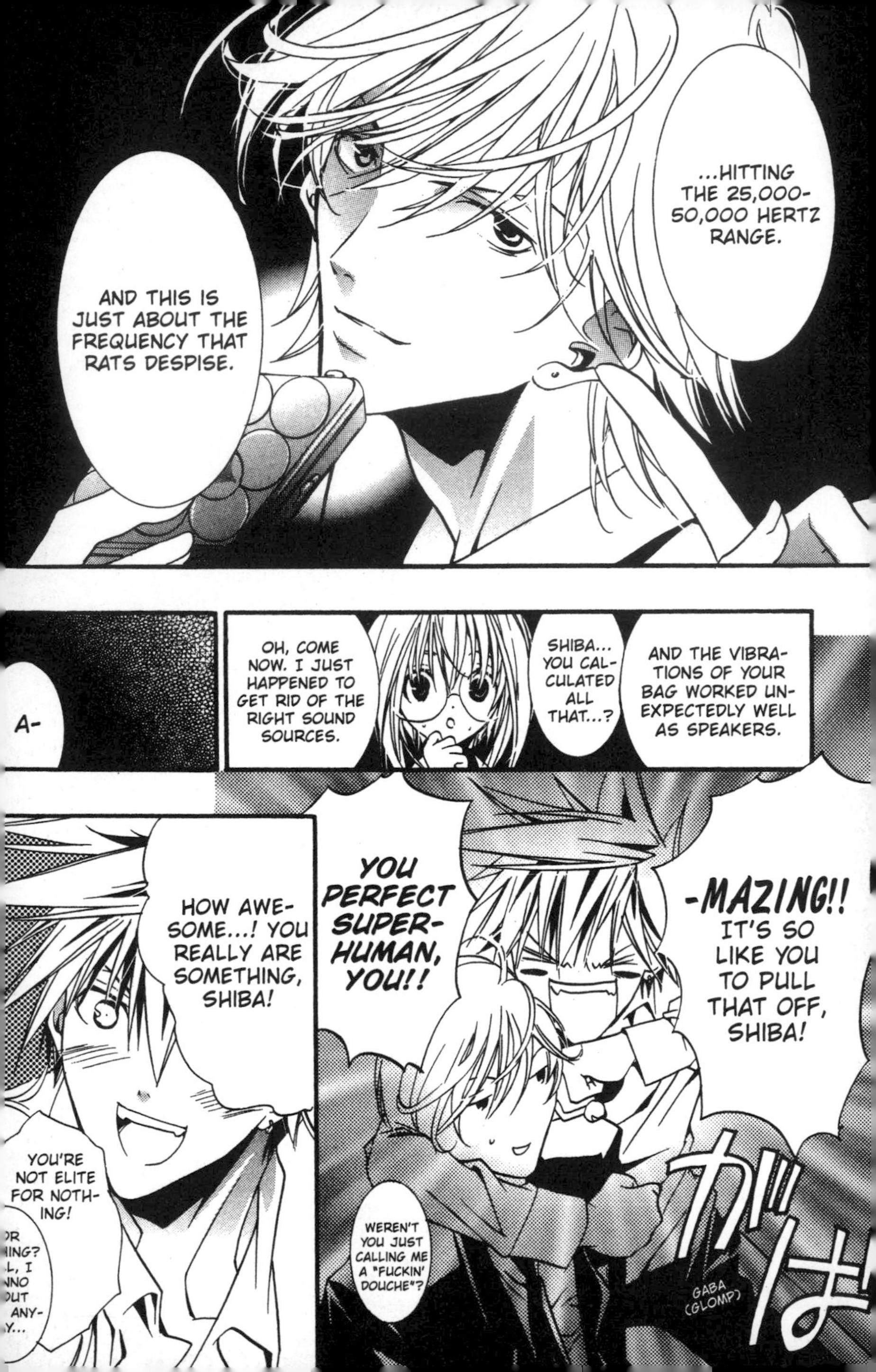
...HITTING THE 25,000-50,000 HERTZ RANGE.
AND THIS IS JUST ABOUT THE FREQUENCY THAT RATS DESPISE.
AND THE VIBRATIONS OF YOUR BAG WORKED UNEXPECTEDLY WELL AS SPEAKERS.
SHIBA... YOU CALCULATED ALL THAT...?
OH, COME NOW. I JUST HAPPENED TO GET RID OF THE RIGHT SOUND SOURCES.
A-
-MAZING!! IT'S SO LIKE YOU TO PULL THAT OFF, SHIBA!
YOU PERFECT SUPER-HUMAN, YOU!!
GABA (GLOMP)
WEREN'T YOU JUST CALLING ME A "FUCKIN' DOUCHE"?
HOW AWESOME...! YOU REALLY ARE SOMETHING, SHIBA!
YOU'RE NOT ELITE FOR NOTHING!

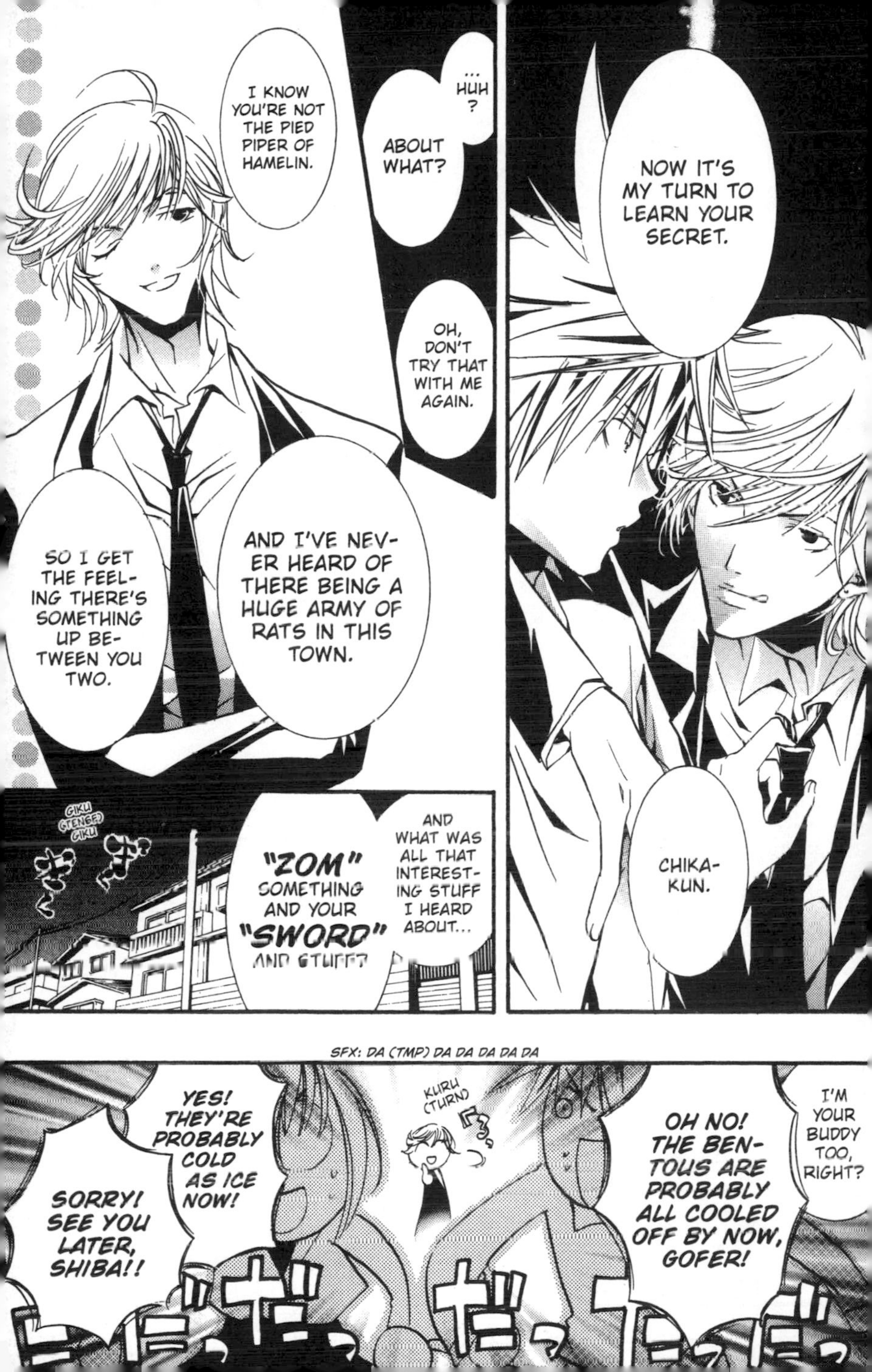
NOW IT'S MY TURN TO LEARN YOUR SECRET.
CHIKA-KUN.
... HUH?
ABOUT WHAT?
I KNOW YOU'RE NOT THE PIED PIPER OF HAMELIN.
OH, DON'T TRY THAT WITH ME AGAIN.
AND I'VE NEVER HEARD OF THERE BEING A HUGE ARMY OF RATS IN THIS TOWN.
SO I GET THE FEELING THERE'S SOMETHING UP BETWEEN YOU TWO.
AND WHAT WAS ALL THAT INTERESTING STUFF I HEARD ABOUT...
"ZOM" SOMETHING AND YOUR "SWORD" AND STUFF
GIKU (TENSE) GIKU
SFX: DA (TMP) DA DA DA DA DA
I'M YOUR BUDDY TOO, RIGHT?
OH NO! THE BENTOUS ARE PROBABLY ALL COOLED OFF BY NOW, GOFER!
KURU (TURN)
YES! THEY'RE PROBABLY COLD AS ICE NOW!
SORRY! SEE YOU LATER, SHIBA!!

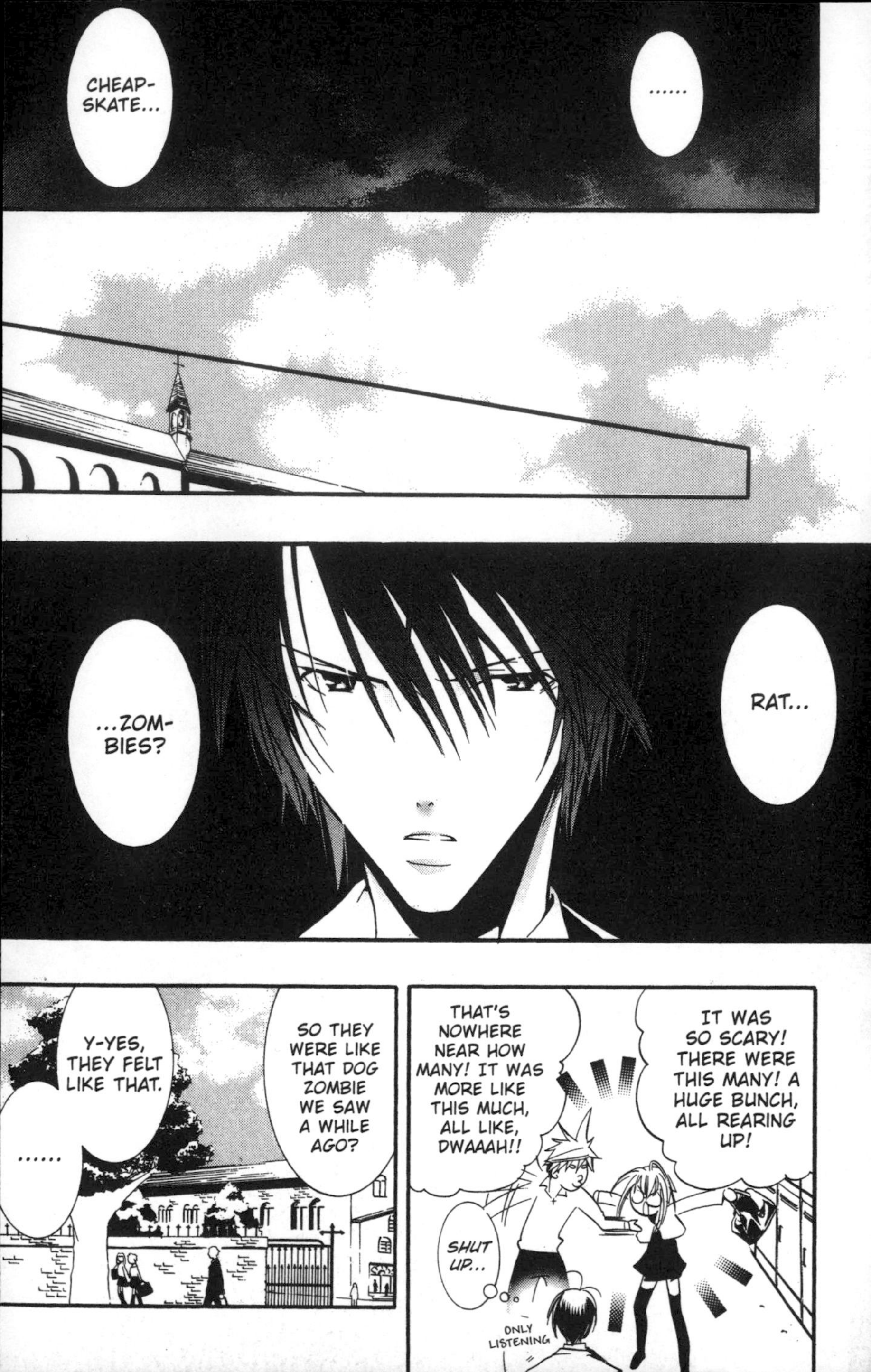
......
CHEAP-SKATE...
RAT...
...ZOMBIES?
IT WAS SO SCARY! THERE WERE THIS MANY! A HUGE BUNCH, ALL REARING UP!
THAT'S NOWHERE NEAR HOW MANY! IT WAS MORE LIKE THIS MUCH, ALL LIKE, DWAAAH!!
SHUT UP...
ONLY LISTENING
SO THEY WERE LIKE THAT DOG ZOMBIE WE SAW A WHILE AGO?
Y-YES, THEY FELT LIKE THAT.
......

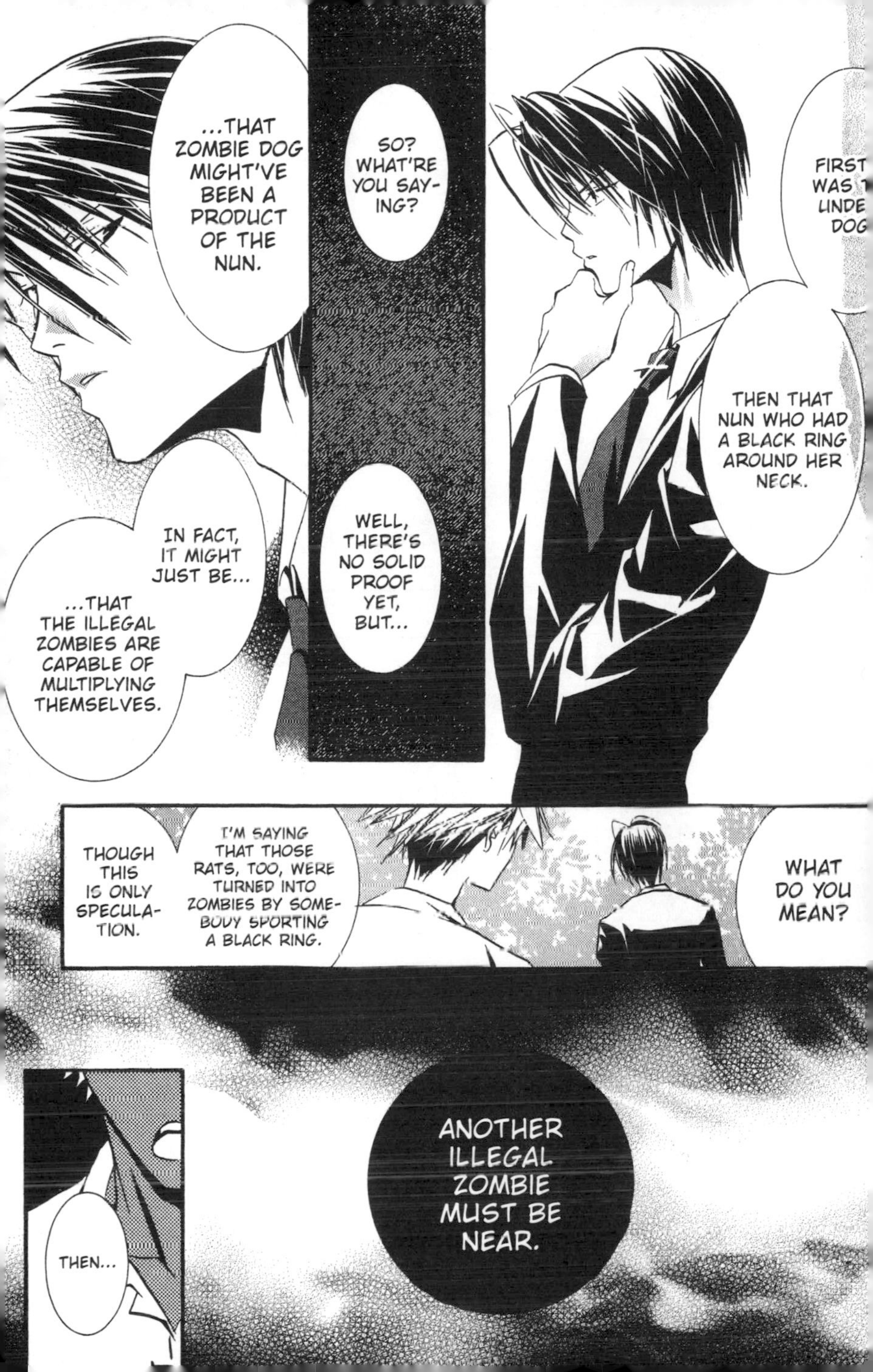
FIRST WAS
THEN THAT NUN WHO HAD A BLACK RING AROUND HER NECK.
SO? WHAT'RE YOU SAY-ING?
WELL, THERE'S NO SOLID PROOF YET, BUT...
...THAT ZOMBIE DOG MIGHT'VE BEEN A PRODUCT OF THE NUN.
IN FACT, IT MIGHT JUST BE...
...THAT THE ILLEGAL ZOMBIES ARE CAPABLE OF MULTIPLYING THEMSELVES.
WHAT DO YOU MEAN?
I'M SAYING THAT THOSE RATS, TOO, WERE TURNED INTO ZOMBIES BY SOME-BODY SPORTING A BLACK RING.
THOUGH THIS IS ONLY SPECULA-TION.
ANOTHER ILLEGAL ZOMBIE MUST BE NEAR.
THEN...

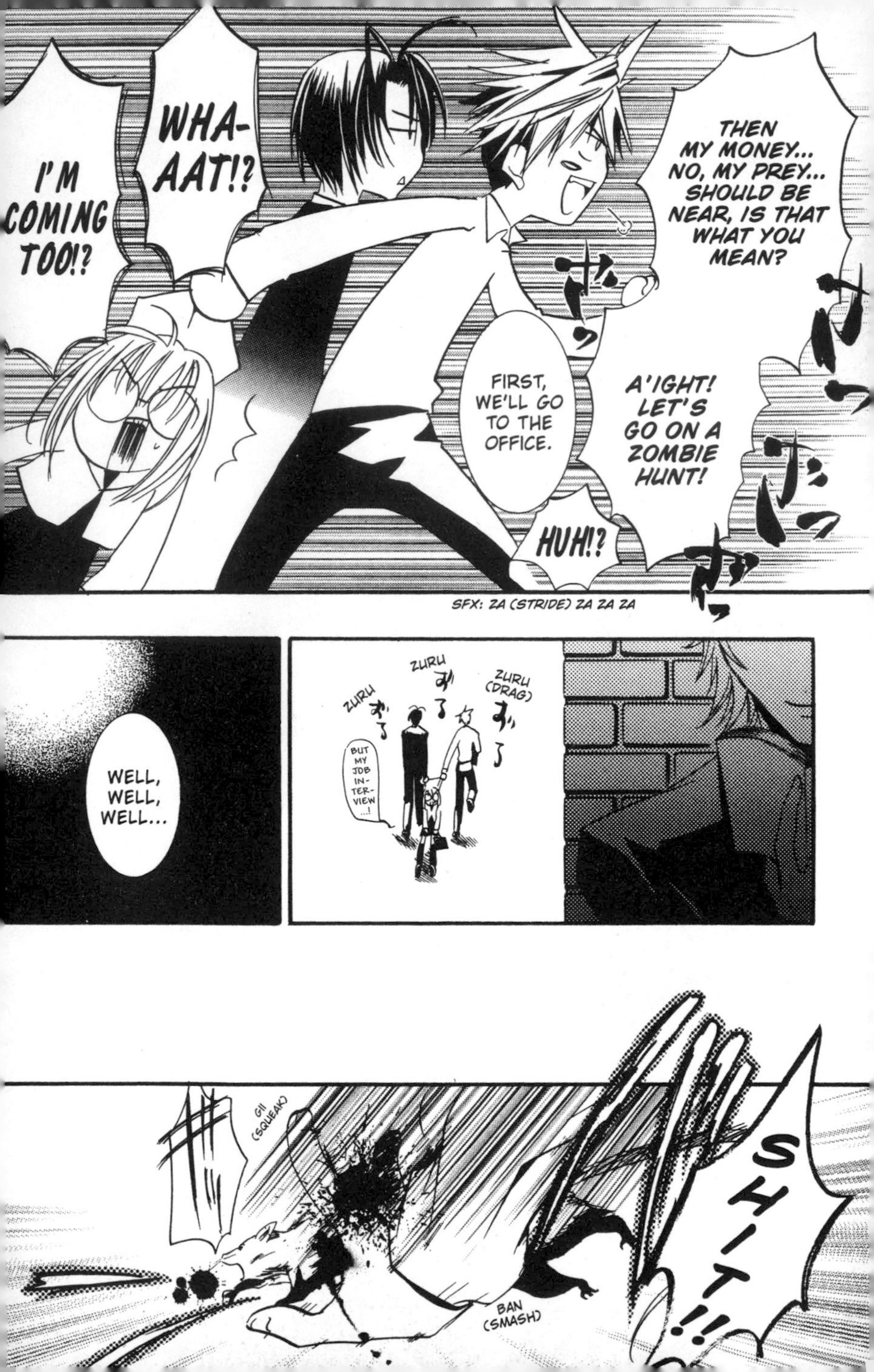
THEN MY MONEY... NO, MY PREY... SHOULD BE NEAR, IS THAT WHAT YOU MEAN?
A'IGHT! LET'S GO ON A ZOMBIE HUNT!
FIRST, WE'LL GO TO THE OFFICE.
HUH!?
WHA-AAT!?
I'M COMING TOO!?
SFX: ZA (STRIDE) ZA ZA ZA
ZURU (DRAG)
ZURU
ZURU
BUT MY JOB INTER-VIEW...!
WELL, WELL, WELL...
SHIT!!!
BAN (SMASH)
GII (SQUEAK)

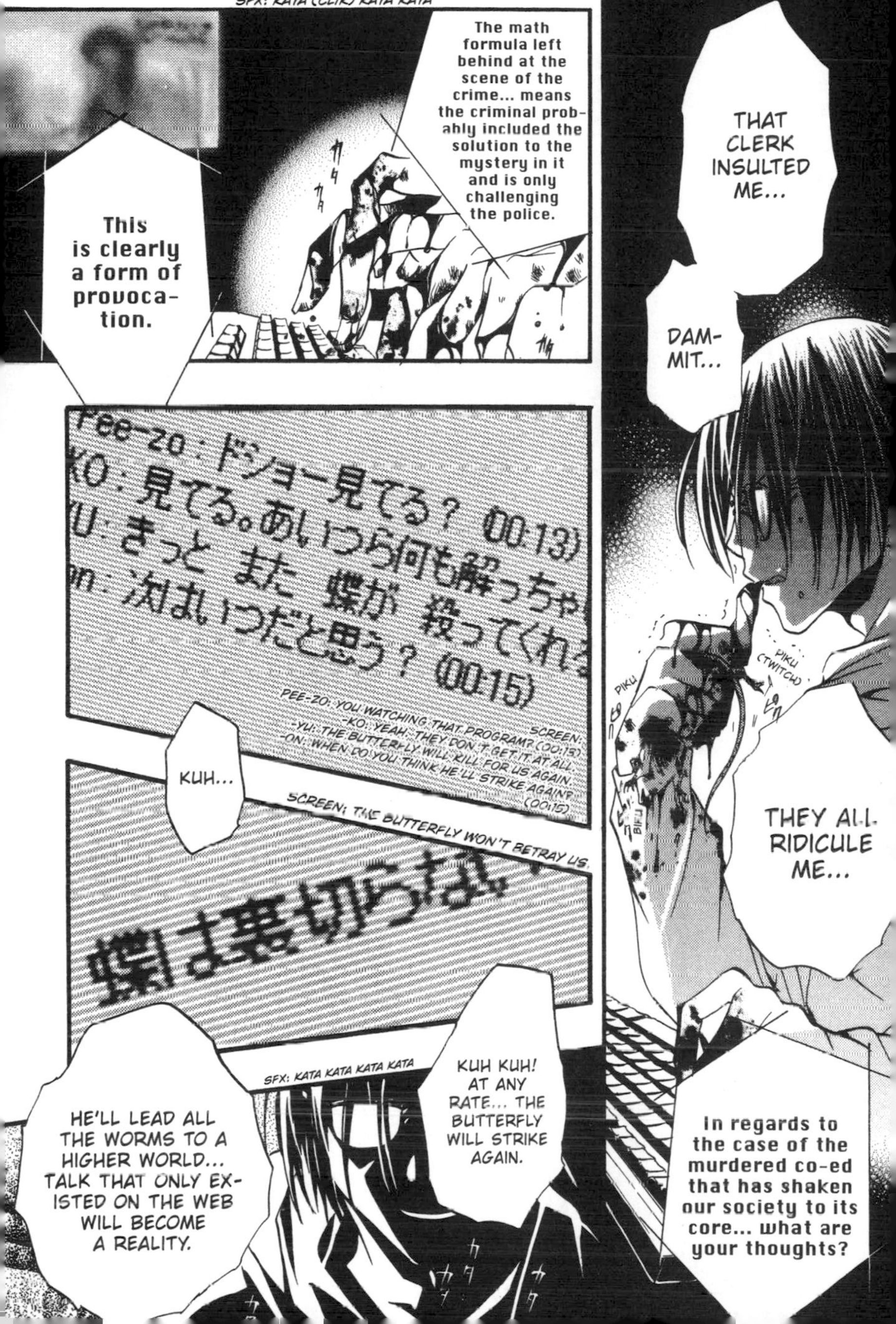
THAT CLERK INSULTED ME...
DAM-MIT...
PIKU (TWITCH)
PIKU
BIKU
THEY ALL RIDICULE ME...
In regards to the case of the murdered co-ed that has shaken our society to its core... what are your thoughts?
SFX: KATA (CLIK) KATA KATA
The math formula left behind at the scene of the crime... means the criminal probably included the solution to the mystery in it and is only challenging the police.
This is clearly a form of provocation.
Pee-zo：ドショー見てる？
KO：見てる。あいつら何も解っちゃ
U：きっと また 蝶が 殺ってくれ
n：次はいつだと思う？(00:15)
SCREEN: PEE-ZO: YOU WATCHING THAT PROGRAM? (00:15)
-KO: YEAH. THEY DON'T GET IT AT ALL.
-YU: THE BUTTERFLY WILL KILL FOR US AGAIN.
-ON: WHEN DO YOU THINK HE'LL STRIKE AGAIN? (00:15)
KUH...
SCREEN: THE BUTTERFLY WON'T BETRAY US.
蝶は裏切らない
SFX: KATA KATA KATA KATA
KUH KUH! AT ANY RATE... THE BUTTERFLY WILL STRIKE AGAIN.
HE'LL LEAD ALL THE WORMS TO A HIGHER WORLD... TALK THAT ONLY EXISTED ON THE WEB WILL BECOME A REALITY.

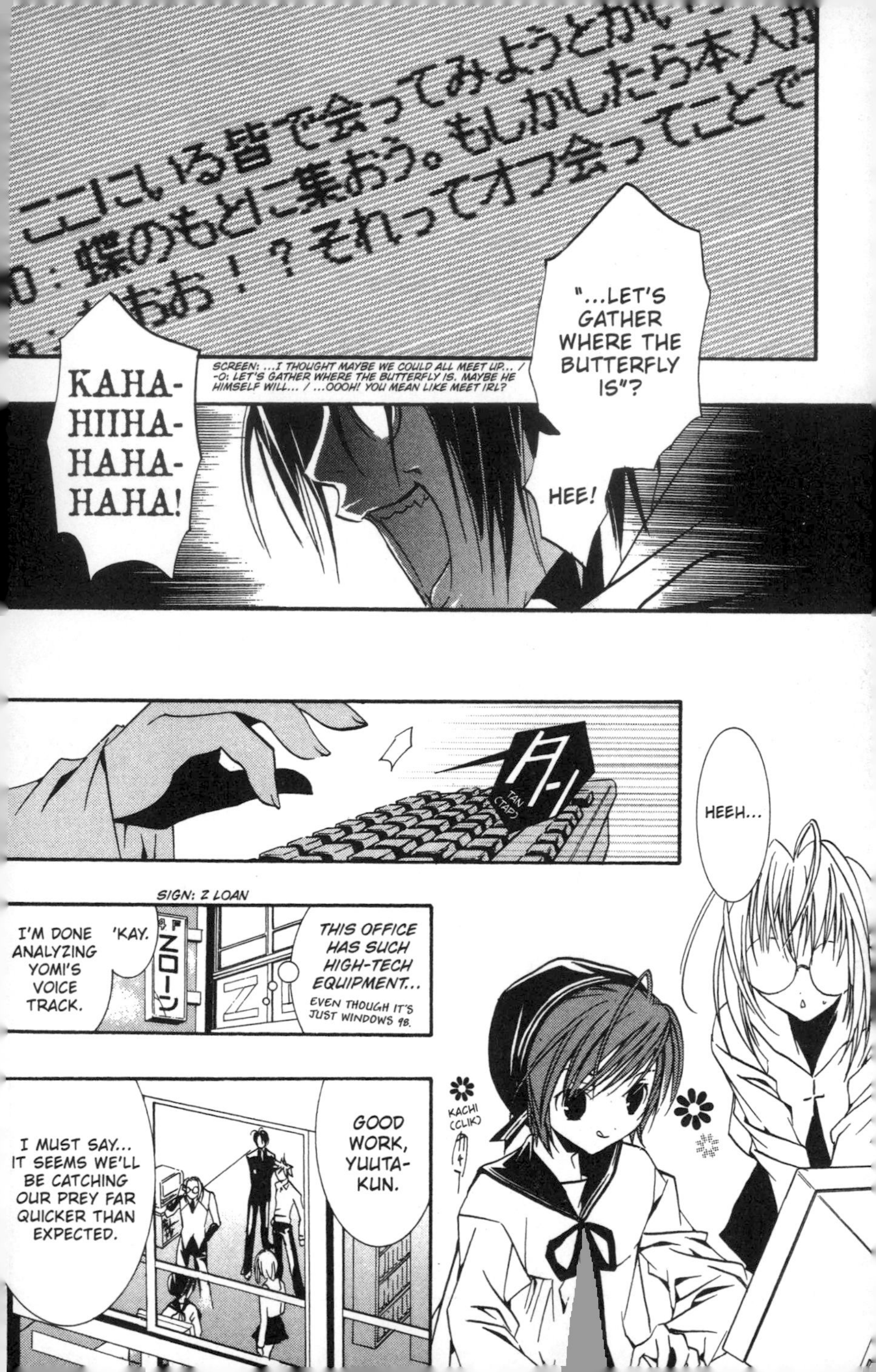
ここにいる皆で会ってみようとか
蝶のもとに集おう。もしかしたら本人が
ちあお！？それってオフ会ってことで
"...LET'S GATHER WHERE THE BUTTERFLY IS"?
SCREEN: ...I THOUGHT MAYBE WE COULD ALL MEET UP... / -O: LET'S GATHER WHERE THE BUTTERFLY IS. MAYBE HE HIMSELF WILL... / ...OOOH! YOU MEAN LIKE MEET IRL?
KAHA-HIIHA-HAHA-HAHA!
HEE!
HEEH...
KACHI (CLIK)
TAN (TAP)
SIGN: Z LOAN
THIS OFFICE HAS SUCH HIGH-TECH EQUIPMENT...
EVEN THOUGH IT'S JUST WINDOWS 98.
'KAY.
I'M DONE ANALYZING YOMI'S VOICE TRACK.
GOOD WORK, YUUTA-KUN.
I MUST SAY... IT SEEMS WE'LL BE CATCHING OUR PREY FAR QUICKER THAN EXPECTED.

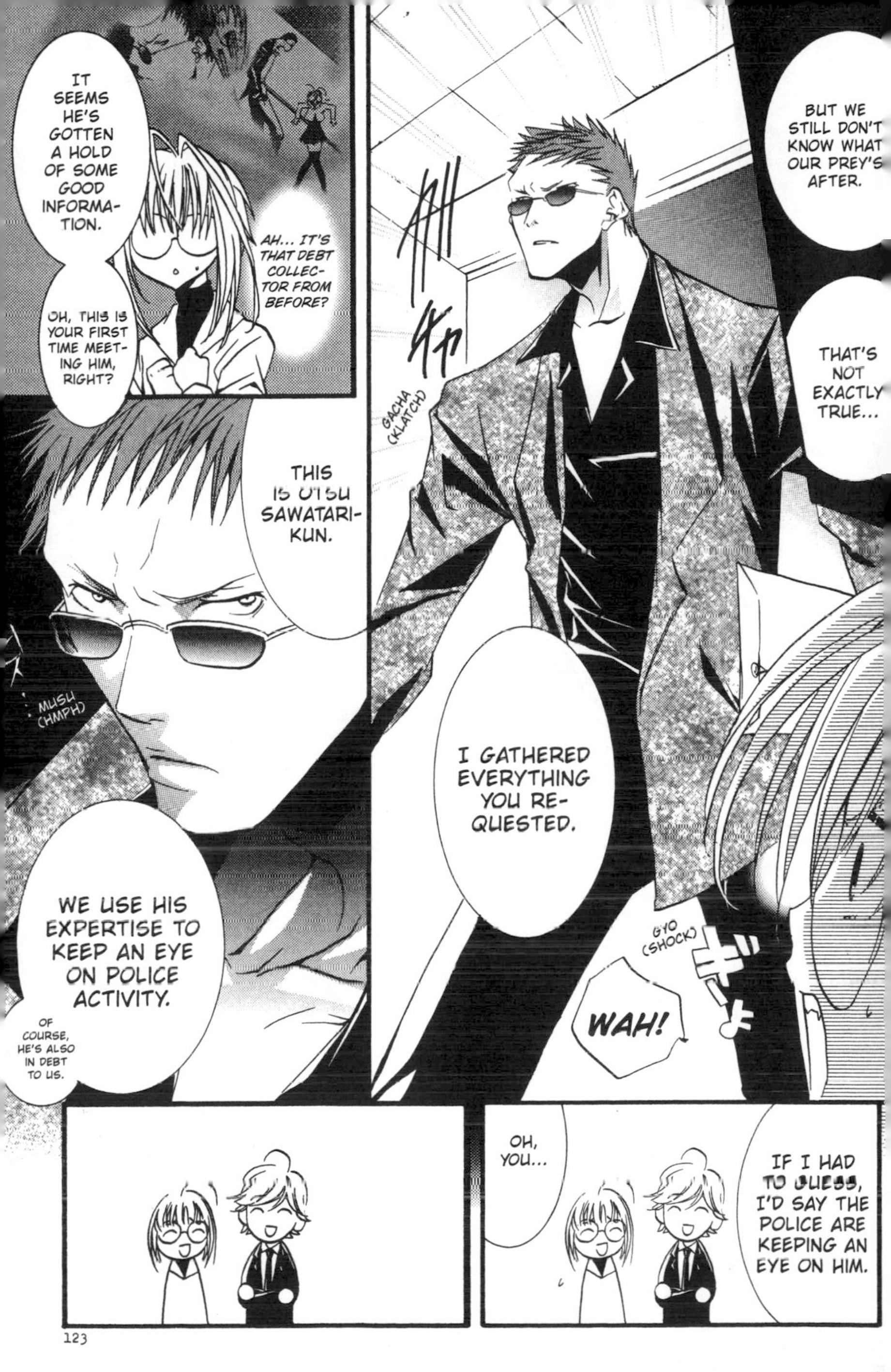
BUT WE STILL DON'T KNOW WHAT OUR PREY'S AFTER.
THAT'S NOT EXACTLY TRUE...
GACHA (KLATCH)
I GATHERED EVERYTHING YOU RE-QUESTED.
GYO (SHOCK)
WAH!
IT SEEMS HE'S GOTTEN A HOLD OF SOME GOOD INFORMA-TION.
AH... IT'S THAT DEBT COLLEC-TOR FROM BEFORE?
OH, THIS IS YOUR FIRST TIME MEET-ING HIM, RIGHT?
THIS IS OTSU SAWATARI-KUN.
MUSU (HMPH)
WE USE HIS EXPERTISE TO KEEP AN EYE ON POLICE ACTIVITY.
OF COURSE, HE'S ALSO IN DEBT TO US.
IF I HAD TO GUESS, I'D SAY THE POLICE ARE KEEPING AN EYE ON HIM.
OH, YOU...

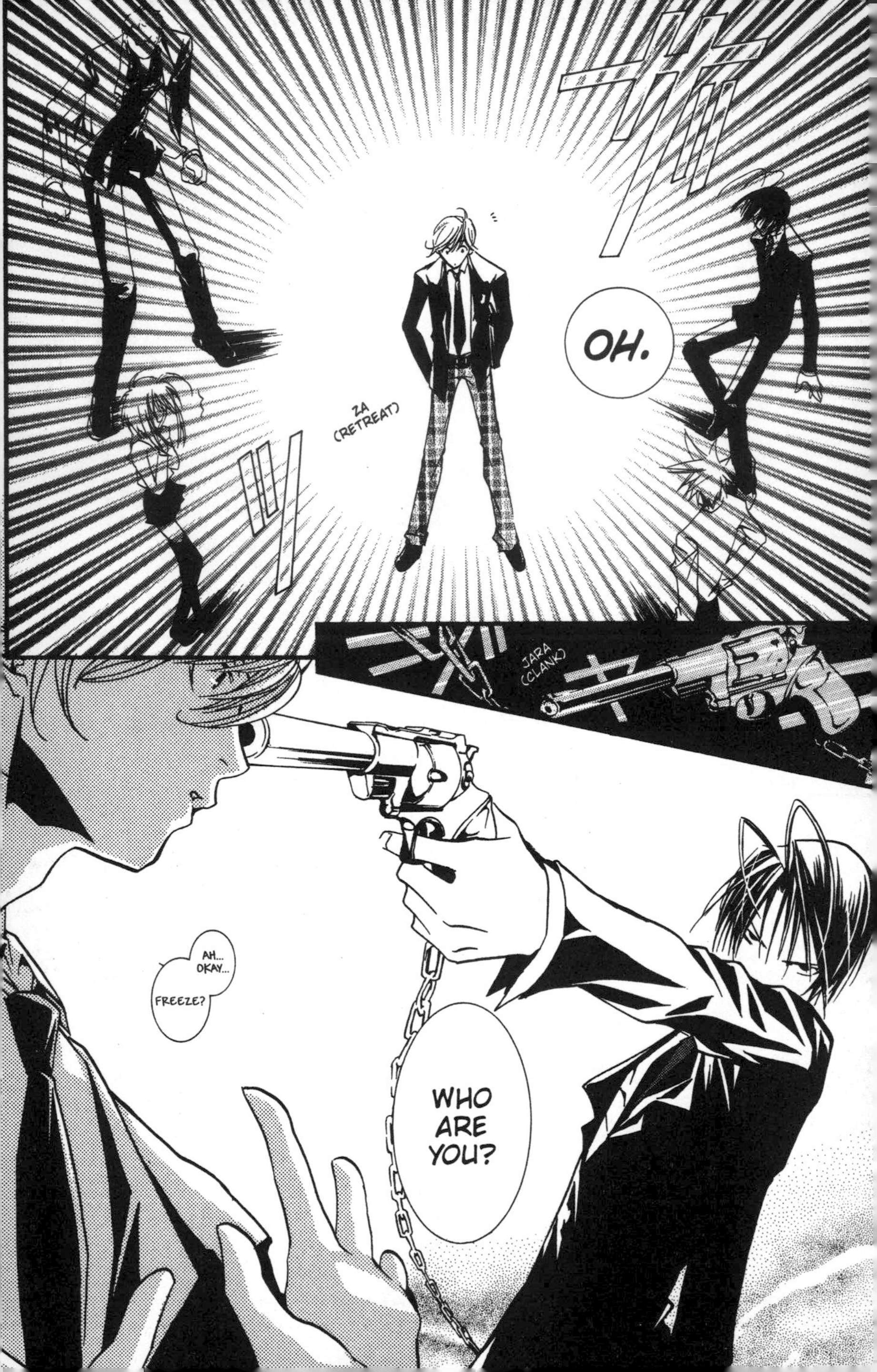
OH.
ZA (RETREAT)
JARA (CLANK)
WHO ARE YOU?
AH... OKAY...
FREEZE?

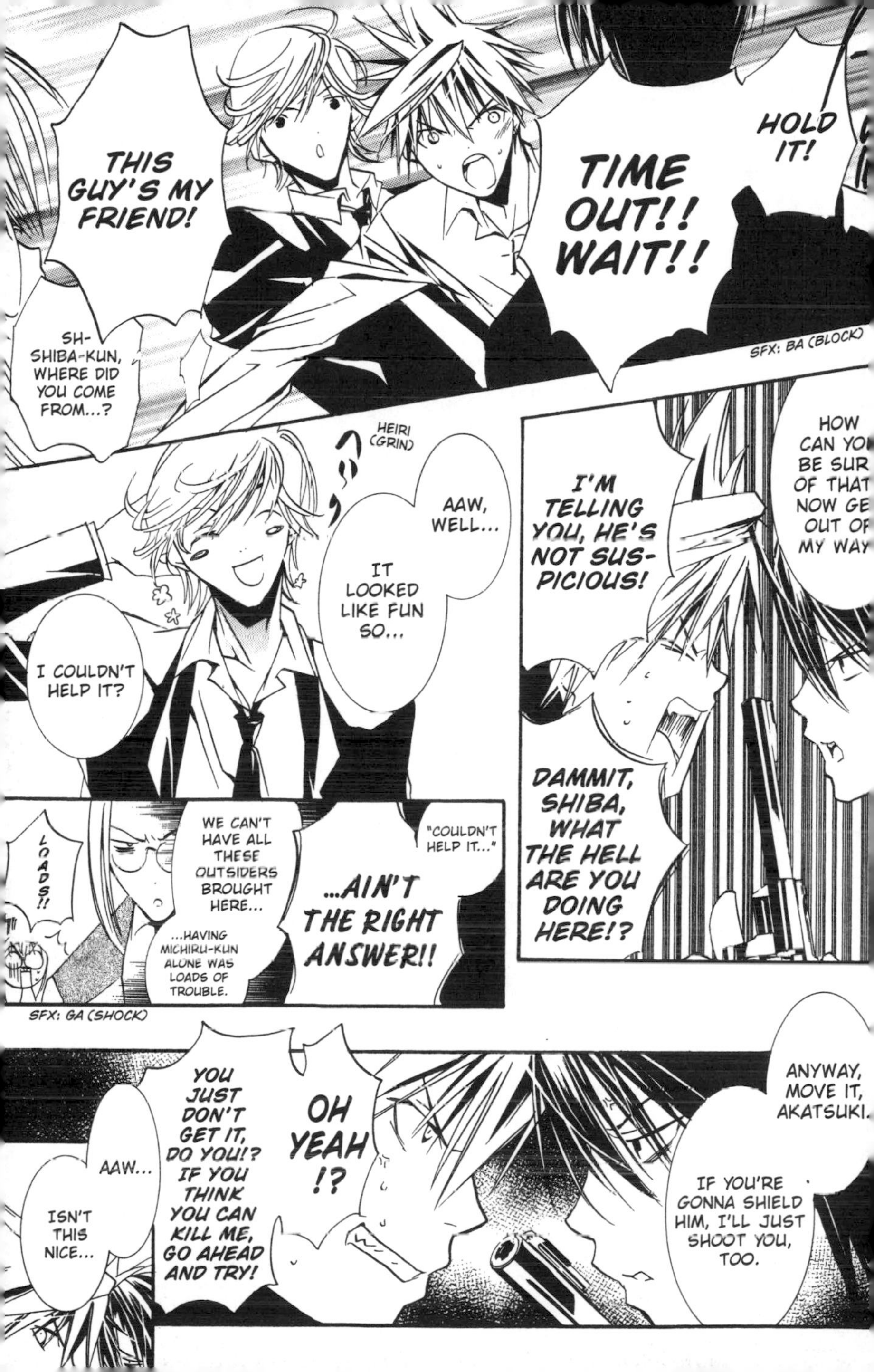
HOLD IT!
TIME OUT!! WAIT!!
THIS GUY'S MY FRIEND!
SH- SHIBA-KUN, WHERE DID YOU COME FROM...?
SFX: BA (BLOCK)
HOW CAN YO BE SUR OF THAT NOW GE OUT OF MY WAY
I'M TELLING YOU, HE'S NOT SUS-PICIOUS!
DAMMIT, SHIBA, WHAT THE HELL ARE YOU DOING HERE!?
HEIRI (GRIN)
AAW, WELL...
IT LOOKED LIKE FUN SO...
I COULDN'T HELP IT?
"COULDN'T HELP IT..."
...AIN'T THE RIGHT ANSWER!!
WE CAN'T HAVE ALL THESE OUTSIDERS BROUGHT HERE...
...HAVING MICHIRU-KUN ALONE WAS LOADS OF TROUBLE.
LOADS!!
SFX: GA (SHOCK)
ANYWAY, MOVE IT, AKATSUKI.
IF YOU'RE GONNA SHIELD HIM, I'LL JUST SHOOT YOU, TOO.
OH YEAH !?
YOU JUST DON'T GET IT, DO YOU!? IF YOU THINK YOU CAN KILL ME, GO AHEAD AND TRY!
AAW...
ISN'T THIS NICE...

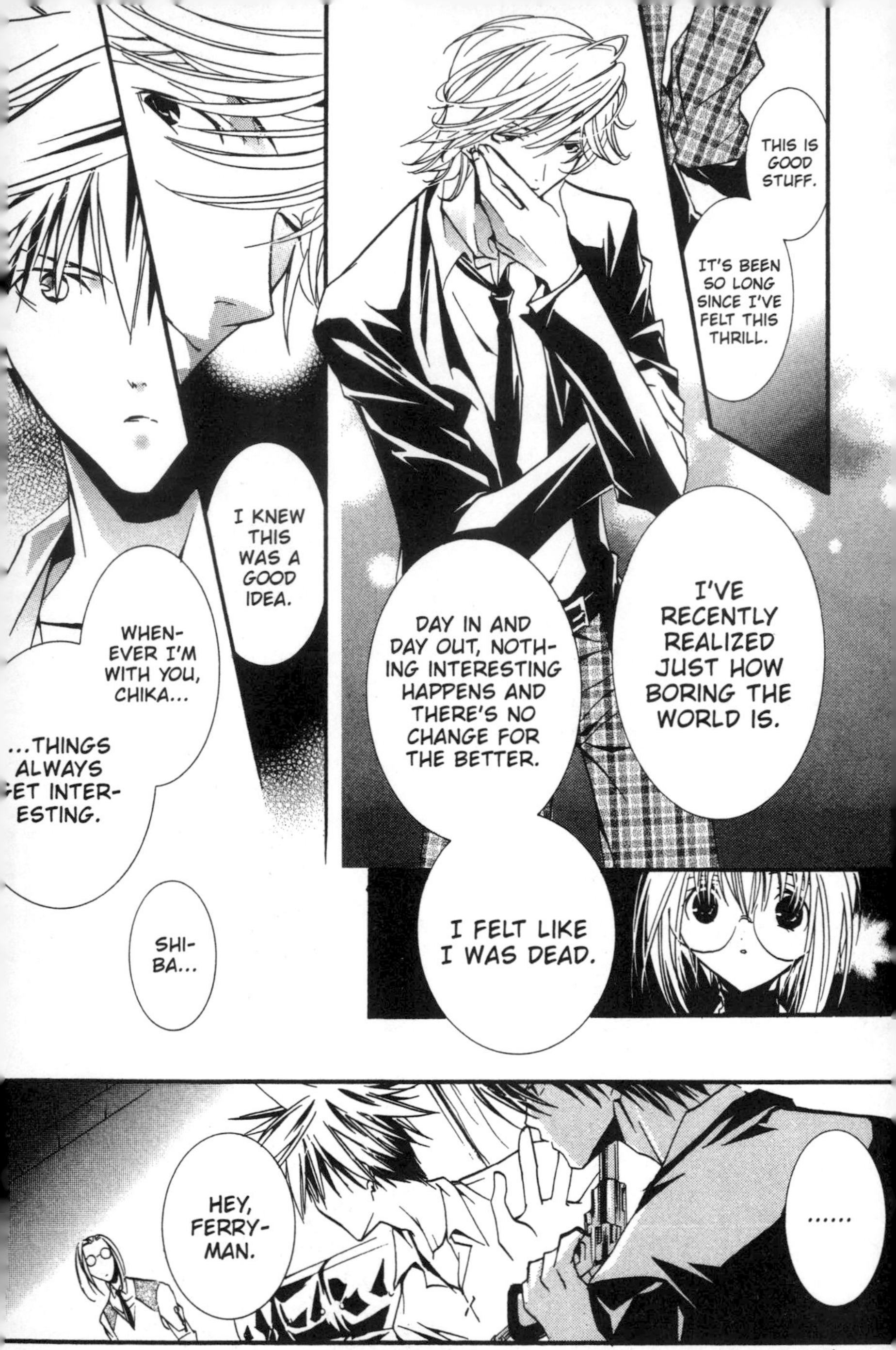
THIS IS GOOD STUFF.
IT'S BEEN SO LONG SINCE I'VE FELT THIS THRILL.
I'VE RECENTLY REALIZED JUST HOW BORING THE WORLD IS.
DAY IN AND DAY OUT, NOTHING INTERESTING HAPPENS AND THERE'S NO CHANGE FOR THE BETTER.
I FELT LIKE I WAS DEAD.
I KNEW THIS WAS A GOOD IDEA.
WHENEVER I'M WITH YOU, CHIKA...
...THINGS ALWAYS GET INTERESTING.
SHIBA...
......
HEY, FERRYMAN.

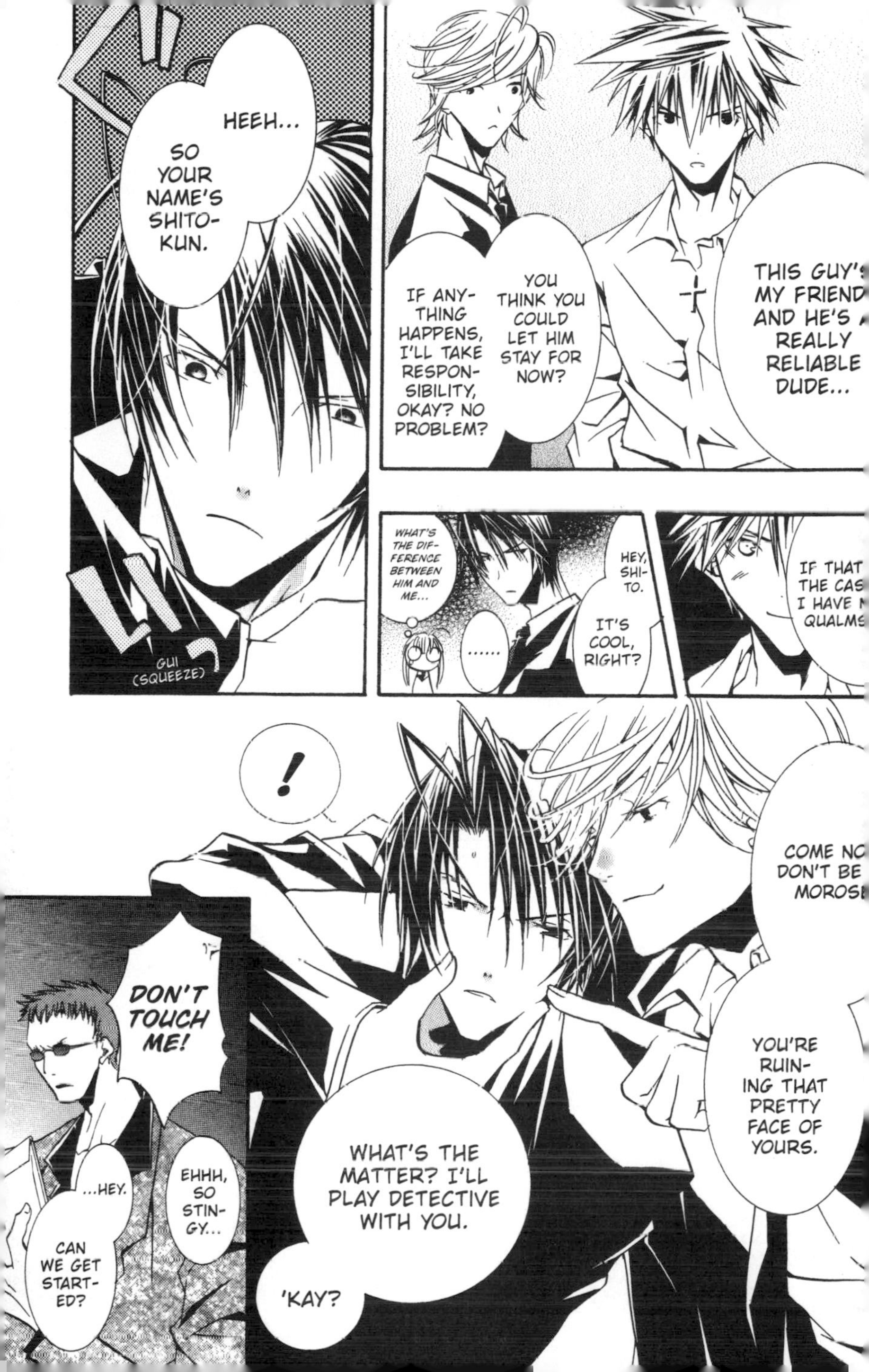
THIS GUY'S MY FRIEND AND HE'S A REALLY RELIABLE DUDE...
YOU THINK YOU COULD LET HIM STAY FOR NOW?
IF ANY-THING HAPPENS, I'LL TAKE RESPON-SIBILITY, OKAY? NO PROBLEM?
IF THAT THE CAS I HAVE N QUALMS
HEY, SHI-TO.
IT'S COOL, RIGHT?
......
WHAT'S THE DIF-FERENCE BETWEEN HIM AND ME...
HEEH...
SO YOUR NAME'S SHITO-KUN.
GUI (SQUEEZE)
!
COME NO DON'T BE MOROS
YOU'RE RUIN-ING THAT PRETTY FACE OF YOURS.
WHAT'S THE MATTER? I'LL PLAY DETECTIVE WITH YOU.
'KAY?
DON'T TOUCH ME!
EHHH, SO STIN-GY...
...HEY.
CAN WE GET START-ED?

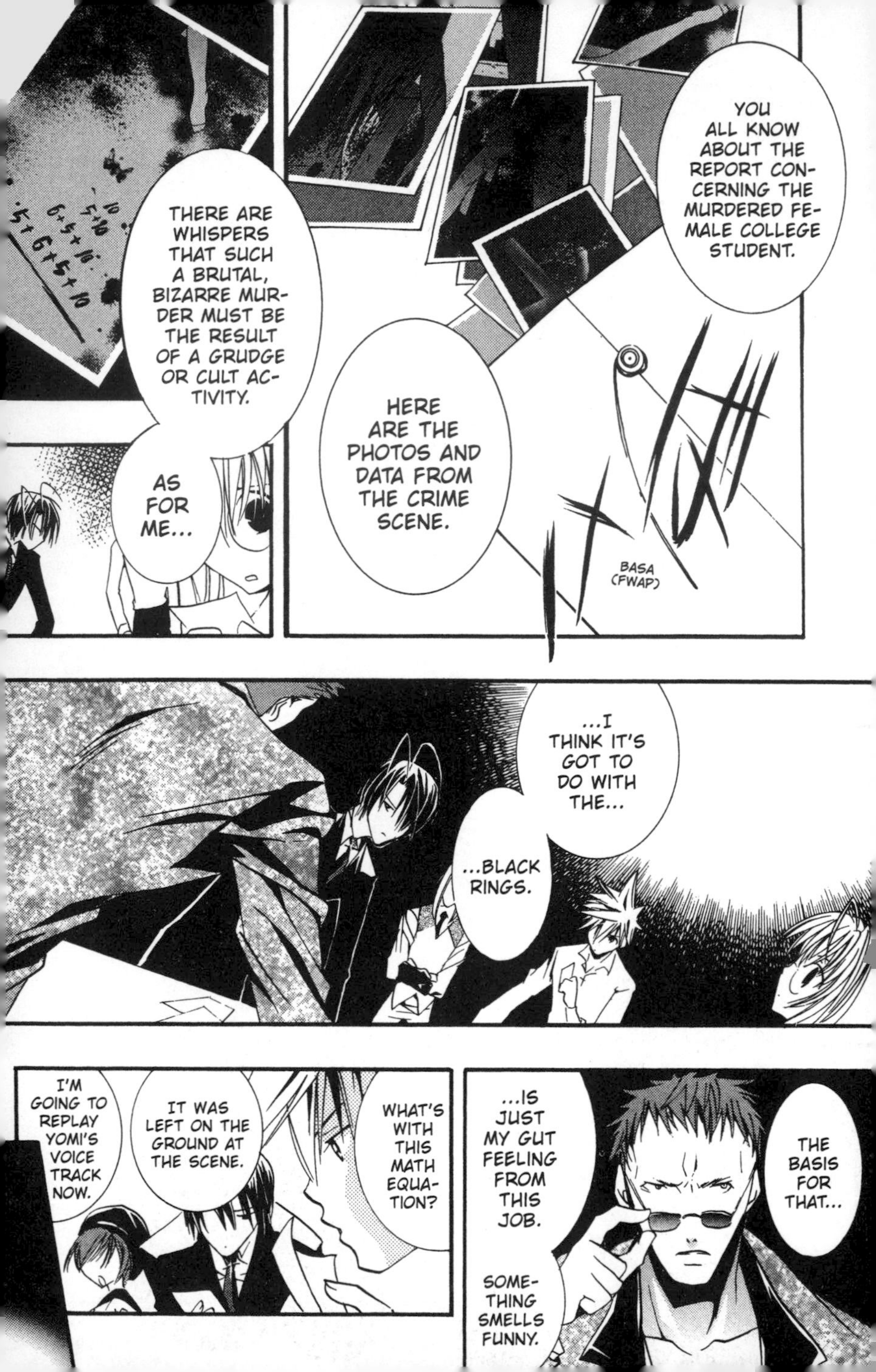
YOU ALL KNOW ABOUT THE REPORT CONCERNING THE MURDERED FEMALE COLLEGE STUDENT.
HERE ARE THE PHOTOS AND DATA FROM THE CRIME SCENE.
BASA (FWAP)
THERE ARE WHISPERS THAT SUCH A BRUTAL, BIZARRE MURDER MUST BE THE RESULT OF A GRUDGE OR CULT ACTIVITY.
AS FOR ME...
...I THINK IT'S GOT TO DO WITH THE...
...BLACK RINGS.
THE BASIS FOR THAT...
...IS JUST MY GUT FEELING FROM THIS JOB.
SOMETHING SMELLS FUNNY.
WHAT'S WITH THIS MATH EQUATION?
IT WAS LEFT ON THE GROUND AT THE SCENE.
I'M GOING TO REPLAY YOMI'S VOICE TRACK NOW.

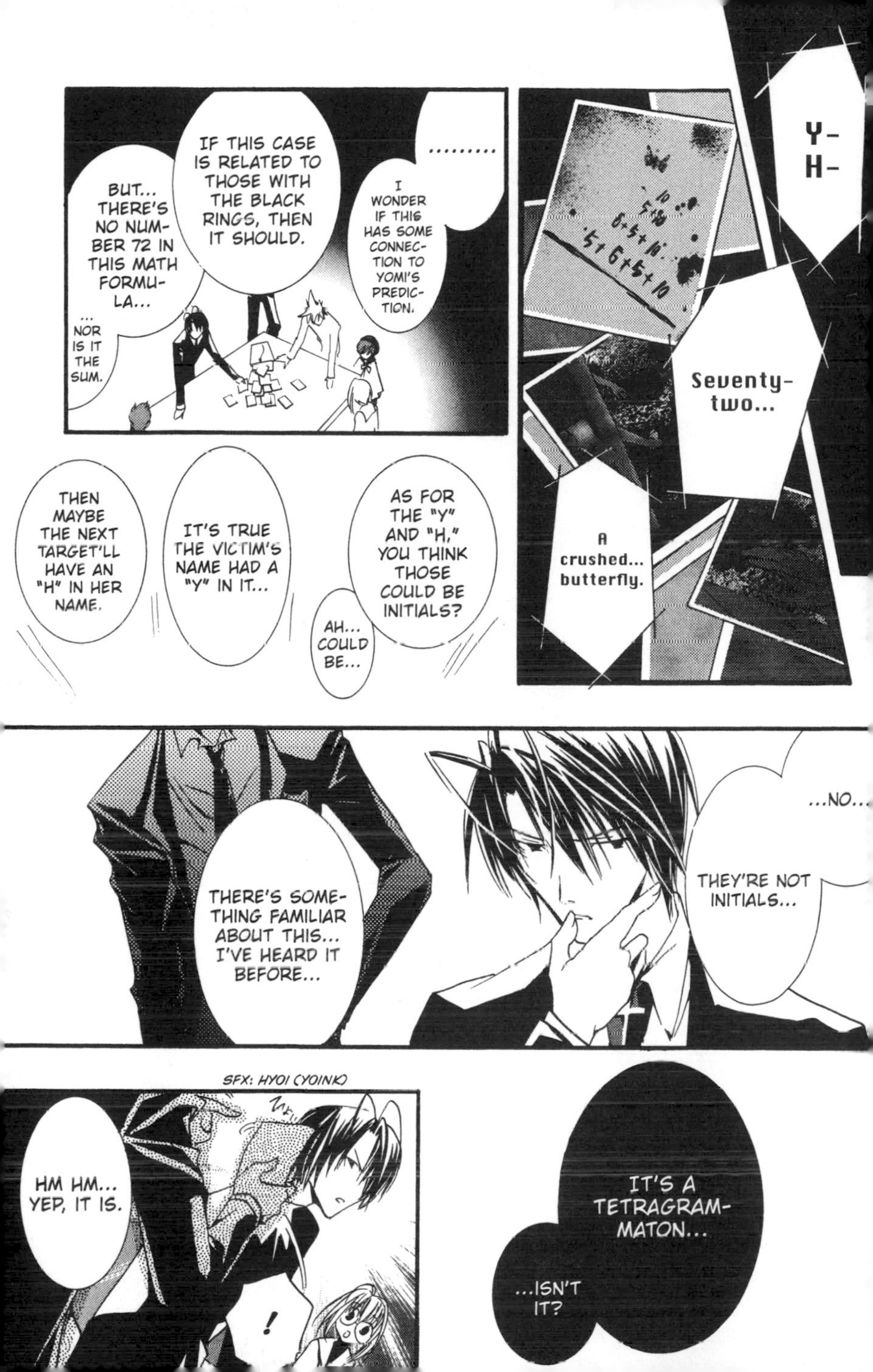
Y-
H-
Seventy-two...
A crushed... butterfly.
....
I WONDER IF THIS HAS SOME CONNECTION TO YOMI'S PREDICTION.
IF THIS CASE IS RELATED TO THOSE WITH THE BLACK RINGS, THEN IT SHOULD.
BUT... THERE'S NO NUMBER 72 IN THIS MATH FORMULA...
...NOR IS IT THE SUM.
AS FOR THE "Y" AND "H," YOU THINK THOSE COULD BE INITIALS?
AH... COULD BE...
IT'S TRUE THE VICTIM'S NAME HAD A "Y" IN IT...
THEN MAYBE THE NEXT TARGET'LL HAVE AN "H" IN HER NAME.
...NO...
THEY'RE NOT INITIALS...
THERE'S SOMETHING FAMILIAR ABOUT THIS... I'VE HEARD IT BEFORE...
IT'S A TETRAGRAMMATON...
...ISN'T IT?
SFX: HYOI (YOINK)
HM HM... YEP, IT IS.
!

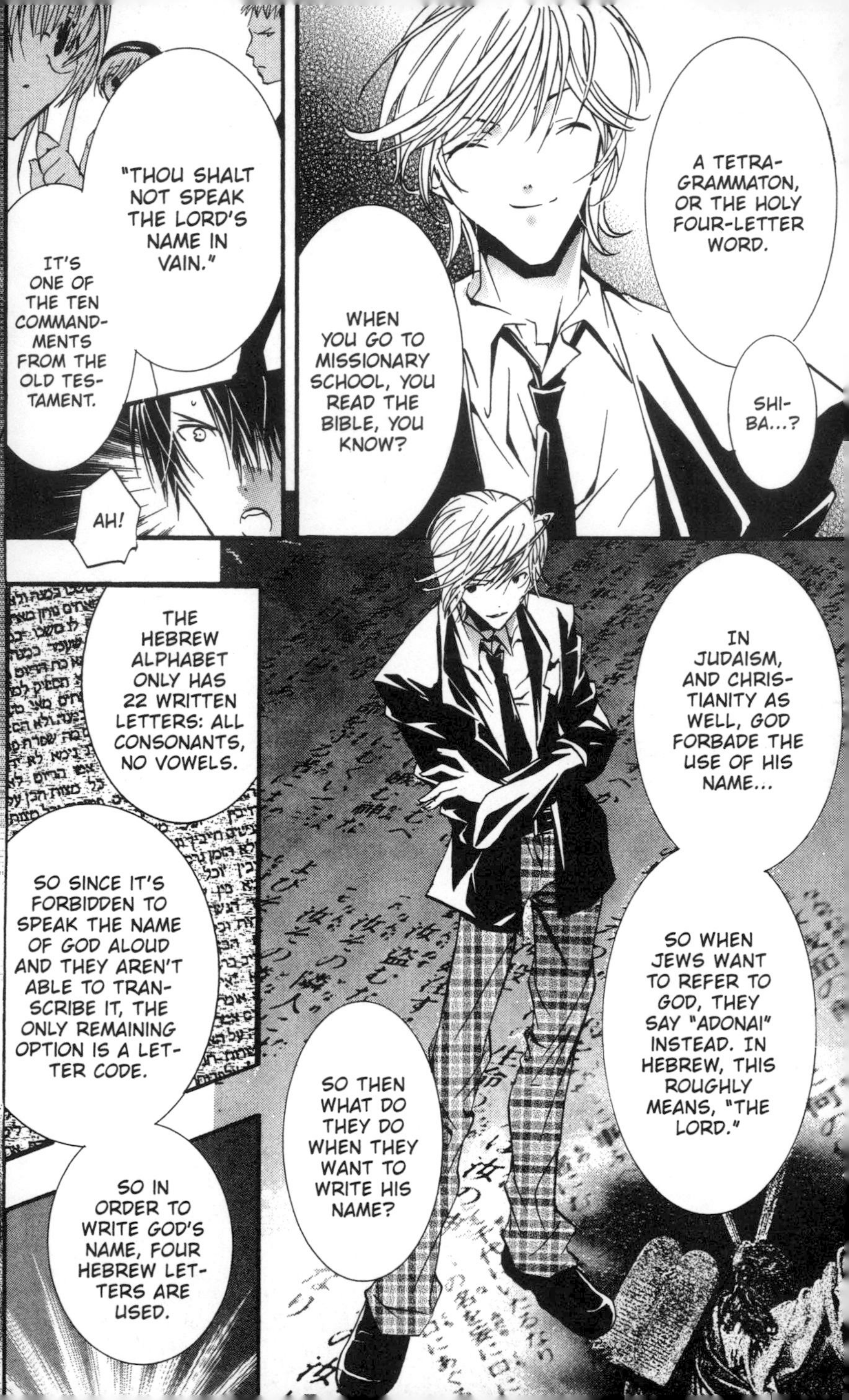
A TETRA-GRAMMATON, OR THE HOLY FOUR-LETTER WORD.
SHI-BA...?
WHEN YOU GO TO MISSIONARY SCHOOL, YOU READ THE BIBLE, YOU KNOW?
"THOU SHALT NOT SPEAK THE LORD'S NAME IN VAIN."
IT'S ONE OF THE TEN COMMAND-MENTS FROM THE OLD TES-TAMENT.
AH!
IN JUDAISM, AND CHRIS-TIANITY AS WELL, GOD FORBADE THE USE OF HIS NAME...
SO WHEN JEWS WANT TO REFER TO GOD, THEY SAY "ADONAI" INSTEAD. IN HEBREW, THIS ROUGHLY MEANS, "THE LORD."
SO THEN WHAT DO THEY DO WHEN THEY WANT TO WRITE HIS NAME?
THE HEBREW ALPHABET ONLY HAS 22 WRITTEN LETTERS: ALL CONSONANTS, NO VOWELS.
SO SINCE IT'S FORBIDDEN TO SPEAK THE NAME OF GOD ALOUD AND THEY AREN'T ABLE TO TRAN-SCRIBE IT, THE ONLY REMAINING OPTION IS A LET-TER CODE.
SO IN ORDER TO WRITE GOD'S NAME, FOUR HEBREW LET-TERS ARE USED.

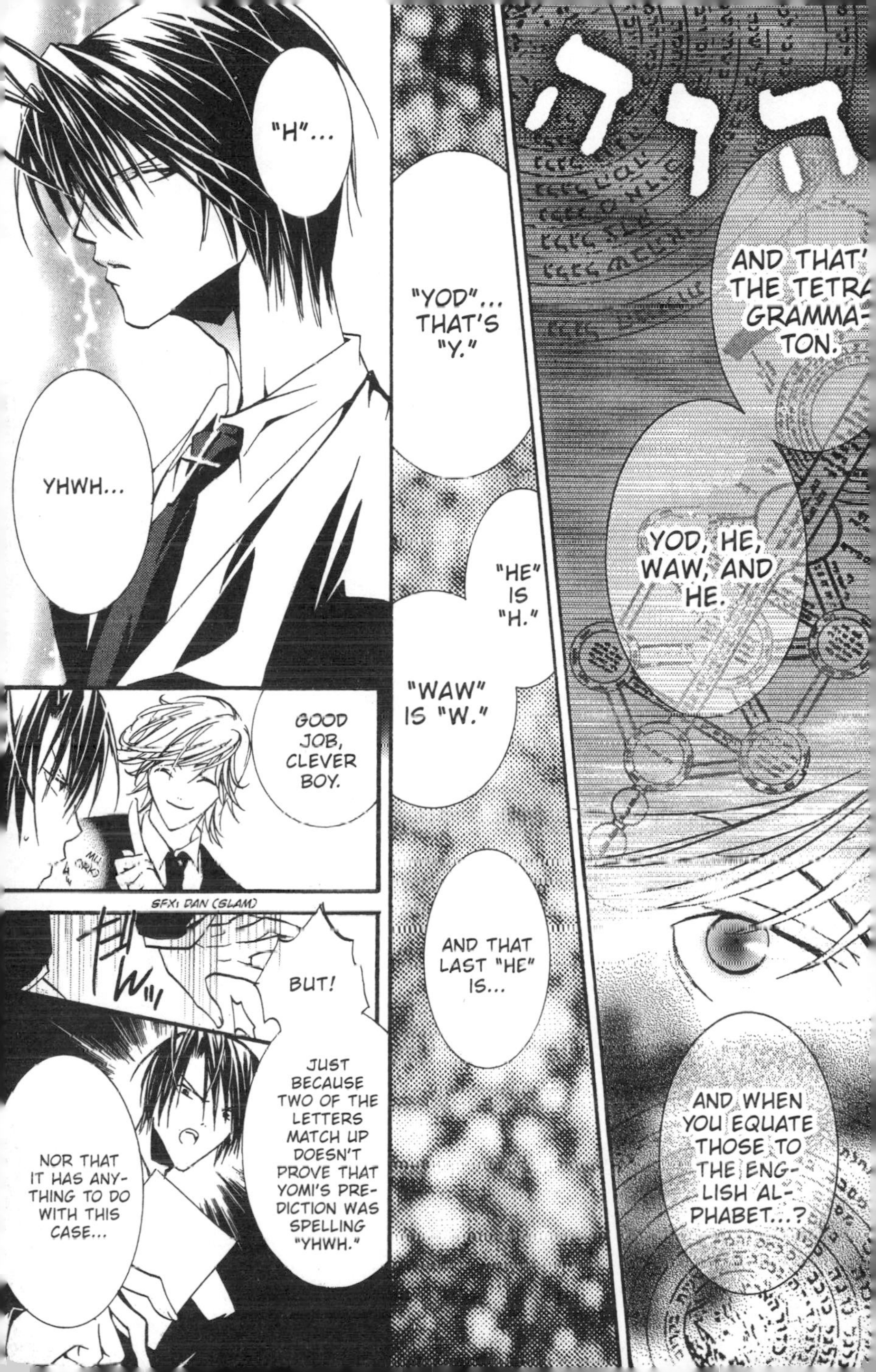
AND THAT' THE TETRA GRAMMA-TON.
YOD, HE, WAW, AND HE.
AND WHEN YOU EQUATE THOSE TO THE ENG-LISH AL-PHABET...?
"YOD"... THAT'S "Y."
"HE" IS "H."
"WAW" IS "W."
AND THAT LAST "HE" IS...
"H"...
YHWH...
GOOD JOB, CLEVER BOY.
SFX: DAN (GLAM)
BUT!
JUST BECAUSE TWO OF THE LETTERS MATCH UP DOESN'T PROVE THAT YOMI'S PRE-DICTION WAS SPELLING "YHWH."
NOR THAT IT HAS ANY-THING TO DO WITH THIS CASE...

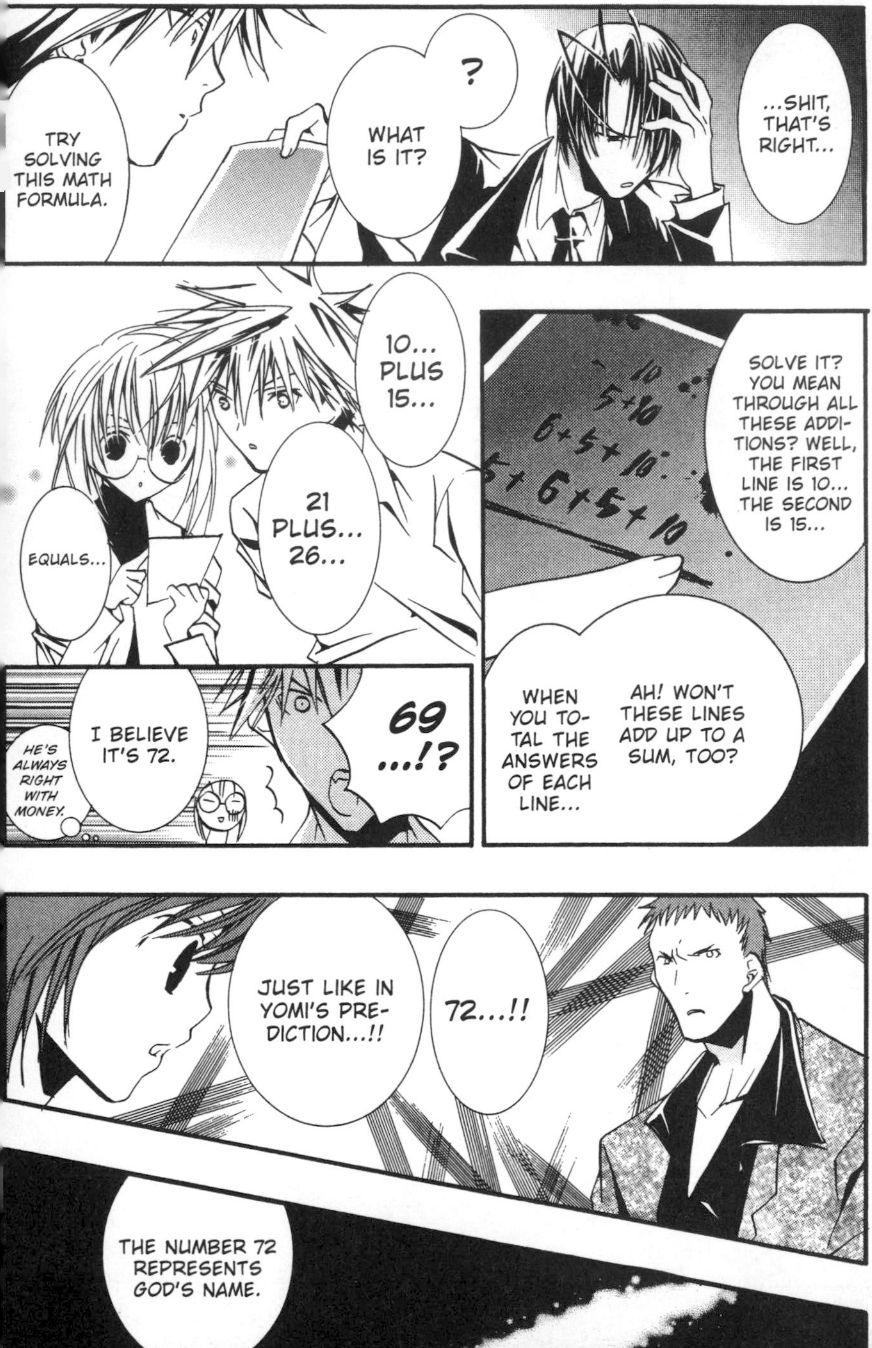
...SHIT, THAT'S RIGHT...
?
WHAT IS IT?
TRY SOLVING THIS MATH FORMULA.
SOLVE IT? YOU MEAN THROUGH ALL THESE ADDITIONS? WELL, THE FIRST LINE IS 10... THE SECOND IS 15...
AH! WON'T THESE LINES ADD UP TO A SUM, TOO?
WHEN YOU TOTAL THE ANSWERS OF EACH LINE...
10... PLUS 15...
21 PLUS... 26...
EQUALS...
69 ...!?
I BELIEVE IT'S 72.
HE'S ALWAYS RIGHT WITH MONEY.
72...!!
JUST LIKE IN YOMI'S PREDICTION...!!
THE NUMBER 72 REPRESENTS GOD'S NAME.

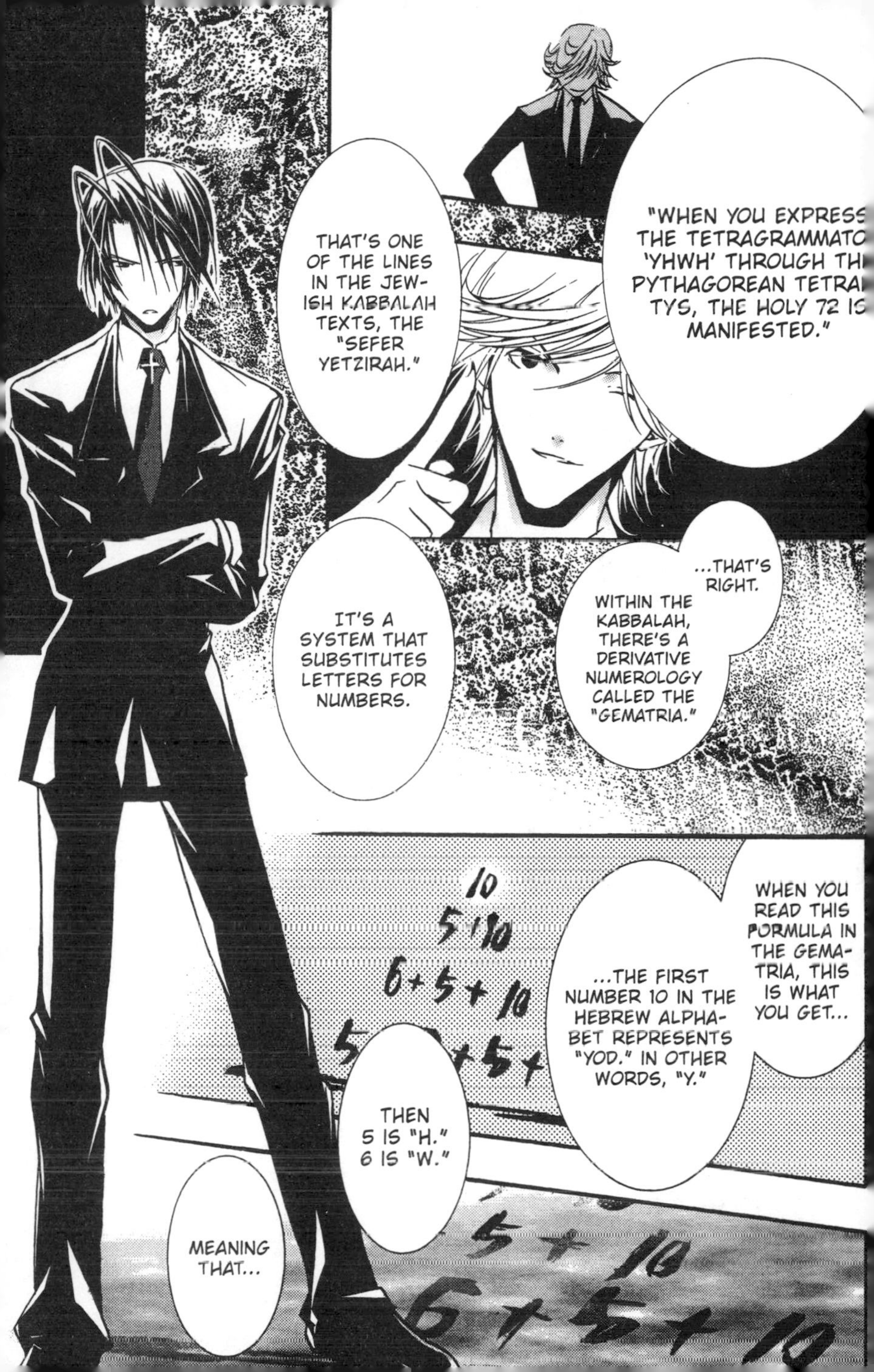
"WHEN YOU EXPRESS THE TETRAGRAMMATON 'YHWH' THROUGH THE PYTHAGOREAN TETRAKTYS, THE HOLY 72 IS MANIFESTED."
THAT'S ONE OF THE LINES IN THE JEWISH KABBALAH TEXTS, THE "SEFER YETZIRAH."
...THAT'S RIGHT.
WITHIN THE KABBALAH, THERE'S A DERIVATIVE NUMEROLOGY CALLED THE "GEMATRIA."
IT'S A SYSTEM THAT SUBSTITUTES LETTERS FOR NUMBERS.
WHEN YOU READ THIS FORMULA IN THE GEMATRIA, THIS IS WHAT YOU GET...
10
5+10
6+5+10
...THE FIRST NUMBER 10 IN THE HEBREW ALPHABET REPRESENTS "YOD." IN OTHER WORDS, "Y."
THEN 5 IS "H." 6 IS "W."
MEANING THAT...

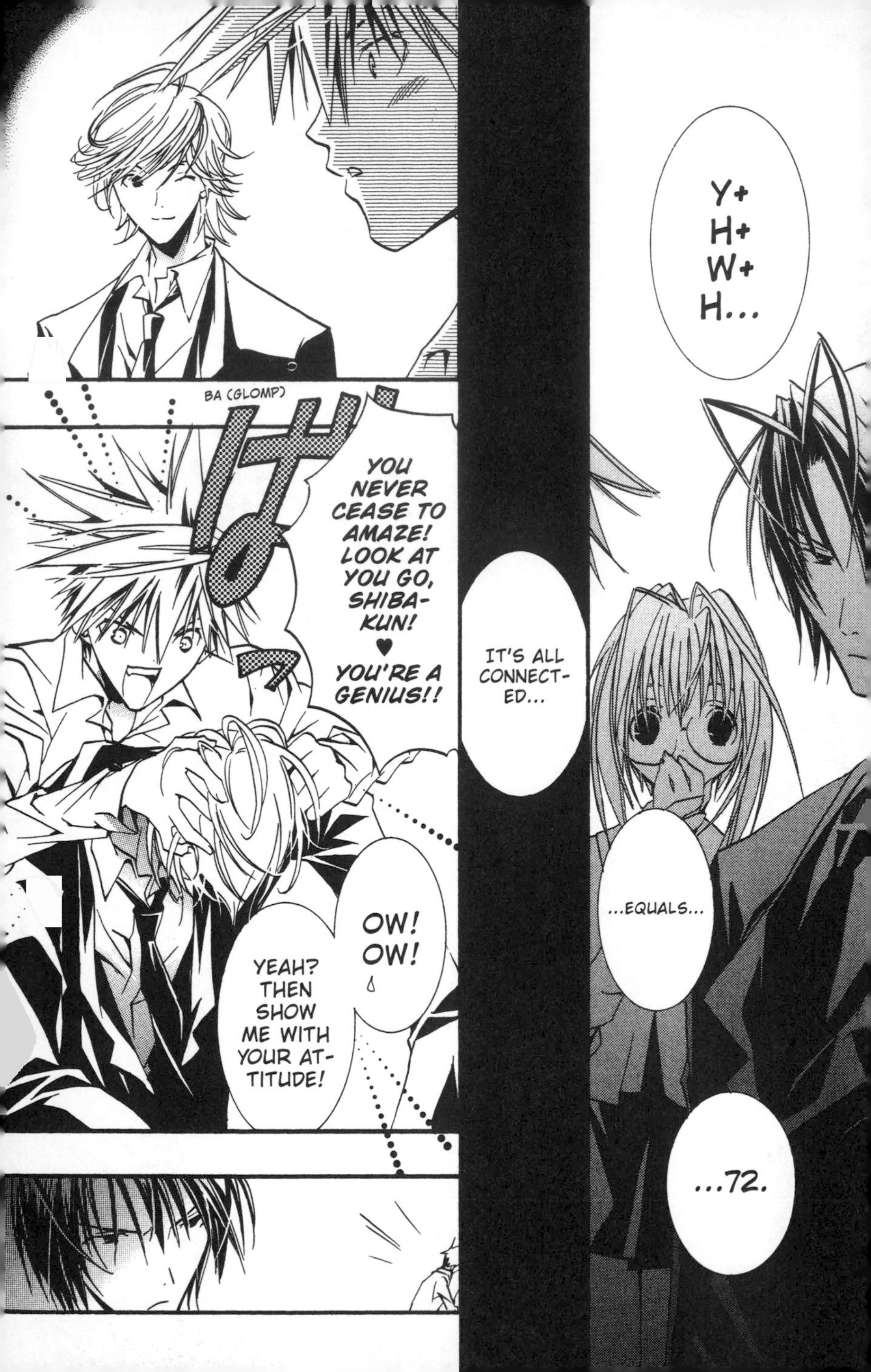
Y+ H+ W+ H...
IT'S ALL CONNECT-ED...
...EQUALS...
...72.
BA (GLOMP)
YOU NEVER CEASE TO AMAZE! LOOK AT YOU GO, SHIBA-KUN! ♥ YOU'RE A GENIUS!!
OW! OW!
YEAH? THEN SHOW ME WITH YOUR AT-TITUDE!

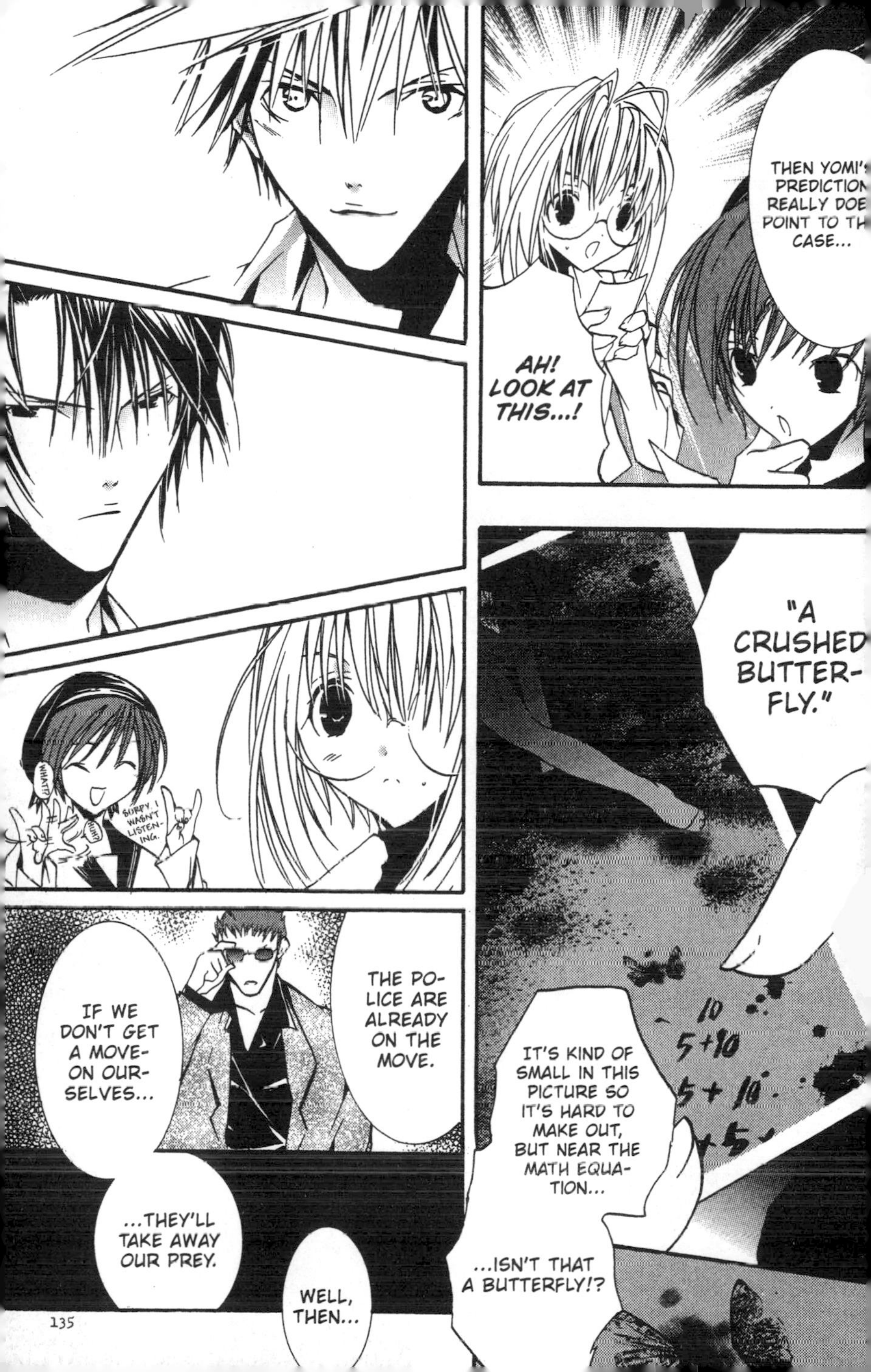
THEN YOMI'S PREDICTION REALLY DOE POINT TO TH CASE...
AH! LOOK AT THIS...!
"A CRUSHED BUTTER-FLY."
IT'S KIND OF SMALL IN THIS PICTURE SO IT'S HARD TO MAKE OUT, BUT NEAR THE MATH EQUA-TION...
10
5+10
5+10
...ISN'T THAT A BUTTERFLY!?
WHAT?!
HUH?
SORRY, I WASN'T LISTEN-ING.
THE PO-LICE ARE ALREADY ON THE MOVE.
IF WE DON'T GET A MOVE-ON OUR-SELVES...
...THEY'LL TAKE AWAY OUR PREY.
WELL, THEN...

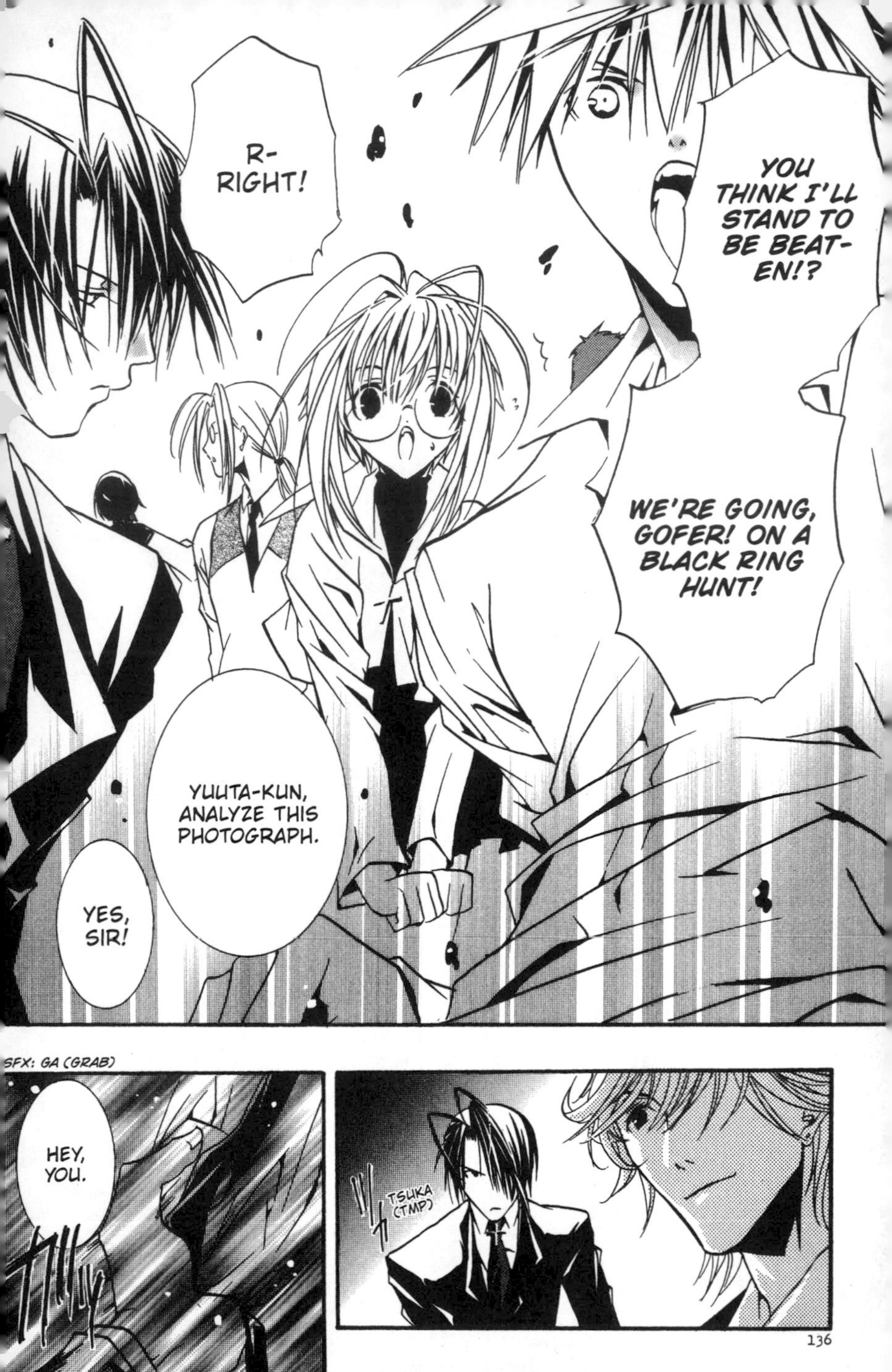
YOU THINK I'LL STAND TO BE BEAT-EN!?
R-RIGHT!
WE'RE GOING, GOFER! ON A BLACK RING HUNT!
YUUTA-KUN, ANALYZE THIS PHOTOGRAPH.
YES, SIR!
SFX: GA (GRAB)
TSUKA (TMP)
HEY, YOU.

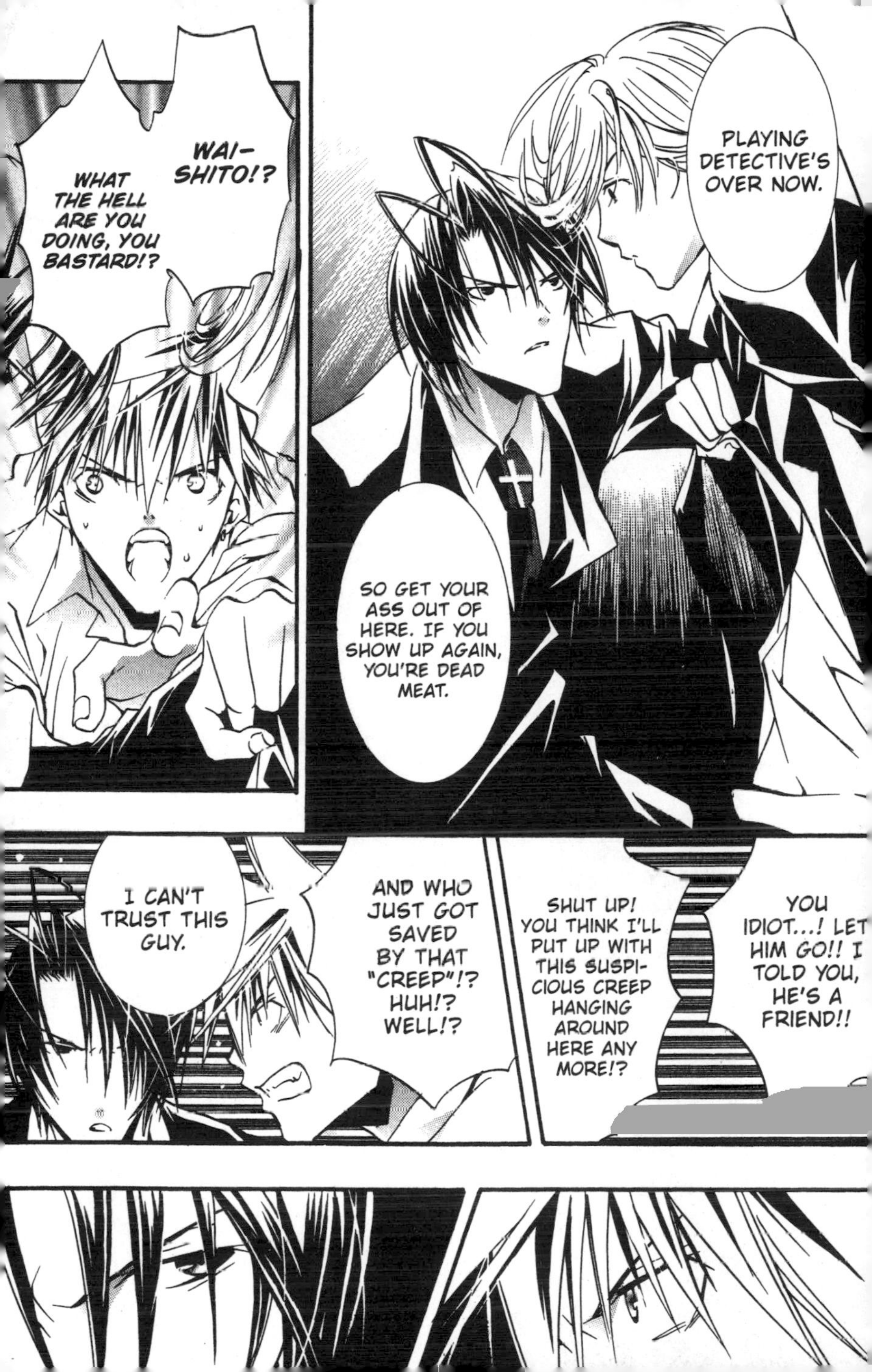
PLAYING DETECTIVE'S OVER NOW.
SO GET YOUR ASS OUT OF HERE. IF YOU SHOW UP AGAIN, YOU'RE DEAD MEAT.
WAI-SHITO!?
WHAT THE HELL ARE YOU DOING, YOU BASTARD!?
YOU IDIOT...! LET HIM GO!! I TOLD YOU, HE'S A FRIEND!!
SHUT UP! YOU THINK I'LL PUT UP WITH THIS SUSPICIOUS CREEP HANGING AROUND HERE ANY MORE!?
AND WHO JUST GOT SAVED BY THAT "CREEP"!? HUH!? WELL!?
I CAN'T TRUST THIS GUY.

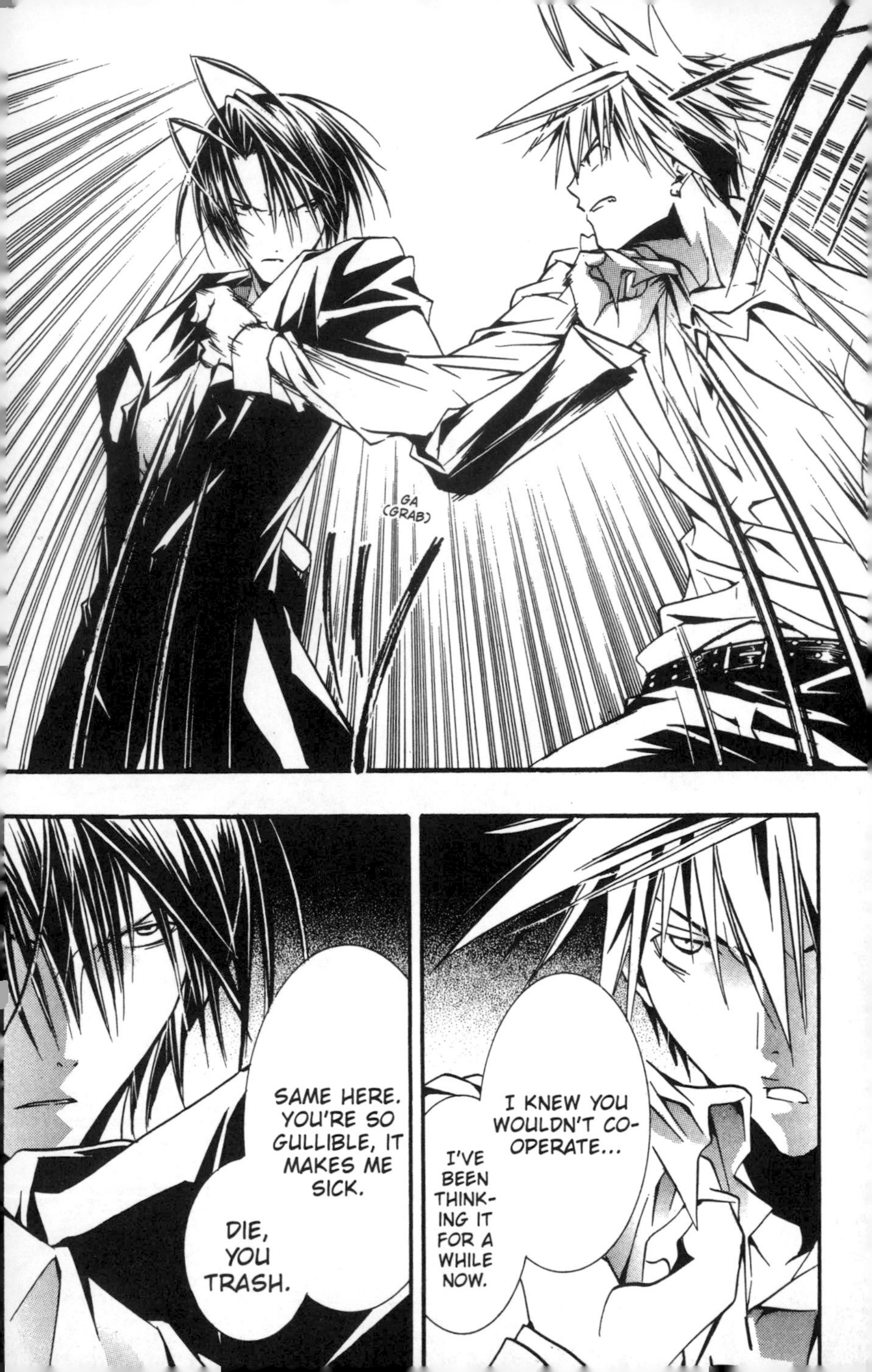
GA (GRAB)
I KNEW YOU WOULDN'T CO-OPERATE...
I'VE BEEN THINKING IT FOR A WHILE NOW.
SAME HERE. YOU'RE SO GULLIBLE, IT MAKES ME SICK.
DIE, YOU TRASH.

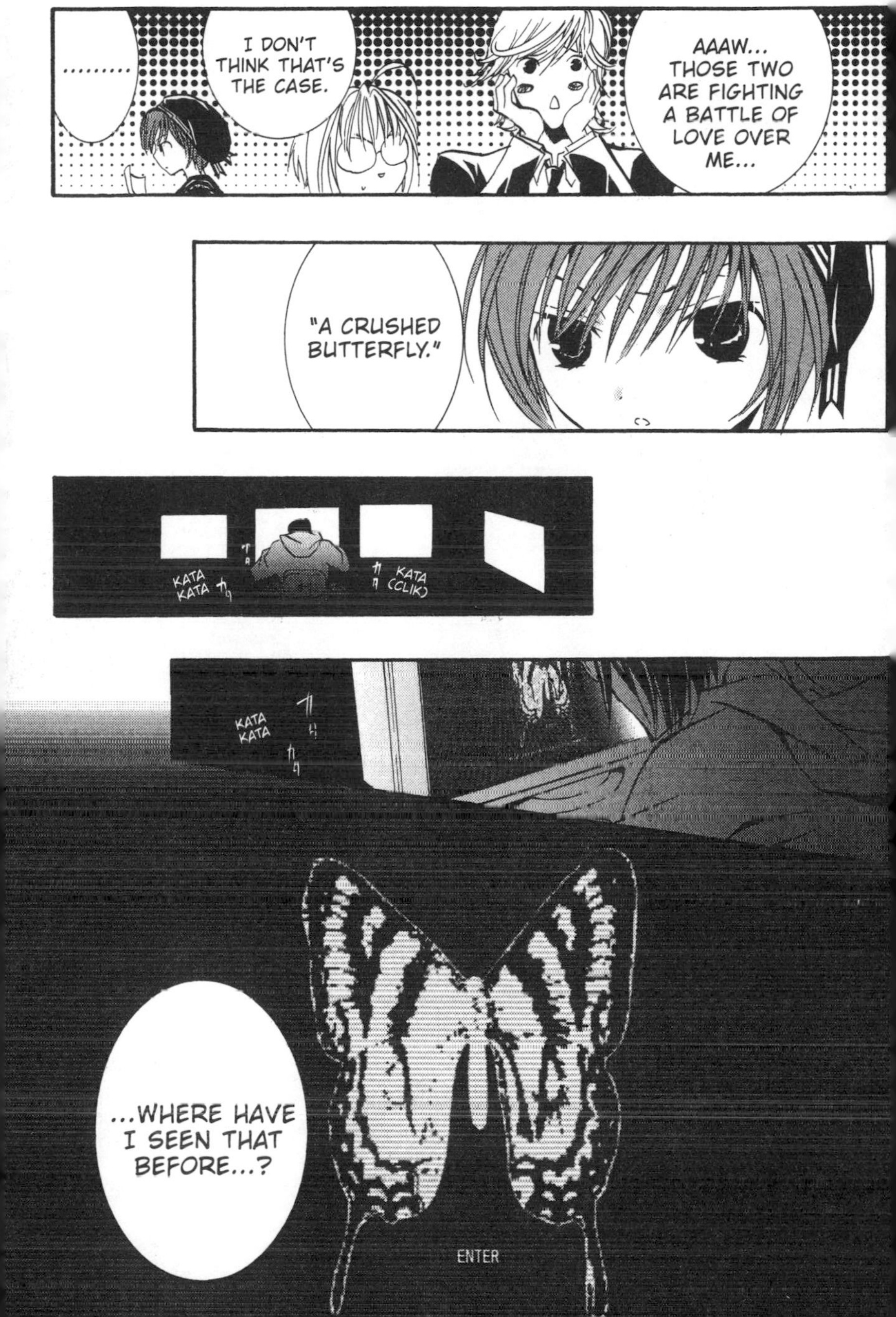
AAAW... THOSE TWO ARE FIGHTING A BATTLE OF LOVE OVER ME...
I DON'T THINK THAT'S THE CASE.
....
"A CRUSHED BUTTERFLY."
KATA (CLIK)
KATA KATA
KATA KATA
ENTER
...WHERE HAVE I SEEN THAT BEFORE...?

SHITO TACHIBANA

5'9.3"/141lb
blood type:AB
birthday:1/21

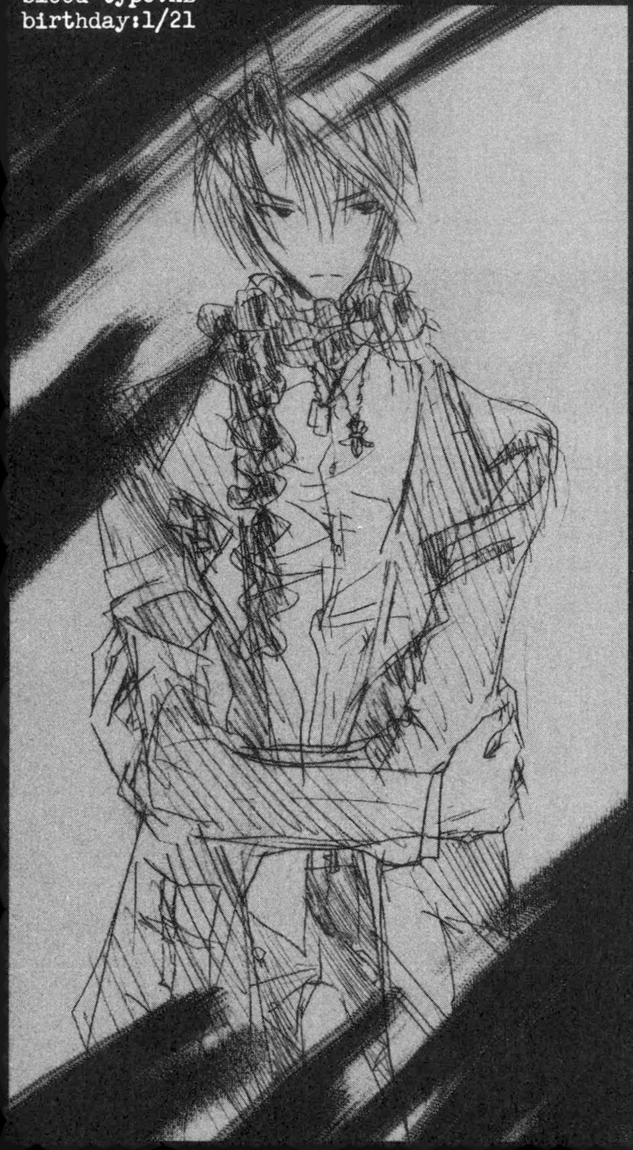

ZOMBIE-LOAN

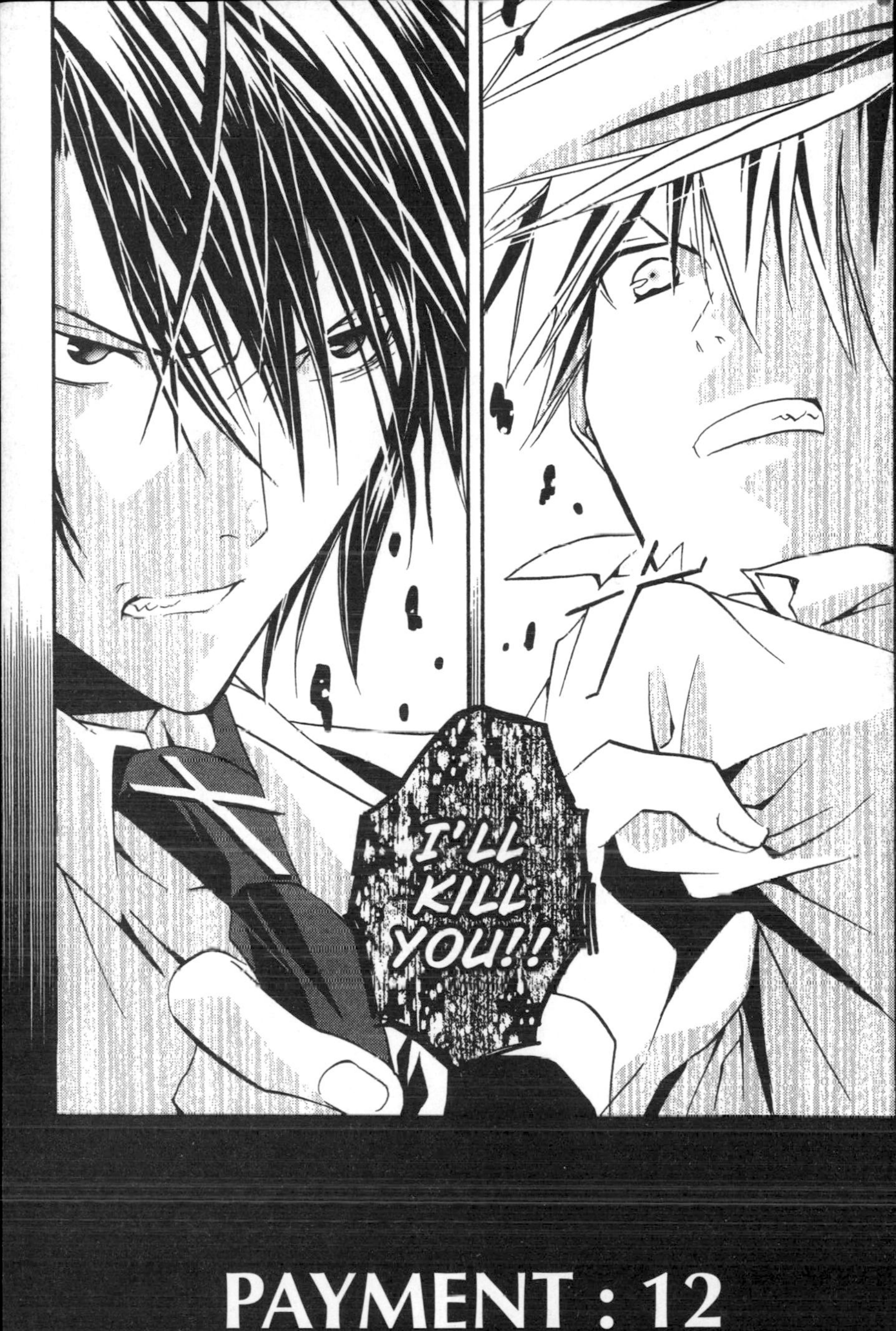
I'LL KILL YOU!!

PAYMENT : 12

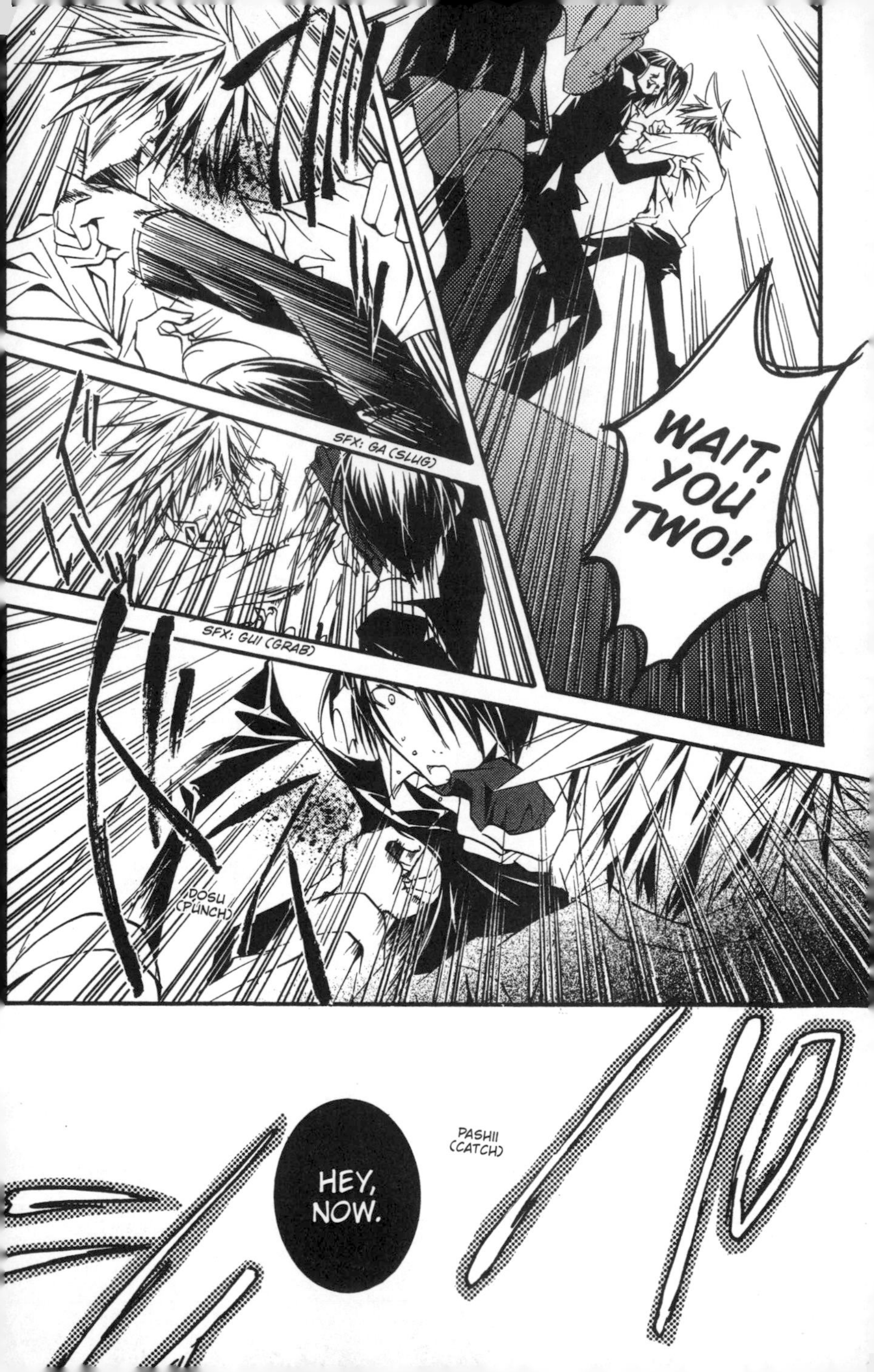
WAIT, YOU TWO!
SFX: GA (SLUG)
SFX: GUI (GRAB)
DOSU (PUNCH)
PASHII (CATCH)
HEY, NOW.

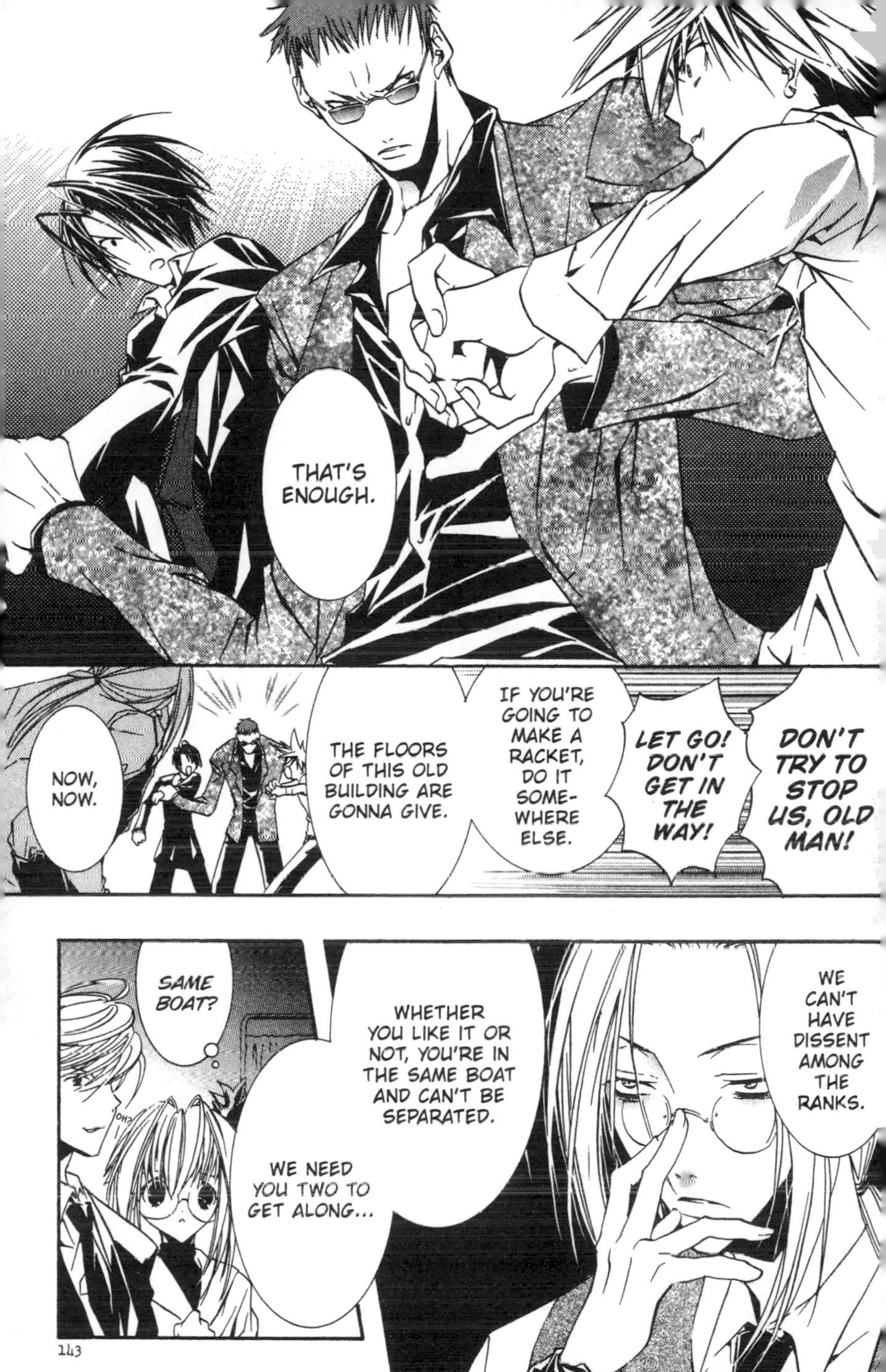
THAT'S ENOUGH.
DON'T TRY TO STOP US, OLD MAN!
LET GO! DON'T GET IN THE WAY!
IF YOU'RE GOING TO MAKE A RACKET, DO IT SOMEWHERE ELSE.
THE FLOORS OF THIS OLD BUILDING ARE GONNA GIVE.
NOW, NOW.
WE CAN'T HAVE DISSENT AMONG THE RANKS.
WHETHER YOU LIKE IT OR NOT, YOU'RE IN THE SAME BOAT AND CAN'T BE SEPARATED.
WE NEED YOU TWO TO GET ALONG...
SAME BOAT?

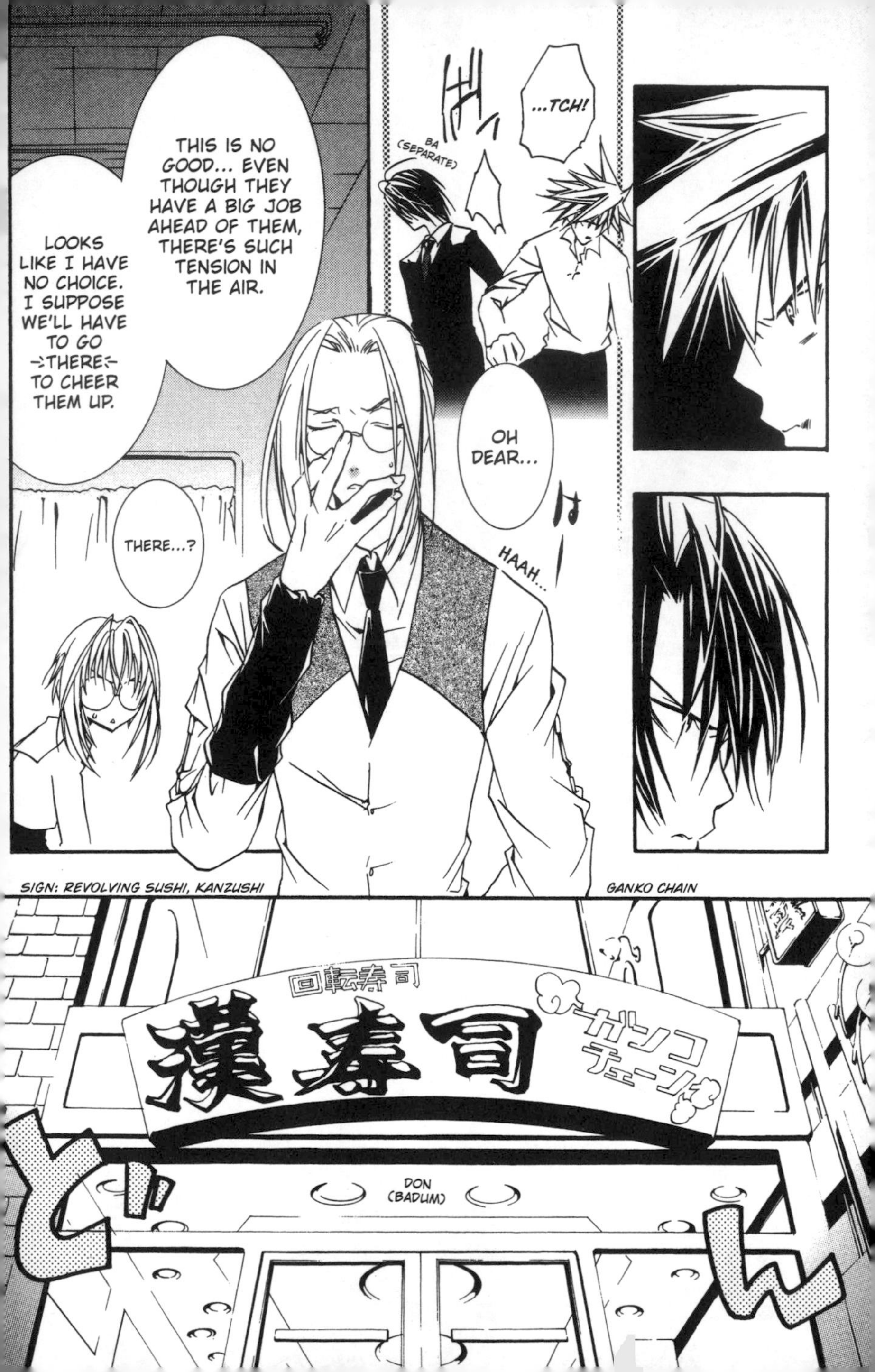
BA
(SEPARATE)
...TCH!
OH DEAR...
HAAH...
THIS IS NO GOOD... EVEN THOUGH THEY HAVE A BIG JOB AHEAD OF THEM, THERE'S SUCH TENSION IN THE AIR.
LOOKS LIKE I HAVE NO CHOICE. I SUPPOSE WE'LL HAVE TO GO ⇝THERE⇜ TO CHEER THEM UP.
THERE...?
GANKO CHAIN
SIGN: REVOLVING SUSHI, KANZUSHI
回転寿司
漢寿司
ガンコチェーン
DON
(BADUM)

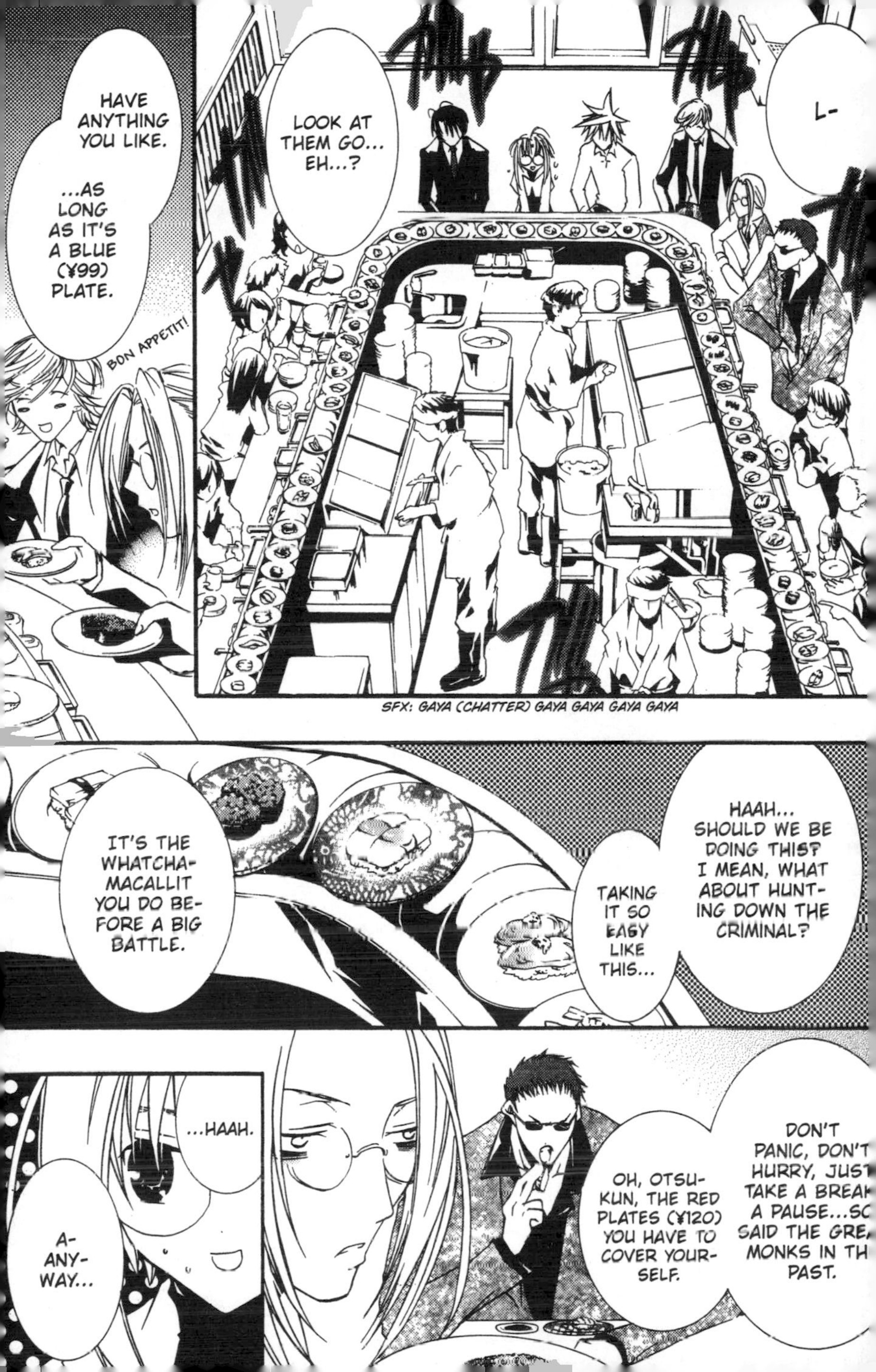
L-
LOOK AT THEM GO... EH...?
SFX: GAYA (CHATTER) GAYA GAYA GAYA GAYA
HAVE ANYTHING YOU LIKE.
...AS LONG AS IT'S A BLUE (¥99) PLATE.
BON APPETIT!
HAAH... SHOULD WE BE DOING THIS? I MEAN, WHAT ABOUT HUNT-ING DOWN THE CRIMINAL?
TAKING IT SO EASY LIKE THIS...
IT'S THE WHATCHA-MACALLIT YOU DO BE-FORE A BIG BATTLE.
DON'T PANIC, DON'T HURRY, JUST TAKE A BREAK A PAUSE...SO SAID THE GREA MONKS IN TH PAST.
OH, OTSU-KUN, THE RED PLATES (¥120) YOU HAVE TO COVER YOUR-SELF.
...HAAH.
A-ANY-WAY...

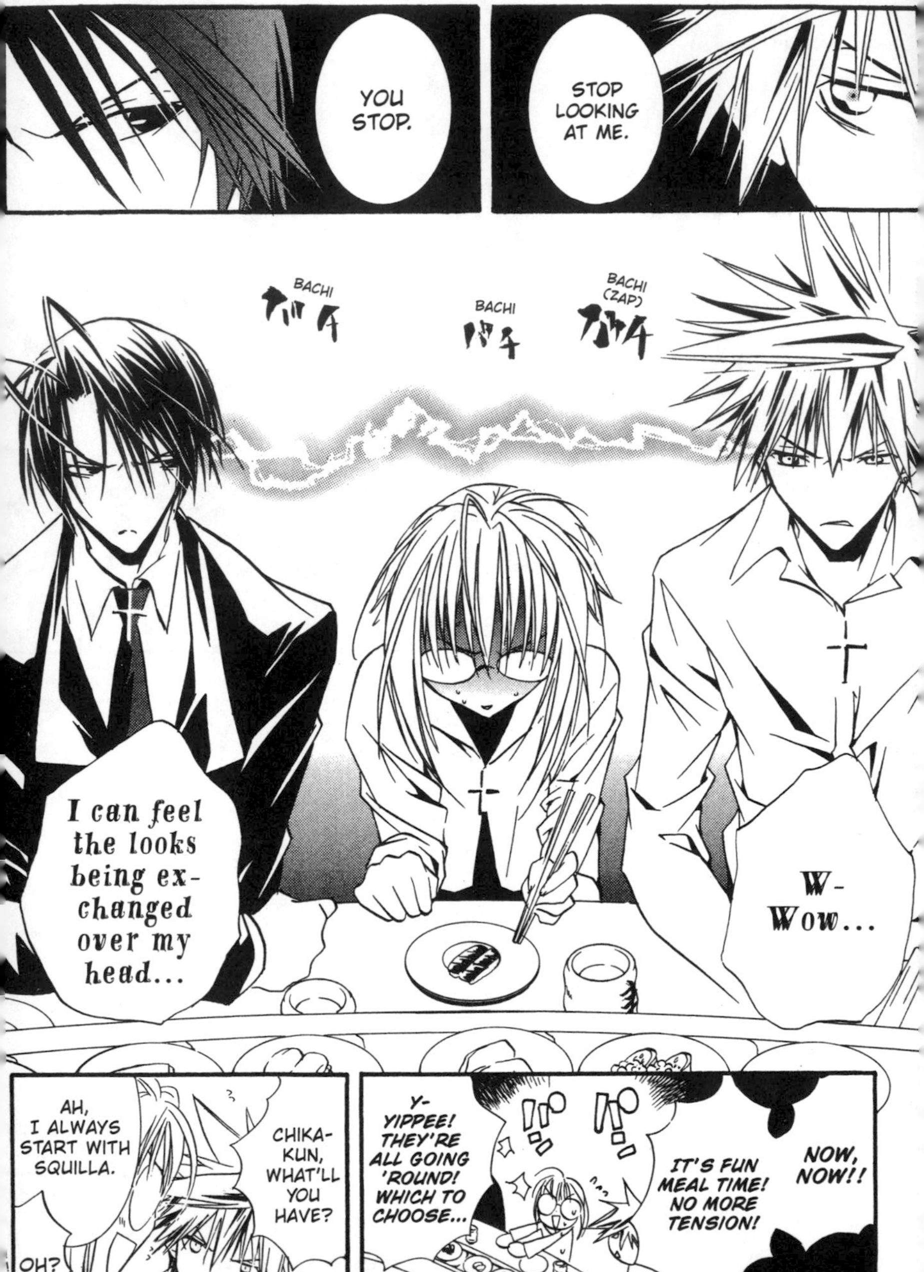
STOP LOOKING AT ME.
YOU STOP.
BACHI (ZAP)
BACHI
BACHI
W-Wow...
I can feel the looks being ex-changed over my head...
NOW, NOW!!
IT'S FUN MEAL TIME! NO MORE TENSION!
Y-YIPPEE! THEY'RE ALL GOING 'ROUND! WHICH TO CHOOSE...
CHIKA-KUN, WHAT'LL YOU HAVE?
AH, I ALWAYS START WITH SQUILLA.
OH?
SFX: PAN (CLAP) PAN

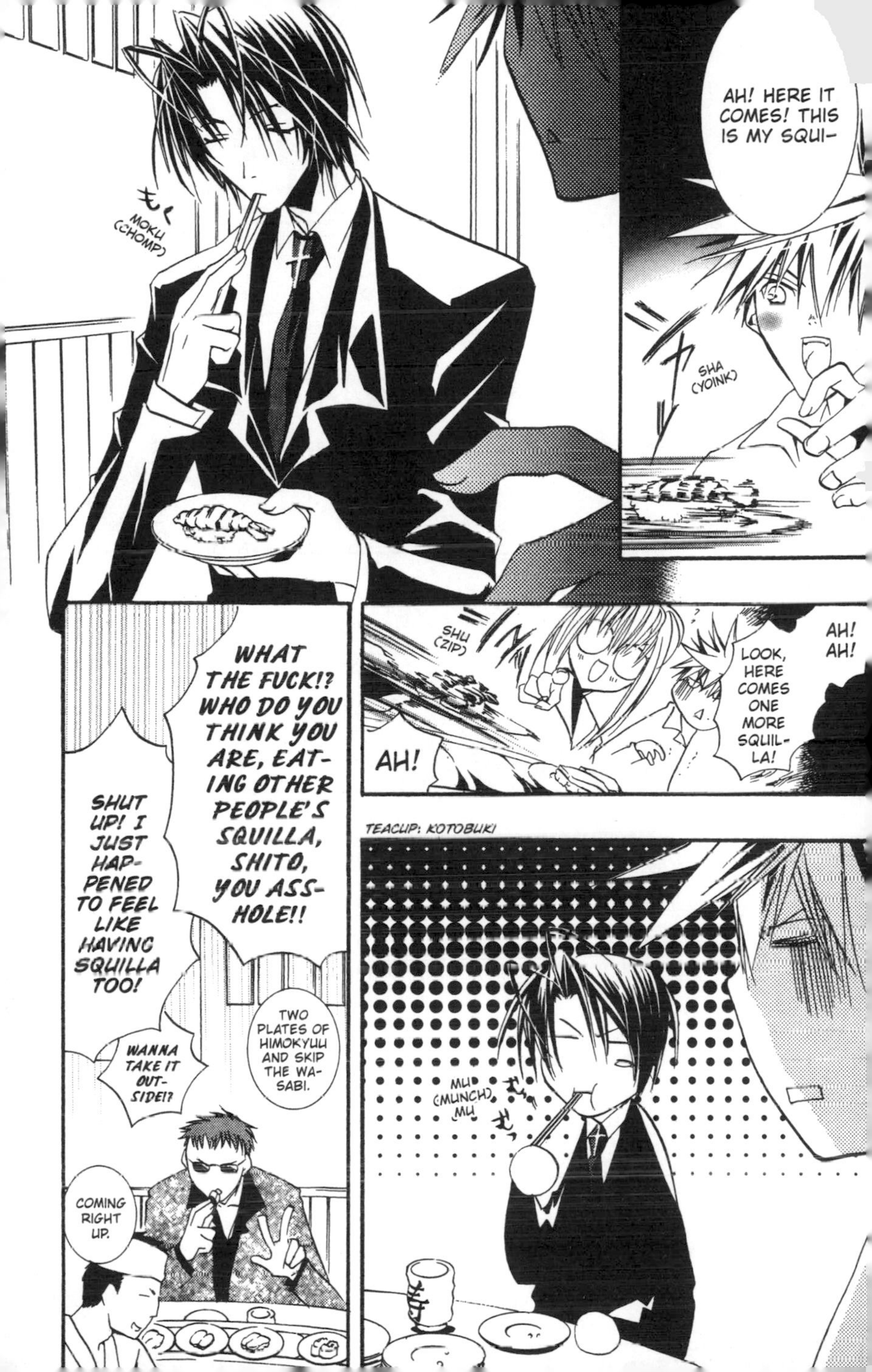
AH! HERE IT COMES! THIS IS MY SQUI-
SHA (YOINK)
もく
MOKU (CHOMP)
AH! AH!
LOOK, HERE COMES ONE MORE SQUIL-LA!
SHU (ZIP)
AH!
TEACUP: KOTOBUKI
MU (MUNCH) MU
WHAT THE FUCK!? WHO DO YOU THINK YOU ARE, EAT-ING OTHER PEOPLE'S SQUILLA, SHITO, YOU ASS-HOLE!!
SHUT UP! I JUST HAP-PENED TO FEEL LIKE HAVING SQUILLA TOO!
TWO PLATES OF HIMOKYUU AND SKIP THE WA-SABI.
WANNA TAKE IT OUT-SIDE!?
COMING RIGHT UP.

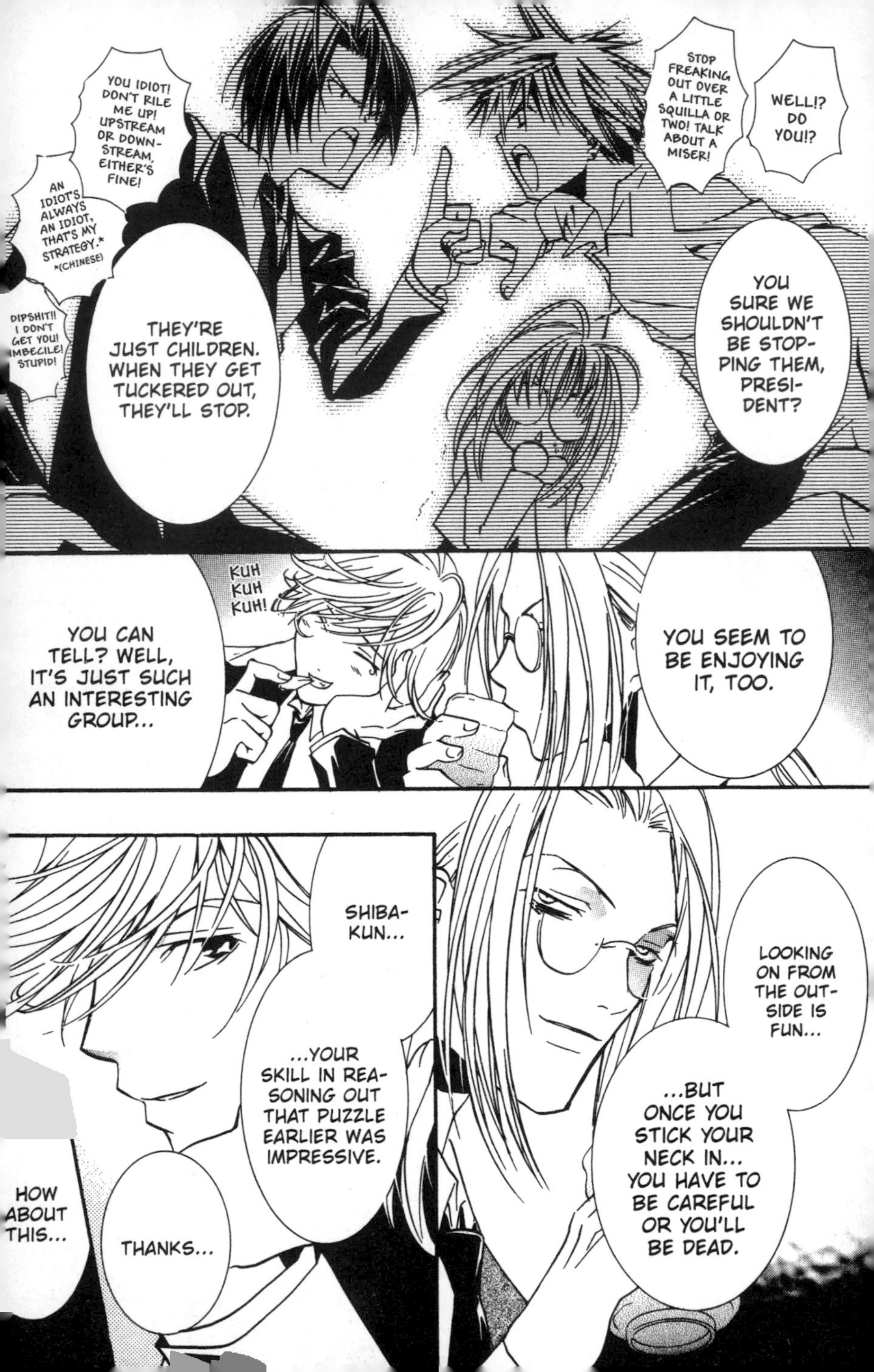
WELL!? DO YOU!?
STOP FREAKING OUT OVER A LITTLE SQUILLA OR TWO! TALK ABOUT A MISER!
YOU IDIOT! DON'T RILE ME UP! UPSTREAM OR DOWN-STREAM, EITHER'S FINE!
AN IDIOT'S ALWAYS AN IDIOT, THAT'S MY STRATEGY.* *(CHINESE)
DIPSHIT!! I DON'T GET YOU! IMBECILE! STUPID!
YOU SURE WE SHOULDN'T BE STOP-PING THEM, PRESI-DENT?
THEY'RE JUST CHILDREN. WHEN THEY GET TUCKERED OUT, THEY'LL STOP.
YOU SEEM TO BE ENJOYING IT, TOO.
KUH KUH KUH!
YOU CAN TELL? WELL, IT'S JUST SUCH AN INTERESTING GROUP...
LOOKING ON FROM THE OUT-SIDE IS FUN...
...BUT ONCE YOU STICK YOUR NECK IN... YOU HAVE TO BE CAREFUL OR YOU'LL BE DEAD.
SHIBA-KUN...
...YOUR SKILL IN REA-SONING OUT THAT PUZZLE EARLIER WAS IMPRESSIVE.
THANKS...
HOW ABOUT THIS...

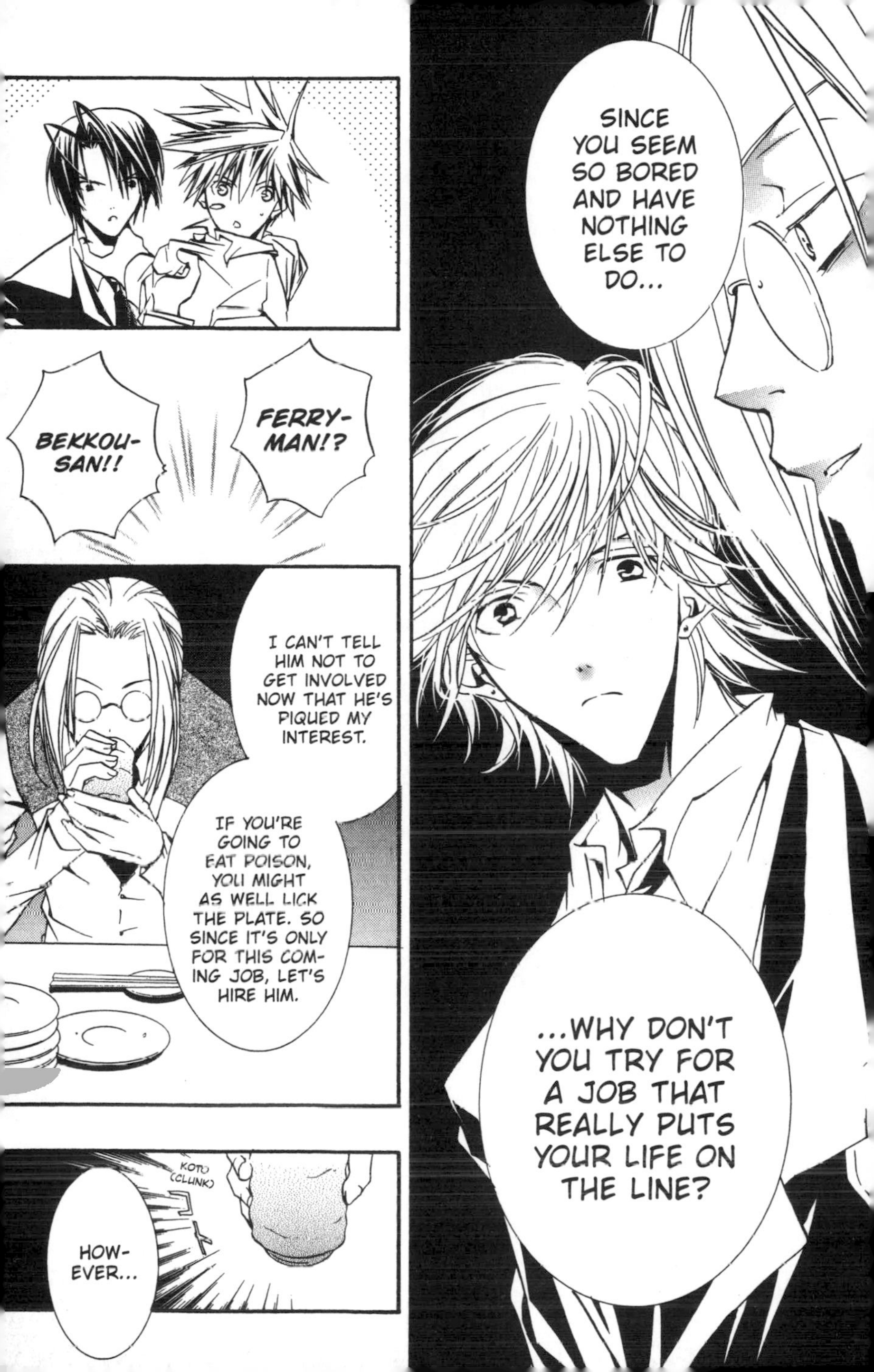
BEKKOU-SAN!!
FERRY-MAN!?
I CAN'T TELL HIM NOT TO GET INVOLVED NOW THAT HE'S PIQUED MY INTEREST.
IF YOU'RE GOING TO EAT POISON, YOU MIGHT AS WELL LICK THE PLATE. SO SINCE IT'S ONLY FOR THIS COMING JOB, LET'S HIRE HIM.
KOTO (CLUNK)
HOW-EVER...
SINCE YOU SEEM SO BORED AND HAVE NOTHING ELSE TO DO...
...WHY DON'T YOU TRY FOR A JOB THAT REALLY PUTS YOUR LIFE ON THE LINE?

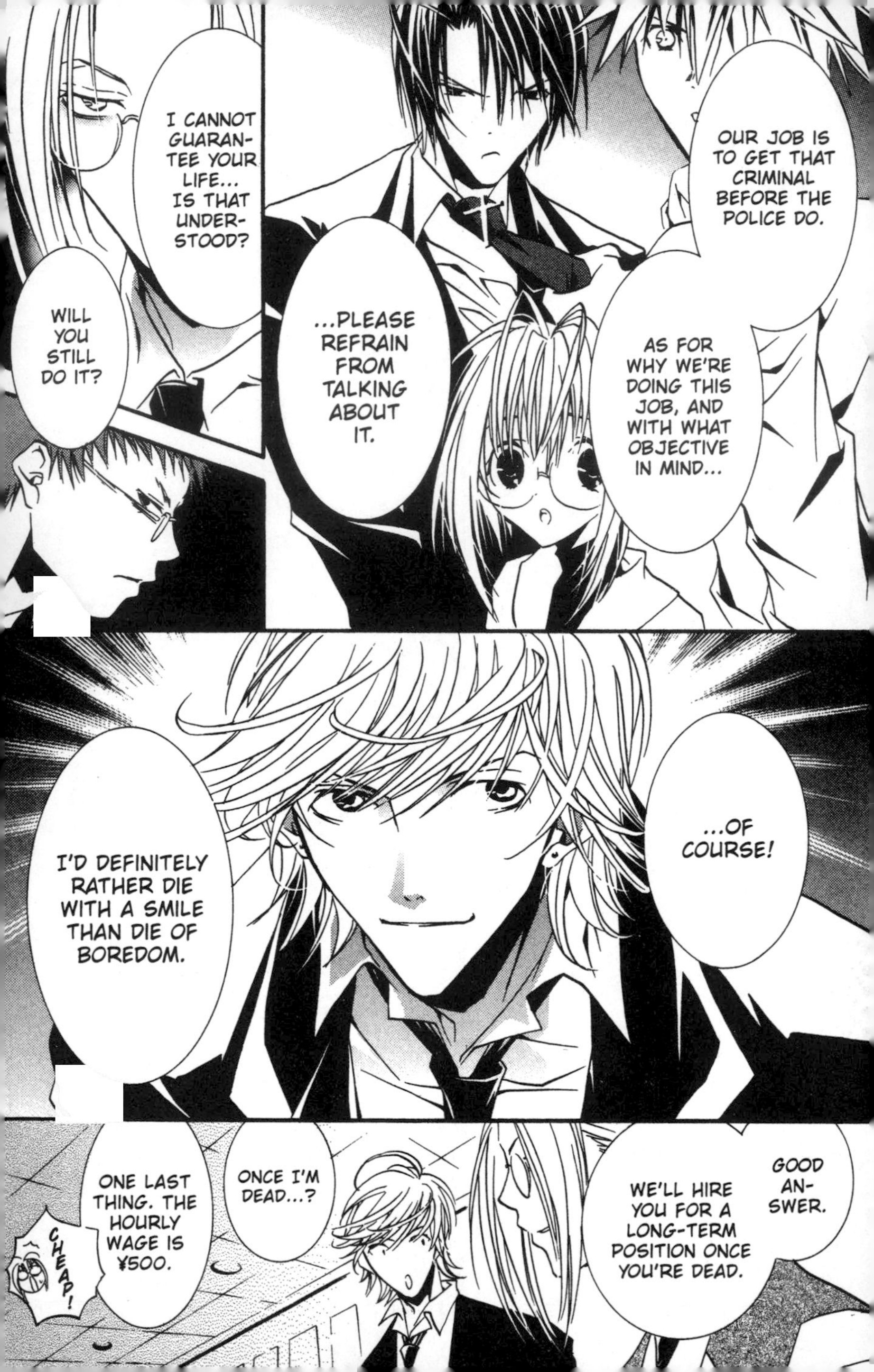
OUR JOB IS TO GET THAT CRIMINAL BEFORE THE POLICE DO.
AS FOR WHY WE'RE DOING THIS JOB, AND WITH WHAT OBJECTIVE IN MIND...
...PLEASE REFRAIN FROM TALKING ABOUT IT.
I CANNOT GUARAN-TEE YOUR LIFE... IS THAT UNDER-STOOD?
WILL YOU STILL DO IT?
...OF COURSE!
I'D DEFINITELY RATHER DIE WITH A SMILE THAN DIE OF BOREDOM.
GOOD AN-SWER.
WE'LL HIRE YOU FOR A LONG-TERM POSITION ONCE YOU'RE DEAD.
ONCE I'M DEAD...?
ONE LAST THING. THE HOURLY WAGE IS ¥500.
CHEAP!

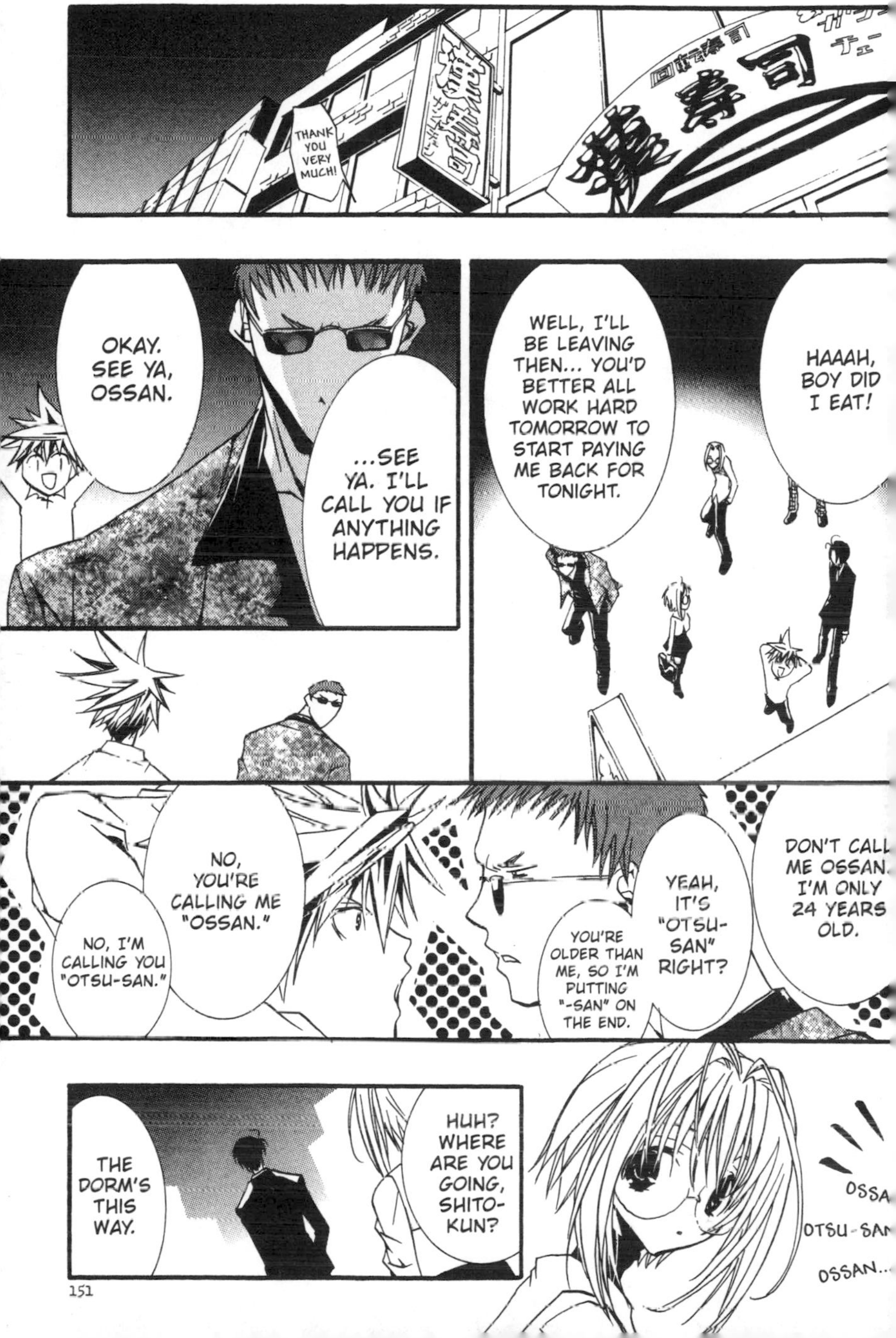
THANK YOU VERY MUCH!
HAAAH, BOY DID I EAT!
WELL, I'LL BE LEAVING THEN... YOU'D BETTER ALL WORK HARD TOMORROW TO START PAYING ME BACK FOR TONIGHT.
...SEE YA. I'LL CALL YOU IF ANYTHING HAPPENS.
OKAY. SEE YA, OSSAN.
DON'T CALL ME OSSAN. I'M ONLY 24 YEARS OLD.
YEAH, IT'S "OTSU-SAN" RIGHT?
YOU'RE OLDER THAN ME, SO I'M PUTTING "-SAN" ON THE END.
NO, YOU'RE CALLING ME "OSSAN."
NO, I'M CALLING YOU "OTSU-SAN."
OSSA
OTSU-SAN
OSSAN...
HUH? WHERE ARE YOU GOING, SHITO-KUN?
THE DORM'S THIS WAY.

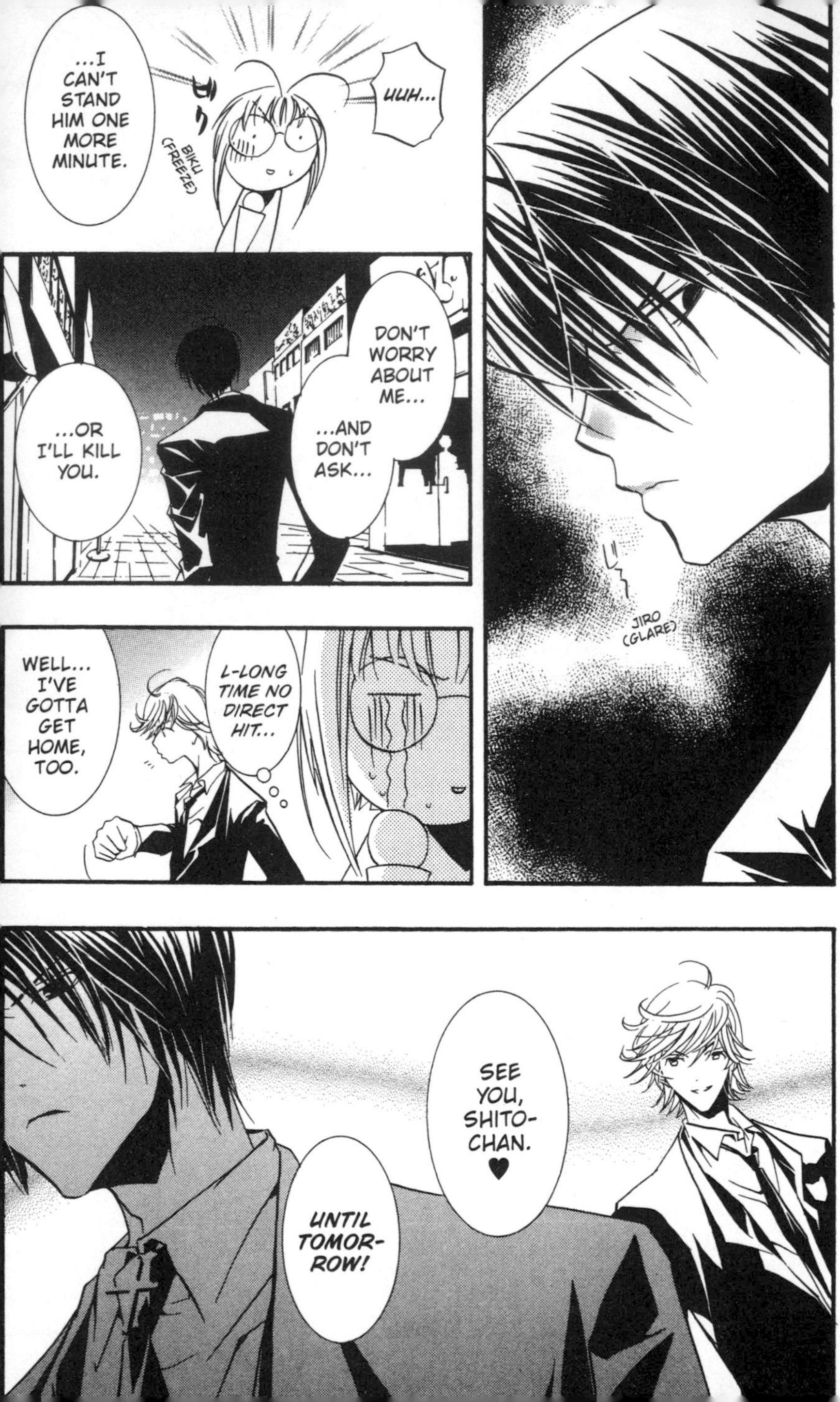
JIRO (GLARE)
UUH...
BIKU (FREEZE)
...I CAN'T STAND HIM ONE MORE MINUTE.
DON'T WORRY ABOUT ME...
...AND DON'T ASK...
...OR I'LL KILL YOU.
L-LONG TIME NO DIRECT HIT...
WELL... I'VE GOTTA GET HOME, TOO.
SEE YOU, SHITO-CHAN. ♥
UNTIL TOMORROW!

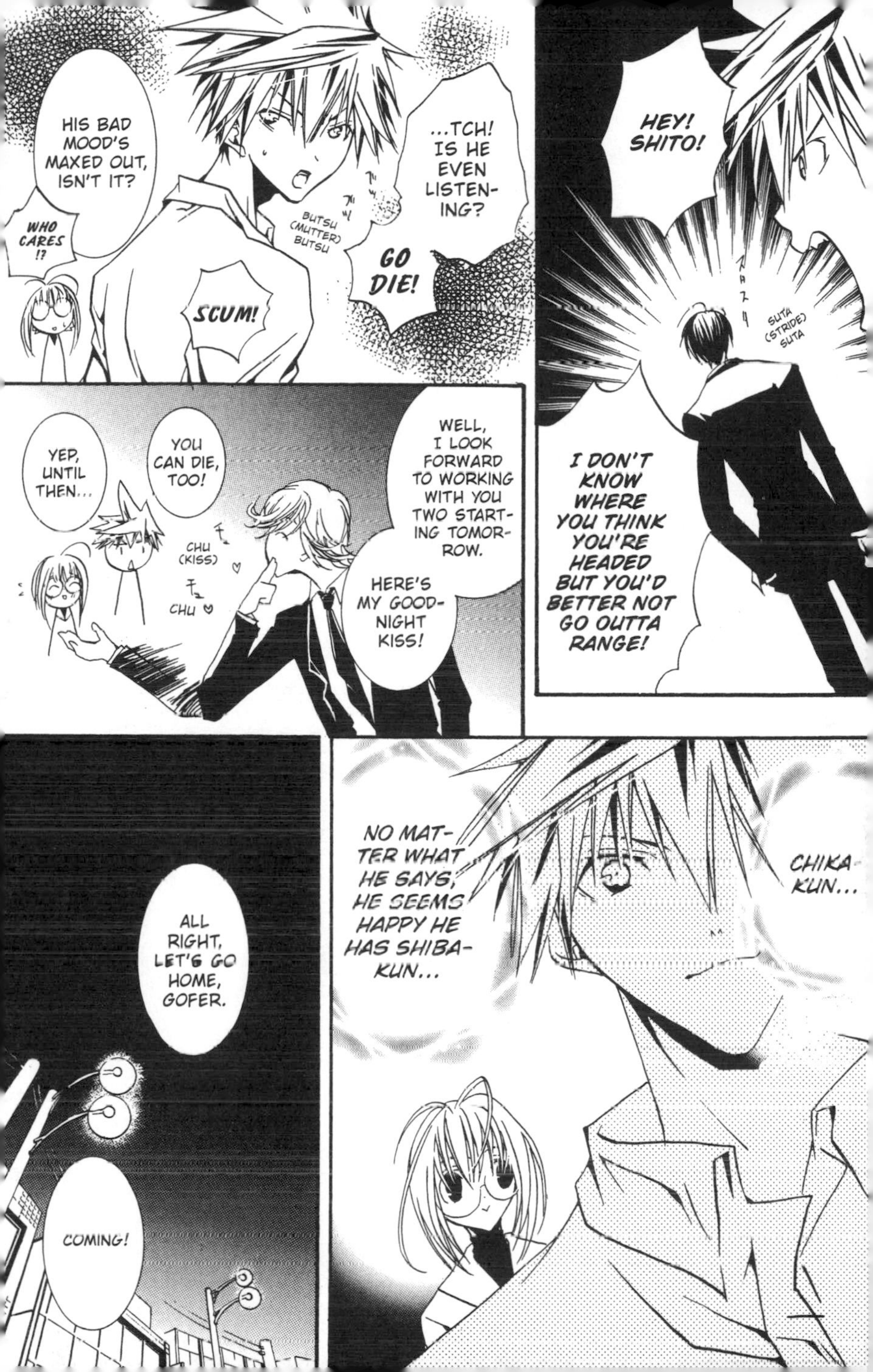
HEY! SHITO!
SUTA (STRIDE) SUTA
I DON'T KNOW WHERE YOU THINK YOU'RE HEADED BUT YOU'D BETTER NOT GO OUTTA RANGE!
...TCH! IS HE EVEN LISTENING?
GO DIE!
BUTSU (MUTTER) BUTSU
HIS BAD MOOD'S MAXED OUT, ISN'T IT?
SCUM!
WHO CARES!?
WELL, I LOOK FORWARD TO WORKING WITH YOU TWO STARTING TOMORROW.
HERE'S MY GOOD-NIGHT KISS!
YOU CAN DIE, TOO!
CHU (KISS)
CHU
YEP, UNTIL THEN...
CHIKA-KUN...
NO MATTER WHAT HE SAYS, HE SEEMS HAPPY HE HAS SHIBA-KUN...
ALL RIGHT, LET'S GO HOME, GOFER.
COMING!

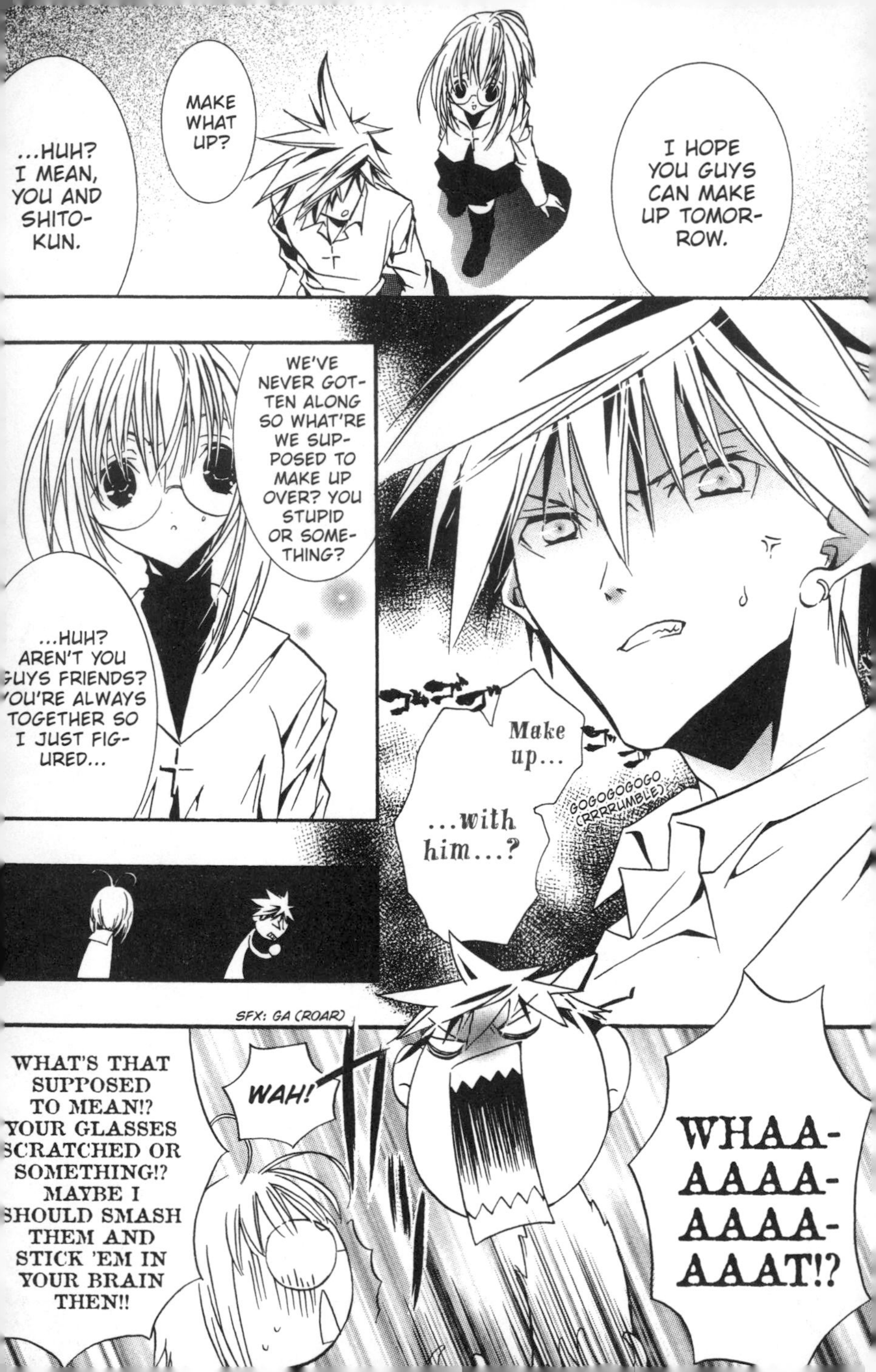
I HOPE YOU GUYS CAN MAKE UP TOMORROW.
MAKE WHAT UP?
...HUH? I MEAN, YOU AND SHITO-KUN.
Make up...
...with him...?
GOGOGOGOGO (RRRRUMBLE)
WE'VE NEVER GOTTEN ALONG SO WHAT'RE WE SUPPOSED TO MAKE UP OVER? YOU STUPID OR SOMETHING?
...HUH? AREN'T YOU GUYS FRIENDS? YOU'RE ALWAYS TOGETHER SO I JUST FIGURED...
WHAAAAAAAAAAAAT!?
WAH!
SFX: GA (ROAR)
WHAT'S THAT SUPPOSED TO MEAN!? YOUR GLASSES SCRATCHED OR SOMETHING!? MAYBE I SHOULD SMASH THEM AND STICK 'EM IN YOUR BRAIN THEN!!

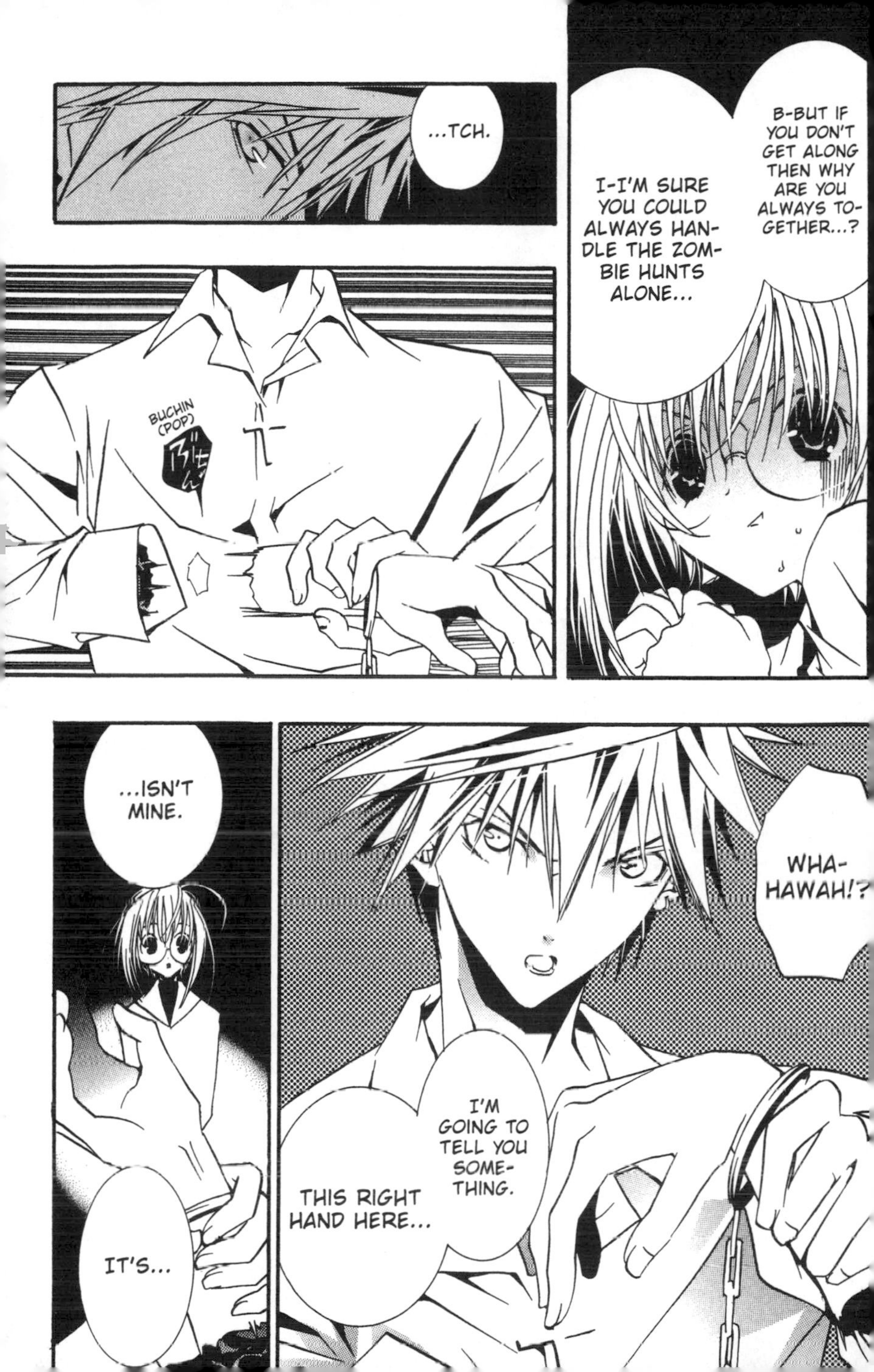

B-BUT IF YOU DON'T GET ALONG THEN WHY ARE YOU ALWAYS TO-GETHER...?
I-I'M SURE YOU COULD ALWAYS HAN-DLE THE ZOM-BIE HUNTS ALONE...
...TCH.
BUCHIN (POP)
WHA-HAWAH!?
I'M GOING TO TELL YOU SOME-THING.
THIS RIGHT HAND HERE...
IT'S...
...ISN'T MINE.

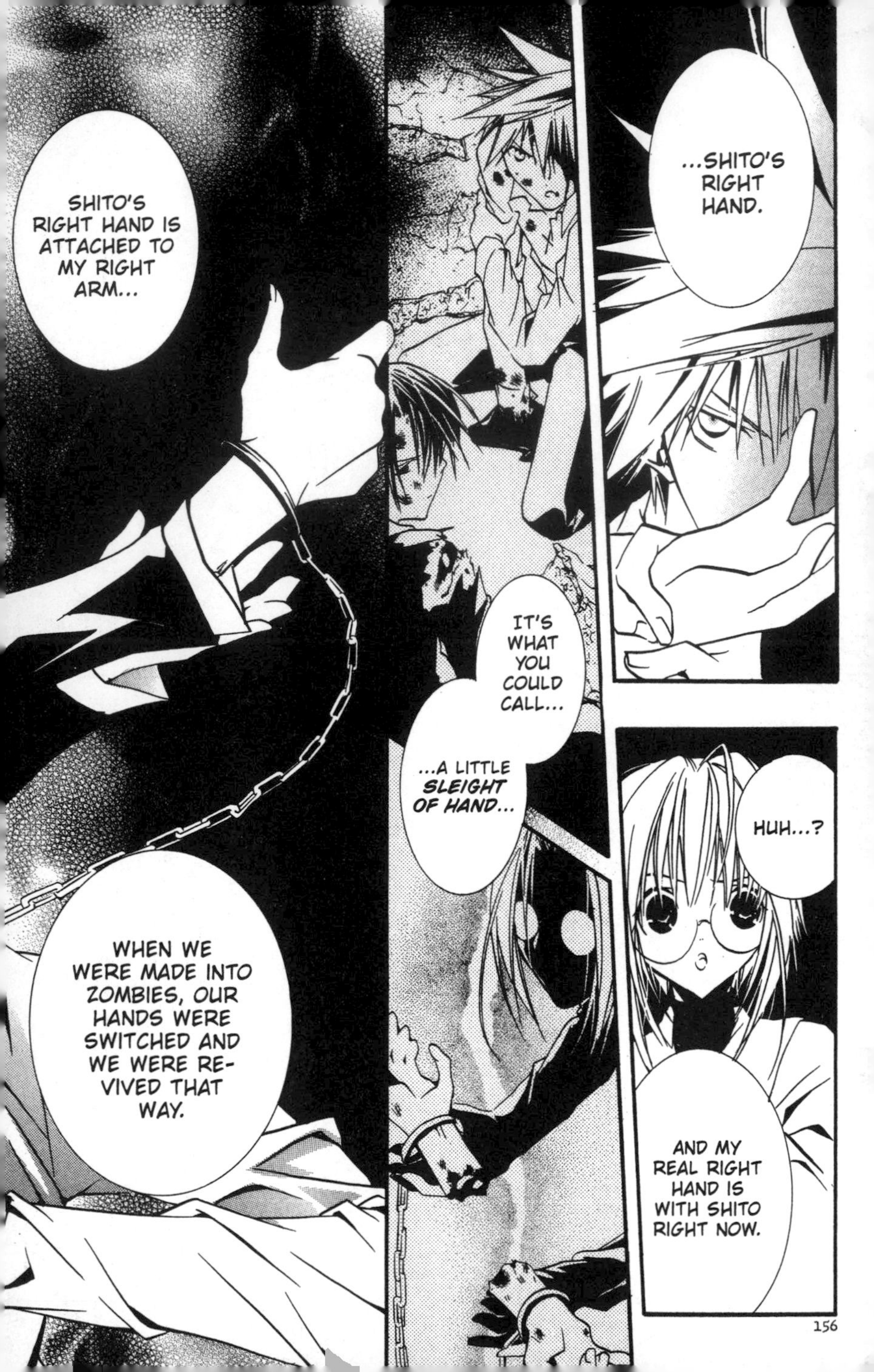
...SHITO'S RIGHT HAND.
HUH...?
AND MY REAL RIGHT HAND IS WITH SHITO RIGHT NOW.
IT'S WHAT YOU COULD CALL...
...A LITTLE *SLEIGHT OF HAND*...
SHITO'S RIGHT HAND IS ATTACHED TO MY RIGHT ARM...
WHEN WE WERE MADE INTO ZOMBIES, OUR HANDS WERE SWITCHED AND WE WERE RE-VIVED THAT WAY.

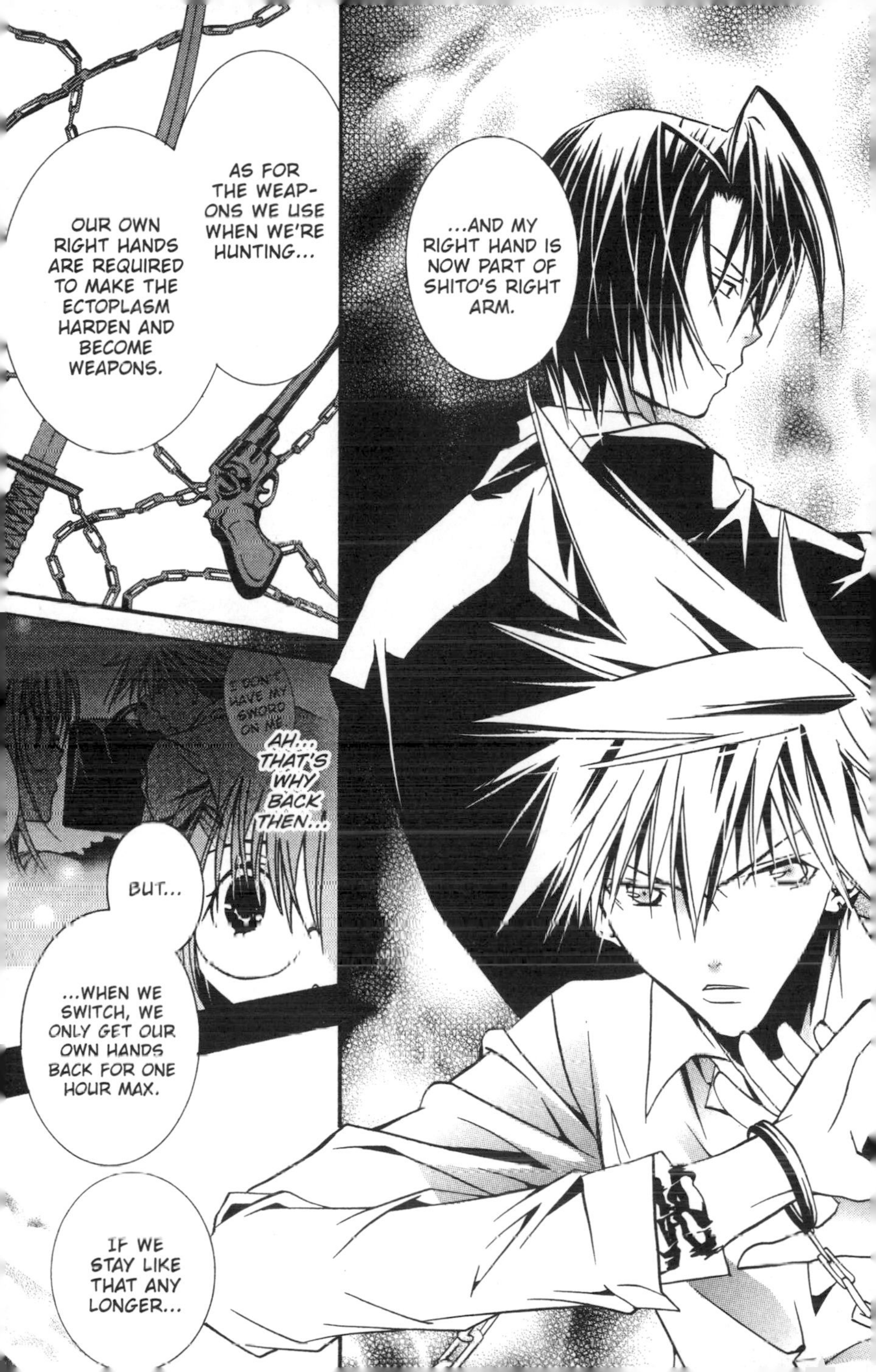
...AND MY RIGHT HAND IS NOW PART OF SHITO'S RIGHT ARM.
AS FOR THE WEAPONS WE USE WHEN WE'RE HUNTING...
OUR OWN RIGHT HANDS ARE REQUIRED TO MAKE THE ECTOPLASM HARDEN AND BECOME WEAPONS.
I DON'T HAVE MY SWORD ON ME
AH... THAT'S WHY BACK THEN...
BUT...
...WHEN WE SWITCH, WE ONLY GET OUR OWN HANDS BACK FOR ONE HOUR MAX.
IF WE STAY LIKE THAT ANY LONGER...

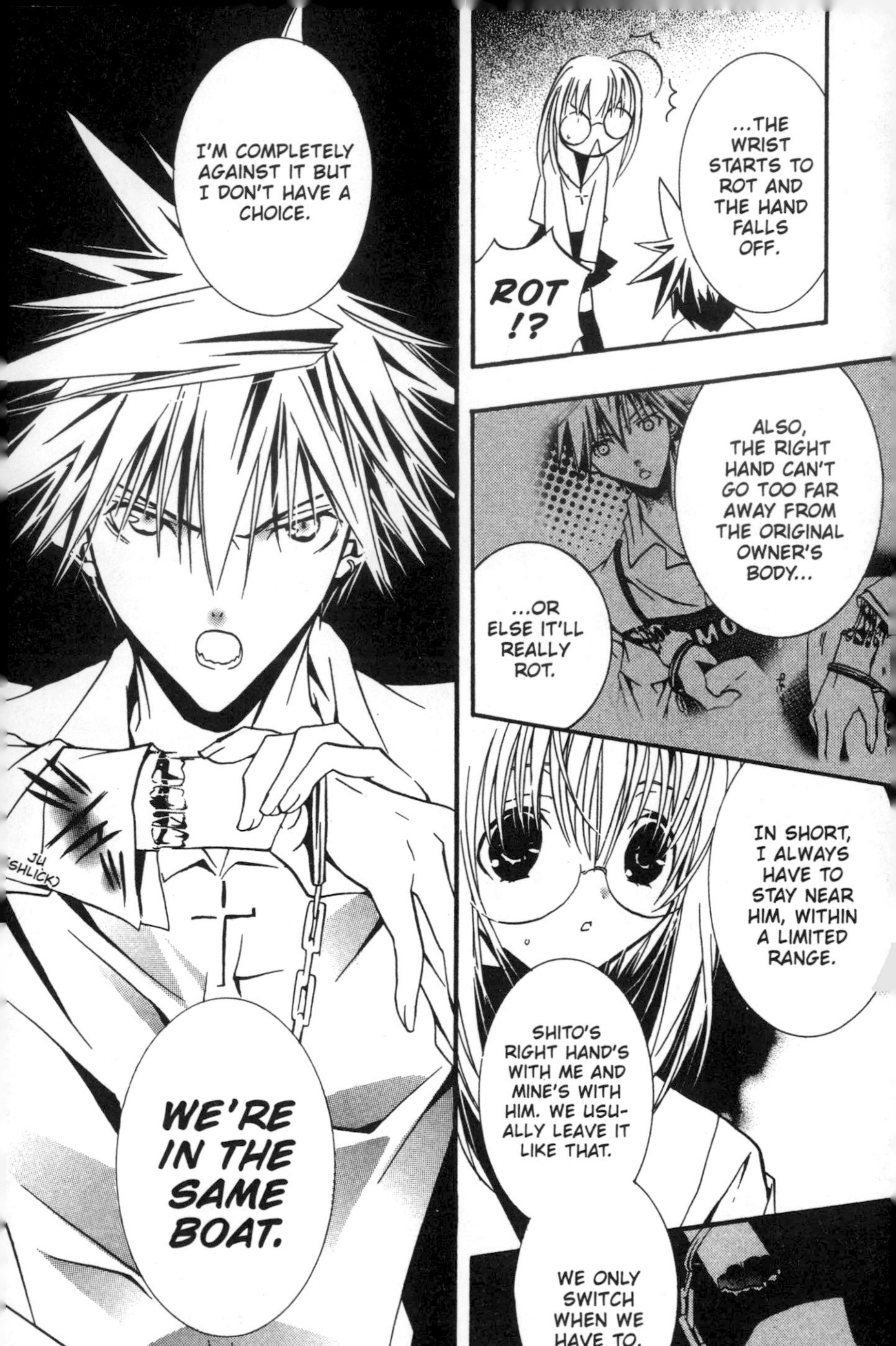
...THE WRIST STARTS TO ROT AND THE HAND FALLS OFF.
ROT !?
ALSO, THE RIGHT HAND CAN'T GO TOO FAR AWAY FROM THE ORIGINAL OWNER'S BODY...
...OR ELSE IT'LL REALLY ROT.
IN SHORT, I ALWAYS HAVE TO STAY NEAR HIM, WITHIN A LIMITED RANGE.
SHITO'S RIGHT HAND'S WITH ME AND MINE'S WITH HIM. WE USU-ALLY LEAVE IT LIKE THAT.
WE ONLY SWITCH WHEN WE HAVE TO.
I'M COMPLETELY AGAINST IT BUT I DON'T HAVE A CHOICE.
JU (SHLICK)
WE'RE IN THE SAME BOAT.

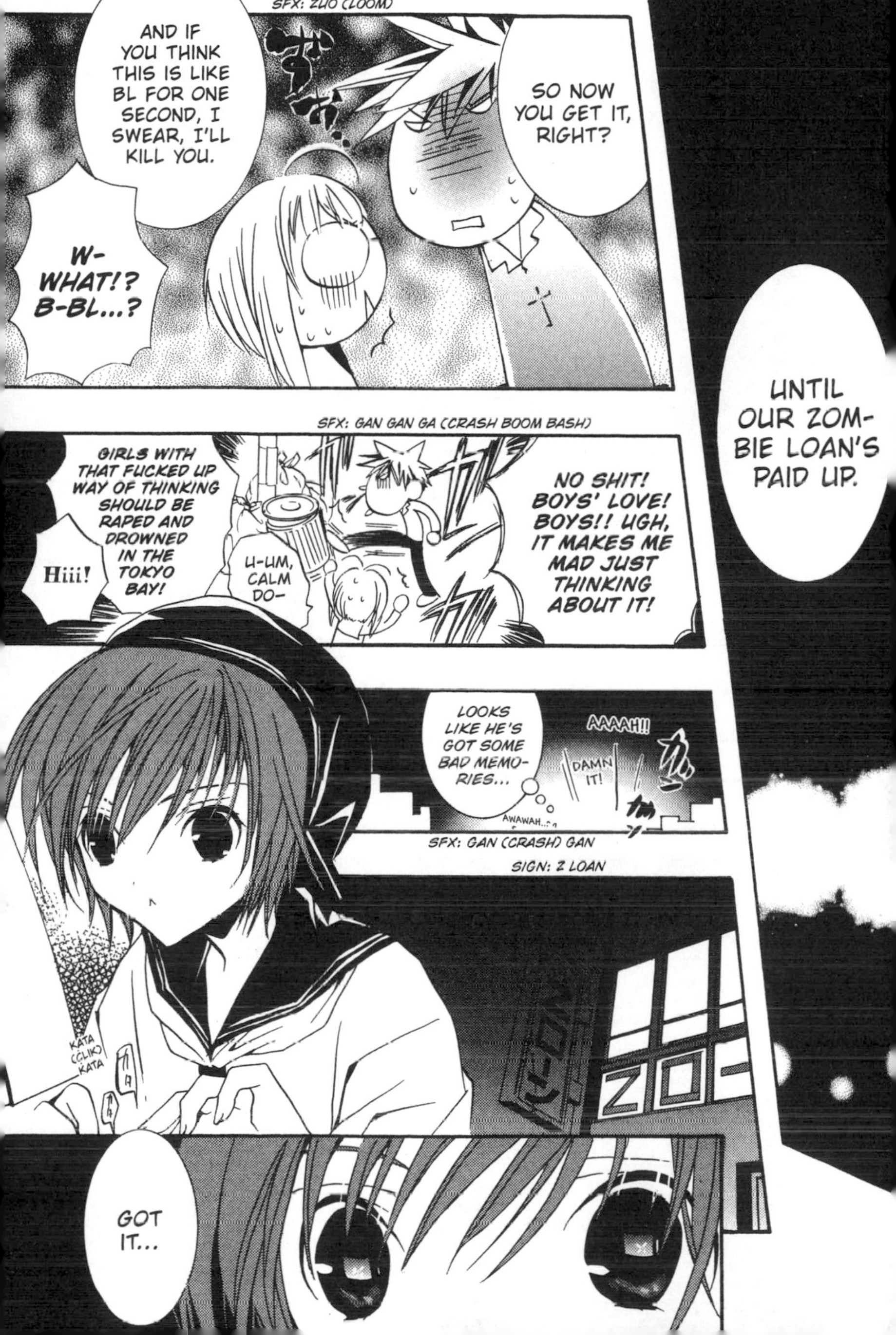
UNTIL OUR ZOM-BIE LOAN'S PAID UP.
SFX: ZUO (LOOM)
SO NOW YOU GET IT, RIGHT?
AND IF YOU THINK THIS IS LIKE BL FOR ONE SECOND, I SWEAR, I'LL KILL YOU.
W-WHAT!? B-BL...?
SFX: GAN GAN GA (CRASH BOOM BASH)
NO SHIT! BOYS' LOVE! BOYS!! UGH, IT MAKES ME MAD JUST THINKING ABOUT IT!
U-UM, CALM DO-
GIRLS WITH THAT FUCKED UP WAY OF THINKING SHOULD BE RAPED AND DROWNED IN THE TOKYO BAY!
Hiii!
AAAAH!!
DAMN IT!
LOOKS LIKE HE'S GOT SOME BAD MEMO-RIES...
SFX: GAN (CRASH) GAN
SIGN: Z LOAN
KATA (CLIK) KATA
GOT IT...

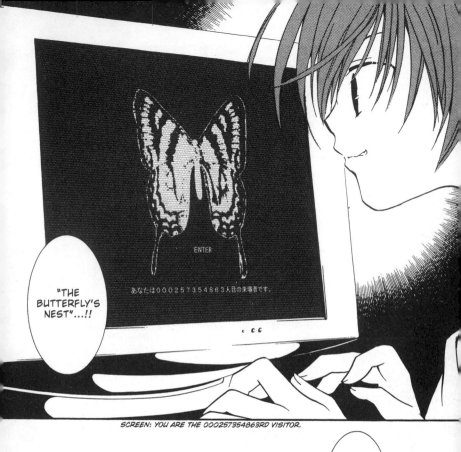

ENTER

あなたは000257354863人目の来場者です。

"THE BUTTERFLY'S NEST"...!!

SCREEN: YOU ARE THE 000257354863RD VISITOR.

SOON... VERY SOON...

IT WILL BE THE ADVENT OF THE BUTTER-FLY.

SFX: KATA (CLIK) KATA KATA

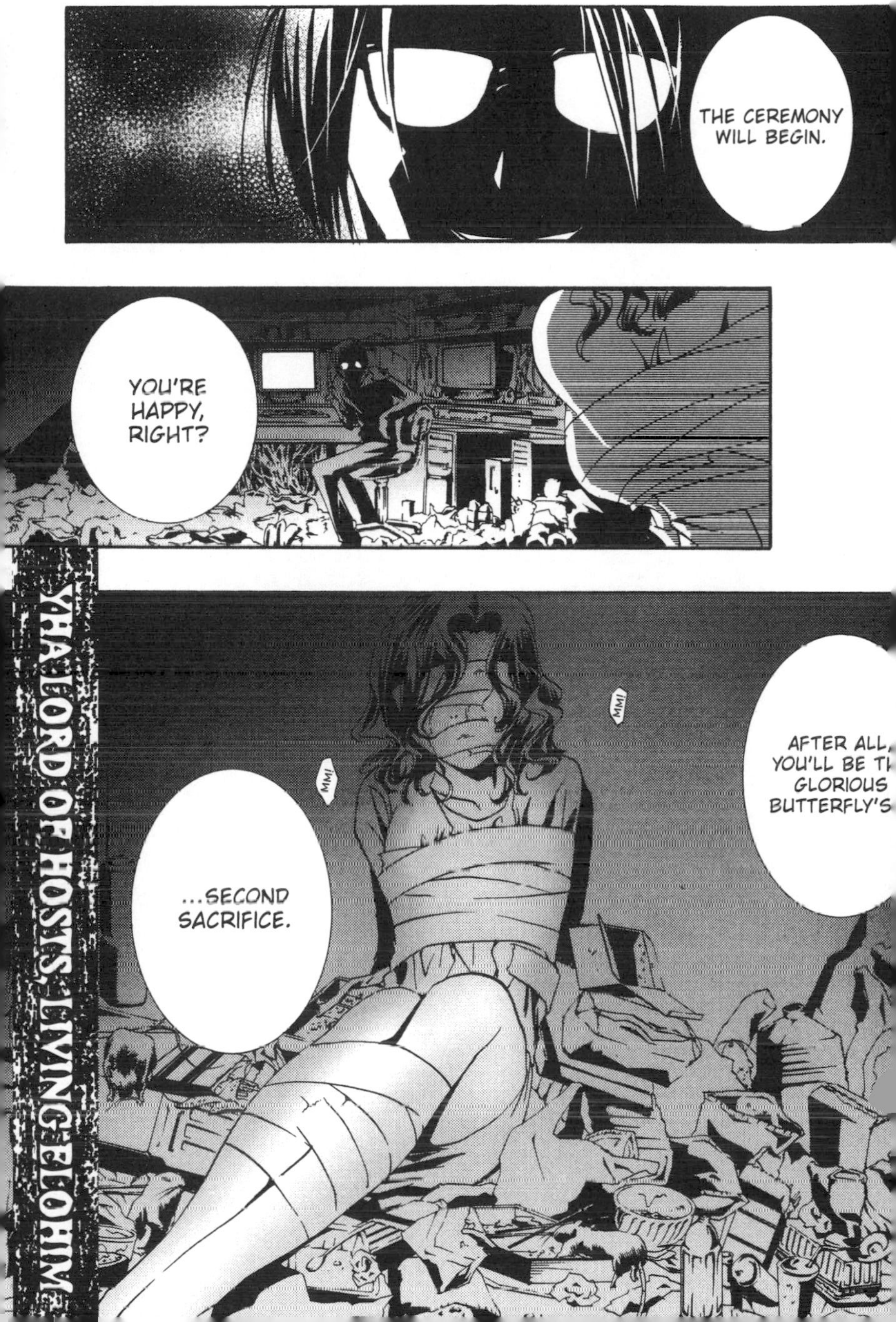
THE CEREMONY WILL BEGIN.
YOU'RE HAPPY, RIGHT?
AFTER ALL, YOU'LL BE T GLORIOUS BUTTERFLY'S
MM!
MM!
...SECOND SACRIFICE.
YHA LORD OF HOSTS, LIVING ELOHIM

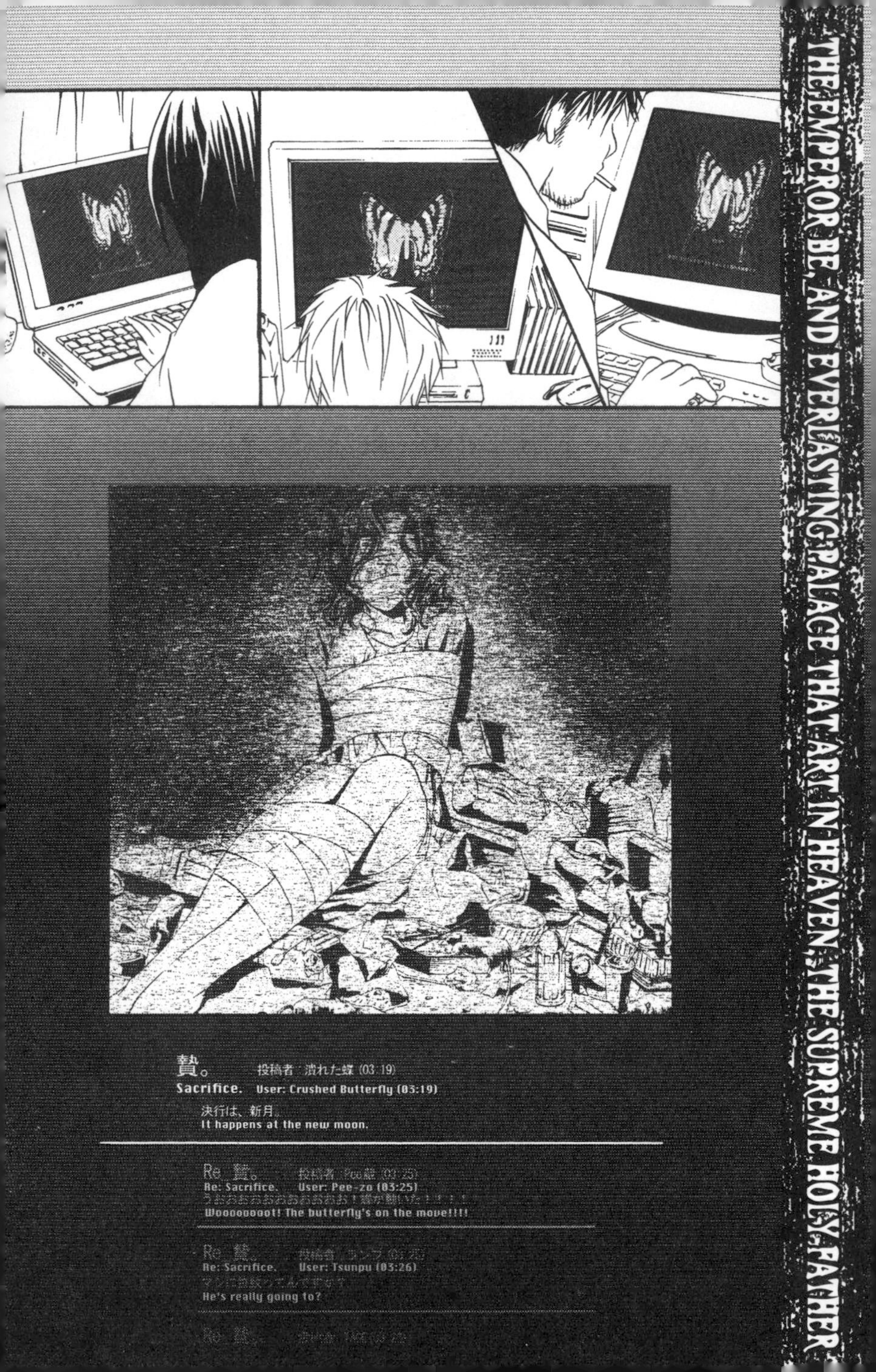
THE EMPEROR BE, AND EVERLASTING PALACE THAT ART IN HEAVEN, THE SUPREME HOLY FATHER
贄。 投稿者：潰れた蝶 (03:19)
Sacrifice. User: Crushed Butterfly (03:19)
決行は、新月。
It happens at the new moon.
Re: Sacrifice. User: Pee-zo (03:25)
Woooooooot! The butterfly's on the move!!!!
Re: Sacrifice. User: Tsunpu (03:26)
He's really going to?

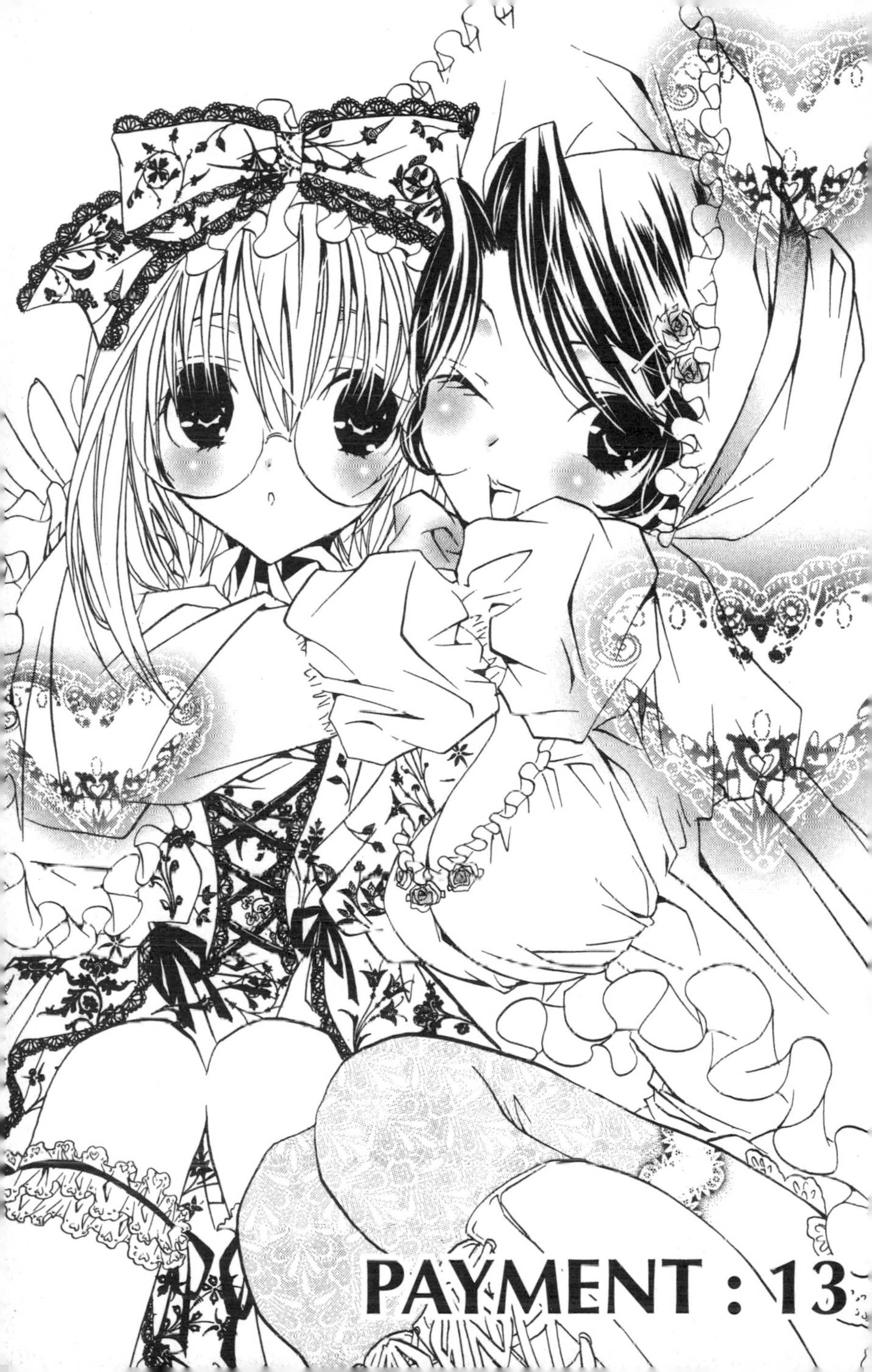
PAYMENT : 13

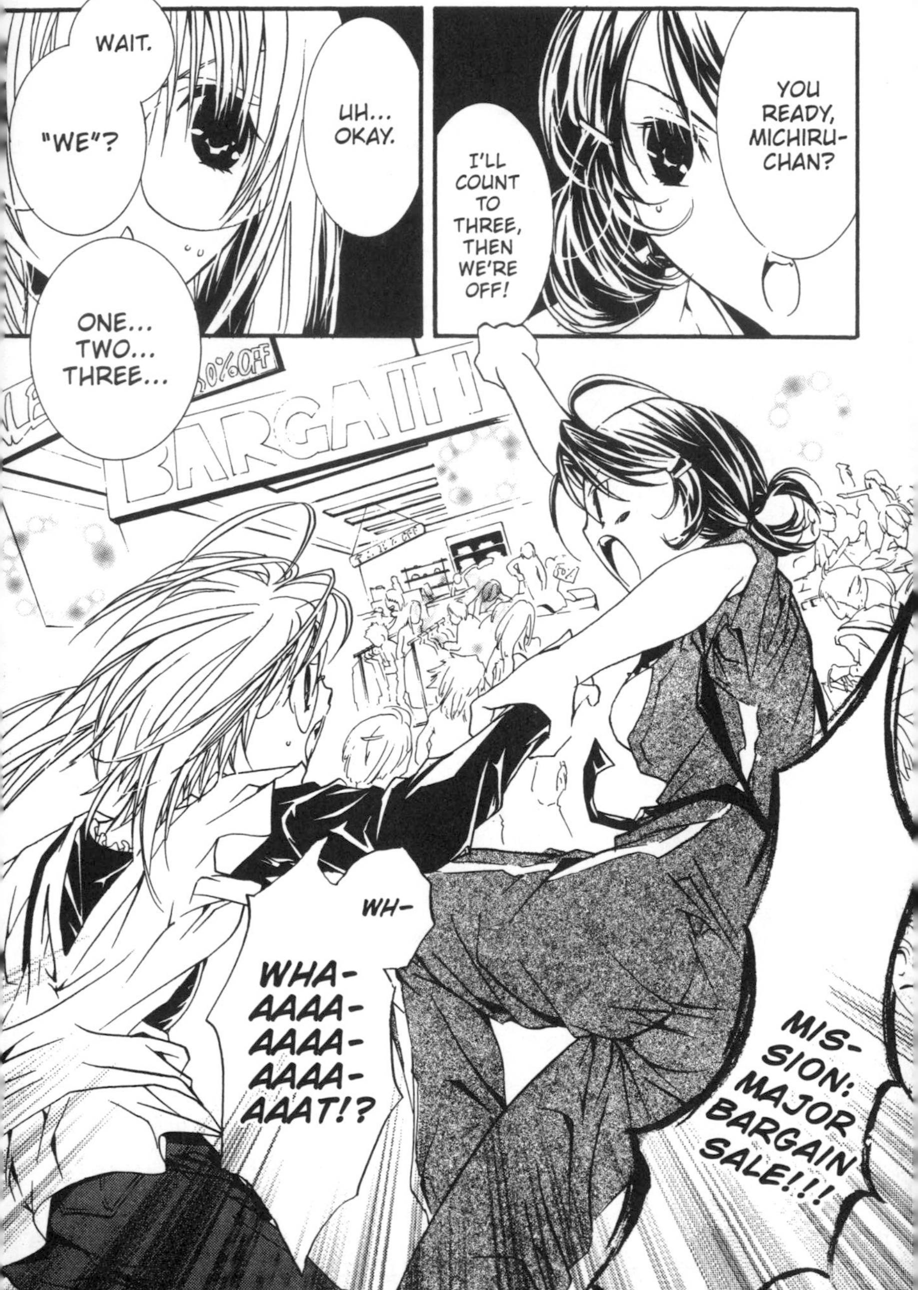
YOU READY, MICHIRU-CHAN?
I'LL COUNT TO THREE, THEN WE'RE OFF!
UH... OKAY.
WAIT.
"WE"?
ONE... TWO... THREE...
BARGAIN
MIS-SION: MAJOR BARGAIN SALE!!!
WH-
WHA-AAAA-AAAA-AAAA-AAAT!?

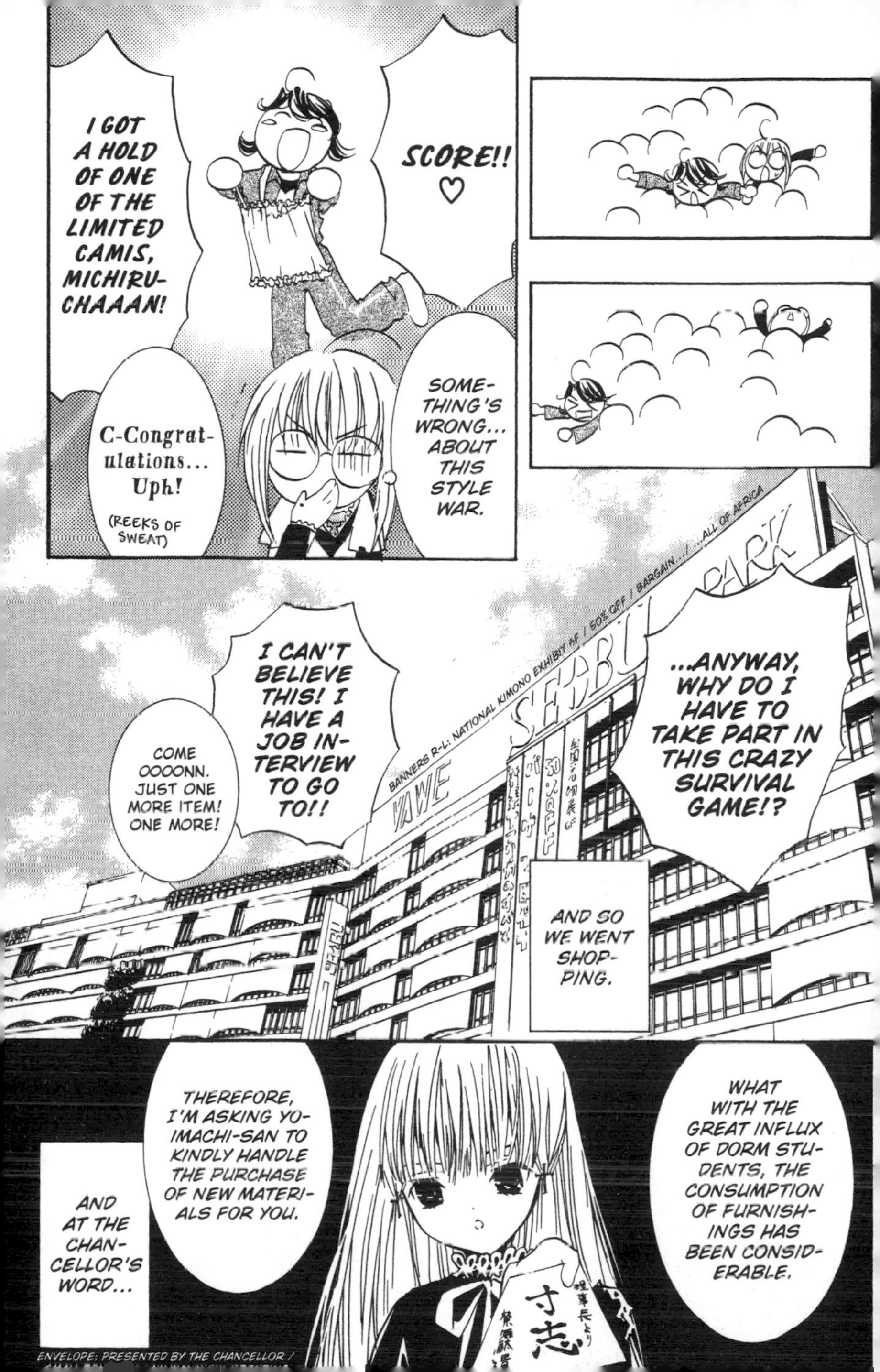
SCORE!! ♡
I GOT A HOLD OF ONE OF THE LIMITED CAMIS, MICHIRU-CHAAAN!
SOME-THING'S WRONG... ABOUT THIS STYLE WAR.
C-Congratulations... Uph!
(REEKS OF SWEAT)
...ANYWAY, WHY DO I HAVE TO TAKE PART IN THIS CRAZY SURVIVAL GAME!?
BANNERS R-L: NATIONAL KIMONO EXHIBIT 4F / 50% OFF / BARGAIN... / ...ALL OF AFRICA
PARK
I CAN'T BELIEVE THIS! I HAVE A JOB INTERVIEW TO GO TO!!
COME OOOONN. JUST ONE MORE ITEM! ONE MORE!
AND SO WE WENT SHOPPING.
WHAT WITH THE GREAT INFLUX OF DORM STUDENTS, THE CONSUMPTION OF FURNISHINGS HAS BEEN CONSIDERABLE.
THEREFORE, I'M ASKING YOIMACHI-SAN TO KINDLY HANDLE THE PURCHASE OF NEW MATERIALS FOR YOU.
AND AT THE CHANCELLOR'S WORD...
ENVELOPE: PRESENTED BY THE CHANCELLOR /

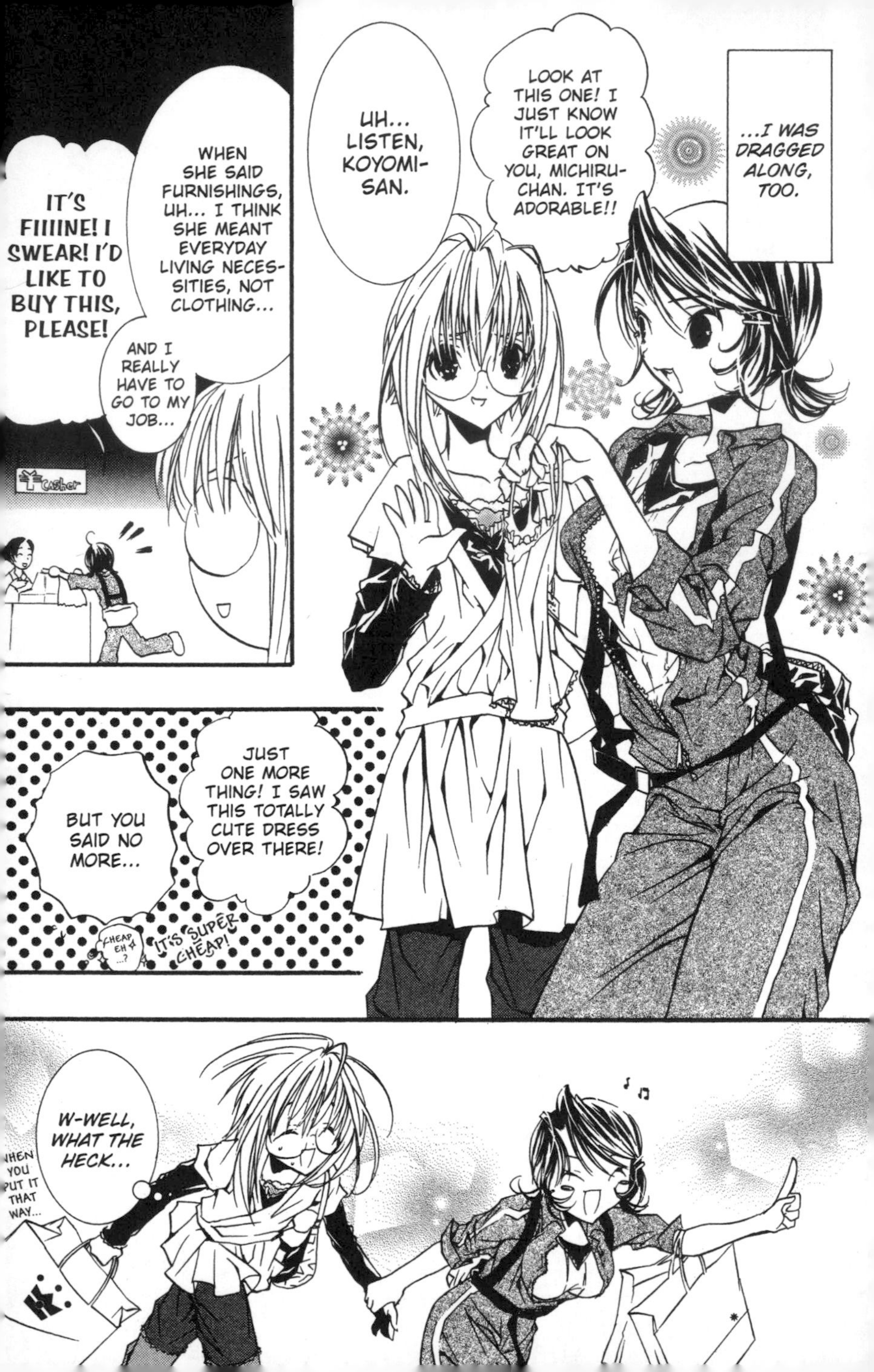
...I WAS DRAGGED ALONG, TOO.
LOOK AT THIS ONE! I JUST KNOW IT'LL LOOK GREAT ON YOU, MICHIRU-CHAN. IT'S ADORABLE!!
UH... LISTEN, KOYOMI-SAN.
WHEN SHE SAID FURNISHINGS, UH... I THINK SHE MEANT EVERYDAY LIVING NECES-SITIES, NOT CLOTHING...
AND I REALLY HAVE TO GO TO MY JOB...
IT'S FIIIINE! I SWEAR! I'D LIKE TO BUY THIS, PLEASE!
Casher
JUST ONE MORE THING! I SAW THIS TOTALLY CUTE DRESS OVER THERE!
BUT YOU SAID NO MORE...
IT'S SUPER CHEAP!
CHEAP, EH ...?
W-WELL, WHAT THE HECK...
HEN YOU PUT IT THAT WAY...

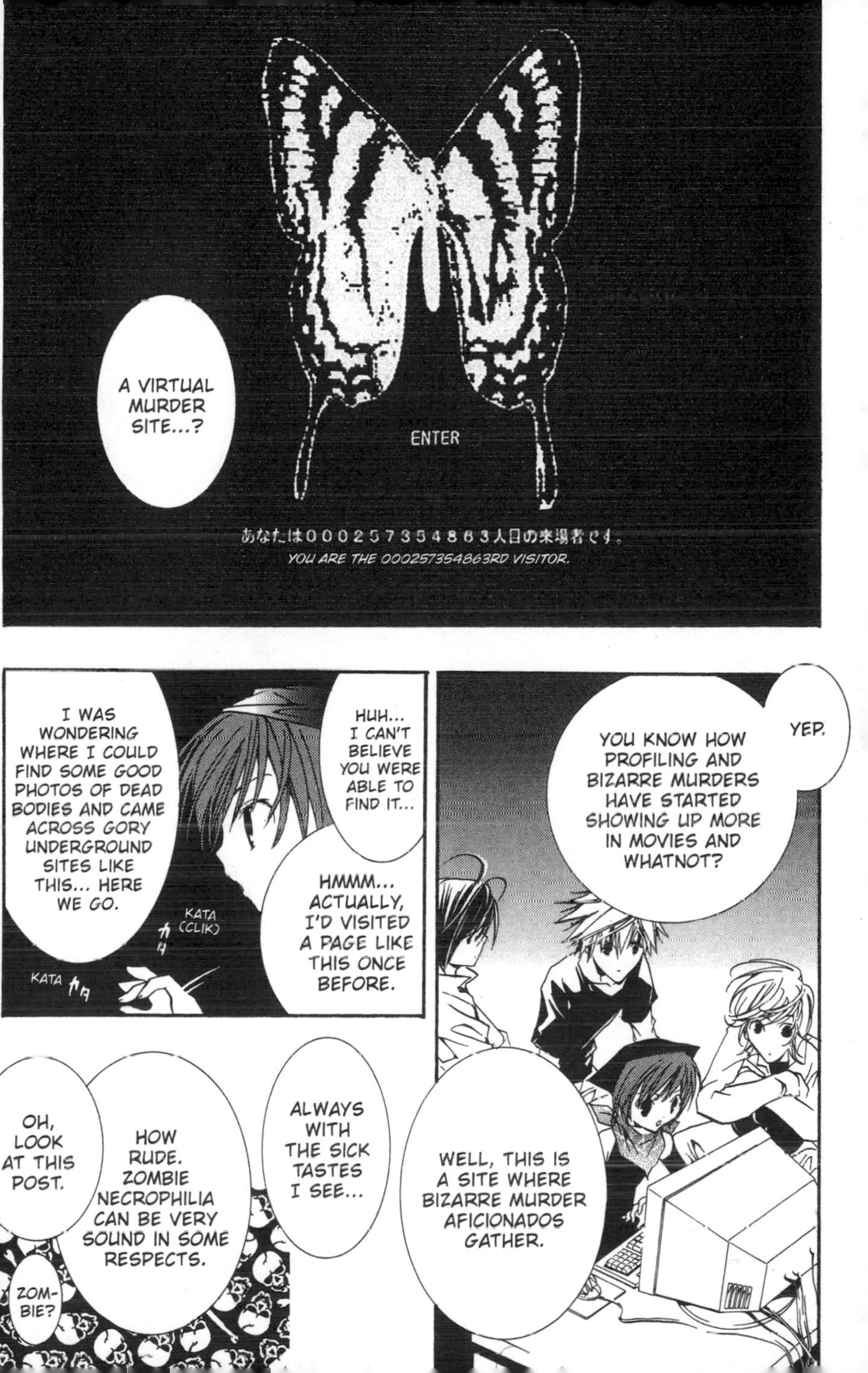
A VIRTUAL MURDER SITE...?
ENTER
あなたは000257354863人目の来場者です。
YOU ARE THE 000257354863RD VISITOR.
YEP.
YOU KNOW HOW PROFILING AND BIZARRE MURDERS HAVE STARTED SHOWING UP MORE IN MOVIES AND WHATNOT?
WELL, THIS IS A SITE WHERE BIZARRE MURDER AFICIONADOS GATHER.
HUH... I CAN'T BELIEVE YOU WERE ABLE TO FIND IT...
HMMM... ACTUALLY, I'D VISITED A PAGE LIKE THIS ONCE BEFORE.
I WAS WONDERING WHERE I COULD FIND SOME GOOD PHOTOS OF DEAD BODIES AND CAME ACROSS GORY UNDERGROUND SITES LIKE THIS... HERE WE GO.
KATA (CLIK) カタ
KATA カタ
ALWAYS WITH THE SICK TASTES I SEE...
HOW RUDE. ZOMBIE NECROPHILIA CAN BE VERY SOUND IN SOME RESPECTS.
OH, LOOK AT THIS POST.
ZOM-BIE?

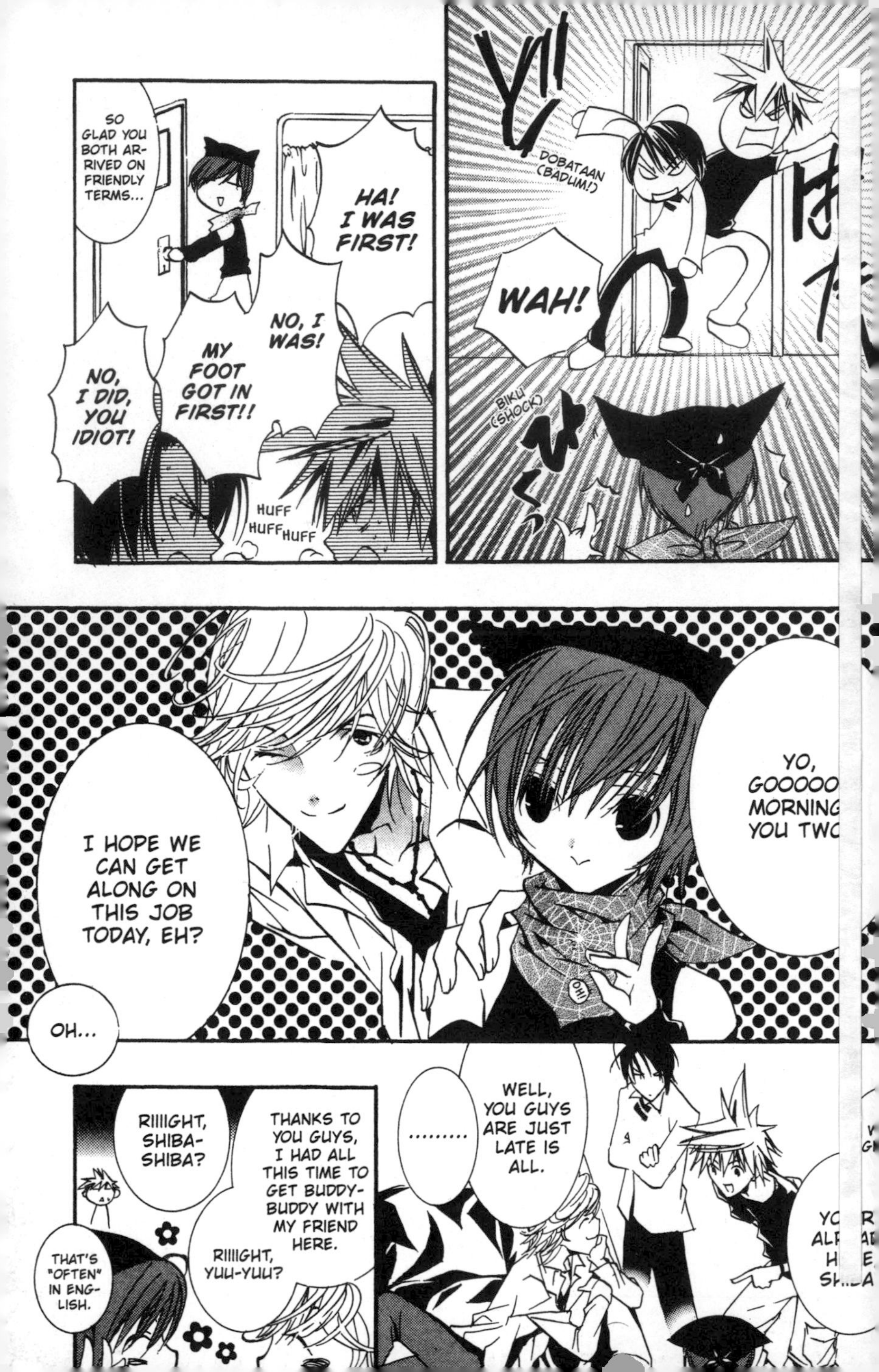
DOBATAAN (BADUM!)
WAH!
BIKU (SHOCK)
HA! I WAS FIRST!
NO, I WAS!
SO GLAD YOU BOTH AR-RIVED ON FRIENDLY TERMS...
MY FOOT GOT IN FIRST!!
NO, I DID, YOU IDIOT!
HUFF HUFF HUFF
YO, GOOOOO MORNING YOU TWO
I HOPE WE CAN GET ALONG ON THIS JOB TODAY, EH?
OH!
OH...
WELL, YOU GUYS ARE JUST LATE IS ALL.
....
THANKS TO YOU GUYS, I HAD ALL THIS TIME TO GET BUDDY-BUDDY WITH MY FRIEND HERE.
RIIIIGHT, SHIBA-SHIBA?
RIIIGHT, YUU-YUU?
THAT'S "OFTEN" IN ENG-LISH.

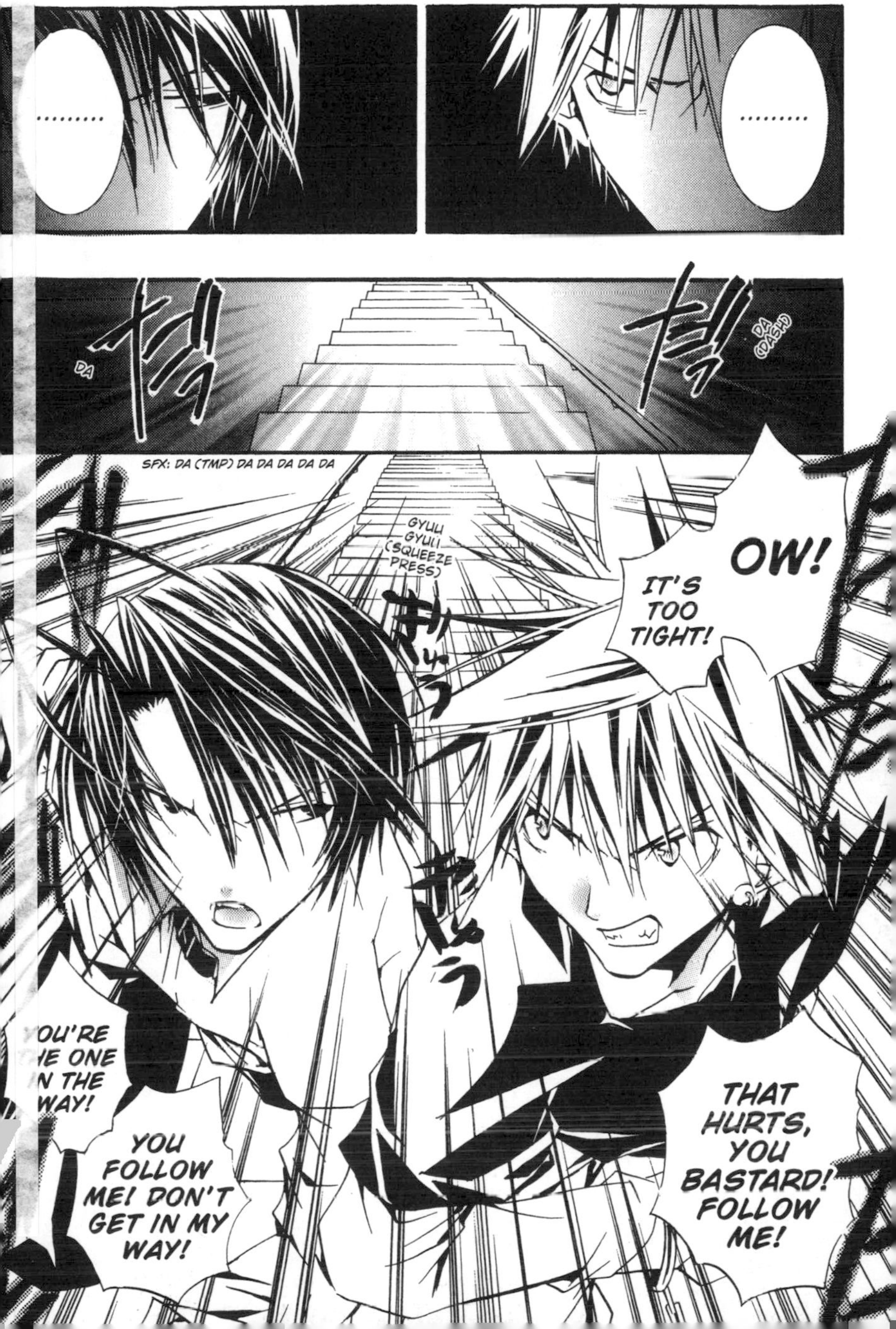
....
....
DA (DASH)
DA
SFX: DA (TMP) DA DA DA DA DA
OW!
IT'S TOO TIGHT!
GYUU GYUU (SQUEEZE PRESS)
THAT HURTS, YOU BASTARD! FOLLOW ME!
YOU FOLLOW ME! DON'T GET IN MY WAY!
OU'RE HE ONE N THE WAY!

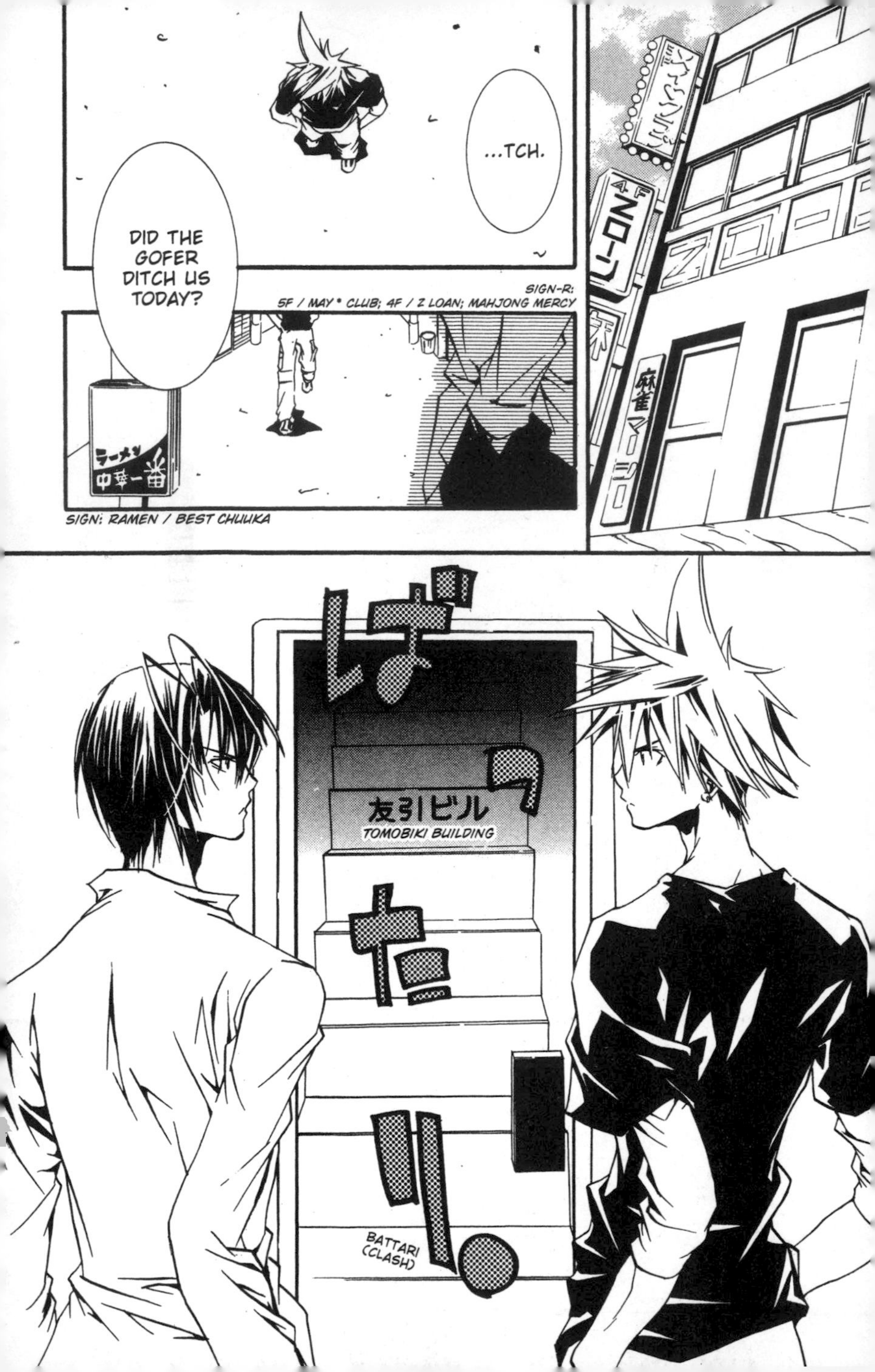
SIGN-R:
5F / MAY * CLUB; 4F / Z LOAN; MAHJONG MERCY
...TCH.
DID THE GOFER DITCH US TODAY?
SIGN: RAMEN / BEST CHUUKA
ばったり
友引ビル
TOMOBIKI BUILDING
BATTARI (CLASH)

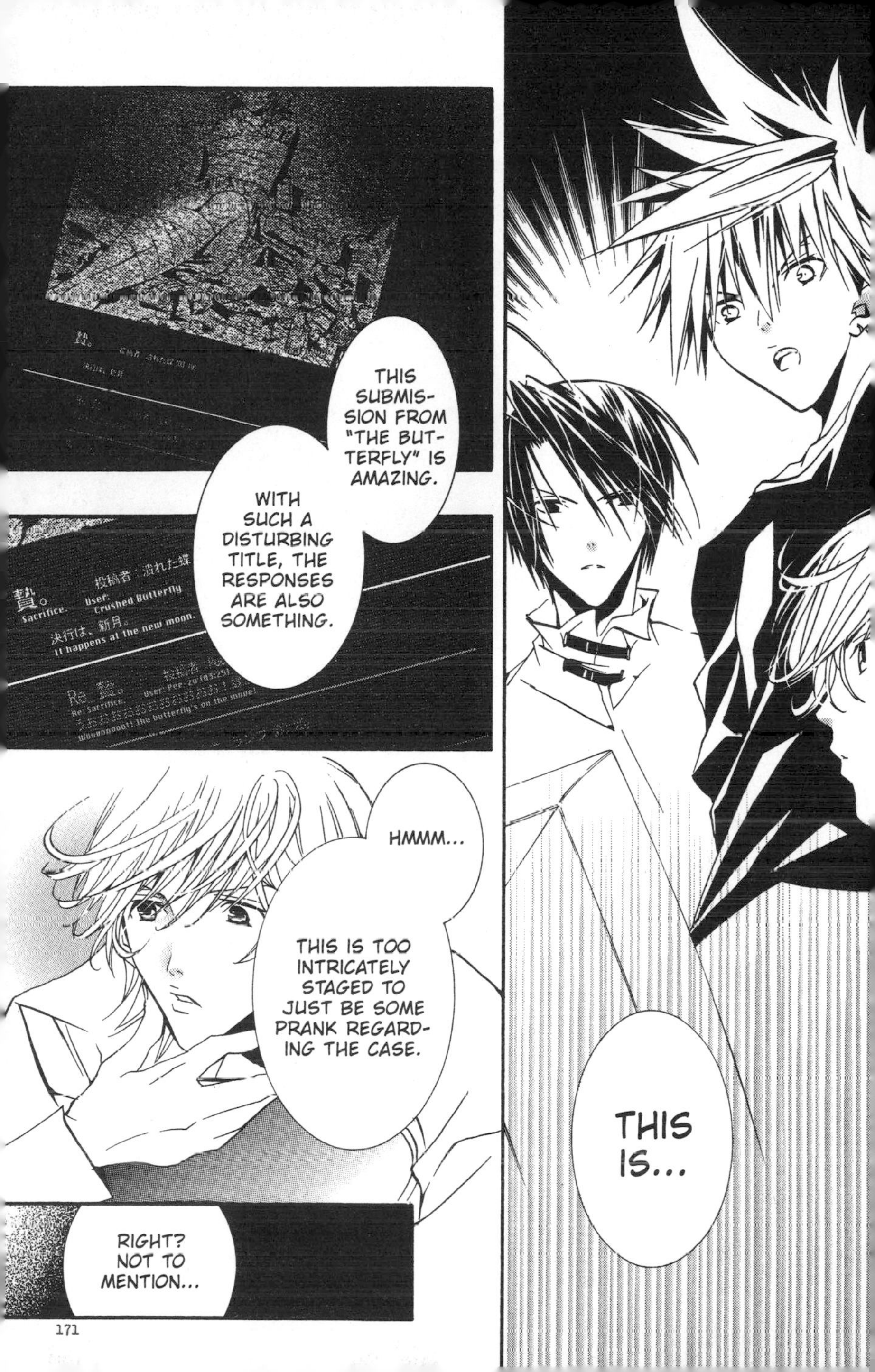
THIS IS...
THIS SUBMISSION FROM "THE BUTTERFLY" IS AMAZING.
WITH SUCH A DISTURBING TITLE, THE RESPONSES ARE ALSO SOMETHING.
贄。 投稿者：潰れた蝶
Sacrifice. User: Crushed Butterfly
決行は、新月。
It happens at the new moon.
Re: Sacrifice.
The butterfly's on the move!
HMMM...
THIS IS TOO INTRICATELY STAGED TO JUST BE SOME PRANK REGARDING THE CASE.
RIGHT? NOT TO MENTION...

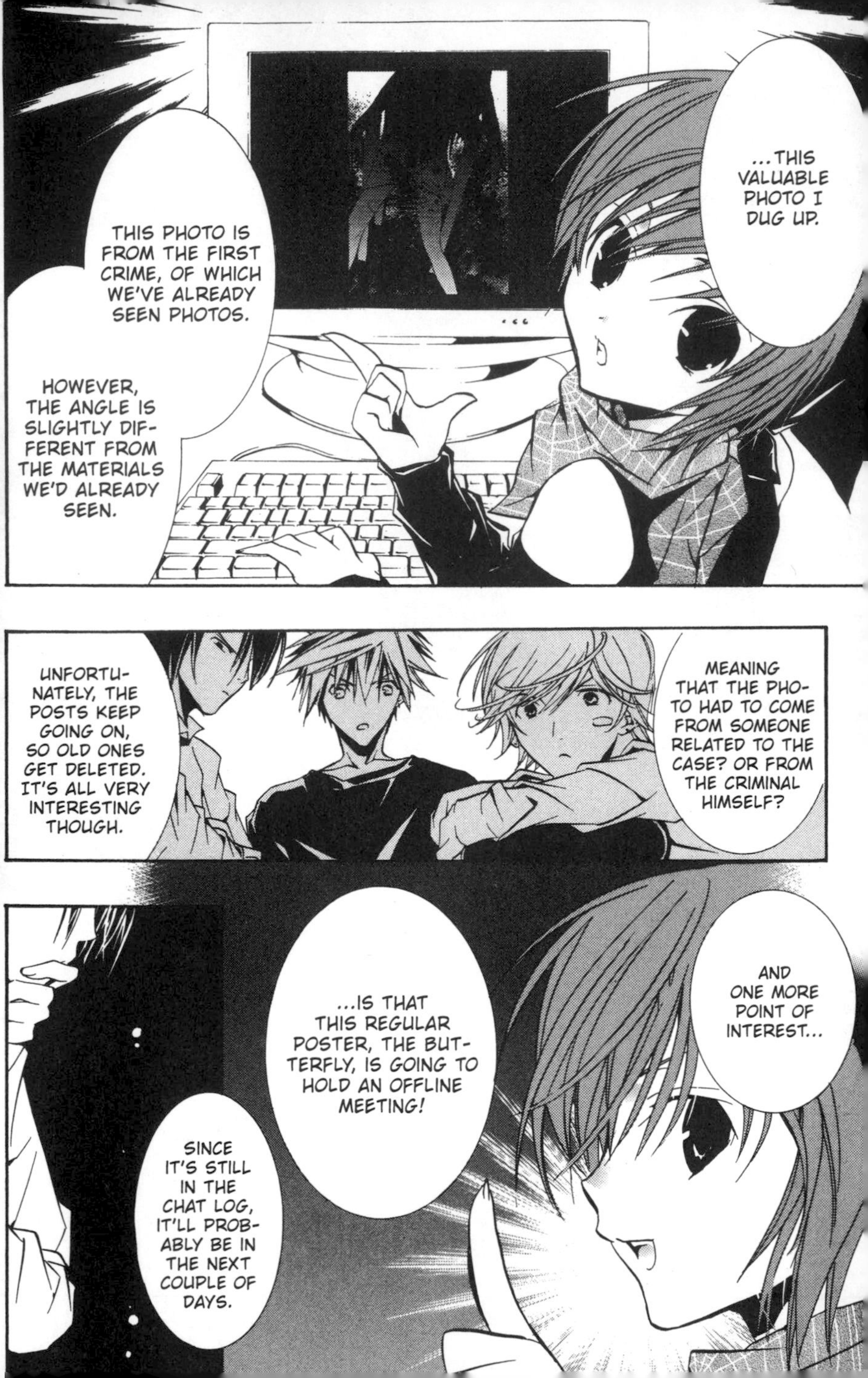
...THIS VALUABLE PHOTO I DUG UP.
THIS PHOTO IS FROM THE FIRST CRIME, OF WHICH WE'VE ALREADY SEEN PHOTOS.
HOWEVER, THE ANGLE IS SLIGHTLY DIF-FERENT FROM THE MATERIALS WE'D ALREADY SEEN.
MEANING THAT THE PHO-TO HAD TO COME FROM SOMEONE RELATED TO THE CASE? OR FROM THE CRIMINAL HIMSELF?
UNFORTU-NATELY, THE POSTS KEEP GOING ON, SO OLD ONES GET DELETED. IT'S ALL VERY INTERESTING THOUGH.
AND ONE MORE POINT OF INTEREST...
...IS THAT THIS REGULAR POSTER, THE BUT-TERFLY, IS GOING TO HOLD AN OFFLINE MEETING!
SINCE IT'S STILL IN THE CHAT LOG, IT'LL PROB-ABLY BE IN THE NEXT COUPLE OF DAYS.

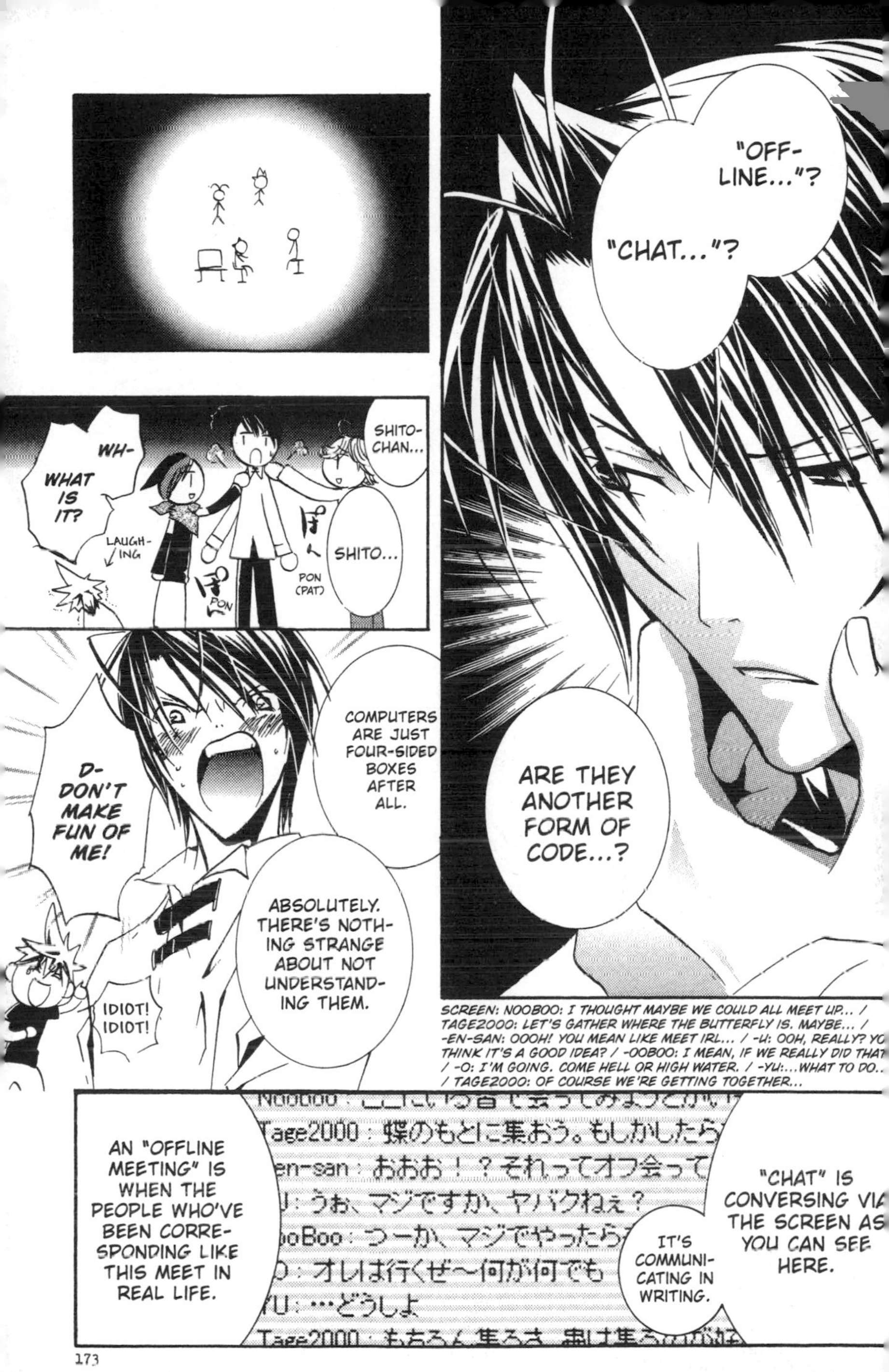
"OFF-LINE..."?
"CHAT..."?
ARE THEY ANOTHER FORM OF CODE...?
SHITO-CHAN...
SHITO...
PON (PAT)
ぽん
PON
ぽん
WH- WHAT IS IT?
LAUGHING
COMPUTERS ARE JUST FOUR-SIDED BOXES AFTER ALL.
ABSOLUTELY. THERE'S NOTHING STRANGE ABOUT NOT UNDERSTANDING THEM.
D-DON'T MAKE FUN OF ME!
IDIOT! IDIOT!
SCREEN: NOOBOO: I THOUGHT MAYBE WE COULD ALL MEET UP... / TAGE2000: LET'S GATHER WHERE THE BUTTERFLY IS. MAYBE... / -EN-SAN: OOOH! YOU MEAN LIKE MEET IRL... / -U: OOH, REALLY? YOU THINK IT'S A GOOD IDEA? / -OOBOO: I MEAN, IF WE REALLY DID THAT / -O: I'M GOING. COME HELL OR HIGH WATER. / -YU:...WHAT TO DO... / TAGE2000: OF COURSE WE'RE GETTING TOGETHER...
"CHAT" IS CONVERSING VIA THE SCREEN AS YOU CAN SEE HERE.
IT'S COMMUNICATING IN WRITING.
Tage2000：蝶のもとに集おう。もしかしたら
en-san：おおお！？それってオフ会って
U：うお、マジですか、ヤバクねぇ？
ooBoo：つーか、マジでやったら
O：オレは行くぜ〜何が何でも
YU：…どうしよ
AN "OFFLINE MEETING" IS WHEN THE PEOPLE WHO'VE BEEN CORRESPONDING LIKE THIS MEET IN REAL LIFE.

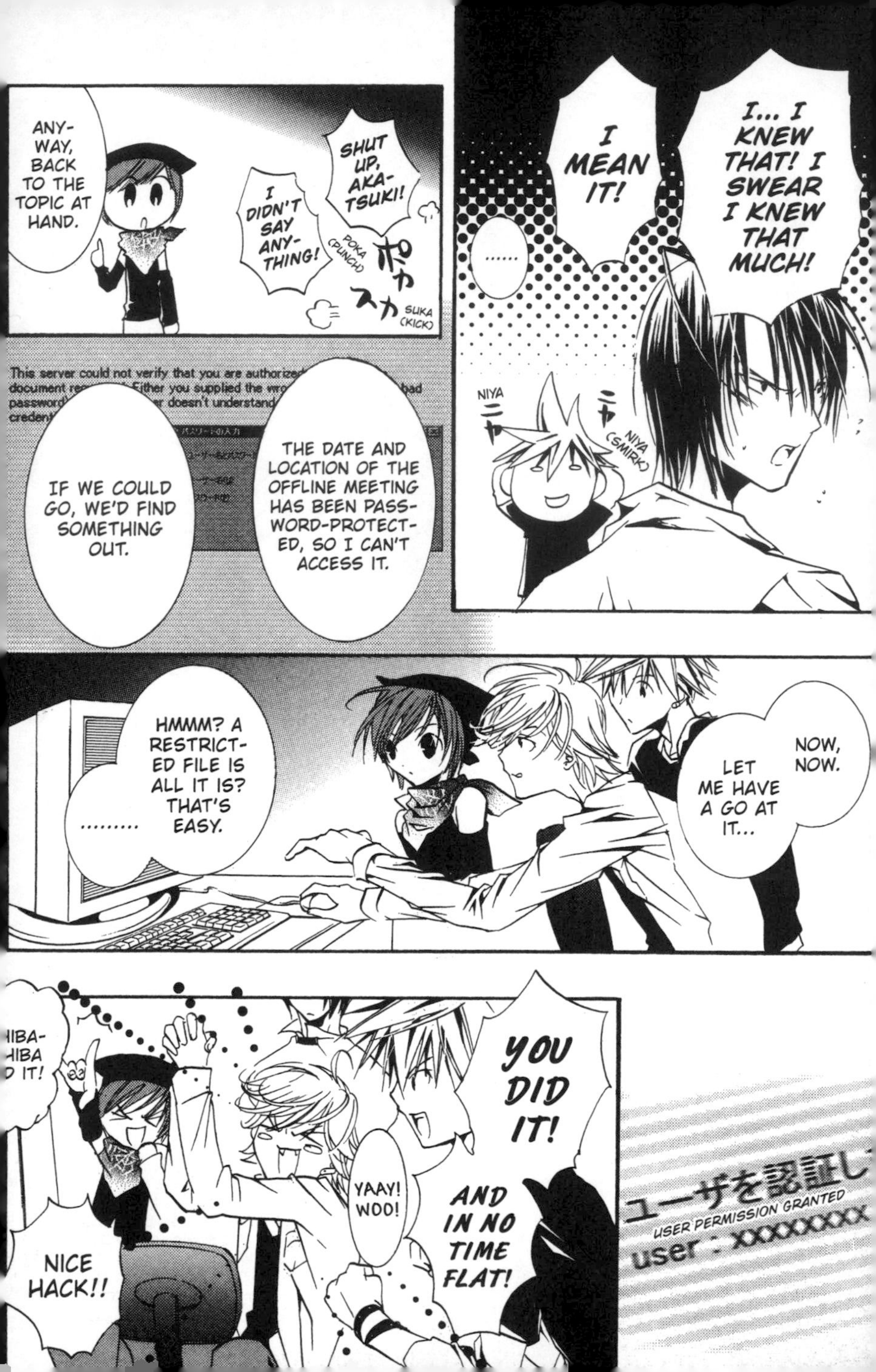
I... I KNEW THAT! I SWEAR I KNEW THAT MUCH!
I MEAN IT!
......
NIYA (SMIRK)
NIYA
SHUT UP, AKA-TSUKI!
I DIDN'T SAY ANY-THING!
POKA (PUNCH)
SUKA (KICK)
ANY-WAY, BACK TO THE TOPIC AT HAND.
This server could not verify that you are authorized
THE DATE AND LOCATION OF THE OFFLINE MEETING HAS BEEN PASS-WORD-PROTECT-ED, SO I CAN'T ACCESS IT.
IF WE COULD GO, WE'D FIND SOMETHING OUT.
NOW, NOW.
LET ME HAVE A GO AT IT...
HMMM? A RESTRICT-ED FILE IS ALL IT IS? THAT'S EASY.
....
USER PERMISSION GRANTED
user : XXXXXXXX
YOU DID IT!
AND IN NO TIME FLAT!
YAAY! WOO!
NICE HACK!!

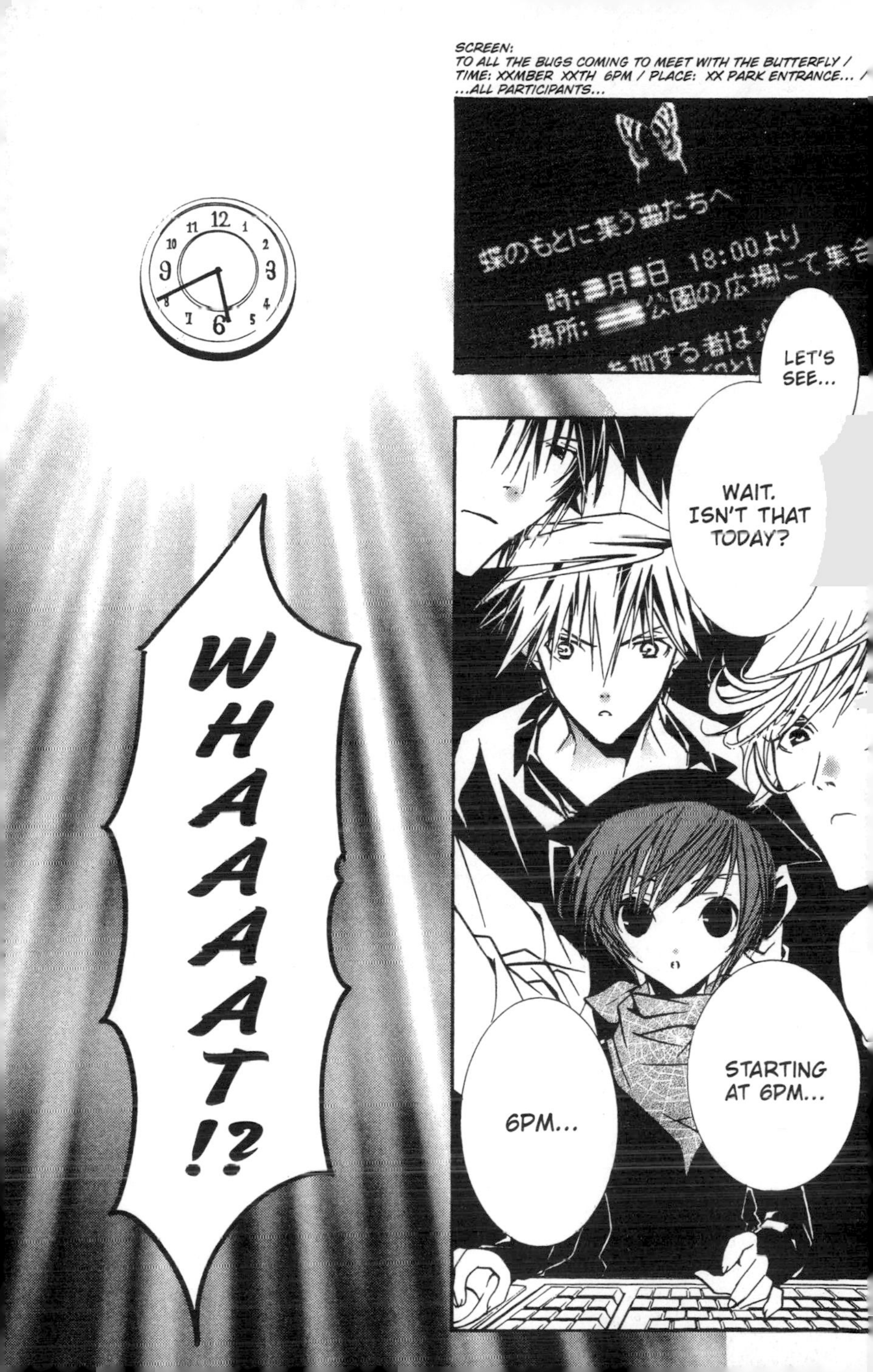
SCREEN:
TO ALL THE BUGS COMING TO MEET WITH THE BUTTERFLY / TIME: XXMBER XXTH 6PM / PLACE: XX PARK ENTRANCE... / ...ALL PARTICIPANTS...
LET'S SEE...
WAIT. ISN'T THAT TODAY?
STARTING AT 6PM...
6PM...
WHAAAAT!?

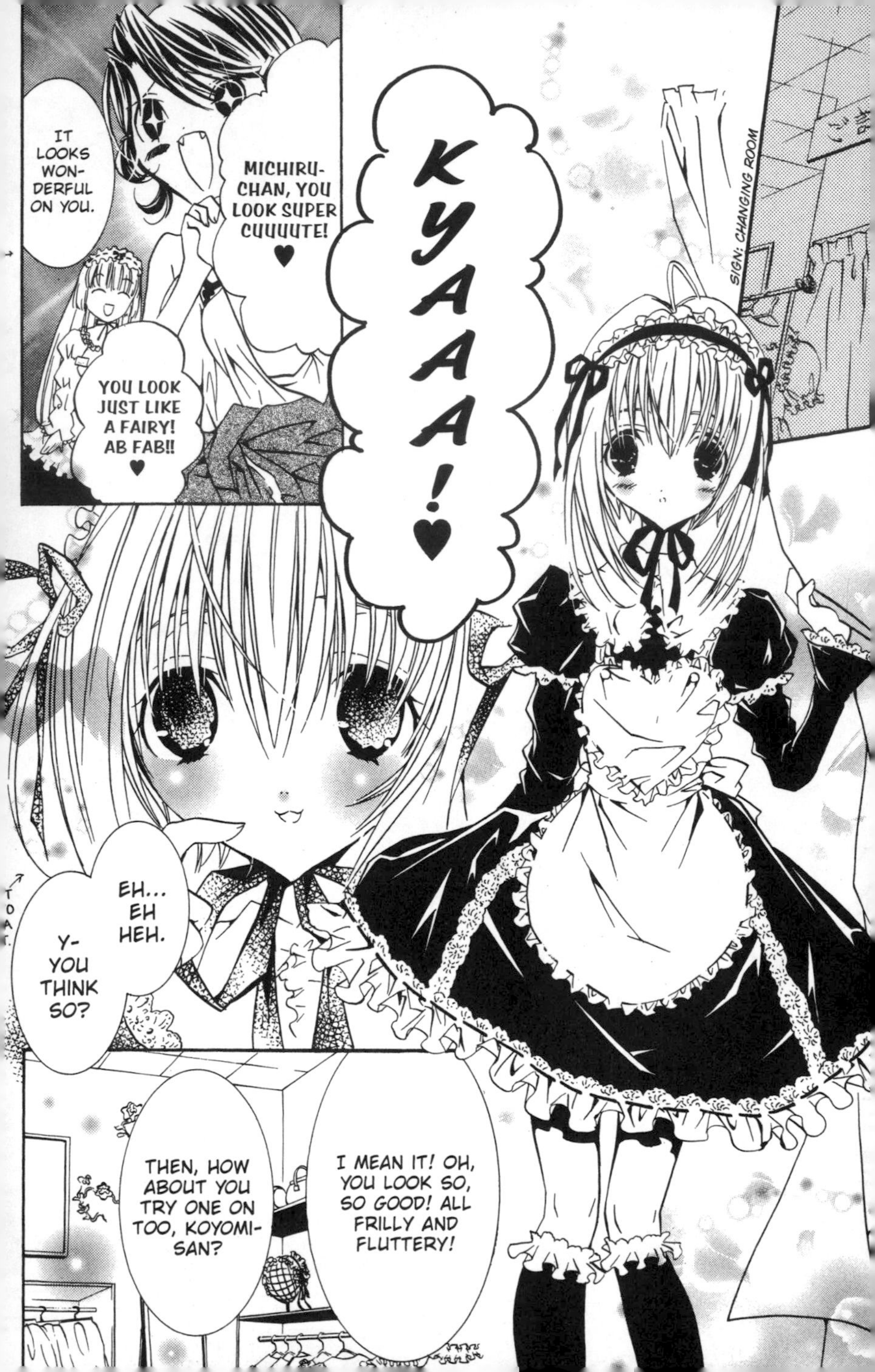

SIGN: CHANGING ROOM
KYAAA! ♥
MICHIRU-CHAN, YOU LOOK SUPER CUUUUTE! ♥
IT LOOKS WONDERFUL ON YOU.
YOU LOOK JUST LIKE A FAIRY! AB FAB!! ♥
EH... EH HEH.
Y-YOU THINK SO?
I MEAN IT! OH, YOU LOOK SO, SO GOOD! ALL FRILLY AND FLUTTERY!
THEN, HOW ABOUT YOU TRY ONE ON TOO, KOYOMI-SAN?

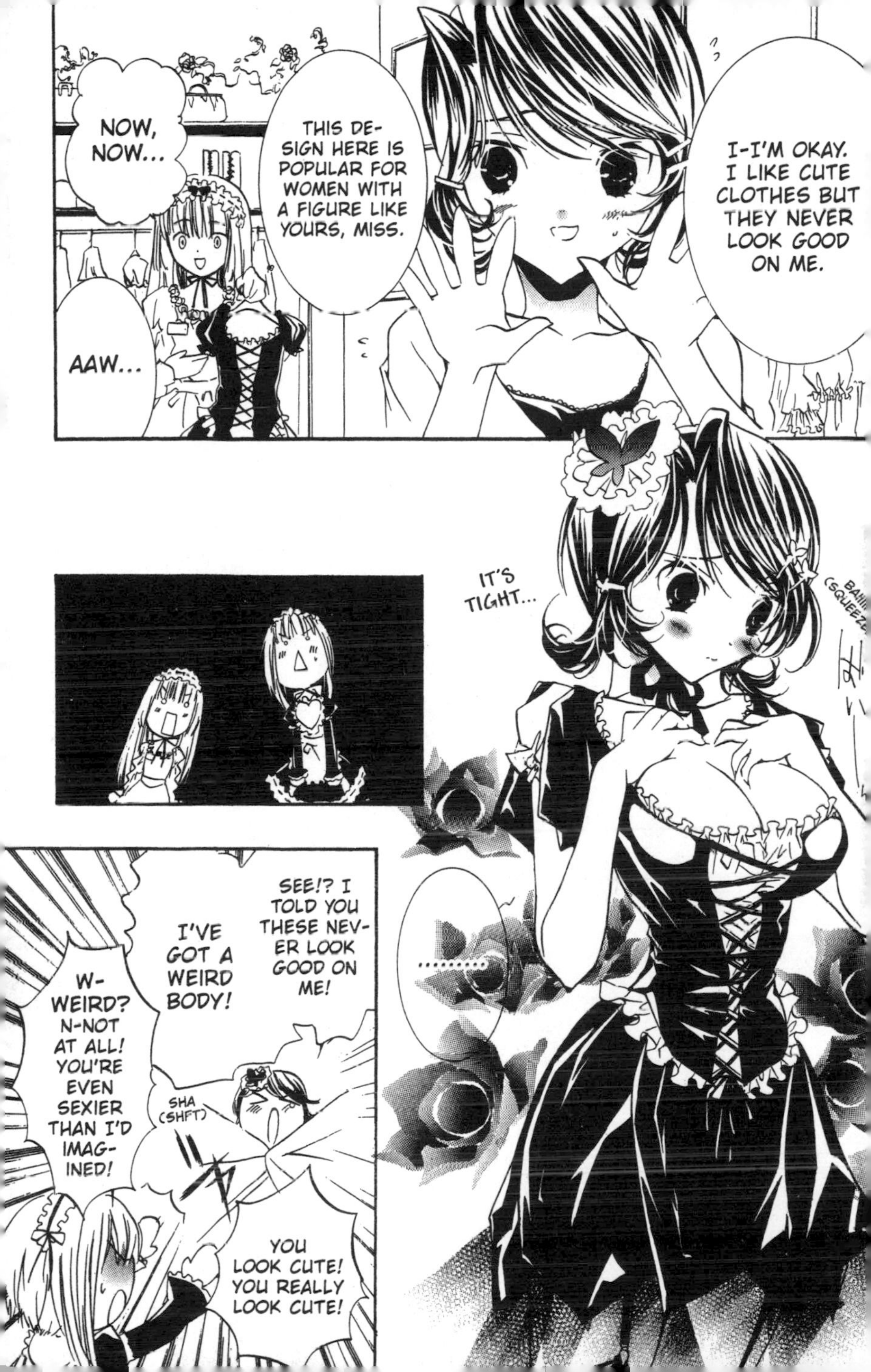
I-I'M OKAY. I LIKE CUTE CLOTHES BUT THEY NEVER LOOK GOOD ON ME.
THIS DESIGN HERE IS POPULAR FOR WOMEN WITH A FIGURE LIKE YOURS, MISS.
NOW, NOW...
AAW...
IT'S TIGHT...
....
SEE!? I TOLD YOU THESE NEVER LOOK GOOD ON ME!
I'VE GOT A WEIRD BODY!
W-WEIRD? N-NOT AT ALL! YOU'RE EVEN SEXIER THAN I'D IMAGINED!
SHA (SHFT)
YOU LOOK CUTE! YOU REALLY LOOK CUTE!

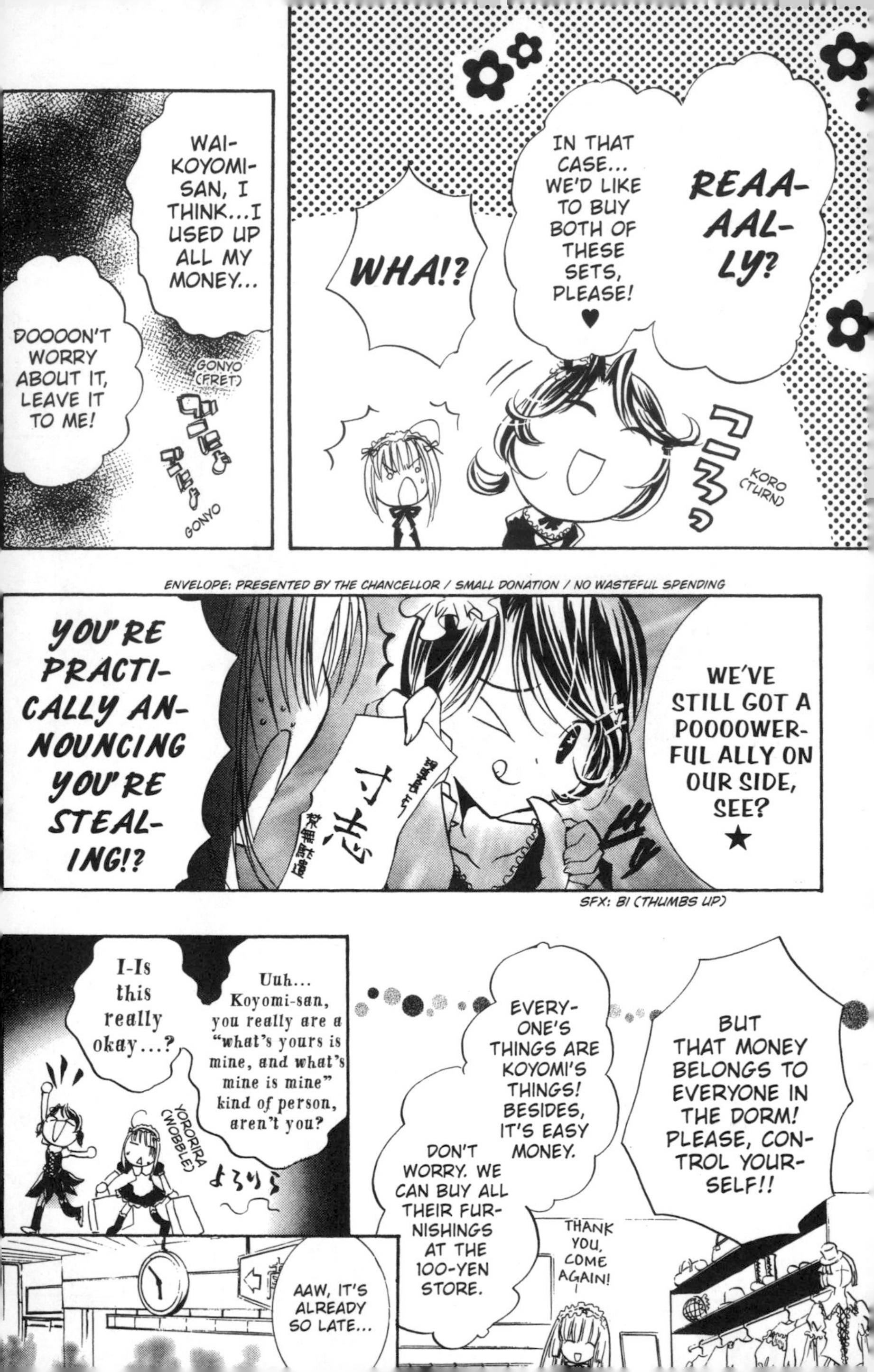
REAAA-AAL-LY?
IN THAT CASE... WE'D LIKE TO BUY BOTH OF THESE SETS, PLEASE! ♥
WHA!?
KORO (TURN)
WAI-KOYOMI-SAN, I THINK...I USED UP ALL MY MONEY...
DOOOON'T WORRY ABOUT IT, LEAVE IT TO ME!
GONYO (FRET)
GONYO
ENVELOPE: PRESENTED BY THE CHANCELLOR / SMALL DONATION / NO WASTEFUL SPENDING
WE'VE STILL GOT A POOOOWERFUL ALLY ON OUR SIDE, SEE? ★
YOU'RE PRACTI-CALLY AN-NOUNCING YOU'RE STEAL-ING!?
SFX: BI (THUMBS UP)
BUT THAT MONEY BELONGS TO EVERYONE IN THE DORM! PLEASE, CON-TROL YOUR-SELF!!
EVERY-ONE'S THINGS ARE KOYOMI'S THINGS! BESIDES, IT'S EASY MONEY.
DON'T WORRY. WE CAN BUY ALL THEIR FUR-NISHINGS AT THE 100-YEN STORE.
THANK YOU, COME AGAIN!
I-Is this really okay...?
Uuh... Koyomi-san, you really are a "what's yours is mine, and what's mine is mine" kind of person, aren't you?
YORORIRA (WOBBLE)
AAW, IT'S ALREADY SO LATE...

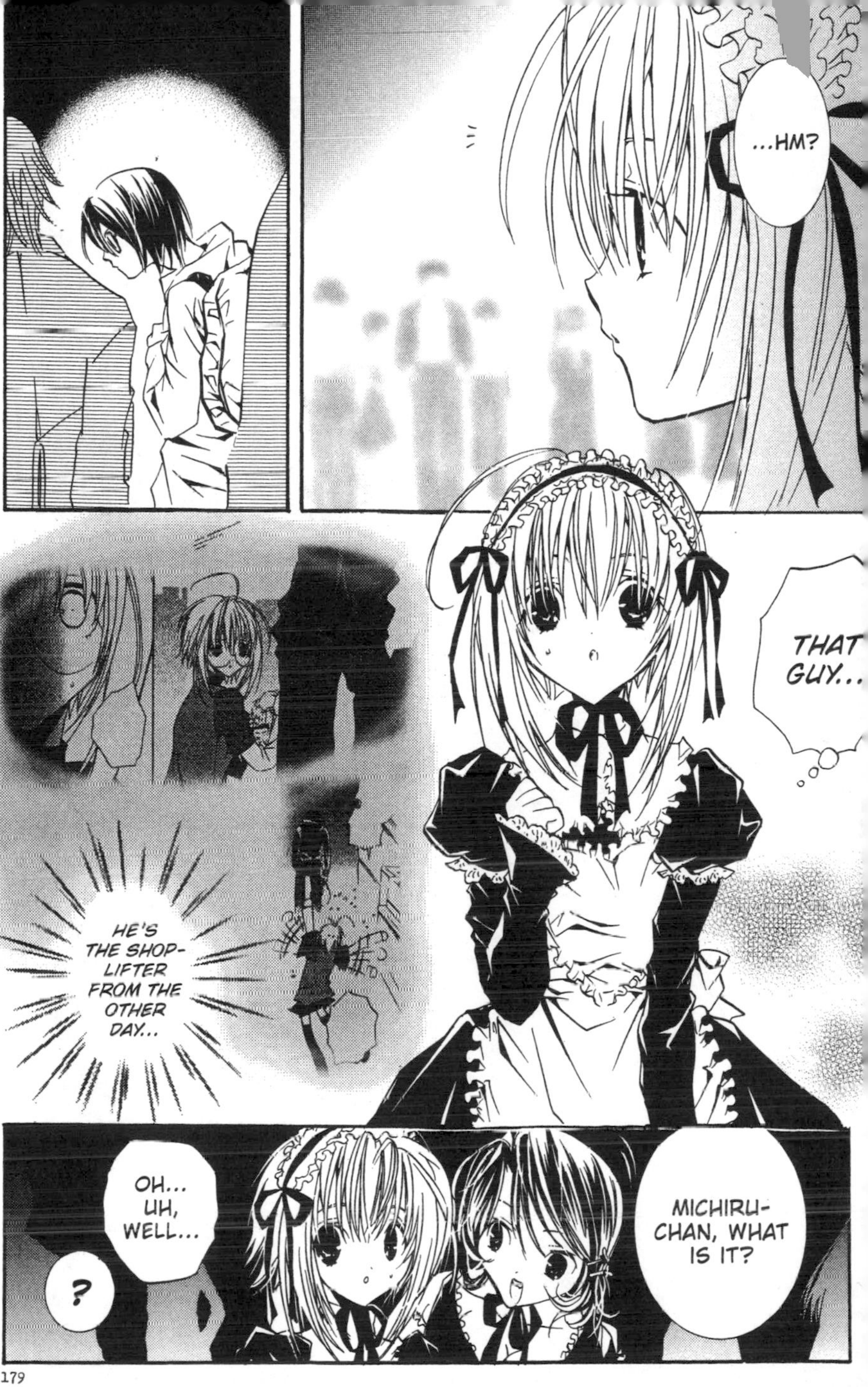
...HM?
THAT GUY...
HE'S THE SHOP-LIFTER FROM THE OTHER DAY...
MICHIRU-CHAN, WHAT IS IT?
OH... UH, WELL...
?

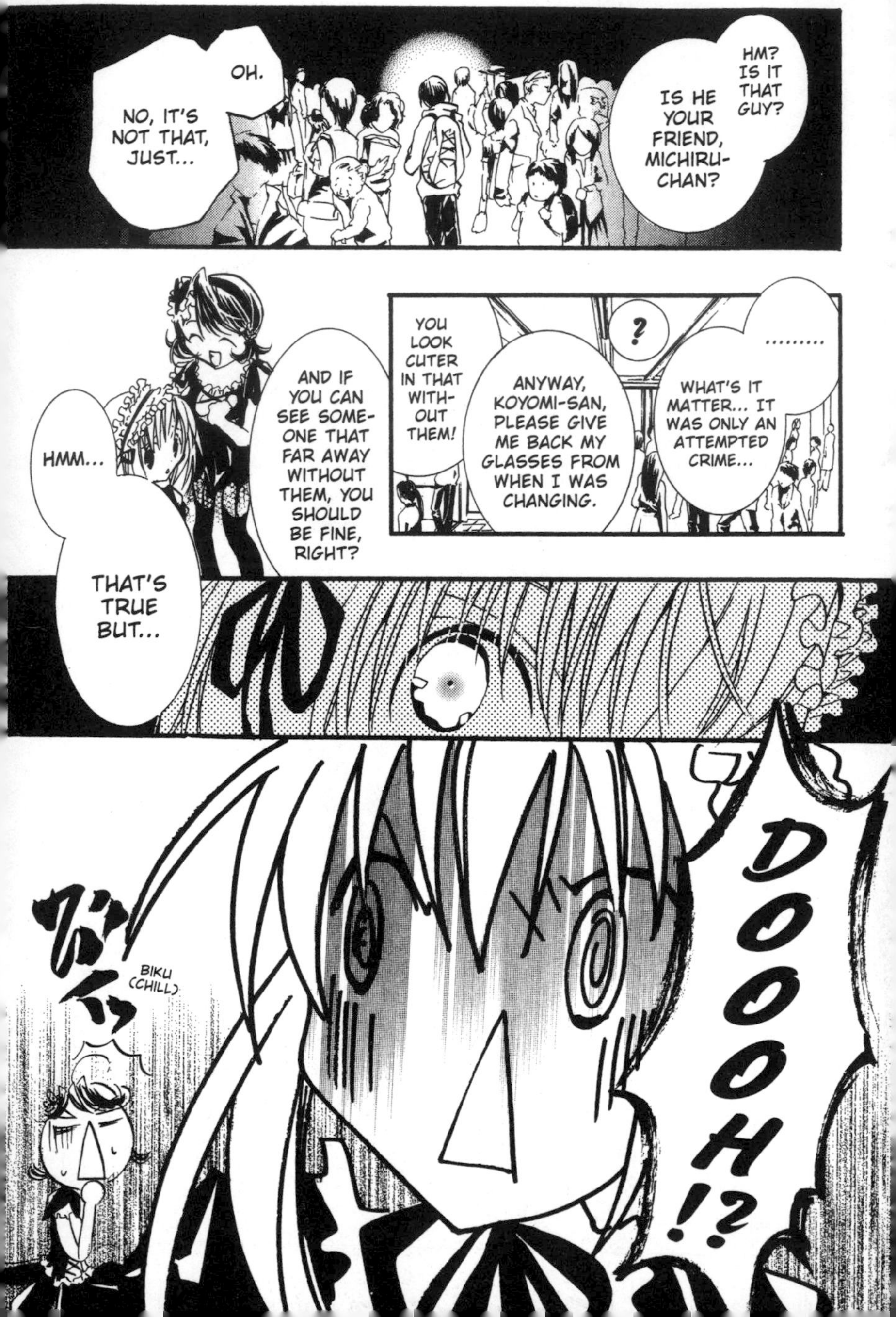
HM? IS IT THAT GUY?
IS HE YOUR FRIEND, MICHIRU-CHAN?
OH.
NO, IT'S NOT THAT, JUST...
....
WHAT'S IT MATTER... IT WAS ONLY AN ATTEMPTED CRIME...
?
ANYWAY, KOYOMI-SAN, PLEASE GIVE ME BACK MY GLASSES FROM WHEN I WAS CHANGING.
YOU LOOK CUTER IN THAT WITH-OUT THEM!
AND IF YOU CAN SEE SOME-ONE THAT FAR AWAY WITHOUT THEM, YOU SHOULD BE FINE, RIGHT?
HMM...
THAT'S TRUE BUT...
DOOOOH!?
BIKU (CHILL)

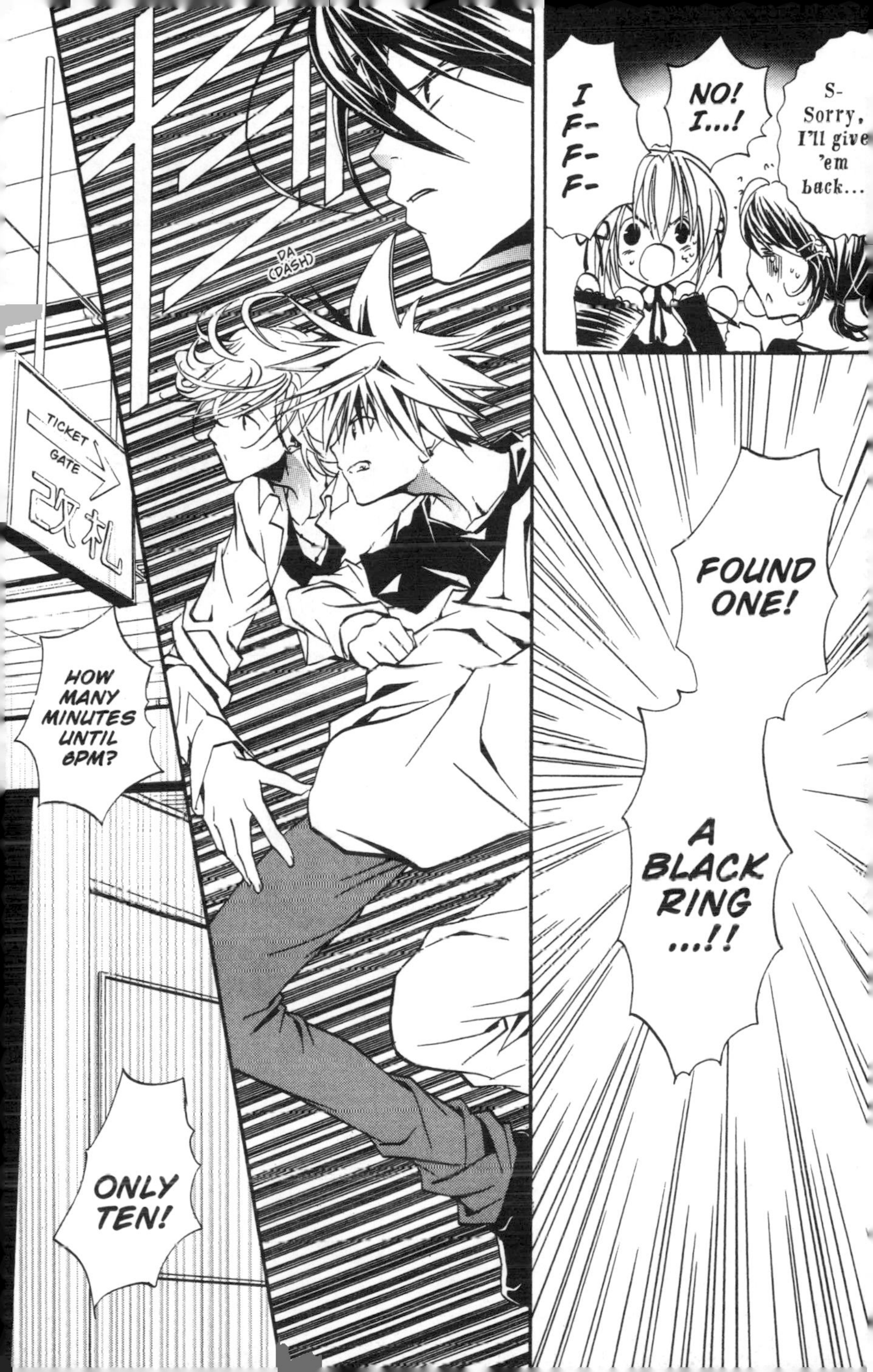
S- Sorry, I'll give 'em back...
NO! I...!
I F-F-F-
FOUND ONE!
A BLACK RING ...!!
DA (DASH)
TICKET GATE
改札
HOW MANY MINUTES UNTIL 6PM?
ONLY TEN!

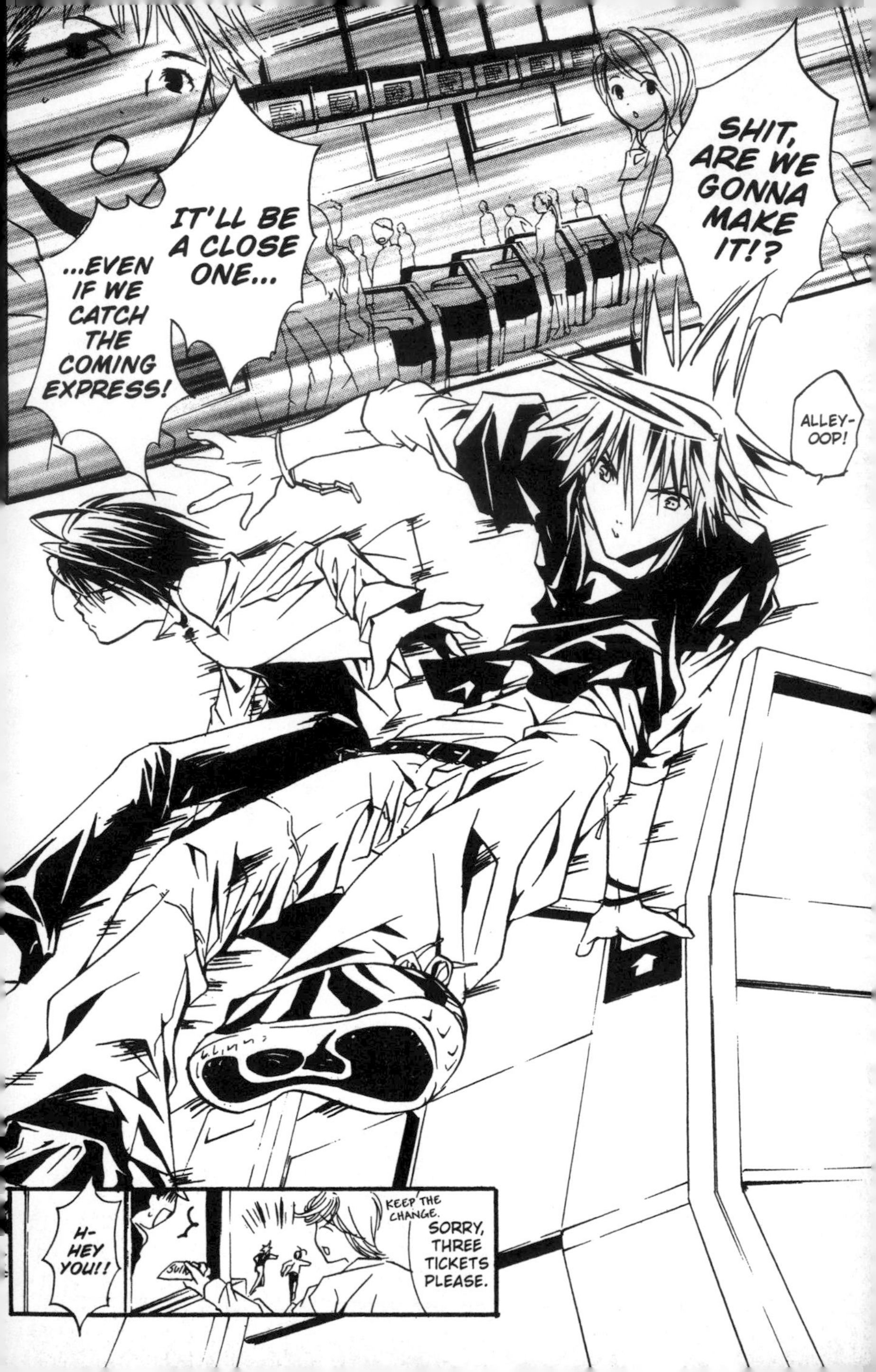
SHIT, ARE WE GONNA MAKE IT!?
IT'LL BE A CLOSE ONE...
...EVEN IF WE CATCH THE COMING EXPRESS!
ALLEY-OOP!
SORRY, THREE TICKETS PLEASE.
KEEP THE CHANGE.
H-HEY YOU!!

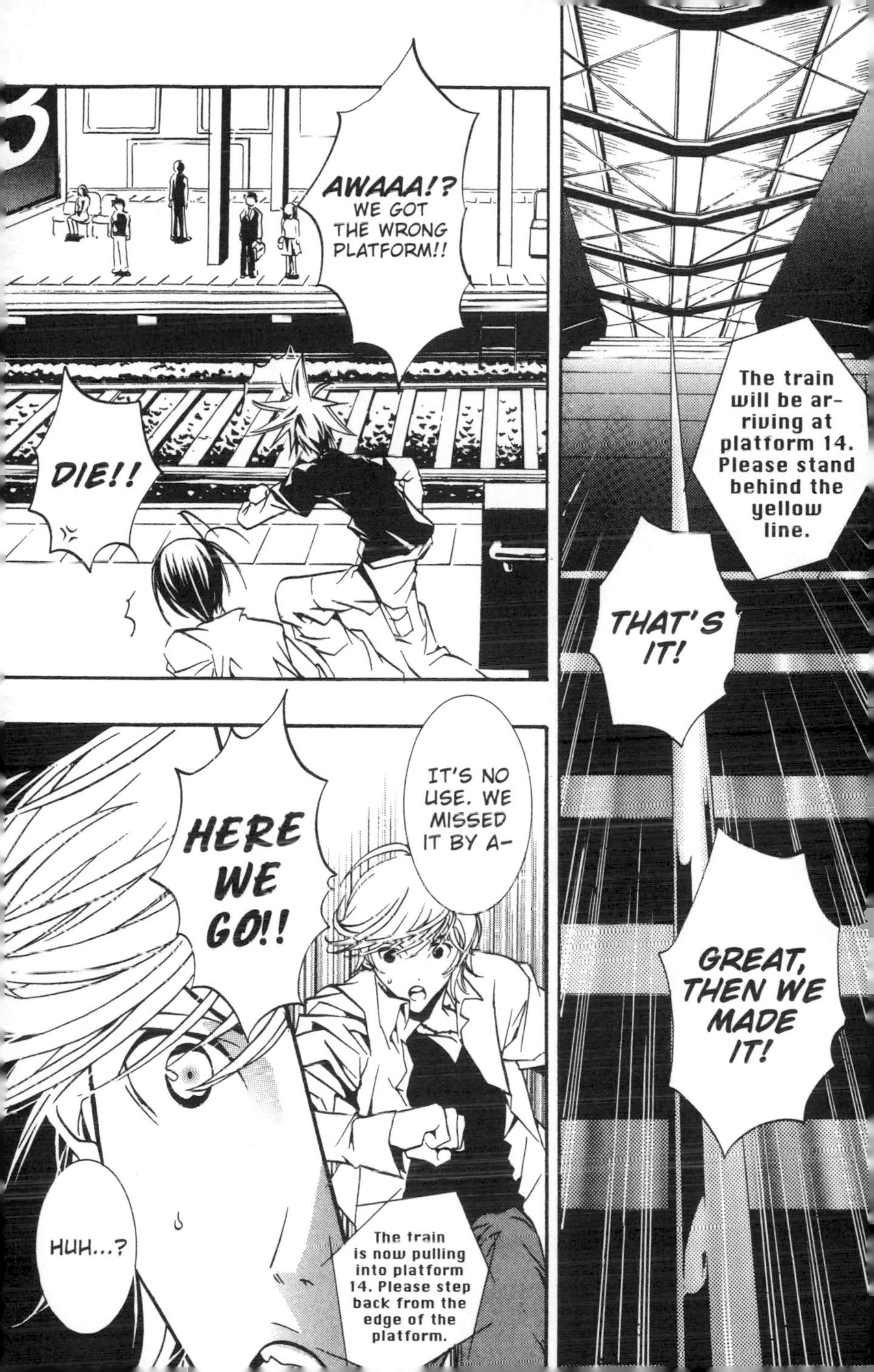
The train will be ar-riving at platform 14. Please stand behind the yellow line.
THAT'S IT!
GREAT, THEN WE MADE IT!
AWAAA!? WE GOT THE WRONG PLATFORM!!
DIE!!
IT'S NO USE. WE MISSED IT BY A-
HERE WE GO!!
The train is now pulling into platform 14. Please step back from the edge of the platform.
HUH...?

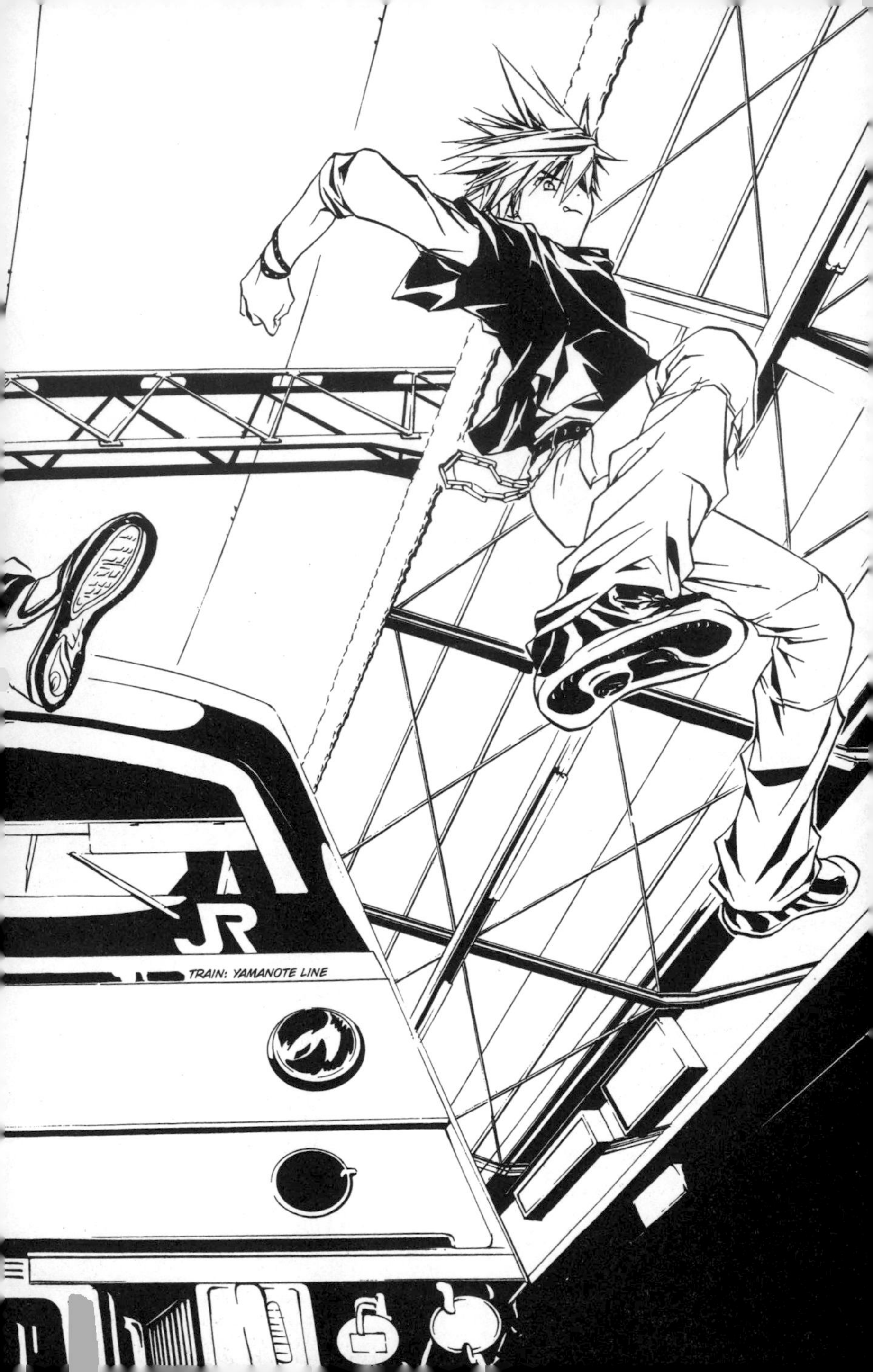
TRAIN: YAMANOTE LINE

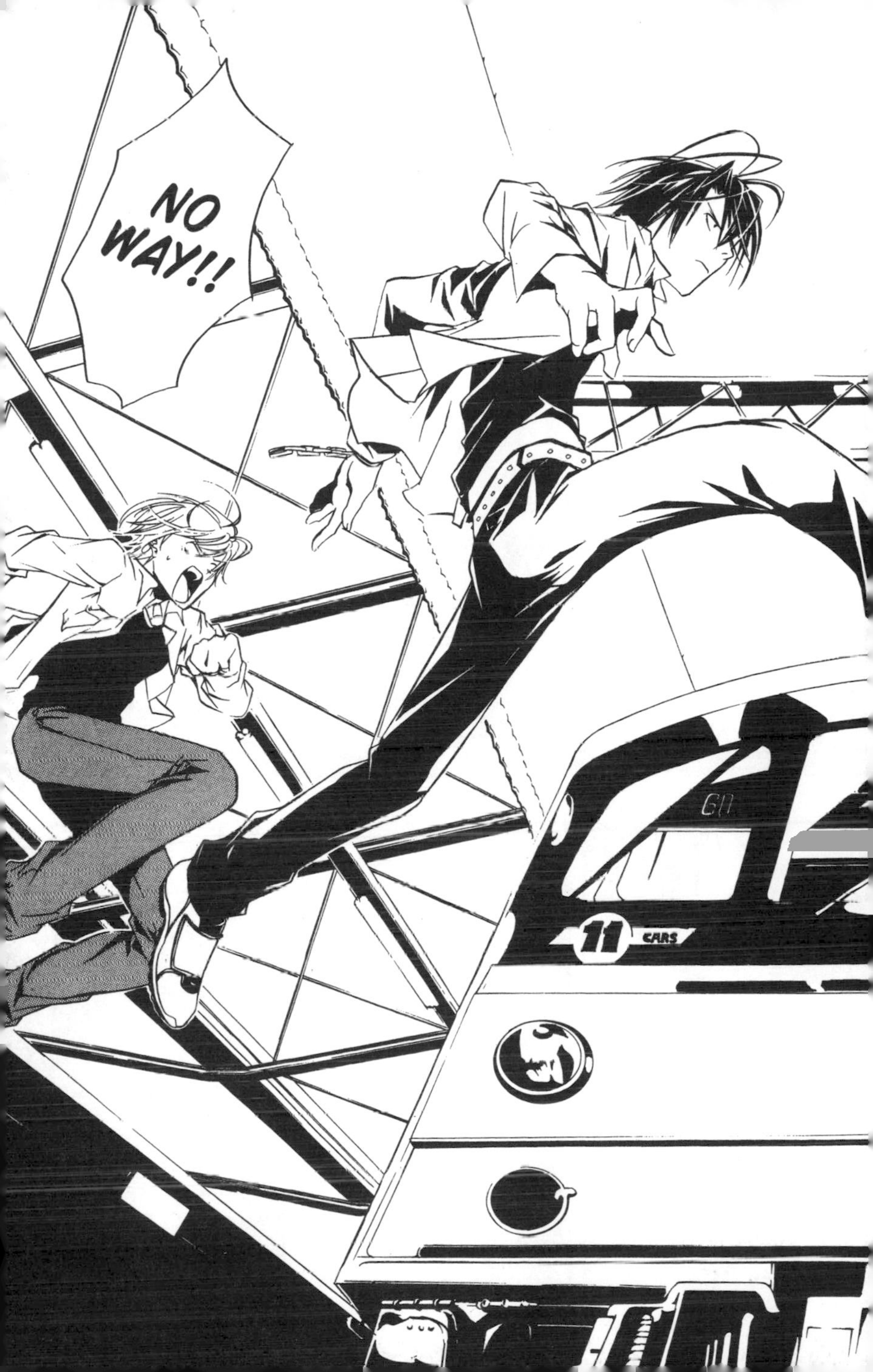
NO WAY!!
11 CARS

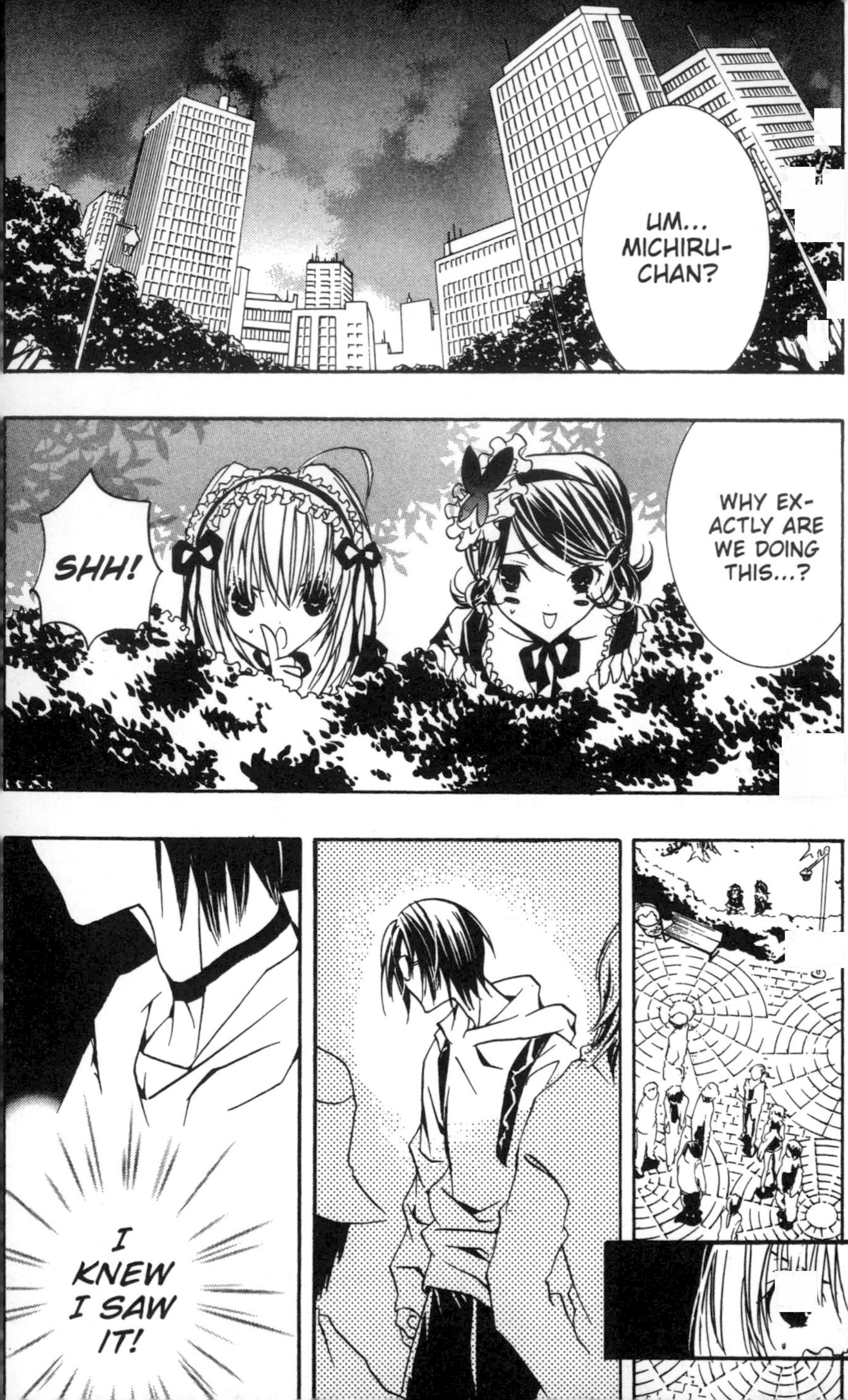
UM... MICHIRU-CHAN?
WHY EX-ACTLY ARE WE DOING THIS...?
SHH!
I KNEW I SAW IT!

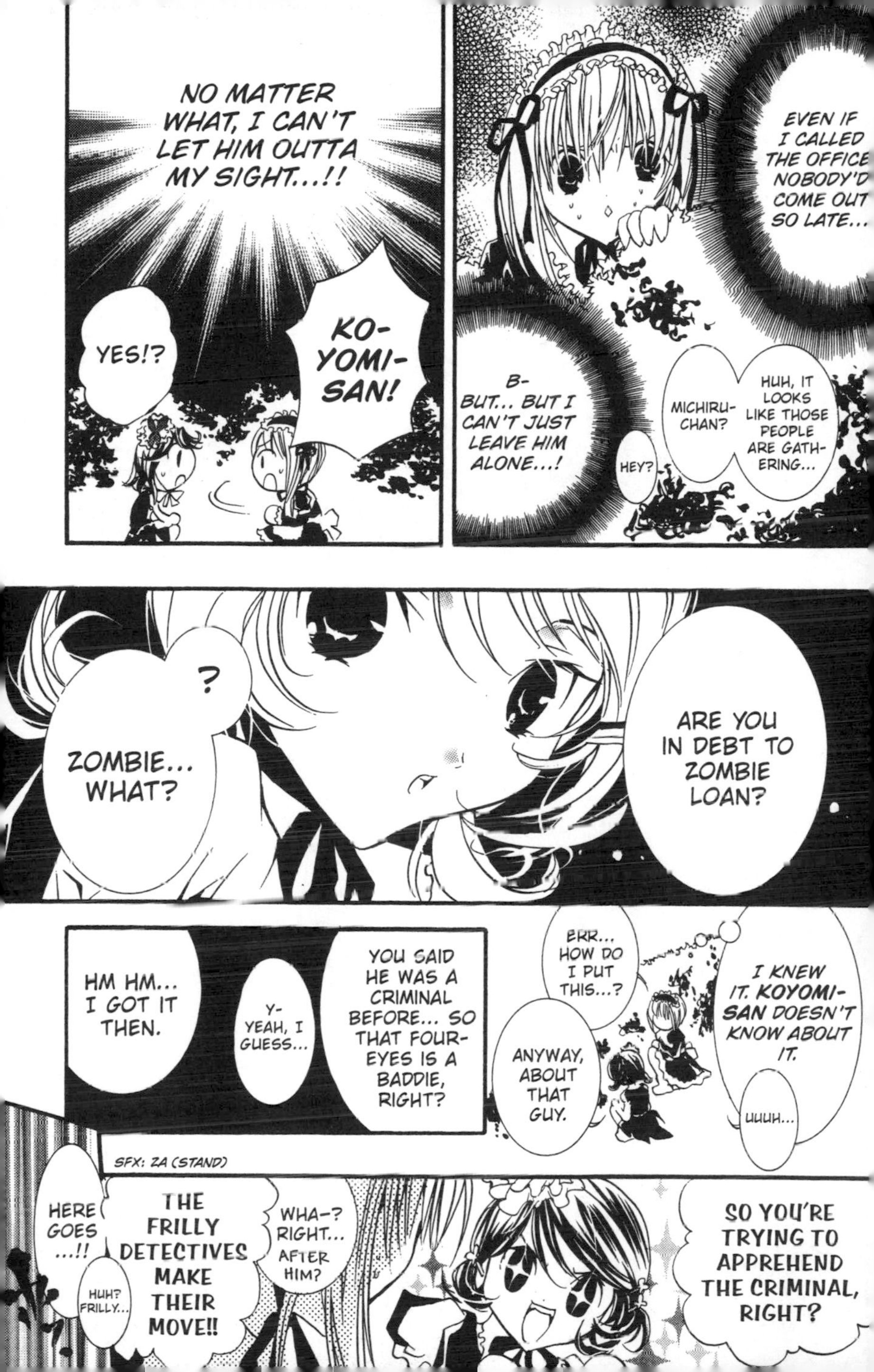
EVEN IF I CALLED THE OFFICE NOBODY'D COME OUT SO LATE...
HUH, IT LOOKS LIKE THOSE PEOPLE ARE GATHERING...
MICHIRU-CHAN?
HEY?
B- BUT... BUT I CAN'T JUST LEAVE HIM ALONE...!
NO MATTER WHAT, I CAN'T LET HIM OUTTA MY SIGHT...!!
KO-YOMI-SAN!
YES!?
ARE YOU IN DEBT TO ZOMBIE LOAN?
?
ZOMBIE... WHAT?
I KNEW IT. KOYOMI-SAN DOESN'T KNOW ABOUT IT.
ERR... HOW DO I PUT THIS...?
UUUH...
ANYWAY, ABOUT THAT GUY.
YOU SAID HE WAS A CRIMINAL BEFORE... SO THAT FOUR-EYES IS A BADDIE, RIGHT?
Y-YEAH, I GUESS...
HM HM... I GOT IT THEN.
SFX: ZA (STAND)
SO YOU'RE TRYING TO APPREHEND THE CRIMINAL, RIGHT?
WHA-? RIGHT... AFTER HIM?
THE FRILLY DETECTIVES MAKE THEIR MOVE!!
HERE GOES ...!!
HUH? FRILLY...

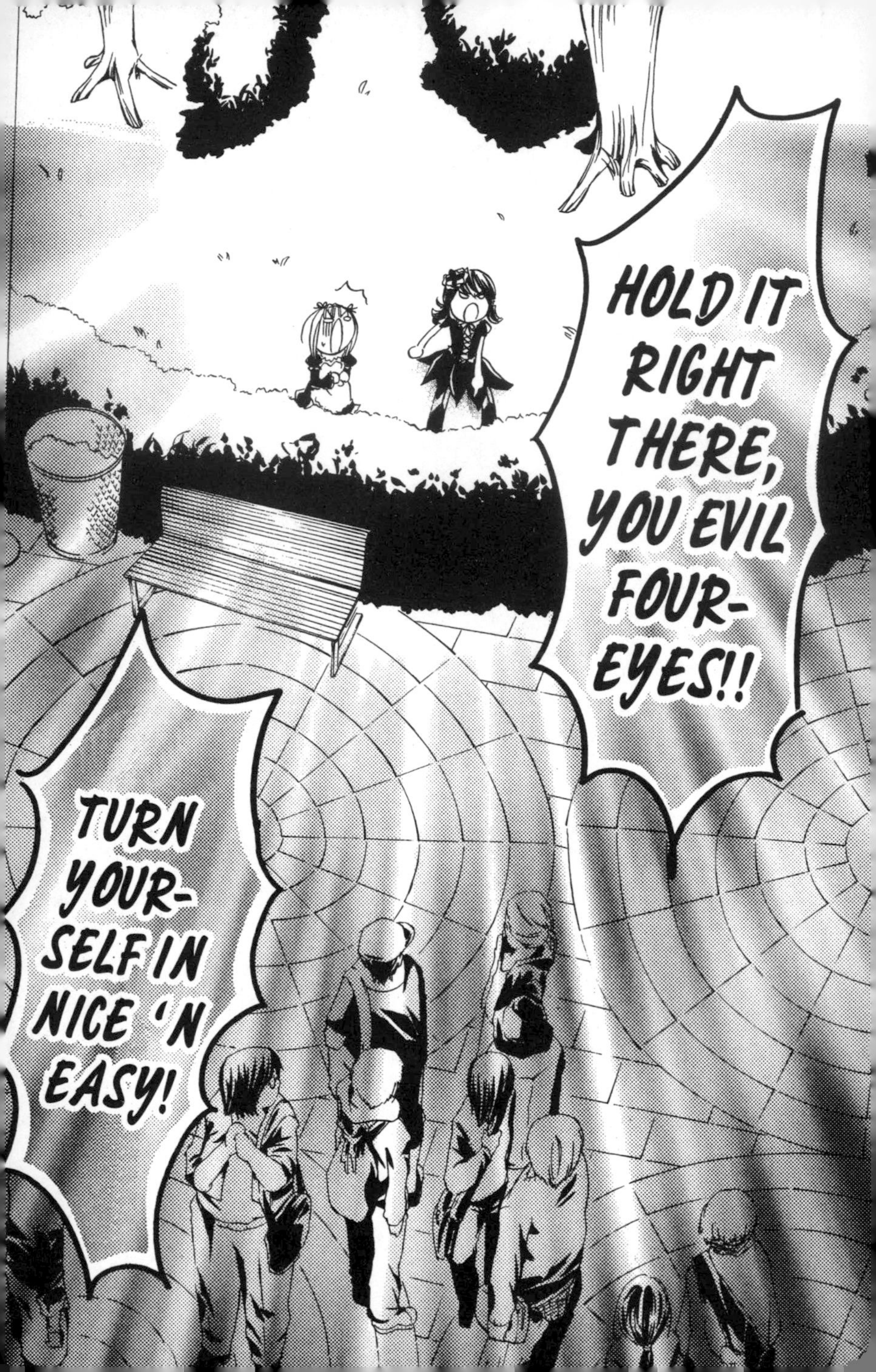
HOLD IT RIGHT THERE, YOU EVIL FOUR-EYES!!
TURN YOUR-SELF IN NICE 'N EASY!

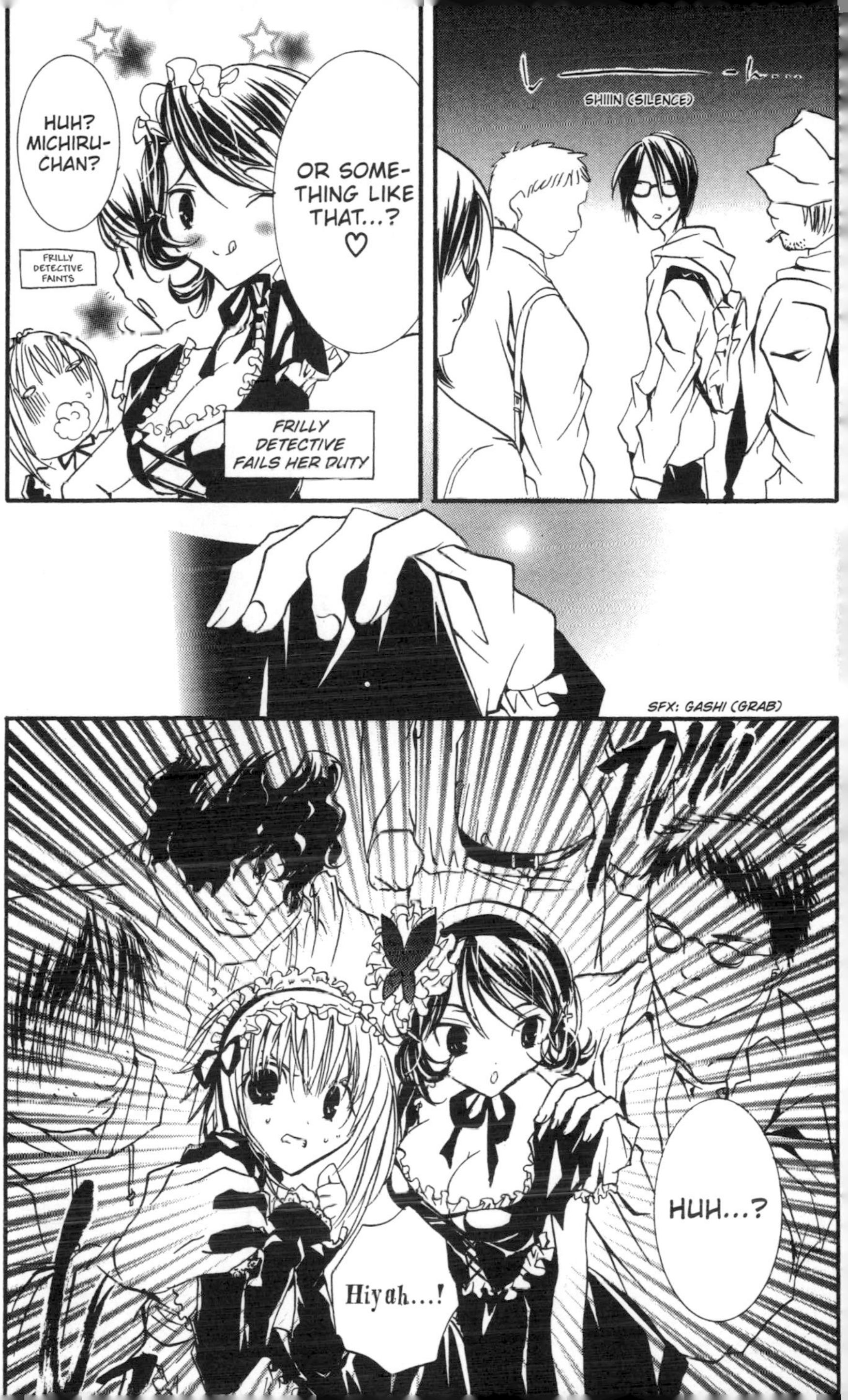
SHIIIN (SILENCE)
OR SOME-THING LIKE THAT...? ♡
HUH? MICHIRU-CHAN?
FRILLY DETECTIVE FAINTS
FRILLY DETECTIVE FAILS HER DUTY
SFX: GASHI (GRAB)
HUH...?
Hiyah...!

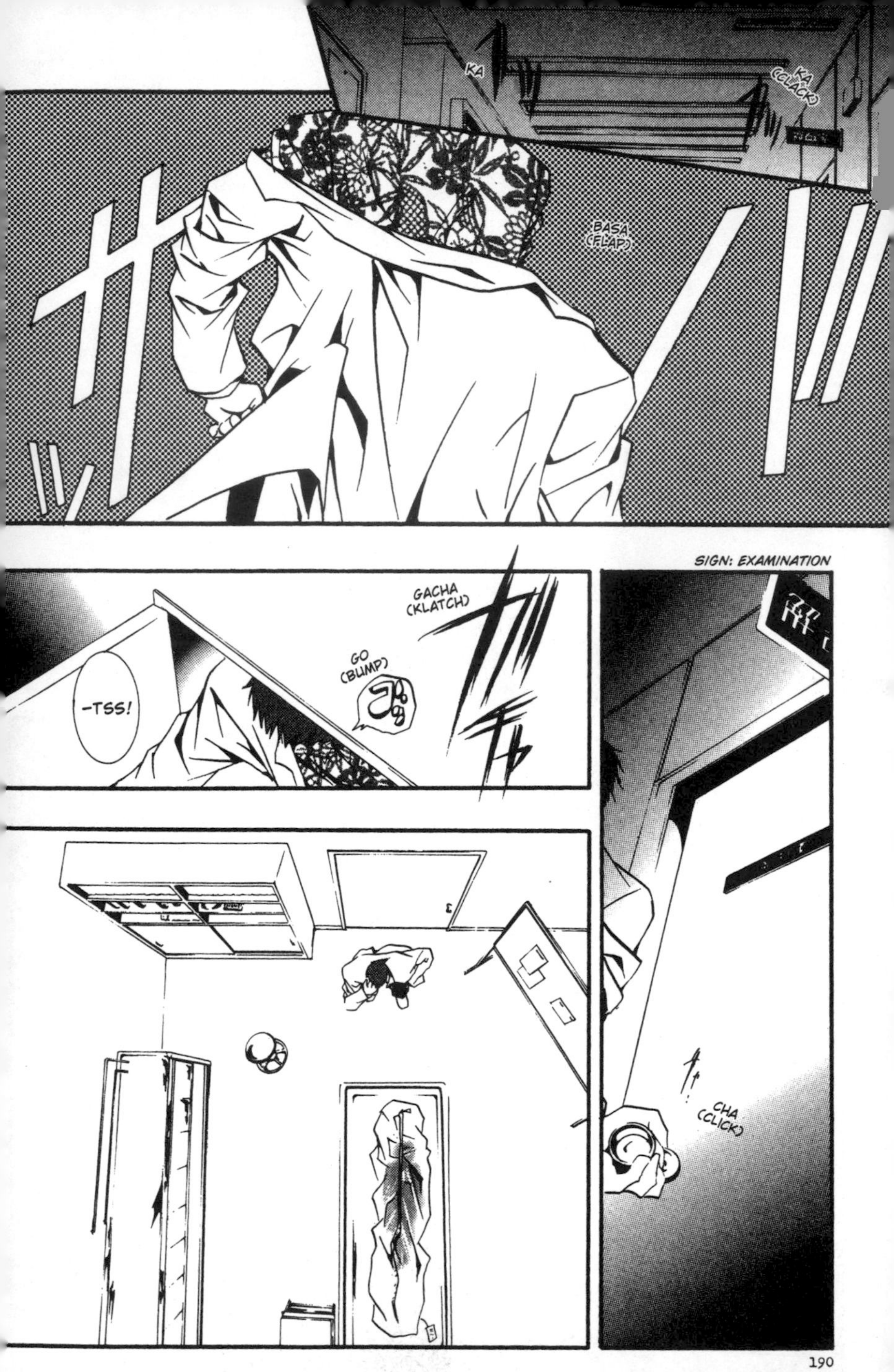
KA (CLACK)
KA
BASA (FLAP)
SIGN: EXAMINATION
CHA (CLICK)
GACHA (KLATCH)
GO (BUMP)
-TSS!

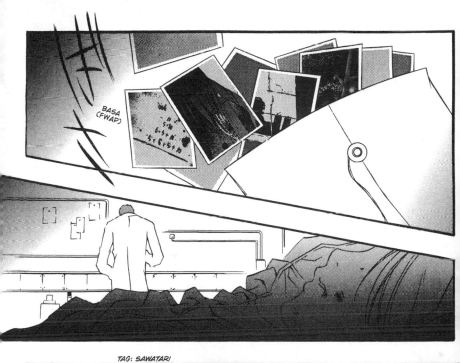

BASA
(FWAP)

TAG: SAWATARI

....

沢渡

ZURU
(SCRAPE)

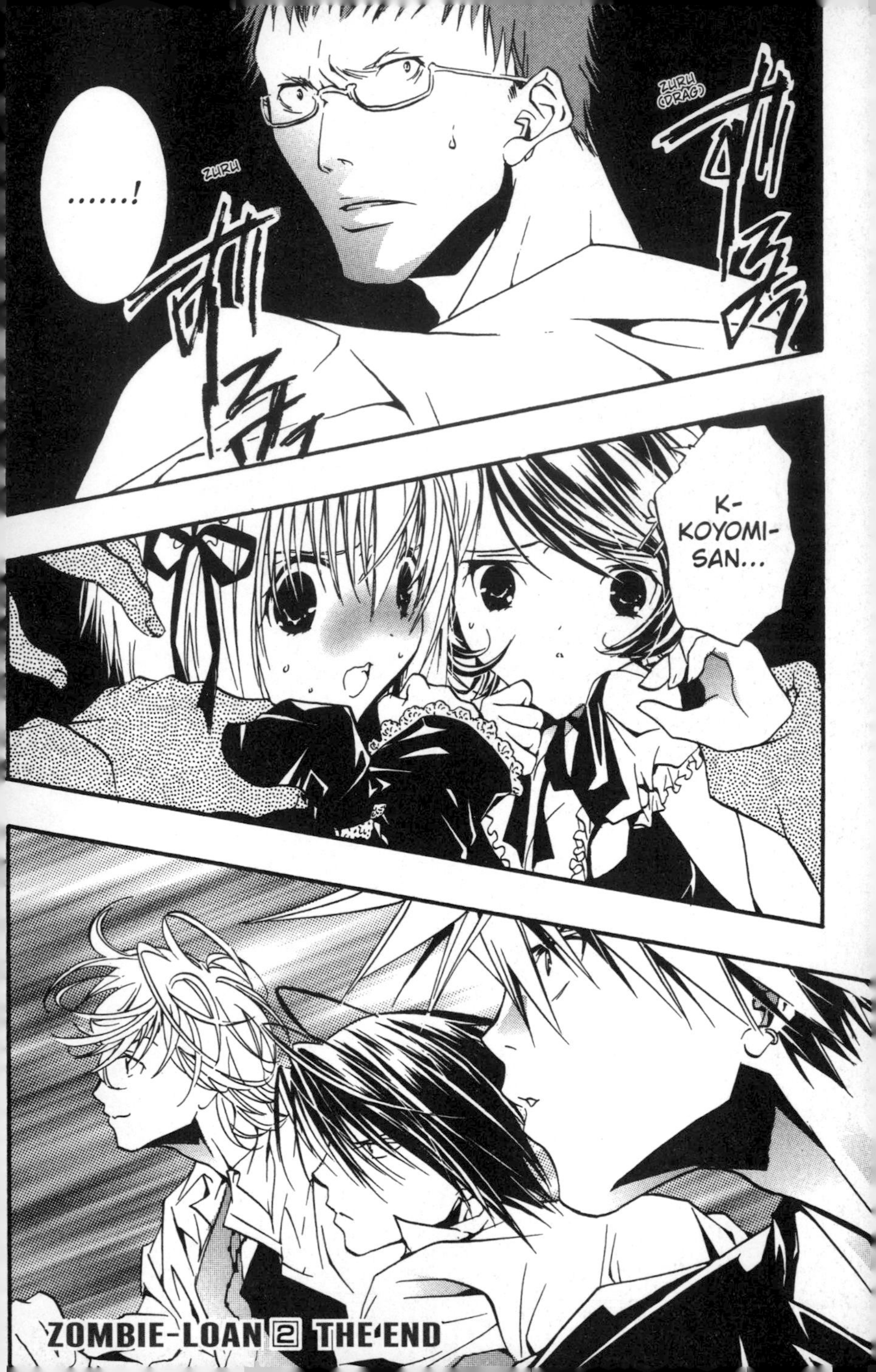
ZURU (DRAG)
......!
ZURU
K-KOYOMI-SAN...
ZOMBIE-LOAN 2 THE END